Paul D. Sheriff & Ken Getz

ASP.NET
Developer's
JumpStart

✦ Addison-Wesley

Boston • San Francisco • New York • Toronto • Montreal
London • Munich • Paris • Madrid
Capetown • Sydney • Singapore • Mexico City

ASP.NET Developer's JumpStart

Many of the designations used by manufacturers and sellers to distinguish their products are claimed as trademarks. Where those designations appear in this book, and Addison-Wesley were aware of a trademark claim, the designations have been printed in initial capital letters or in all capitals.

The author and publisher have taken care in the preparation of this book, but make no expressed or implied warranty of any kind and assume no responsibility for errors or omissions. No liability is assumed for incidental or consequential damages in connection with or arising out of the use of the information or programs contained herein.

The publisher offers discounts on this book when ordered in quantity for special sales.

For more information, please contact:

Pearson Education Corporate Sales Division
201 W. 103rd Street
Indianapolis, IN 46290
(800) 428-5331
corpsales@pearsoned.com

Visit AW on the Web: www.awprofessional.com

ISBN 0-672-323-575

Associate Publisher
Linda Engelman

Acquisitions Editor
Sondra Scott

Development Editor
Karen Wachs

Managing Editor
Charlotte Clapp

Project Editor
Elizabeth Finney

Copy Editor
Bart Reed

Indexer
Angie Bess
Ginny Bess

Proofreader
Jessica McCarty

Technical Editor
Ken Cox
Sundar Rajan

Team Coordinator
Lynne Williams

Media Developer
Dan Scherf

Interior Designer
Anne Jones

Cover Designer
Aren Howell

Page Layout
Susan Geiselman

Contents at a Glance

Table of Contents

About the Authors

Paul D. Sheriff has over 17 years experience programming business applications. Paul is considered one of the leading Visual Basic programmers in the industry. Paul has also been very active in the Visual Basic community. He has been the president of the Orange County Visual Basic User Group. He has written over 60 articles for many different publications and is a contributing editor to *Advisor* magazine, writing many articles on Visual Basic 3, 4, 5, 6 and now VB .NET. Paul is the author of the Que book *Paul Sheriff Teaches Visual Basic 6.0*. Paul also speaks at the Advisor Publications Developer's Conferences, Microsoft Tech-Ed, and Microsoft Developer Days. Paul currently is the Microsoft Regional Director for Southern California.

In 1991, Paul started PDSA, Inc., a high-level computer consulting company specializing in high-quality custom software. PDSA, Inc. is a Microsoft Managed Partner. Since starting PDSA, Inc., Paul and his team have consulted in many different industries, such as aerospace, real estate, medicine, hotel, and government.

PDSA, Inc. is available for consulting work and onsite training in Visual Basic, SQL Server, and Internet/intranet applications. Contact PDSA, Inc. toll-free at (888) 899-PDSA (7372) or at (714) 734-9792. Fax: (714) 734-9793. E-mail: Psheriff@pdsa.com. Visit the PDSA Web site at http://www.pdsa.com.

Ken Getz is a senior consultant with MCW Technologies and splits his time between programming, writing, and training. He specializes in tools and applications written in Visual Studio .NET and Visual Basic. Ken is coauthor of several bestselling books, including *Access 2002 Developer's Handbooks with Paul Litwin and Mike Gunderloy*, *Visual Basic Language Developer's Handbook with Mike Gilbert*, and *VBA Developer's Handbook with Mike Gilbert* (Sybex). He cowrote several training courses for Application Developer's Training Company (www.appdev.com), including VB .NET, ASP.NET, Access 2000 and 97, Visual Basic 6, and Visual Basic 5 seminars. He has also recorded video training for AppDev covering VB .NET, ASP.NET, VB6, Access 2000, and Access 97. Ken is a frequent speaker at technical conferences and has spoken often at Microsoft's Tech-Ed conference. Ken also is a technical editor for *Access-VB-SQL Advisor* magazine and a columnist for Informant Publications' *asp.netPRO* magazine. You can reach Ken at keng@mcwtech.com, www.mcwtech.com, or at www.developershandbook.com.

Dedication

For my wife, Ann, and everyone at PDSA, Inc. Also for my coauthor and good friend Ken Getz. PDS

For Melanie Spiller and Peter Mason: I think of you both as I write each paragraph. Different reasons, of course. KNG

Acknowledgments

We would like to thank a few people who helped us get this book put together. Many people contributed to this book, and they deserve some of the credit for making it a reality:

- The editorial staff at Sams, especially Sondra Scott, Acquisitions Editor; Karen Wachs, Development Editor; Bart Reed, Copy Editor; and Elizabeth Finney, Project Editor. Your help and support made it far easier to put together this book.

- The staff at PDSA, Inc. for helping review and tech edit most of these chapters.

- Craig Utley, for some of the material in Chapter 4, "Overview of .NET Framework Classes."

- Stephen Scott and Martin Wasznicky for some of the material in Chapter 26, "Development and Deployment Techniques."

- The input of several of our fellow instructors, including Mike Groh, Tom Howe, Bruce Jones, and Scott Barker.

- Mary Chipman and Andy Baron, for unflagging efforts in helping dig into some of the dark corners of ASP.NET.

- Erik Ruthruff, of Informant Communications Group, for helping us get started on this book by prodding us to write .NET courseware.

If there is useful content in this book, it's due in part to these folks, and to the many others who helped us learn ASP.NET. If there are errors or omissions, of course, it's all the authors' doing!

Introduction

The major benefit you will derive from reading this book is that you will be led, step by step, through the creation of a real-world–style business Web application that takes advantage of many of the new capabilities provided by the .NET platform. After reading this book, you will be able to program .NET applications using ADO.NET, Web Forms, and Web Services. Most of the books on the market do not address a real-world application, and most do not ever use a step-by-step approach. This book uses this approach so you can learn what you need in order to get your job done quicker and more efficiently. This will make your investment in this book pay off right from the beginning chapters.

What Is the Purpose of This Book?

The purpose of this book is to show you how to use ASP.NET and Visual Studio .NET to build real-world business applications on the Web. We will show the practical applications of ASP.NET by illustrating how to build a client/server application using Web Forms and Web Services. Emphasis will be on good programming standards and practices. You will be taken from an introduction of the Visual Basic .NET language to intermediate topics through a step-by-step approach. This lets you try out the practices being set forth in this book.

What This Book Isn't

Given the challenge of writing about a huge technology like Microsoft's .NET platform, we made specific decisions about what and what not to cover. With that in mind, this book is most definitely not a reference manual, and it is not a rehash of the Microsoft documentation. It is, however, a great place to start digging into the features and power of ASP.NET. The book is also not a resource on advanced features—you'll find many other books that explain the things you'll want to dig into after you've learned the basics. We deliberately avoided topics that you don't need to know right away. Instead, we focused on topics you'll need right away to begin your exploration of ASP.NET and Web development using the .NET platform.

Who Should Read This Book?

This book is designed for anyone who wants to learn how to create a business application using ASP.NET, HTML, and Internet Information Services (IIS). Throughout this book, you will be introduced to the concepts of the Microsoft .NET Framework, how to create a Web application using SQL Server, ASP.NET, ADO.NET, and Web Services, as well as good programming principles.

Prerequisites

This book is designed for programmers who need to know how to program a Web application. If you are a programmer and/or Web designer who has some experience with VBScript or ColdFusion, you will get a lot out of this book. Even if you're not, there is enough in here to get you started. To get the most out of this book, it is recommended that you have experience using a programming language such as Visual Basic 6.0. Some experience with Visual Basic .NET would be helpful, but it's not required. You should also be familiar with relational database concepts and have access to the Northwind sample database that comes with SQL Server and Access. You must be familiar with Windows 2000, or later, and have access to Windows NT, Windows 2000, or Windows XP to effectively use this book. Familiarity with IIS is also recommended, because this book will assume you know how to set up virtual directories in IIS.

Assumptions

You will need several tools at your disposal so you can try out the many exercises contained in this book. Here is a list of the tools you should have on your computer:

- Microsoft SQL Server 7.0 or later or Microsoft Access

- The Northwind sample database, which comes with SQL Server and Access

- Microsoft Windows 2000, or XP

- Microsoft .NET Common Language Runtime (CLR) Framework SDK

- Microsoft Visual Studio .NET

- Microsoft Mobile Internet Toolkit (optional)

Getting and Running .NET

The .NET Framework and the Visual Studio .NET IDE can both be purchased from many vendors, including directly from Microsoft. Although the .NET Framework will run on Microsoft Windows XP, Windows 2000, Windows NT 4.0, Windows 98 second edition, and Windows Millennium Edition (Windows Me), you'll need to have Windows NT with Service Pack 6, Windows 2000, Windows XP, or Windows .NET Server in order to develop applications. Microsoft Internet Explorer 6.0 or later is required. For server-side installs, Microsoft Data Access Components 2.7 is required. You need at least a PII 450MHz processor with a minimum of 128MB of RAM and at least 800×600 resolution.

You will find that you need at least a PIII 650MHz processor with 384MB of RAM or better to be really productive. The more memory you have, the better off you will be. Given the choice, adding memory should have a higher priority than upgrading your processor.

Making the Most of This Book

To download the examples discussed in this book, and to find updates and fixes, visit our Web site, www.pdsa.com/aspnetjumpstart. Because this book focuses on building an application that looks and feels like a simple business-oriented Web site, you'll get the flavor of the types of issues that will affect every ASP.NET developer. Rather than focusing on features or technology, we've focused on tasks and solutions. Although there may be other ways to accomplish some of the techniques we've proposed in this book, given the examples shown here, you'll have a running head start toward building your own sites and applications.

We suggest that you work your way through this book, from start to finish. There may be some chapters along the way that cover material you're already familiar with (for example, the chapters on HTML and XML). In that case, skim on past. Don't worry about missing out on steps in building the sample application—we've included, along with the sample application, a finished version of the application after each chapter. If you skip a chapter, you can simply copy the contents of the finished version for the chapter into your working folder. (See Chapter 1, "Getting Started with the Sample Application," for more details.) In a perfect world, after working through the examples in each chapter, you would take the time to review the documentation on the objects and techniques covered and then add your own functionality to the application.

PART I

Introduction to Microsoft .NET and ASP.NET

IN THIS PART

1

Getting Started with the Sample Application

OBJECTIVES

- Become acquainted with the sample application you will build in this book

- Learn how to use the application sample code

This book focuses on creating applications in ASP.NET, and to help you get started creating your own applications as quickly as possible, we've supplied a full working application that shows off as many ASP.NET features as we could cram into one application. As you work through the book, you'll create and study many pages all related to the Northwind sample database that comes with Microsoft SQL Server. In this chapter, you'll preview the various pages in the main application as well as those from some of the subsidiary applications (we couldn't fit everything we wanted to cover into the one single application). You can think of this chapter as an orientation to the applications, so you'll be familiar with each chapter's example before you begin.

Preparing for the Sample Application

The sample application is built using Microsoft SQL Server's Northwind sample database. If you do not have Microsoft SQL Server available, you can use the Access/Jet version of the same database, Northwind.mdb file supplied with the sample files for this book.

TIP

If you're going to use the Northwind database, you'll need to change the connection string in DataHandler.vb to point to the Northwind.mdb file supplied with the examples. You can find the connection string in the DataHandler.vb file in the completed Northwind sample project. You will be unable to run the examples that involve stored procedures, because Microsoft Access (and the Jet database engine) doesn't support stored procedures.

Installing the Examples

We have supplied a Microsoft Installer 2.0 (MSI) file that will create all the sample applications for this book on your machine. Before you can install the examples, the following items must be installed on your computer:

- **Operating system.** You must be running Windows NT Workstation or Server, Windows 2000 Professional or Server, Windows XP Professional, or Windows .NET Server. If you have any other OS, you may not be able to run Visual Studio .NET. Check with Microsoft to see if your operating system will run Visual Studio .NET. Some operating systems (such as Windows NT) require additional service packs in order for Visual Studio to run.

- **Visual Studio .NET.** Every example in this book requires you to have Visual Studio .NET 2002 installed on your computer.

- **Internet Information Server.** IIS is an optional component in non-server operating systems (such as Windows XP Professional, Windows 2000 Professional, and so on). Use the Control Panel's Add or Remove Programs option to install IIS.

- **SQL Server.** Although this database system is highly recommended, you can also use the supplied Access MDB file.

If you have all the installation criteria, you should be able to run all the examples for this book. To install the sample files, follow these steps:

1. Go to http://www.pdsa.com/ASPNETJumpstart. You can download the sample files (and any updates) from this Web site.

2. Download ASPNETJumpstart.MSI to a location on your local hard drive.

3. Execute the MSI file by double-clicking it in Windows Explorer.

4. Follow the prompts presented by Windows Installer, as it installs the examples.

Once you're done installing the examples, you'll find a new folder tree, starting with <d>:\ASP.NET Jumpstart. Under this folder, you will find other folders that are described in the next section.

Before You Get Started

Before you get going, it's important to review some issues that will affect you as you follow the examples and create your own Web pages throughout the book. We'd like to take this opportunity to mention some important general instructions that apply to all the following chapters. Not all these issues will seem relevant as you're getting ready to start working through the chapters, but you may want to refer back to this section later on—make sure you at least skim through this list before proceeding so you know what's covered here:

- **Folder structure.** We've supplied three directory "trees": Jumpstart, Jumpstart-Completed, and Jumpstart-SampleCode. The Jumpstart folder contains completed projects, ready for you to run (for example, the Debugger, ErrorHandling, FrameworkClasses, and VBLanguage folders). These projects exist outside the main Northwind example and show off particular features that didn't fit into the main project. This folder also includes the Northwind-Completed subfolder, which contains the finished sample project you'll create as you work through this book. You'll also create your Northwind sample project in this folder, as well as other projects throughout the book. The Jumpstart-Completed folder contains a series of subfolders, one corresponding to each chapter in the book in which you modify the Northwind sample project. Each subfolder contains a full copy of the Northwind sample project, up to the point of completion at the end of the corresponding chapter. See the "Typing code" bulleted point for more information about the third directory tree.

- **Building the sample project.** Our intent, when writing this book, was that you would work through the chapters in order, building the sample application as you go. (Some chapters load other projects or have you create projects not directly related to the Northwind sample project, but the majority of the chapters focus on creating this one example.) When you start building the example, you'll create a virtual root named Northwind, and you'll add pages to this root as you work through the book. In some chapters, you will build the sample pages yourself; in others, you will bring in a completed page or a partially completed page and finish it by following the steps in the book.

- **Using the finished versions of projects.** If you want to skip ahead to a particular chapter, you can find the appropriate subfolder for the chapter right before the one you're skipping to in the Jumpstart-Completed tree. Copy the contents of the folder to your Northwind folder (the location where you placed the Northwind virtual root) and continue from that point, as if you had worked through all the chapters up to that point. At any time, you can wipe out the contents of the Northwind folder (if you're going to do this, make sure and delete all the files and folders, as well); then add in the contents of any of the subfolders in the Jumpstart-Completed tree. Table 1.1 lists the chapters for which we've supplied finished versions of the Northwind sample project. (The Jumpstart-Completed/Northwind folder contains all the sample pages, including all the code.) If you work through the book in order, you won't need to worry with any of these details.

TIP

If, for example, you had completed up to Chapter 8, (`ValidationControls`) and you now wanted to skip ahead to Chapter 15 (`StoredProcedures`), you would need to find the most recent previous chapter that provides a full copy of the sample project (in this case, Chapter 14: `WorkingWithData`) and copy the contents from the `Jumpstart-Completed/ WorkingWithData` folder into your working project's folder. You could then continue with Chapter 15 as if you had worked through all the chapters up to that point.

- **Loading the projects.** To load the sample projects, look for `*.sln` in the folder associated with each of the chapters. A Visual Studio .NET solution can contain multiple projects, and the SLN file contains information about each of the individual project files (`*.vbproj`) included in the solution. You can double-click an SLN file to load the solution into Visual Studio .NET. If, for some reason, you can't find an SLN file, you can also double-click the project's VBPROJ file to load the single project into Visual Studio .NET.

- **Handling virtual roots.** Each SLN file contains information about the virtual roots where it can find each of the VBPROJ files it needs to load. Normally, if you use the Microsoft Installer (MSI) file we've supplied to install the examples, the virtual roots you need will already be created for you. If there's a problem finding a virtual root, Visual Studio .NET won't be able to load your project. You can always open the SLN file for your solution within a text editor (such as Notepad) and view or edit the virtual root the solution requires.

TIP

The virtual root information is also embedded in the `*.vbproj.webinfo` file associated with a project. The information in this file is transient and will be re-created for you when you restart Visual Studio .NET. If you find that you're having trouble loading a project, and you need to re-create or modify virtual roots, you can always delete this file so that you only need to worry about the one file that contains path information: the `*.sln` file.

- **Adding existing pages.** Some chapters require you to add existing pages to your sample project. In each case, instructions in the chapter will direct you to a particular folder within the `Jumpstart` directory tree. You'll be asked to copy files from the specific folder (using Windows Explorer) and then to paste the files into your project, within Visual Studio .NET. When you do this, Visual Studio .NET will place a copy of each file into the folder containing your project—you needn't worry about modifications you make affecting the originals, which remain intact.

- **Using existing projects.** When you load an existing project and then press F5 to begin running the project, Visual Studio .NET must know what the start page is for your project. If you receive an error message from Visual Studio .NET as you begin running your project, you can right-click the start page in the Solution Explorer window and then select Set as Start Page from the context menu. For most chapters, the start page will be `Main.aspx`. Some of the chapters may use a different start page, but those instances are called out appropriately in the text.

- **Typing code.** Some chapters contain a significant amount of code. You may want to type all the code yourself (it's all printed in the book—there's no "hidden" code), but you may want to copy and paste it into your project, instead. Although we find that we learn a great deal by actually typing the code, we've provided all the code in files named `Code.txt`, within the folder `Jumpstart-SampleCode`. You can locate the file named `Code.txt` in the subfolder listed in the `SampleCode` column of Table 1.1. Load the file into any text editor and then copy/paste the appropriate chunk of text into your project.

- **Flow layout versus grid layout.** Although Visual Studio .NET supports two ways to lay out pages (you control which you want by setting the page's `pageLayout` property), we suggest that, for the most part, you use the flowLayout setting. Selecting the gridLayout setting makes page designing experience "feel" more like designing in Visual Basic 6, but the rigidity of the exact placement of controls doesn't work quite as well in a Web page. You're welcome to choose whichever layout you like, but for the examples we've created, we always set the `pageLayout` property to flowLayout.

- **Adding controls using flow layout.** When working in flow layout, you may find it tricky to insert controls "in front of" other controls—that is, to insert a control earlier on the page than an existing control. The trick is to click the existing control and then press the left-arrow key to move the insertion point to the left of the control. Double-click the control you'd like to add, and Visual Studio .NET will place it immediately before the existing control.

- **Setting up debugging.** You'll want to be able to debug your ASP.NET applications, and Visual Studio .NET makes this easy. If you installed VS .NET under any other user ID than the one you use to log in to your computer, you will need to make sure your user ID is a member of the Debugger users group. This won't be a problem if you run under the same ID you used when installing. Also, if you have a problem debugging, make sure you've edited the project properties. Also, on the Configuration Properties, Debugging page, ensure that the ASP.NET Debugging option is selected.

TABLE 1.1   Find Sample Code and Finished Projects Using the Folders Listed in This Table

Chapter	Finished Project Folders Under \Jumpstart-Completed	Code.txt Files in Folders Under \Jumpstart-SampleCode
Chapter 1: Getting Started with the Sample Application		
Chapter 2: Introduction to Microsoft .NET		
Chapter 3: Introduction to Visual Studio .NET		
Chapter 4: Overview of .NET Framework Classes		
Chapter 5: Introduction to Internet Programming	InternetBasics	
Chapter 6: Introduction to ASP.NET	ASPIntro	ASPIntro
Chapter 7: Working with ASP.NET and VB .NET	VBLanguage	VBLanguage
Chapter 8: Validation Controls	ValidationControls	ValidationControls
Chapter 9: Debugging in Visual Studio .NET		
Chapter 10: Introduction to ADO.NET		
Chapter 11: Data Binding on Web Forms	DataBinding	DataBinding
Chapter 12: Error Handling		
Chapter 13: ADO.NET Connection and Command Objects	ConnectionCommands	ConnectionCommands
Chapter 14: Working with Data	WorkingWithData	WorkingWithData
Chapter 15: Using Stored Procedures with ADO.NET	StoredProcs	
Chapter 16: Using the DataGrid Control	DataGrid	DataGrid
Chapter 17: Editing Data Using the DataGrid Control	DataGridEditing	DataGridEditing
Chapter 18: Using the Repeater Control	Repeater	Repeater
Chapter 19: Using the DataList Control	DataList	DataList
Chapter 20: Using Crystal Reports	CrystalReports	CrystalReports
Chapter 21: Creating User Controls	CreatingControls	CreatingControls
Chapter 22: Rich ASP.NET Controls		

TABLE 1.1   Continued

Chapter	Finished Project Folders Under \Jumpstart-Completed	Code.txt Files in Folders Under \Jumpstart-SampleCode
Chapter 23: State Management in ASP.NET		
Chapter 24: Introduction to Web Security	Security	Security
Chapter 25: Creating Mobile Web Applications		Mobile
Chapter 26: Development and Deployment Techniques		
Chapter 27: Introduction to XML	XMLIntro	XMLIntro
Chapter 28: Introduction to XML Web Services		
Chapter 29: Creating and Consuming XML Web Services		WebService
Chapter 30: Investigating Web Service Consumers		WebServiceAsync
Chapter 31: Securing Web Services		WebServiceSecurity

SETTING UP FOLDERS CORRECTLY

When you are working on Web projects on your local machine, it is NOT a good idea to create all your folders underneath the \inetpub\wwwroot folder. This folder can become cluttered over time. In addition, in most medium-to-large Web applications you create, you will most likely not create the whole application under just one virtual root. We suggest that you create your own virtual root, somewhere outside of the \inetpub\wwwroot folder, and store your application in this new location.

If you've created a new virtual root named MyASPApps, for example, you can browse to this root as http://localhost/MyASPApps. From within Visual Studio .NET, you can create new projects under that same root by specifying the root when prompted for a project location.

To have Visual Studio .NET select your folder as its default project location, follow these steps:

1. Load Visual Studio .NET.

2. Select the Tools, Options menu item.

3. Select Environment, Projects and Solutions.

4. Change the Visual Studio Projects Location setting to the same folder where you created the virtual root.

5. Select Projects, Web Settings.

6. Change the location of the Web project cache to a folder you can find easily (for example, `D:\MyASPApps\VSWebCache`). This folder will become cluttered, and you want to put it somewhere you can find it and periodically clean it out.

TIP

Although we've covered a lot of material in this book, there's a lot more depth and breadth of material available. We suggest you start by visiting Microsoft's .NET site, `http://www.gotdotnet.com`. Also, make sure you investigate the Quickstart examples that ship as part of the .NET Framework. Look in the documentation for more information.

Introducing the Sample Application

In this section, we'll introduce the major portions of the sample application you'll be building and investigating as you work through this book. To get the most out of this book, we assume you are able to perform the following tasks:

- Create programs in some programming language (preferably Visual Basic or VBScript)

- Create a virtual directory in IIS

- Create basic HTML Web pages

- Write basic SQL statements

At this point, it's worth taking a few minutes to see what types of pages you'll be creating and how they display data from the Northwind sample database. We've described the functionality of each page and what you can expect to learn from each example.

The Main Page

The main page, shown in Figure 1.1, provides a jumping-off place for the rest of the application. On this page, you'll learn:

- How to create hyperlinks using HyperLink controls

- How to use LinkButton controls

- How to dynamically choose which hyperlinks to display

- How to navigate to other pages

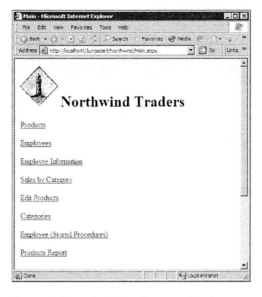

FIGURE 1.1 Use main.aspx to navigate to all your other pages.

The Login Page

You'll use the login page, shown in Figure 1.2, to allow users to log in to your application. In the beginning of this book, you will use this page to restrict access to certain menu items. Later, you'll learn to use this page as a required login page, disallowing access to the site until the user has successfully authenticated. (In the sample application, one of the valid login ID/password pairs is King/465.)

On this page, you'll learn:

- How to respond to Click events on Button controls

- How to set Session variables

- How to use Forms-based authentication

- How to redirect to a starting page if a user enters valid authentication information

- How to authenticate users against data in a database

The Products Page

The Products.aspx page, shown in Figure 1.3, uses a number of different controls and displays data from Microsoft SQL Server. You'll fill DropDownList controls, a

DataGrid control, and Label controls with data from several tables in the Northwind database.

FIGURE 1.2   The Login page helps you to secure your site against unwanted intruders.

On this page, you'll learn:

- How to react to handle control events
- How to use the ADO.NET DataSet object
- How to configure a DataAdapter so that it can retrieve data
- How to fill a DropDownList control using a DataReader
- How to use Connection and Command objects
- How to execute action queries

The Employees and Orders Page

The Employees.aspx page, shown in Figure 1.4, displays a drop-down list containing employee names. When you select an employee, the page displays orders for the selected employee in a DataGrid control.

On this page, you'll learn:

- How to build a DataSet containing multiple DataTable objects
- How to add a relationship between DataTable objects
- How to retrieve orders based on a selected employee, using parent/child relationships
- How to store and retrieve a DataSet using a Session variable

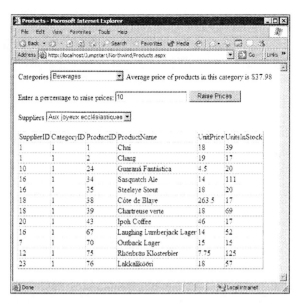

FIGURE 1.3   The Products.aspx page shows how to respond to many different events on different controls.

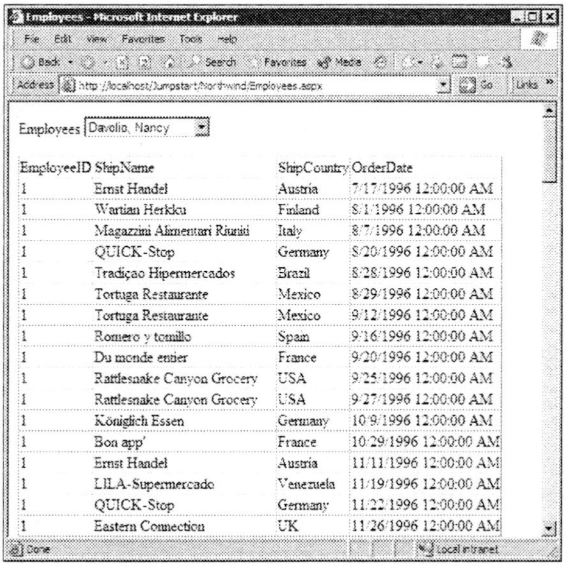

FIGURE 1.4   The Employees.aspx page shows that setting relationships between tables is easy with the DataSet object.

The Employees (Stored Procedures) Page

The EmployeeSP.aspx page, shown in Figure 1.5, will show you how to work with SQL Server stored procedures. This page demonstrates calling several stored procedures that you'll add to the Northwind sample database.

On this page, you'll learn:

- How to call stored procedures

- How to pass parameters to stored procedures

- How to retrieve output parameters returned from a stored procedure

- How to use both the OleDb and SqlClient namespaces, and why you would use one or the other

- Differences between the OleDb and SqlClient namespaces, with regards to stored procedures

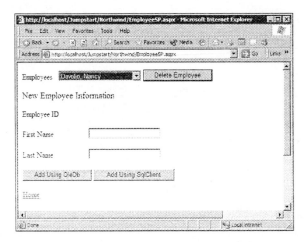

FIGURE 1.5   The EmployeeSP.aspx page shows you how to call stored procedures using both OleDb and SqlClient namespaces.

The Sales by Category Page

The CategorySales.aspx page, shown in Figure 1.6, shows you techniques for formatting, sorting, and selecting items within the DataGrid control. The DataGrid control is incredibly powerful, and this page demonstrates many of the useful features of this control.

On this page, you'll learn:

- How to format columns in a DataGrid control

- How to sort a DataGrid's data by clicking the column header

- How to select an item and respond to the ItemCommand event procedure

- How to pass information to the ItemCommand event procedure

- How to enable paging on a DataGrid control

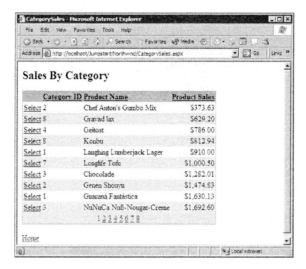

FIGURE 1.6   The DataGrid control can be formatted in many different ways, and you'll use several useful techniques on this page.

The Edit Products Page

The DataGrid control not only allows you to display data, it allows you to edit data in place, as well. The ProductsEdit.aspx page, shown in Figure 1.7, will allow you to edit product information within the grid as well as edit detail information on a separate page.

On this page, you'll learn:

- How to edit data "in place" in the DataGrid control

- How to delete a row from a DataGrid and the underlying database table

- How to add a row to a DataGrid control and the underlying database table

- How to add a hyperlink to a column of data so that selecting an item from the column navigates to a detail editing page

- How to use template columns in a DataGrid control

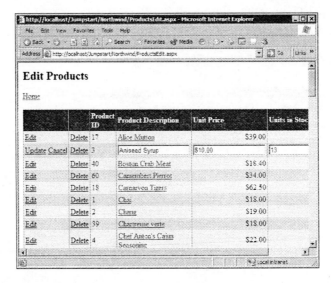

FIGURE 1.7   The tasks of adding, editing, and deleting on a DataGrid control are relatively easy, but they do require some care. This page shows you how.

The Product Details Page

When you select a link on the ProductsEdit.aspx page, shown in Figure 1.7, you navigate to the ProductDetail.aspx page, shown in Figure 1.8. This page shows you how to add or edit data on a "detail page" and save that data back to the underlying database table.

On this page, you'll learn:

- How to add or edit data retrieved from a DataGrid control

- How to submit data back to the database

- How to position a DropDownList control to a specified value

The Categories Page

The Categories.aspx page, shown in Figure 1.9, demonstrates how to display bound lists, drawing items from a data source.

FIGURE 1.8   A detail page is somewhat easier to enter data into than editing directly on the DataGrid control. This page shows how you can link a detail page and a DataGrid control.

On this page, you'll learn:

- How to use the Repeater control

- How to create header, footer, and item templates

- How to load data into the Repeater control

- How to display links using the Repeater control

FIGURE 1.9   Using the Repeater allows you to customize the display of the data using any HTML templates. In this case, the item template displays a bulleted list.

The Category Detail Page

The CategoryDetail.aspx page, shown in Figure 1.10, shows another use of the Repeater control. In this case, the item template is more complex and displays data in a nontabular format.

On this page, you'll learn:

- How to use the Repeater control to display a nontabular data layout

- How to select an item in the Repeater and display data based on the item selected

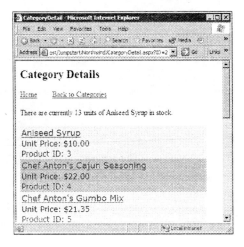

FIGURE 1.10   You can create complex formatting using the Repeater control because you decide how to lay out the various data elements.

The Employee Information Page

The EmployeeInfo.aspx page, shown in Figure 1.11, shows you how to display images and detail information and how to edit the data. This page also demonstrates how to display data in multiple rows and columns (as you might when displaying data for a phone list or items available for sale).

On this page, you'll learn:

- How to use the DataList control

- How to display rows of data using the DataList control and its HTML templates

- How to use the HTML designers for DataList templates

- How to add, edit, and delete data using the DataList control

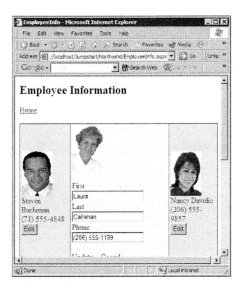

FIGURE 1.11   The DataList control is the most flexible control available if you want to display multiple rows and columns of data.

The Employee Maintenance Page

The EmpMaint.aspx page, shown in Figure 1.12, shows how you can validate data on an ASP.NET page. This page demonstrates several different techniques for validating data, including requiring input, ensuring data is within a certain range, and running your own code in order to validate data.

On this page, you'll learn:

- How to use all the validation controls, including the RequiredFieldValidator, RegularExpressionValidator, and RangeValidator controls

- How to display a validation summary using the ValidationSummary control

- How to create your own validation procedures for use with the CustomValidator control

The Change Password Page

The PwdChange.aspx page, shown in Figure 1.13, shows how you can compare two values and disallow posting the page until the values are the same. This is a common technique used when asking for a new user password. On this page, you'll learn how to use the CompareValidator control.

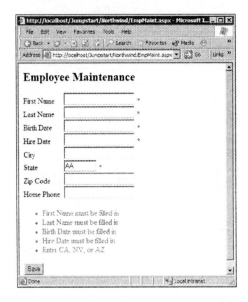

FIGURE 1.12   Validating data is simple using the ASP.NET validation controls.

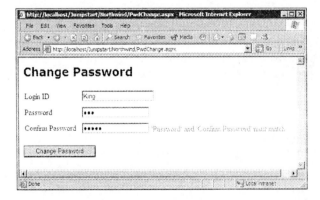

FIGURE 1.13   Use the CompareValidator control to verify that two values match.

Using the Debugger

The `Jumpstart\Debugger\Debugger.sln` solution, shown in Figure 1.14, walks you through using many of the features of the debugger provided by Visual Studio .NET.

In this solution, you'll learn:

- How to set breakpoints
- How to use the Debug class

- How to use `WriteLine` and `Assert`

- How to use conditional compilation

FIGURE 1.14   Learn to use the Visual Studio .NET debugger with this project.

Handling Errors

The `Jumpstart\ErrorHandling\ErrorHandling.sln` solution, shown in Figure 1.15, walks you through structured exception handling, which is new in Visual Basic .NET.

In this solution, you'll learn:

- How to add exception handling to your code

- How to use the `Try` and `Catch` keywords

- How to retrieve exception information

- How to add code that runs whether or not an exception occurs using the `Finally` keyword

Using the Framework Classes

The `Jumpstart\Framework\FrameworkClasses.sln` solution, shown in Figure 1.16, introduces and demonstrates several objects and namespaces (selected from the thousands of available objects and namespaces) provided by the .NET Framework.

In this solution, you'll learn:

- How to use the `OleDb` and `SqlClient` namespaces

- How to write to a file using the `System.IO` namespace

- How to use the `StringBuilder` class

- How to use the `Collection` classes

- How to use XML classes

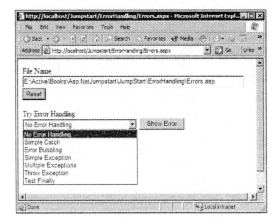

FIGURE 1.15   Demonstrate various types of exception handling using this sample project.

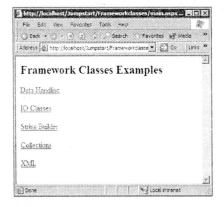

FIGURE 1.16   This page navigates to sample pages, testing out several of the .NET Framework classes.

Using Other ASP.NET Controls

The `Jumpstart\MiscWebControls\MiscWebControls.sln` solution, shown in Figure 1.17, walks you through using many of the ASP.NET controls not covered elsewhere in this book. The .NET Framework provides a rich palette of server controls, and some of them just didn't fit into the Northwind project you'll create.

In this solution, you'll learn:

- How to use the CheckBoxList and RadioButtonList controls to select from a list of values

- How to use the Calendar control to select dates

- How to use the AdRotator control to display randomly selected images from an XML file containing a list of available images

- How to use the Literal control to inject HTML into a page

- How to use the Placeholder control to reserve space for dynamically created controls

FIGURE 1.17   Learn how to use the RadioButtonList, CheckBoxList, AdRotator, Calendar, Literal, and Placeholder controls in this solution.

Using the Mobile Internet Toolkit

The Jumpstart\MITSample\MITSample.sln solution, shown in Figure 1.18, walks you through creating a simple page using the Mobile Internet Toolkit, showing you how to create Web applications that can be browsed from multiple handheld devices.

In this solution, you'll learn:

- How to build a Web application targeted to mobile devices

- How to use the server controls provided by the Microsoft Mobile Internet Toolkit

- How to display data on mobile Web forms

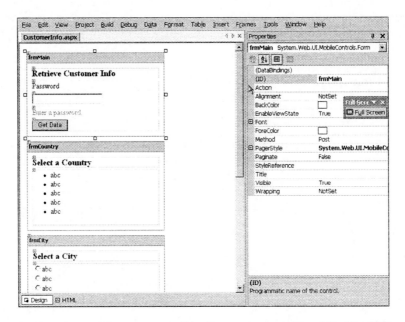

FIGURE 1.18 The Mobile Internet Toolkit allows you to use Visual Studio .NET to create mobile applications.

Using State Management

The Jumpstart\StateMgmt\StateMgmt.sln solution, shown in Figure 1.19, demonstrates using the built-in features of state management in the .NET Framework.

In this solution, you'll learn:

- How to manage state using cookies

- How to manage state using StateBag objects

- How to manage state using the ASP.NET State service

- How to manage state using SQL Server

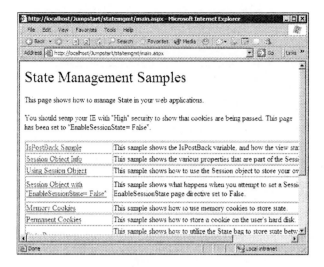

FIGURE 1.19   The .NET Framework provides multiple ways in which you can manage state within your applications. This solution walks you through several of these techniques.

Introducing Visual Basic .NET Language Basics

The Jumpstart\VBLanguage\VBLanguage.sln solution, shown in Figure 1.20, introduces you to many of the new features of the Visual Basic .NET language.

In this solution, you'll learn:

- How to respond to events

- Which data types are available in VB .NET

- How to convert data from one type to another

- How to create procedures

- How to create classes

- How to use Shared methods in classes

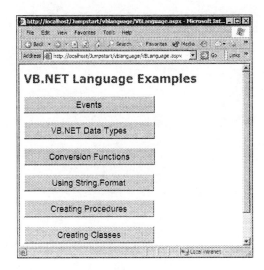

FIGURE 1.20   Learn features of Visual Basic .NET using this project.

Summary

In this chapter, you saw an overview of each of the Web pages and projects you'll build or investigate as you work through this book. Here's what you saw:

- All the important pages from the Northwind sample project that you'll be building

- An introduction to each of the subsidiary projects you'll investigate, in order to learn the topics not covered in the Northwind sample project

2

Introduction to Microsoft .NET

OBJECTIVES

- Learn about the Microsoft .NET Framework

- Learn about the Common Language Runtime (CLR)

.NET is Microsoft's platform for XML Web Services—the next generation of software that connects our world of information, devices, and people in a unified, personalized way. The .NET platform enables the creation and use of XML-based applications and Web sites as services that share and combine information. These services can target any platform or smart device to provide tailored solutions for organizations and individuals.

The .NET platform includes a comprehensive family of products, built on industry XML and Internet standards. This family of products includes tools such as Visual Studio .NET, servers such as SQL Server and BizTalk server, and building block services such as .NET Passport and .NET MyServices. These all help developers create applications that are rich in features. .NET will become part of the Microsoft applications, tools, and servers you already use today as well as new products that extend XML Web Service capabilities to all of your business needs.

In addition to these XML Web Services, .NET will also allow you to build more traditional applications. Using .NET, you can build Windows desktop applications, Windows Services, Web sites, console applications, and components for use in other applications. Any of these applications can also be used in conjunction with the XML Web Services applications you create.

.NET and XML

The .NET platform requires XML—specifically XML Web Services—to achieve its vision of applications communicating seamlessly across disparate networks, hardware, and software. XML Web Services enable applications to communicate and share data over the Internet, regardless of operating system or programming language. XML Web Services are not complex. In fact, it's their simplicity that makes them so powerful. They are no more than XML text messages passing back and forth between computers via the same network or across the Internet.

The key to making XML Web Services work is to agree to a simple data description format—and that format is XML. Specifically, XML Web Services use XML for three things:

- **Wire format: SOAP.** At the lowest level, systems need to speak the same language. In particular, communicating applications need to have a set of rules for how they are going to represent different data types (such as integers and arrays) and how they are going to represent commands (that is, what should be done with the data). Also, the applications need a way to extend this language if they have to. The Simple Object Access Protocol (SOAP), now on its way to becoming a W3C standard, is a common set of rules about how data and commands will be represented and extended.

- **Description: Web Services Description Language.** Once applications have general rules for how they will represent data types and commands, they need a way to describe the specific data and commands they accept. It's not enough for an application to say that it accepts integers; somehow, there must be a way to deterministically say that, if you give it two integers, it will multiply them. The Web Services Description Language (WSDL), also working its way through W3C standardization, is an XML grammar that developers and development tools can use to represent the capabilities of an XML Web Service.

- **Discovery: UDDI.** The final layer needed is a set of rules for how to locate a service's description—where does a human or tool look by default to discover a service's capabilities? The Universal Description, Discovery, and Integration (UDDI) specification provides a set of rules so that a human or development tool can automatically discover a service's WSDL description.

Once these three layers are in place, a developer can easily find an XML Web Service, instantiate it as an object, integrate it into an application, and build enough infrastructure so that the resulting application can easily use this XML Web Service.

Overview of the .NET Framework

Clearly, a considerable amount of infrastructure is required to make XML Web Services transparent to the developers and users. The .NET Framework provides that infrastructure. To the .NET Framework, all components can be XML Web Services, and XML Web Services are just a kind of component. In effect, the .NET Framework takes the best aspects of the Microsoft Component Object Model (COM) and combines them with the best aspects of loosely coupled, XML-based computing. The result is a powerful, productive Web component system that simplifies programmer plumbing, deeply integrates security, introduces an Internet-scale deployment system, and greatly improves application reliability and scalability.

The .NET Framework consists of two main parts: the Common Language Runtime (CLR) and a set of unified class libraries. The class libraries include versions of many of Microsoft's existing development technologies, such as an advanced version of Active Server Pages, called ASP.NET, a set of classes for rich user interface development, called Windows Forms, and a data-access subsystem called ADO.NET. All these existing libraries have been updated to be XML aware within the .NET Framework.

The Common Language Runtime

Despite its name, the Common Language Runtime actually has a role in a component's development time and runtime experiences. While the component is running, the runtime is responsible for managing memory allocation, starting up and killing threads and processes, enforcing security policy, and satisfying any dependencies that the component may have on other components. At development time, the runtime's role changes slightly. Because it automates so much (for example, memory management), the runtime makes the developer's experience very simple, especially when compared to COM today. In particular, features such as reflection dramatically reduce the amount of code a developer must write in order to turn business logic into a reusable component.

Runtimes are nothing new for languages—virtually every programming language has a runtime. Visual Basic has the most obvious runtime (the aptly named VBRUN), but Visual C++ has one (MSVCRT), as do FoxPro, JScript, Smalltalk, Perl, Python, and Java. The .NET Framework's critical role, and what really sets it apart, is that it provides a unified runtime and development environment across all programming languages.

The .NET Classes

The .NET Framework's classes provide a unified, object-oriented, hierarchical, extensible set of class libraries (APIs) for developers to use. Today, C++ developers will use the Microsoft Foundation Classes, Java developers will use the Windows Foundation Classes or J2EE, and Visual Basic developers will use VB's APIs. Simply put, the .NET

CLR unifies the disparate frameworks Microsoft has today. The result is that developers no longer have to learn multiple frameworks when working in multiple languages. By creating a common set of APIs across all programming languages, the .NET Framework enables cross-language inheritance, error handling, and debugging. In effect, all programming languages, from JScript to C++, become equals, and developers are free to choose the language they want to use.

Here are some of the key benefits of the .NET Framework for developers:

- **Can use any .NET-enabled programming language.** The .NET Framework enables developers to use any .NET-enabled programming language, and it enables applications written in these languages to integrate deeply with each other, which means current development skills can be used right away within the same project and future projects.

- **Can write less code.** The .NET Framework uses a highly "componentized," plumbing-free design that enables developers to focus on writing business logic. Developers don't need to write Interface Definition Language (IDL) or Registry code anymore. ASP.NET, for example, includes dozens of controls that encapsulate common programmer tasks, such as user validation, creating calendars and ad rotators, and much more.

- **Can use XML and SOAP without learning these technologies.** The .NET Framework was built for delivering software as a service, so it is built on XML and the SOAP family of integration standards. Simply annotate method calls and the .NET Framework turns them into full XML Web Services. You do not need to learn these underlying technologies because the .NET Framework wraps classes around them.

- **Can run more reliable applications.** The .NET Framework includes technologies to make applications more reliable. For example, memory, threads, and processes are managed by the .NET Framework to ensure that memory leaks don't occur. Also, ASP.NET monitors running Web applications and can automatically restart them at administrator-defined intervals. In addition, when applications are upgraded (versioned), the .NET Framework includes technologies to avoid version conflicts (often called *DLL hell*).

- **Can improve performance.** The .NET Framework improves the performance of typical Web applications. ASP.NET includes advanced compilation and caching features that improve performance by a factor of two to three over existing Active Server Pages applications.

Figure 2.1 gives you an overview of how the different pieces of the .NET Framework relate to one another.

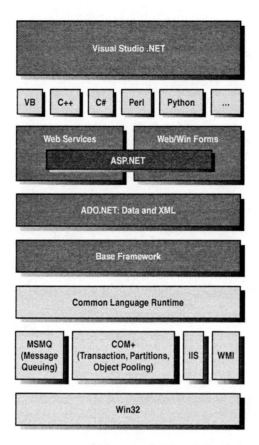

FIGURE 2.1   All the layers of the .NET platform, from the OS all the way up to the
highest-level classes.

The Win32 APIs are at the lowest level in this platform. Above are the common
services built in to the OS, with which you can interact. These include the message
queuing services, transactions, Internet Information Server (IIS), and the Windows
Management Instrumentation (WMI). The CLR in the .NET Framework interacts with
these lower-level services so all .NET languages can interact with these services using
a common interface. On top of the CLR is a framework of classes, including
ADO.NET and ASP.NET.

Next comes the set of languages that have been written to take advantage of the
.NET Framework. These languages are most of the common languages in use today,
including Visual Basic, C++, C# (a new language), COBOL, Perl, Python, Eiffel, and
many others.

Common Language Specification

The Common Language Specification (CLS) is a contract that states how a language that interacts with the CLR will behave. When languages use the CLS, they are said to be using *managed code*. Managed code is a set of language constructs that all .NET languages must contain, including data types, error handling, metadata, and so forth.

Managed code can be broken down by a compiler into a set of *bytecodes*, known as the *Microsoft Intermediate Language* (MSIL or IL). The MSIL is stored, along with some metadata about the program itself, in a portable executable (EXE or DLL).

Intermediate Language

Intermediate Language (IL) is used so that a compiler can translate the program into the final code, which can, in turn, be interpreted by the OS and the hardware. Using IL makes it easier to create a compiler for that IL for any OS and hardware platform.

The compiler for .NET is called a Just-In-Time (JIT) compiler. When you distribute a DLL or EXE file, it is not in an executable format. Instead, it is in a Microsoft IL (MSIL) format that will be compiled into native code for the target operating system. This compilation can either be done at runtime (JIT) or when the program is installed for the first time. In either case, it is the JIT compiler that performs this compilation, as shown in Figure 2.2.

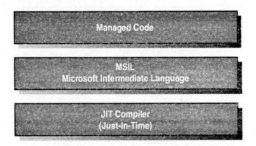

FIGURE 2.2   Managed code is compiled down to MSIL, which is then compiled by the JIT compiler.

Services in .NET

The .NET Framework supplies many services to a developer. Here are some of the most notable ones:

- Memory management
- Threads

- Garbage collection

- Exception handling

- Security

- Application isolation

- Data interaction

- Encryption services

- Deployment

In the past, to get all these sophisticated services, you either had to build them yourself or use a higher-level language. The problem with building these services yourself is they are ancillary to the actual program. Most customers just want a business problem solved; they do not want you spending your time developing security systems and garbage-collection routines. In other words, they just want you to give them a program that solves their problem. Therefore, in a low-level language, you might end up spending twice as long to get an application that accomplishes the business purpose because you have to spend so long on designing all of these infrastructure services.

If you use a high-level language, most of these services are built in. However, if they are not built in to the language, you might not be able to build these services because the language is so far removed from the OS. This means that it is difficult, if not impossible, to take advantage of threading or security from that language.

All these services can be used from any language that works with the CLR. So now your choice of language does not matter so much, because everything compiles down to the same Intermediate Language.

Data Services (ADO.NET)

One of the new services built in to the .NET Framework is a complete new data-access model called ADO.NET. Although it has the same name as an earlier data-access technique, called ADO, it is very different. You might recognize some of the objects that are similar to the Connection and Command objects in ADO, but there are enough different methods and properties to keep you on your toes.

The biggest difference between the two models is how the data is stored in memory after it is read from the database. In ADO, the recordsets were stored in a binary format. In ADO.NET, they are stored as XML. Another big change is that ADO.NET is disconnected. That is, ADO.NET does not keep any connections open after reading the data in from a data source.

There are several new classes, such as `Command`, `DataAdapter`, `DataReader`, and `DataSet`. The `Recordset` object is gone, and all records are read either from the `DataReader` or the `DataSet` object.

`DataSet` objects allow you to read in several tables into one object. You can then set relationships between the tables in memory as well as add, edit, and delete the data in these tables, and you can store the data back in the database. The schema for the tables is also read in and stored in an XML format.

ADO.NET has the capability to natively read and write to XML. In addition, you can use OLE DB or native providers to read data from data sources such as SQL Server, Oracle, and Access.

Security Services

Security is pervasive throughout the .NET Framework. Table 2.1 shows some of the different types of security that you can set up for your applications.

TABLE 2.1   The Different Security Types in .NET

Security Type	Description
Access Control	Secures objects, such as files, Registry keys, and directory service objects
Security Support Provider Interface	Establishes authenticated connections
Logon Authenticated	Provides for password filtering, Windows logon, and local security authentication
Certificate Services and Components	Issues and manages certificates
Cryptography	Provides a set of classes based on the Crypto API functions in Windows 2000
Smart Card	Allows you to integrate with smart card–based authentication
Policy Management	Programmatically sets and manages local security policies

Common Type System and Standard Data Types

As part of the .NET Framework and the CLR, it is important that all languages have access to common data types. This makes the interoperability between languages much easier. To accomplish this, Microsoft has created the Common Type System with a standard set of data types that each language can utilize.

Data types in .NET are no longer defined by each language. Instead, they are a core part of the CLR. Each data type is itself an object. Each language has the choice to implement all of them or just a subset.

Table 2.2 lists each of the different data types and tells which languages implement each one.

TABLE 2.2   Each Data Type in the .NET Framework Is Actually Implemented as a Class

Data Type	Description	Language Usage
Byte	8-bit unsigned integer	Visual Basic: Byte C#: Byte Visual C++: Char
Sbyte	8-bit signed integer	Visual Basic: N/A C#: sbyte Visual C++: signed char
Int16	16-bit signed integer	Visual Basic: Short C#: short Visual C++: short
Int32	32-bit signed integer	Visual Basic: Integer C#: int C++: int or long
Int64	64-bit signed integer	Visual Basic: Long C#: long Visual C++: _int64
Unint16	16-bit unsigned integer	Visual Basic: N/A C#: ushort Visual C++: unsigned short
Uint32	32-bit unsigned integer	Visual Basic: N/A C#: uint Visual C++: unsigned int or unsigned long
Uint64	64-bit unsigned integer	Visual Basic: N/A C#: ulong Visual C++: unsigned __int64
Single	32-bit floating-point number	Visual Basic: Single C#: float Visual C++: float
Double	64-bit floating-point number	Visual Basic: Double C#: double Visual C++: double
Boolean	True (1) or False (0)	Visual Basic: Boolean C#: bool Visual C++: bool
Object	The base type of any class or data type	Visual Basic: Object C#: object Visual C++: Object
Char	Unicode character (16 bit)	Visual Basic: Char C#: Char Visual C++: __wchar_t

TABLE 2.2   Continued

Data Type	Description	Language Usage
String	A string of Unicode characters	Visual Basic: String
		C#: string
		Visual C++: String
Decimal	96-bit decimal value	Visual Basic: Decimal
		C#: decimal
		Visual C++: Decimal

Types of Applications You Can Build

With the .NET Framework, you can build many different types of applications, including the following:

- Windows applications

- Windows Services

- ASP.NET Web applications

- ASP.NET Web Services (XML Web Services)

- Class libraries

- Windows Forms custom controls

- Web Forms custom controls

In this book, you will learn how to build ASP.NET Web applications and ASP.NET Web Services. You will be shown how to create Class Library (DLLs) projects to help you "componetize" your applications. This section describes each of these project types in a little more detail.

Windows Applications

A Windows application involves a rich user interface (UI) client that runs on a Windows OS. It uses the Windows Forms engine to create the UI. Windows applications are best suited for client/server database applications, numerical control, graphical programs, or any application that needs to have a rich UI.

Windows Forms

Windows Forms are the new form engine for Windows development. You can use Windows Forms with any CLR language. Windows Forms can be ported from one language to another easily. Windows Forms come with a rich set of standard controls built in, and you can build your own controls as well.

Windows Services

A Windows Service is an application that runs under Windows NT, Windows 2000 Server, or Advanced Server. These types of applications do not typically have a UI. Instead, they are used to perform some ongoing service without any interaction from a user. The OS starts a Windows Service application when the OS itself starts up. You may need to supply a security context for this service. You can create these types of applications very easily with .NET.

Web Applications

A Web application is an interactive set of HTML pages that run programs on a Web server. Web applications can either have a UI or not. You will be using this type of application most often as you read through this book. ASP.NET is at the heart of Web applications and is the replacement for the older Active Server Pages (ASP) technology.

ASP.NET

ASP.NET is an enhanced version of ASP. If you have programmed in ASP before, you will find the move to ASP.NET very easy. Porting your old ASP applications to ASP.NET may prove to be somewhat of a challenge, so you might choose to rewrite as you go. ASP and ASP.NET can run side by side within the same IIS computer.

ASP.NET provides the following enhancements:

- Better session statement management

- Better handling of Web farms

- Two to three times faster performance than ASP

- Uses compiled code, as opposed to an interpreted scripting language like ASP does

- Better caching techniques

- Includes both Web Forms and XML Web Services for developing either a UI or non-UI application

ASP.NET Web Forms

ASP.NET Web Forms are the Internet equivalent of Windows Forms. Server-side controls have a lot of flexibility, including the capability to bind to a data source and generate a lot of HTML that otherwise would be very tedious to code. These server-side controls can generate standard HTML 3.2 or include Internet Explorer (IE) extensions for a richer UI. These server-side controls have a rich programming interface too.

XML Web Services

An XML Web Service is an application that exposes its features through XML, specifically SOAP. You use both XML and SOAP to call these services. With the .NET tools, you only need to use built-in classes to interact with and build XML Web Services—you never have to see or use the XML or SOAP specifications.

You can return many types of information to users with XML Web Services, including the following:

- Authorization on credit cards
- Shipment status
- Order confirmations
- Stock quotes
- Catalog/product information

Class Libraries

A class library is a collection of classes that you build into one project, and you compile that project as a DLL. These libraries can then be reused in any application that you build. In Visual Basic 6.0, these Class Library projects are called *COM DLLs*. Although they are still DLLs in .NET, they no longer rely on COM.

Migrating to .NET

.NET takes advantage of the best of all the technologies you have used to date, and it improves upon them. If you have an existing application in Visual Basic 6.0, you can attempt to migrate to Visual Basic .NET. There are several methods you can use to migrate, including simply reusing any COM components you already have developed, creating new components in .NET and using them from your VB 6.0 applications, or using the Migration Wizard.

Migration Tools

NET allows you to leverage your existing code by providing a nice interface to your COM components. With just a couple mouse clicks within the Visual Studio environment, you can bring in your COM component and use it just as if it were a class library you developed in .NET.

The Migration Wizard will help you migrate from an existing Visual Basic 6.0 application to a VB .NET application. The Migration Wizard will convert many common elements of your Visual Basic 6.0 applications, but it cannot convert everything. You will still need to make many changes to your code by hand. You may also need to rewrite certain sections to take full advantage of new tools.

The Migration Wizard will also attempt to convert common ActiveX controls into .NET controls. In those cases where there is no equivalent, it will attempt to use the ActiveX control on the Windows Form (WinForm) in .NET. Many ActiveX controls will work on a .NET WinForm, but there are no guarantees.

Reasons to Migrate

The .NET Framework includes many interlanguage integration features, such as inheritance, debugging, common data types, and Windows and Web Forms. Creating Web applications has never been easier, and cross-platform capabilities using XML Web Services makes communication with non-Windows applications a breeze.

The installation and removal of programs is much easier now that .NET applications no longer have to be registered like previous COM applications did. Installations can be done by using a simple copy command, and uninstalling is as simple as deleting the files. Of course, this assumes that the .NET Framework and the CLR are already installed.

SHOULD YOU REWRITE?

In most cases, you might want to leave your older applications in their original language. But if you find that an application that started out as a departmental-level application now needs to be an enterprise-wide application, you might want to rewrite.

The Internet has changed society and business as we know it. You now need to think about all programs as being "global" and "distributed." Doing this with the tools before .NET was not easy; in global distribution cases, you will probably want to migrate your old applications. In most cases, you will probably find that you can remove large sections of your code and replace them with just a few objects in the new .NET Framework.

Benefits of Using the .NET Framework

.NET provides advantages for everyone involved with the application-development process. The discussion in this section takes into account the people who will be directly affected by you choosing to use the .NET Framework. When making the decision to go with .NET, you will need to consider the benefits for the users, developers, and managers involved with the project.

What's in It for Users

Users will be able to get fast information using XML Web Services and by collaborating via the Internet. Their personal information may be stored in one central database, and they can access it from their work machine, home machine, or maybe even their cell phone.

What's in It for Developers

The .NET Framework allows developers to build the types of applications that users demand. With a common set of system tools, they will be able to write code once and have it delivered to a wide range of devices faster than ever.

Instead of developers having to learn complicated tools such as XML and SOAP, the .NET Framework wraps up these interfaces into an easy-to-use object-oriented structure. This accelerates the learning curve for new developers while allowing advanced developers to create Web applications in a fraction of the time they could before.

Because installations are much easier, time-to-market will diminish for newly developed applications.

What's in It for Managers

Managers are often faced with too many projects, not enough time, and not enough programmers to get their projects done. Because most of the core services are already in place within the .NET Framework, programmers will be able to create applications faster than before, thus allowing more projects to be completed.

In a large corporate environment, managers may also be faced with the challenge of integrating many disparate systems. Using XML can help these different systems talk back and forth. Before the .NET Framework, if systems needed to run across the Internet, getting outside the corporate firewall with proprietary protocols or binary data was difficult, if not impossible. The use of XML in all transmissions within the .NET Framework ensures that you can talk across an open standard such as HTTP.

As companies grow, the need to scale distributed applications becomes an issue. In the .NET Framework, scalability is built in to all core services. Threading across all languages will help with this scalability as well.

Security is another area that will help put managers' minds at ease. There are many different security models in the .NET Framework that should satisfy almost anyone's needs.

.NET also offers benefits for managing personnel resources. For instance, training is always an issue when advanced developers use proprietary or new technologies and new developers are brought in to maintain these systems. The .NET Framework's OOP approach makes learning its classes much easier.

Additionally, with so many languages that can use the .NET Framework, managers will be able to utilize many different programmers with different language skills. Yet, all programmers can use each others' code. This is the ultimate in flexibility and productivity from a manager's standpoint.

Summary

The .NET Framework is a major step forward in the evolution of programming. You will find that using the .NET classes, tools, and other features will help speed up your development cycle. It also means that you'll adhere to the foundation that Microsoft has set forth, and you are sure to find it to be a well-laid foundation. This chapter provided you with a brief overview of many of the new features of the .NET Framework. Here are some of the major points you should understand from reading this chapter:

- .NET will help make the creation and consumption of XML Web Services very easy.

- You can create many different types of applications using the .NET platform.

- XML is an integral part of .NET and the future of communication between applications.

- You will derive many benefits out of using the new .NET platform.

3

Introduction to Visual Studio .NET

OBJECTIVES

- Learn about creating and working with projects in Visual Studio .NET

- Learn how to configure the Visual Studio .NET development environment

Visual Studio .NET provides an incredibly rich working environment. Although creating applications using the .NET Framework doesn't require the use of Visual Studio .NET, it's a lot easier, and more fun, to use Visual Studio .NET as your development environment. To get the most out of Microsoft Visual Studio .NET, you will most likely wish to tailor it to suit your style of working. With the wide variety of configuration options, both familiar and new, you'll want to take the time to examine some of the various options.

In this chapter, you will be introduced to many of the different configurations and learn about the various settings in Visual Studio .NET. Along the way, you'll also learn about many of the different tools provided by Visual Studio .NET that make your job of creating applications easier.

This chapter introduces many of the tools and windows provided, presented in the order you will most likely encounter them as you work with the product.

Configuring Visual Studio .NET

The first time you start Visual Studio .NET, you will be presented with a profile page. On this page, you can create a profile of yourself as a developer. Although you could keep the default (Visual Studio Developer), you might want to select the Visual Basic Developer profile so that the environment will automatically adapt a look and feel similar to the old Visual Basic 6.0 Integrated Development Environment (IDE). Figure 3.1 shows an example of the My Profile page.

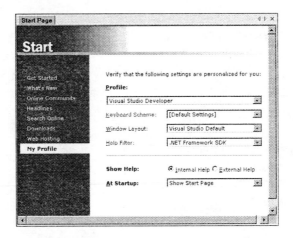

FIGURE 3.1   Setting the configuration on the My Profile screen.

> **TIP**
>
> Although you can use any profile you like, we've selected the Visual Basic Developer profile, and when we describe keystrokes throughout this book, they may not work if you've selected a different profile. In addition, you can always return to this page by selecting the My Profile link on the Visual Studio .NET Start page.

The My Profile Page

In addition to the profile, the My Profile page allows you to set some overall environment defaults. You can, for example, select an existing profile and then modify the window or keyboard layouts individually.

Table 3.1 provides a list of some of the options on the My Profile screen.

TABLE 3.1 Fields on the My Profile Screen

Field	Description
Profile	Set this field to the general window and keyboard layout you'd like to use. You can modify any of the specifics (window or keyboard layout) individually, as well. You have the option of choosing from Visual Studio, Visual Basic, Visual C++, Visual InterDev, VS Macro, Student, and Visual C# developer.
Keyboard Scheme	Select the keyboard mappings you're comfortable with. You can select from Visual Studio Default, Visual Basic 6, Visual C++ 2, Visual C++ 6, and Visual Studio 6.
Window Layout	Set the default window layout to one of the following: Visual Studio Default, Visual Basic 6, Visual C++ 6, Student Window Layout, or No Tools Window Layout.
Help Filter	Set the default filter for help content. This determines which language definitions and examples show up in the Help window when you press F1 or view any help topics.
Show Help	Choose to view help in a separate window or integrated into the IDE.
At Startup	Select the item that's displayed when you start Visual Studio .NET. You have the option of showing one of the following: Show Start Page, Load Last Loaded Solution, Show Open Project Dialog Box, Show New Project Dialog Box, or Show Empty Environment.

Visual Studio Start Page

The Visual Studio Start page, shown in Figure 3.2, is the page you'll see when you start Visual Studio, if you've selected to show this page at startup.

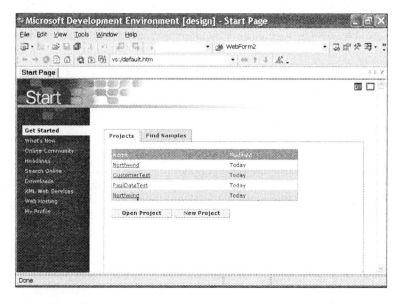

FIGURE 3.2 The Visual Studio Start page allows you to start a recent project, open an existing project, or create a new project.

The menu on the left side of this page includes a number of links, including "What's New" help topics. You can see a list of online community links, where you can get assistance with Visual Studio .NET and many other Microsoft products. You can get the headlines for MSDN news, search the MSDN site for information related to Visual Studio, download sample code and tutorials, check out what's new in XML Web Services, and even get a list of service providers that can host your ASP.NET Web sites. You can get back to the My Profile page to modify your profile from this menu, as well. Note that many of these links will only work when you are connected to the Internet.

In the body of this page, you can select a recent project, create a new project, or open an existing project by selecting it from the file system.

> **TIP**
>
> After you have loaded a project, the Start Page will disappear from your IDE. To bring it back, right-click in the toolbar area of VS .NET and choose the Web toolbar. In the address area of the Web toolbar, type `vs:/default.htm`.

Creating a New Project

If you choose File, New, Project from the Visual Studio .NET menu bar, you will see a dialog box like the one shown in Figure 3.3. When putting together an application in Visual Studio .NET, you will choose one or many of the different types of projects to make up your solution. For example, you can create an ASP.NET Web application that also uses a Class Library project and an ASP.NET Web Service project as well. A solution can therefore be made up of one or more projects.

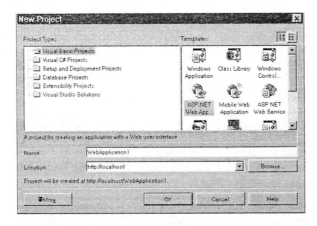

FIGURE 3.3   The New Project dialog box allows you to create a new solution starting with a particular project type.

On the left side of this screen, you can choose the language you will use to create your new project. Depending on the options you selected when you installed your Visual Studio environment, you can choose from Visual Basic .NET, C#, C++, and any other .NET programming language you have installed. Microsoft isn't the only supplier of .NET-supported languages—other vendors have written languages that work just as well in Visual Studio .NET as the languages provided by Microsoft.

On the right side of this screen, you can choose a default template for the type of project you will be creating. You have many different templates to choose from, as described in the next section.

If you choose the ASP.NET Web Application project type, you will be asked to provide a project name. You will also be prompted to specify the Web server name where you wish to place this new Web site. The example in Figure 3.2 is creating a Web root in `http://localhost/` on the current machine. Whichever Web server you choose, you must have installed the .NET Framework on that machine prior to creating a Web project using Visual Studio .NET.

In this book, you will investigate the ASP.NET Web Application project type in great detail. In addition, you will also look at creating mobile Web applications, ASP.NET Web Services, and Class Library projects.

Project Templates

The .NET platform supports a variety of project types. Visual Studio .NET provides you with templates that make the task of creating and getting started with a new project simpler. Table 3.2 lists a variety of project types you can create with Visual Studio .NET.

TABLE 3.2 Project Types You Can Create with Visual Studio .NET

Project Type	Description
Windows Application	A template for creating a Windows desktop application using Windows Forms.
Class Library	A template for creating a DLL of one or more classes that can be used and reused in multiple applications.
Control Library	A template for creating controls that will be used on Windows Forms.
ASP.NET Web Application	A template for creating a Web site with static or dynamic HTML pages as the user interface.
Mobile Web Application	A template for creating mobile Web applications, targeting PDA and phone devices. (This template will only be displayed if you have installed the Microsoft Mobile Internet Toolkit.)
ASP.NET Web Service	A template for creating XML Web Services.

TABLE 3.2   Continued

Project Type	Description
Web Control Library	A template for creating your own ASP.NET server controls.
Console Application	A template for creating command-line applications.
Windows Service	A template for creating your own Windows services.
Empty Project/Empty Web Project	A template that creates an empty project. Use this template to create any type of project.

Visual Studio Integrated Development Environment (IDE)

When you start a new project in Visual Studio .NET, you will see a group of windows opened within the development environment (one possible layout is shown in Figure 3.4). The following subsections describe each of these windows.

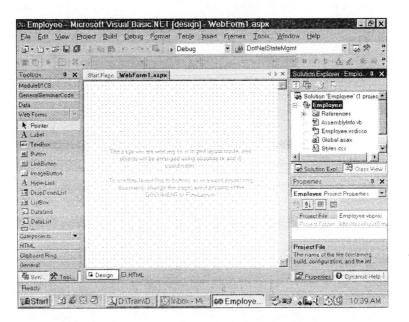

FIGURE 3.4   Several windows will be open when you start a new Visual Studio .NET project.

Toolbox Window

The Toolbox window contains a list of controls or components that you can drag and drop onto your design surface. The Toolbox window contains several tabs that make different sets of components available, depending on the type of designer active in the editor window (the window in the middle of the environment). If you are designing a Windows Form, you will get a specific set of tools that work with Windows Forms. If you are designing a Web Form, you will get a specific set of tools for working with Web Forms. If you are designing an XML document, there will be other options you can choose. To view the Toolbox window, select View, Toolbox from the Visual Studio .NET menu bar. Figure 3.5 shows the Toolbox window displaying controls available on Windows Forms.

FIGURE 3.5   The Toolbox holds a list of controls.

TIP

In addition to providing the standard tools and tabs that Visual Studio .NET provides, you can add tabs, as well as your own code snippets, to the Toolbox. Right-click the Toolbox window to add or delete tabs. You can drag code from the code editor onto the Toolbox, as well, for later use.

If you wish to customize the list of tools displayed in the Toolbox window, or if you wish to add any additional .NET components, ActiveX controls, or third-party controls, choose the Tools, Customize Toolbox menu item to display the Customize Toolbox dialog box, as shown in Figure 3.6 and Figure 3.7. Figure 3.6 shows a list of available COM components, and Figure 3.7 shows the available .NET Framework components.

Solution Explorer Window

In Visual Studio .NET, a *solution* is a set of one or more projects that are part of the same application. The Solution Explorer window shows you an expandable list of projects, each project's references, and each project's components. If this window is closed, you can open it by selecting the View, Solution Explorer menu item. Components may be made up of forms, classes, modules, and any other file types it takes to create your application. Double-click an item in order to edit that item within the IDE. Figure 3.8 shows the Solution Explorer window displaying the contents of a sample Windows application solution.

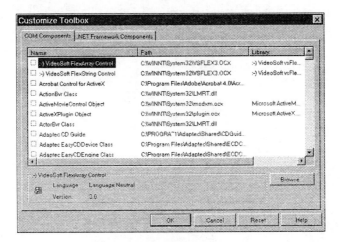

FIGURE 3.6 Customize Toolbox lets you add COM components to your Toolbox.

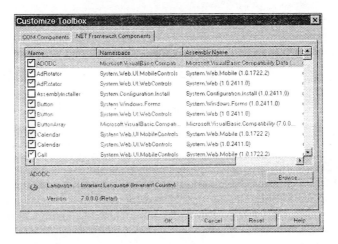

FIGURE 3.7 Use Customize Toolbox to choose which .NET Framework components are displayed in the Toolbox window.

The Solution Explorer window displays a series of buttons across its top, and these buttons dynamically change based on the item you have selected in the Solution Explorer window. Table 3.3 describes some of these buttons, starting with the left-most and proceeding right.

FIGURE 3.8   The Solution Explorer gives you a graphical representation of all the files that make up your project(s).

TABLE 3.3   Buttons on the Solution Explorer Window

Button	Description
View Code	Displays the code for the file that has focus in the Solution Explorer
View Designer	Displays the designer for the specific file that has focus in the Solution Explorer
Refresh	Refreshes the Solution Explorer
Show All Files	Displays all files associated with the project, including files normally hidden by Visual Studio
Properties	Displays the Properties window, which shows properties for the selected file

Class View Window

When you start creating your own classes, you may want to see a list of all the properties and methods available in those classes. You can use the Class View window, as shown in Figure 3.9, to get an overview of these items. You can bring up this window using the View, Class View menu item. Once the window is displayed, you can expand each item in the list to see the members of the class. If you choose any of these members, you can right-click and see a menu of actions that apply directly to the definition of that member. Double-click any of the members of the class to display a code window with the item definition displayed in the editor.

Server Explorer Window

The Server Explorer window (accessed using the View, Server Explorer menu) allows you to view the various services available on a particular server. These services include Crystal Services (for working with Crystal Reports), Event Logs, Message Queues, Performance Counters, and SQL Servers.

For most of these services, you can drill down and see a list of existing items—and you can even add new items. You can drag and drop a service from the Server Explorer window, shown in Figure 3.10, onto a design surface so that you can interact with the element programmatically in your application. For example, you can drag a performance counter onto a Web Form and use that component to interact with the counter. You could also drag a database table onto a page, and it will automatically create the necessary "plumbing" so that you can work with data from that table.

FIGURE 3.9   The Class View is an excellent way to view all the properties and methods of your classes.

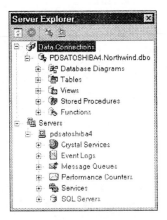

FIGURE 3.10   The Server Explorer window shows a list of servers, Windows services, databases, event logs, and more, available on your server or any server to which you can attach.

Properties Window

The Properties window provides a visual means of investigating and altering the properties of any object within the Visual Studio .NET environment. You can display the Properties window using the View, Properties Window menu item. Once this window is visible, you can either view the list alphabetically or categorized by attribute. Some properties within this window can be selected from a list; others allow you to click a button that brings up a dialog box. Still others require you to supply text by typing into a text box. Figure 3.11 shows the Properties window.

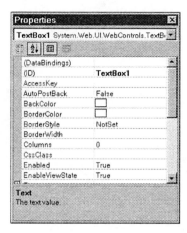

FIGURE 3.11   The Properties window is where you will spend a lot of time.

Object Browser Window

Similar to the Class View window, the Object Browser window shows you a list of classes and their respective members. The main difference between these two tools is that the Object Browser allows you to browse all referenced components, not just the components for the current project like the Class View window does. A nice feature of the Object Browser is that it also shows you the full declaration for the method or property. Bring up the Object Browser by using the View, Other Windows, Object Browser menu item. Figure 3.12 shows the Object Browser window in use.

Task List Window

The Task List window displays, among other items, any To Do items that you have entered in your code. In addition, you'll see information about build errors in this window. Bring up the Task List window using the View, Other Windows, Task List menu item. You will then see a window in your design environment similar to the one shown in Figure 3.13. To add a new task, you can click where the window reads "Click here to add a new task," or you can add comments in a specific format right in your project code. The default comment that adds to the Task List looks like this:

```
'TODO: Write the RepeaterBind procedure here
```

Use TODO: after the comment mark (the apostrophe), and the Task List will display your comment. You can double-click a task in the Task List window to take you directly to the associated comment in your code.

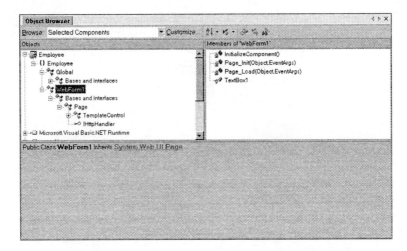

FIGURE 3.12   The Object Browser shows you a complete list of all classes, properties, and methods in your project.

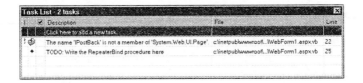

FIGURE 3.13   Tasks can help you organize your thoughts on what needs to be done to complete your project.

TIP

You can create your own Task List items using the Tools, Options menu item. Within the Options dialog box, select Environment, Task List in the left pane. In the right pane, add new items. By default, Visual Studio .NET uses HACK, TODO, and UNDONE as Task List indicators. Add your own tag items to this list and click the Add button to make them available as tags that link comments in your code with the Task List.

Using Help

At any time during your Visual Studio .NET session, you can press F1 to display context-sensitive help as you are working. The help system in Visual Studio .NET will attempt to determine the window or object you are currently positioned on and will bring up the appropriate help for you. There are a number of other ways you can search for help on a specific topic, as described in the following subsections.

Dynamic Help Window

The Dynamic Help window displays context-sensitive links to help topics, dynamically updated as you enter code or move around the environment. (You may notice a slight delay in the response as you move from task to task, perhaps because of the Dynamic Help window recalculating.) Figure 3.14 shows an example of the Dynamic Help window in use. You can bring up this window by choosing the Help, Dynamic Help menu item.

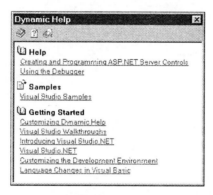

FIGURE 3.14   The Dynamic Help window is constantly updated as you move around the Visual Studio .NET IDE.

Although the Dynamic Help window can be useful, it also can be a hindrance on slower computers. You may decide to turn off Dynamic Help. Use the Tools, Options menu item to bring up the Options dialog box. Select the Environment folder, and then select Dynamic Help to modify the behavior of this tool.

Contents Window

If you wish to read the .NET Framework or Visual Studio .NET help like a manual, you can choose the Contents window by selecting the Help, Contents menu item. The top-level help might look like what's shown in Figure 3.15, depending on the version of the help topics you have installed and whether you're displaying internal or external help.

Index Window

The Index window displays the individual help topics, with links to display each item. You will probably use the Index help window more than any other type of help. You can bring up this window by choosing the Help, Index menu item. This window lets you drill down to a help topic simply by typing letters within the combo box at the top, as shown in Figure 3.16.

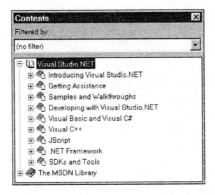

FIGURE 3.15   The Contents menu is for reading the help like a book or just perusing the contents of the help.

FIGURE 3.16   The Index window is excellent for drilling down to a help topic.

Search Window

If you want to perform a full-text search within online help, you will use the Search window. Bring up this window by choosing the Help, Search menu item. Figure 3.17 shows the Search window, ready to perform a full-text search.

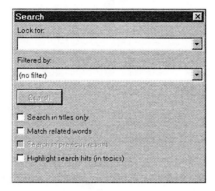

FIGURE 3.17   The Search window is useful for finding help topics based on keywords or phrases within those topics.

Types of Windows

There are two types of windows in the Visual Studio .NET IDE: tool windows and document windows. Tool windows are listed in the View menu and change based on the current application and the various add-ins you may have installed. Document windows are those windows that you open in order to edit some item in your project.

Tool Windows

The windows you have learned about in this chapter, including Toolbox, Solution Explorer, Properties, Help, and Server Explorer, are all tool windows. You can manipulate and arrange these tool windows in the development environment in various ways. You can make these windows automatically hide or show themselves. You can have a group of them display in a tabbed format. You can dock them against the edges of the environment or have them free-floating, by first selecting a window and then selecting or clearing the Dockable option on the Window menu. You can even display these windows on a second monitor if you have dual-monitor capability. (To place tool windows on different monitors, use the display settings in the Control Panel to set up your multiple-monitor configuration. You can then drag the tool window to the other monitor. Only tool windows in a floating mode can be moved outside of the application frame.)

TIP

Normally, dockable windows snap into place when you drag them near a dockable location. If you want to drag a window without having the window snap into place, hold the Ctrl key down as you drag the window.

Tool windows provide some special features, including the following:

- You can open multiple instances of certain tool windows. For example, you can have more than one Web Browser window open at one time. Use the Window, New Window menu to create new instances of windows.

- Docked tool windows can be set to hide automatically when you select another window. When you set a tool window to auto-hide, the window slides to one of the sides of the development environment and only displays a tab showing the window icon and name. You can click or hover over the window's tab to unhide the window. Once you've opened the window, you can click the pushpin icon on the title bar of the window to keep it open and docked.

TIP

Double-click a docked window's title bar to undock the window. Double-click it again to dock the window.

Document Windows

Visual Studio .NET uses document windows (as opposed to tool windows) for all editable documents. These windows never dock. You'll use document windows for all your code editing and all design surfaces. You will be using many of the different document windows as you read through this book, so we will not spend a lot of time on them right now.

Visual Studio .NET supports two different interface modes for document windows: Multiple Document Interface (MDI) and Tabbed Documents. You can change modes using the Tools, Options dialog box. Select the Environment options and then the General pane. In MDI mode, the IDE provides a parent window that serves as a visual and logical container for all tool and document windows. Tabbed Documents mode displays all document windows maximized, and a tab strip on top shows the names of the open documents for quick navigation.

TIP

Once you start playing with your windows, you may find that getting them back to the default setting is rather difficult. Not to worry: Simply select Tools, Options, Environment, Reset Window Layout to return to your default window layout.

Using the Editor

The Visual Studio .NET environment includes a powerful text editor. This editor includes a number of features aimed at making your code-writing experience more productive and as flexible as possible. The following subsections describe some of the Visual Studio .NET code editor features.

Using IntelliSense to Enter Code

Programming in Visual Studio .NET, even at the very beginning, involves working with members (properties and methods) of objects. To make it easier for you, when you enter the name of any object, Visual Studio .NET provides a drop-down list of the members of that class of object. In addition, when you type the name of a method, Visual Studio .NET provides a description of the method signature, including a list of all the parameters you need to supply for the method and a list of all the various ways you can call the method. This technology is named IntelliSense. In addition, IntelliSense allows you to auto-complete any syntax by pressing the space bar or the Tab key once the command you wish to use is highlighted.

Splitting the Editing Window

At times, you may want to view locations within the same code window, as shown in Figure 3.18. You can select the Window, Split menu item to insert a horizontal splitter bar into the code window. You can scroll each pane of the window individually, allowing you to view two locations within the same file. You can also split the editing window by grabbing the divider bar in the upper-right corner of the editing window and dragging it downward. Double-clicking the same area acts as if you'd selected the Window, Split menu item.

TIP

If you need a full-height split of a document window, use the Window, New Window menu item to create a second window. Then position it however you like.

Finding Text

You can search for text anywhere in the current procedure, the current module, or within a highlighted block of code. From any code window, you can select the Edit, Find and Replace, Find menu item or press Ctrl+F to bring up the Find dialog box, as shown in Figure 3.19. If you highlight a piece of text in your code window and then select the Find window, the text will be automatically added to the Find What combo box.

Enter a piece of text in the Find What combo box and click the Find Next command button to find the next location in the code that matches the string. You can keep this dialog box open and keep clicking Find Next to find the next occurrence of the string. You can also close the Find dialog box and press F3 to repeat the search.

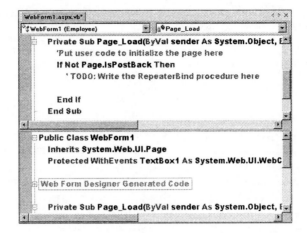

FIGURE 3.18   You can split the window to see two different areas of your code at the same time.

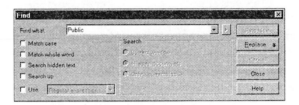

FIGURE 3.19   The Find dialog box will help you search for text in your project.

There are other options you can use to find a particular string in your source code. You can narrow your search to the current procedure or the current module, or you can search across all open documents. You can find a whole word that matches the string you input, you can perform a case-sensitive search, or you can enter wildcards, such as * and ?, to perform pattern matching.

Replacing Text

Replace text using the Replace dialog box. To bring up the Replace dialog box, select Edit, Find and Replace, Replace, press Ctrl+H from within a code window, or click the Replace command button in the Find window. Figure 3.20 shows an example of the Replace dialog box.

This dialog box is essentially the same as the Find dialog box, but it allows you to replace one piece of text at a time. You can also find the next occurrence of the Find What text by clicking Find Next. If you wish to replace all the values within the scope specified, you can click Replace All.

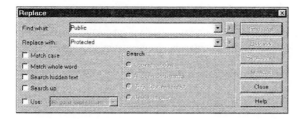

FIGURE 3.20 Find and Replace can come in handy for changing one variable name to another.

Finding Text in All Project Files

The Find dialog box is useful if you are searching open documents, but if you need to search for items in any file in your current project or in your whole solution, you will need to use the Find in Files dialog box shown in Figure 3.21. This dialog box allows you to search all files, regardless of whether they are open, across the current project, or even across the whole solution.

FIGURE 3.21 Find in Files allows you to look for text in all files, regardless of whether they are open.

Replacing Text in All Project Files

The Replace in Files dialog box, shown in Figure 3.22, allows you to perform a search-and-replace operation throughout the files in your project or within a folder. A nice feature of the Replace in Files dialog box is the Keep Modified Files Opened on Replace All option. If you choose to make a bulk change and click Replace All, this option (if checked) will open each modified file so that you can review the change and undo it if it's not what you intended.

Searching for Symbols

A *symbol* is a definition of a variable, such as you might find in your own classes or structures. Searching for symbols is different from searching for normal text in that searching for symbols only involves looking for definitions and references to those definitions based on the symbols you specify. The definitions and references are displayed in the Find Symbol Result window shown in Figure 3.23, which resembles the Search Results window you see in Windows Explorer.

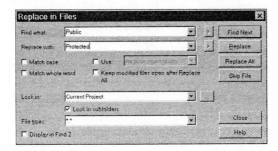

FIGURE 3.22   Search-and-replace operations can be performed within files using this dialog box.

FIGURE 3.23   The Find Symbol dialog box allows you to find the definition of classes.

Incremental Searching

Under the Edit, Advanced menu is an item named Increment Search (Ctrl+Alt+I when using the VB keyboard scheme). You enter an incremental search mode in the code editor so you can press any of the alphanumeric keys and drill down to the selection in your file that matches what you have typed so far. The Incremental Search feature interacts with the main Find tool by sharing the last Find pattern. You can typically press the Shift key instead of the Alt key to initiate a reverse incremental search or to toggle between a forward search and a reverse search.

NOTE

A regular Find operation searches for text in hidden regions when you've selected the Search Hidden Text option, but an incremental search does not.

Using Bookmarks to Locate Code

A bookmark allows you to mark a certain line of code and then find it quickly later. When you close a document, bookmarks in that document are discarded. If you want pointers to code that are persistent, use the Edit, Bookmarks, Add Task List Shortcut menu item. The Task List shortcuts will be saved with your solution, regardless of whether the documents are open. Task List shortcuts also display as items in the Task List, making navigation to those locations even easier.

Commenting/Uncommenting Blocks of Code

This handy tool allows you to highlight a block of text and then comment or uncomment it using the Edit, Advanced, Comment Selection or Uncomment Selection menu item. This tool becomes even more handy when you realize that lines of code that contain line continuation (that is, logical lines of code broken into multiple physical lines using the " _" characters) don't "comment out" as well as they did in Visual Basic 6 (where commenting out the first line of the block commented out the whole block). Now, you must add an apostrophe to comment out each line, in turn. Using these menu items (or their corresponding toolbar buttons) makes it easy to comment and uncomment blocks of code.

Dragging and Dropping Text

Highlight the text you want to move, click and hold your mouse, and then drag the text to the new location. To copy the text, press and hold down the Ctrl key while you are dragging the text.

Word Wrapping

Word Wrap is a feature that removes the horizontal scroll bar and ensures that all text is visible in the document window by wrapping long lines at word boundaries. You can enter this mode by selecting the Edit, Advanced, Word Wrap menu item. No carriage returns or line feeds are inserted into your document—Word Wrap is a visual display effect only.

TIP

To be honest, we find Word Wrap to be a feature of limited value. Turning this feature on makes it difficult to decipher Visual Basic .NET code, because Visual Basic relies on line breaks to delimit code. Word Wrap would be more useful in a language such as C#, where semicolons delimit logical lines of code, not line breaks.

Toggling Full Screen Mode

Your Visual Studio .NET design environment can sometimes get cluttered with the multitude of open windows and toolbars. This clutter can cause a problem when you wish to see more than a few lines of your source code at the same time. You can use the Full Screen mode provided by Visual Studio .NET to see more of your source code. To enter this mode, open a code editor window and select the View, Full Screen menu item. To return to normal mode, you can select the View, Full Screen menu item again.

Tabbing Between Windows

To move quickly among the various open windows in your Visual Studio .NET session, press Ctrl+Tab to iterate forward and Shift+Ctrl+Tab to iterate backward. This keeps your hands on the keyboard instead of having to use the mouse to select a specific window.

Managing the Clipboard Using the Clipboard Ring

Although the Windows Clipboard can hold only a single piece of text at a time, Visual Studio provides the Clipboard Ring, in which you can store up to 20 items at a time. If you add another item, the Clipboard Ring will remove the first item you added so that it maintains at most 20 items. To view the items in the Clipboard Ring, place your cursor somewhere in a code window and use the Edit, Cycle Clipboard Ring menu item. You can also look at the hotkey combination next to this menu item to determine the keystrokes you should use. Whichever keystrokes you use, do not release these keys but keep pressing the final key in your sequence. This allows you to cycle through all the items in the Clipboard Ring. When you find the one you want, release the keys, and the selected item will stay in your code window.

You may also view the Clipboard Ring by selecting the Clipboard Ring tab in the Toolbox window. You can then view each of the items and even drag and drop from the Toolbox into the code editor.

Going Back

Most Visual Basic 6.0 users are familiar with using the Shift+F2 key to take them to the definition of the procedure whose name is under the mouse cursor. In Visual Basic 6.0, you can also use the Ctrl+Shift+F2 key to return to the location where the procedure was called. (These keystrokes also work in Visual Studio .NET, if you've selected the Visual Basic 6.0 keyboard layout. If you've selected another keyboard layout, you can right-click a procedure name and select Go To Definition on the context menu that appears.)

Visual Studio .NET enhances this capability by creating a stack of "Go Back" locations. Each time you perform a command that takes you away from where you currently are located in a document, that previous location is placed into this Go Back stack. Some of the commands that mark these locations are Incremental Find,

Opening a New Document, GoTo Definition, and others. This means that at any time you may use the Ctrl+Shift+F2 key to return to any of these Go Back locations. You may continue to hit these keystrokes to cycle through the complete stack of Go Back locations.

> **NOTE**
>
> We could not find any documentation on the Go Back feature for any of the keyboard schemes. It works fine for the Visual Basic scheme, but if you are using any of the others, you may just have to experiment.

Creating Macros

If you find yourself performing the same functions over and over again within the Visual Studio .NET IDE, you can take advantage of the environment's capability of recording these steps into a macro. Using this feature is much like recording a macro in the Microsoft Office products. Use the Tools, Macros, Record Temporary Macro menu item to turn on the Macro recorder, perform the steps, and then save the macro either temporarily for this session or permanently within a macro project that you can then add to any solution you work with. Although this is a handy feature, digging deeper here is beyond the scope of this book. Consult the online help facility in Visual Studio .NET for more information on using the Macro Recorder.

Summary

Using Visual Studio .NET, and its Integrated Development Environment, is the most productive way to create .NET applications. You'll find many tools in Visual Studio .NET that will help speed your development and help you build better applications. The editor is one of the most powerful development editors to come with any programming language. Here are some of the most important facts you should come away with in this chapter:

- Visual Studio .NET is very customizable, which can help you be productive no matter what tool you come from.

- Many tools are available in Visual Studio .NET to help speed your development time.

- The editor is one of the most powerful development editors to come with any programming language.

4

Overview of .NET Framework Classes

OBJECTIVES

- Understand the concept of namespaces

- Identify the .NET namespaces you will use most

- Learn how to use the .NET namespaces in your code

- Examine examples of the most common classes and methods

Microsoft has created one of the largest class libraries anywhere with the advent of the .NET Framework. This class library, part of the Common Language Runtime (CLR), is the underlying library for all .NET languages. This library of classes, methods, and properties is used both during the development cycle and at runtime. This library allows any .NET language to have access to a wealth of building blocks that shorten the development cycle for developers.

What makes this framework so important is that it allows developers using any .NET language to have access to the same base classes and the same base data types, and those types and classes behave exactly the same way in any .NET language. If you need to create a multithreaded application, for example, you'll find the System.Threading classes in the .NET Framework. You do not need to "roll your own" solutions using the underlying Windows API. The actual syntax you will use to interact with the objects varies from language to language, but the base classes themselves will be the same.

Microsoft .NET developers will spend a large percentage of their time working with .NET Framework objects, because there are classes to help with almost any type of application you might develop. The .NET Framework will make programming easier in the long run no matter what .NET language you are using.

.NET Framework Namespaces

What is a namespace? If Microsoft had simply provided a list of several thousand classes, attempting to find or work with any specific class would be next to impossible. Although we're speculating, Microsoft might have ended up using class names such as `SystemDataOleDbDataSet` and `SystemTheadingThread`. Long names would be required in order to provide some sort of groupings and perspective.

Instead, Microsoft chose to group the various classes into a hierarchical set of namespaces. Using a syntax that separates levels in the hierarchy with dots, you'll find yourself referring to classes like this:

```
System.Data.OleDb.OleDbDataReader
```

In this example, the .NET Framework provides a `System` namespace, a `System.Data` namespace, and a `System.Data.OleDb` namespace. Each provides a set of classes, and the `OleDbDataReader` class is a part of the `System.Data.OleDb` namespace.

Imagine this scenario: You'd like to send a letter to a friend named Tom who lives across the country, and you address an envelope to Tom (just "Tom"), slap on a stamp, and drop it into a mailbox. What's the chance that the letter will get to your friend? Next to none. If the U.S. Postal Service had assigned each of us a local "namespace" consisting of *postalcode.state.city.streetaddress*, then you might address your letter to `90012.ca.los angeles.123 Smith Street` and have it reach your friend. Microsoft faced the same sort of issue when developing the .NET Framework. Therefore, each class belongs to a single namespace, and you'll use the .NET Framework documentation to investigate the various classes and namespaces.

You are probably asking yourself, which namespaces will I use most often? This chapter discusses those namespaces you might utilize for typical Web- or Windows-based business applications. This chapter will not (nor could it) provide a full reference of every available namespace—that would take several books itself.

The task of limiting the classes to be discussed in this chapter was daunting—there are well over 1,000 classes provided by the .NET Framework. We decided to focus on classes that you're likely to use in applications that take advantage of Windows Forms, Web Forms, Web Services, databases, and XML. By using these rather broad areas as the basis for choosing the namespaces, the list of classes we've included is large but not overwhelming. Once you understand some of these objects, working with other objects is easier.

Here's a list of the namespaces covered in this chapter:

- `System`
- `System.Data`
- `System.Data.OleDb`
- `System.Data.SqlClient`

- System.IO

- System.Text

- System.Collections

- System.Web.Services

- System.Windows.Forms

- System.Xml

Although this seems like quite a lot of classes to cover, we'll only provide a brief introduction to them in this chapter. You will find more coverage of many of these namespaces in later chapters in the book.

> **TIP**
>
> In order to follow along with the discussion in this chapter, you can load the Jumpstart\FrameworkClasses\FrameworkClasses.sln solution into Visual Studio .NET.

The System Namespace

The System namespace sits at the top of the namespace hierarchy. All the rest of the libraries in this chapter—and in this book—will be descended from the System namespace. (The .NET Framework does include some namespaces that aren't part of the System namespace, but we won't be discussing them in this book.) The most important items contained within the System namespace are the classes that represent the base data types, such as Object, Integer, Long, String, and so on.

In addition to these base data types, there are dozens of classes in the System namespace. These classes cover areas such as data handling (DataSet), garbage collection (GC), and threading (Threading).

The System namespace also contains namespaces that provide the bulk of the .NET Framework functionality. These secondary namespaces are generally grouped into areas of functionality. For example, data access is handled by System.Data, System.Xml, and System.Xml.Serialization, whereas the System.Drawing and System.Windows.Forms namespaces handle user interfaces.

A System.GC (Garbage Collection) Example

As an example of the System namespace, this section takes a look at garbage collection. Garbage collection is one of the important new features you can control when you use the .NET Framework. In COM, instantiated objects are allocated memory automatically. These COM components kept an internal counter of the number of connections being made to them. When this counter drops to zero, the object is supposed to drop out of memory.

In your client code, you can instantiate a COM component (creating an object in memory) and later kill it by setting your object reference to Nothing. As long as you have the only connection to the COM object (the most likely scenario), the object is destroyed immediately.

The problem with using COM reference counting is that it's possible—and actually far too easy—for one component to maintain a reference to another, while the second maintains a reference back to the first. Because neither component can be destroyed (each has a "live" inward reference), neither object can ever remove itself from memory. This circular reference problem has led to many memory leaks.

Memory management is now handled automatically by the .NET Framework, without reliance on reference counting. The circular reference problem is gone, because the Framework decides when objects are to be released from memory, based on their usage. This means that you do not know exactly when objects will be destroyed, so you can't be sure when the memory is to be cleaned up.

If you want more control, you can force garbage collection to occur by calling the Collect method of the GC class. In the following code snippet, you can see the Collect method being called:

```
Dim oCust As New Customer()
oCust.CompanyName = "Microsoft Corporation"
...
oCust = Nothing
GC.Collect()
```

This code instantiates a hypothetical Customer object. It sets the CompanyName property and then might perform other actions on the object. When it's done, the code sets the object reference to Nothing and explicitly calls the Collect method of the GC class. Not calling the Collect method would mean that the object, while no longer referenced, might still be alive in memory. It would be marked for garbage collection but might not be removed until garbage collection is run.

Perhaps you're wondering why you might ever call the garbage collector manually, given that .NET is so good about handling memory for you? Realize that the component, although dereferenced (set to Nothing), may still exist in memory for some time. Not only is it taking up memory, but more importantly, any resources it was accessing may still be held open. For example, database connections and file handles might still be held open until the object is actually dropped from memory. Therefore, you might want to explicitly call the garbage collector and have the object taken out of memory. Of course, a careful programmer would close all open resources before an object is dereferenced.

Working with Namespace Names

The previous example works with the System.GC class, yet it's referred to simply as GC. How is that possible? How can the compiler determine which exact class you're referring to? When referring to members of a namespace (that is, objects provided by a namespace), you must somehow indicate to Visual Basic .NET which exact object you want to use. In general, you must type the entire object name, including its full namespace. For example, to refer to a SqlDataReader object, you would have to write code like this:

```
Dim dr As New System.Data.SqlClient.SqlDataReader()
```

If you refer to objects in the same namespace often, you may want to find some way to simply refer to the objects themselves, rather than the entire namespace. To make this possible, VB .NET provides the Imports statement, which you can place at the top of any file. This statement acts much like a file-wide With...End With statement. If, for example, you have placed the statement

```
Imports System.Data.SqlClient
```

at the top of a file, you could modify the previous code example to look like this:

```
Dim dr As New SqlDataReader()
```

To make this easier for you, VB .NET projects created in Visual Studio .NET always add implicit Imports statements for you. You can check the list of implicit Imports by right-clicking an open project in the Solution Explorer. Select Imports from the list of common properties in the project's property pages, and you'll see a list of Imports statements that VB .NET automatically handles for you.

In your code, you can only refer to objects that are provided by the assemblies your project references. That is, unless Visual Studio .NET has automatically set a reference to an assembly or you've manually added the reference, you won't be able to use an object. Also, you can only add Imports statements for classes you've referenced. To add a reference to an assembly, use the Project, Add Reference menu item and select the .NET tab.

NOTE

The GC class provides only shared members. The shared keyword indicates that you don't need to create an instance of the class before using its methods or properties. Many .NET Framework classes use shared members (such as GC.Collect) rather than requiring you to declare a GC variable and create a new instance. Instance properties and methods (such as the Length property of a specific string) are more common.

The System.Data **Namespace**

This book will take advantage of three namespaces that allow you to work with data within the application in this book: System.Data, System.Data.OleDb, and System.Data.SqlClient. (Microsoft and other vendors will add support for additional data namespaces in the future.) The System.Data namespace contains classes that manage data within memory. System.Data.OleDb and System.Data.SqlClient provide classes that can connect to data sources, read and write data, and fill System.Data objects with data.

The SqlClient **and** OleDb **Namespaces**

Microsoft has provided two namespaces that we'll use for managing data throughout this book. The System.Data.OleDb namespace allows you to work with data using "unmanaged" OLE DB providers (*unmanaged* means that the namespace uses code written outside of the .NET CLR). The System.Data.SqlClient namespace allows you to work with data in Microsoft SQL Server 7.0 or higher, using the SQL Server native API (with no OLE DB provider required). The classes and their members are almost identical in name and functionality. Table 4.1 provides a list of the most commonly used classes from the System.Data.OleDb and System.Data.SqlClient namespaces. To make things simpler, we've removed the namespace-specific prefixes from each object. Add the appropriate prefix ("OleDb" or "Sql") to each of these class names.

TABLE 4.1   ADO.NET Classes

Class	Description
Connection	This class is responsible for making the actual connection to the database. It has methods for starting, committing, and rolling back transactions as well.
Command	This class allows you to submit SQL statements to a data source or to call stored procedures. It can either perform action queries (INSERT, UPDATE, and DELETE) or execute SELECT statements to return a DataReader object.
DataReader	This class provides forward-only, read-only access to data. If you're an ADO developer, you're familiar with this type of data access—it's similar to the default ADO Recordset (often called a *fire hose cursor*).
DataAdapter	This class encapsulates a connection and one or more commands (SELECT, UPDATE, DELETE, and INSERT). It can retrieve and update data and uses its SelectCommand property to fill a DataSet or DataTable object with data.

The System.Data **Classes**

The System.Data class provides a number of classes, but you'll only use a few of them when developing your applications. The classes described here all work with data in memory rather than interacting with any particular data source. You can typically use these in-memory data stores to both view and update data. Table 4.2 provides a list of the most commonly used System.Data classes.

TABLE 4.2 System.Data Classes

Class	Description
DataSet	This data cache is much like an in-memory database. It can contain one or more DataTable objects. You can store the data as well as the schema information for the tables. You may also set relationships between DataTable objects within a DataSet object.
DataTable	A DataTable provides a collection of DataRow objects. Each DataRow object is, in turn, made up of a collection of DataColumn objects. A DataTable is a single table or a single view of data. A DataTable can be populated via a DataAdapter object.
DataView	A DataView object is used to sort or filter the data within a DataTable. You can also use a DataView for searching data as well.

Making database access part of the underlying .NET Framework means that any language targeting the .NET platform will have access to the same set of data classes. In addition, because the data-access classes are part of the .NET Framework, if or when the framework is ported to alternate platforms such as Linux, the same data classes should be available in the new platforms as well.

This set of data classes in .NET is known collectively as *ADO.NET*. ADO.NET is different from previous Microsoft database access technologies in several ways. It's more highly focused on disconnected data access, which makes it easier for Web developers to work with data. ADO.NET separates objects that talk to data sources from objects that just hold data. The data classes also "speak" fluent XML. This makes it easier to transmit data from one application to another, regardless of operating system or transport mechanism.

A Data-Handling Example

The following example reads data from the Products table in the Northwind sample database. It uses a number of the ADO.NET classes, including OleDbDataAdapter and DataSet.

The procedure shown in this section, XMLGet, first creates a connection string and a SQL string. It passes these two strings to the constructor of the OleDbDataAdapter object. The code then calls the OleDbDataAdapter object's Fill method in order to fill the DataSet object with data.

NOTE

You don't need to type System.Data.OleDb.OleDbDataAdapter here because VB .NET automatically includes an Imports statement that imports the System.Data namespace.

The `Fill` method is responsible for creating an implicit `OleDbConnection` object using the supplied connection string. Next, the `Fill` method creates an `OleDbCommand` object and uses the `SELECT` statement to read the data from the data source. The `Fill` method reads the data and fills one table within the `DataSet` object. The code closes the collection, leaving you with just the filled `DataSet` object.

The `DataSet` object's `GetXml` method returns its entire set of data as an XML stream. Your code can handle the XML in any way it requires—the following code snippet places the XML into a text box on the sample page:

```
Private Sub XMLGet()
    Dim strConn As String
    Dim strSQL As String
    Dim da As OleDb.OleDbDataAdapter
    Dim ds As DataSet

    strConn = "Provider=sqloledb;Data
     Source=(local);Initial Catalog=Northwind;User ID=sa"
    strSQL = "SELECT ProductID, ProductName FROM Products"

    da = New OleDb.OleDbDataAdapter(strSQL, strConn)

    ds = New DataSet()
    da.Fill(ds)

    txtXML.Text = ds.GetXml()
End Sub
```

If you know that you are only going to be using SQL Server, you might choose to use the `SqlClient` namespace. The classes in this namespace are specific for SQL Server and will give you a little better performance when working with SQL Server. The following code snippet provides the same functionality, using the `SqlClient` namespace classes:

```
Private Sub XMLGetSqlClient()
    Dim strConn As String
    Dim strSQL As String
    Dim da As SqlClient.SqlDataAdapter
    Dim ds As DataSet

    strConn = "Server=(local);Database=Northwind;" _
     "User ID=sa"
    strSQL = "SELECT ProductID, ProductName FROM Products"
```

```
    da = New SqlClient.SqlDataAdapter(strSQL, strConn)

    ds = New DataSet()
    da.Fill(ds)

    txtXML.Text = ds.GetXml()
End Sub
```

The System.IO Namespace

The System.IO namespace contains classes that allow you to read and write files on disk. File operations can be performed either synchronously or asynchronously. In order to read and write data, you'll work with the base Stream class, which provides a generic technique to access any data without regard to the underlying platform on which the data resides. Streams can support any combination of reading, writing, and seeking (that is, modifying the current position within a stream). Table 4.3 presents a list of some of the more commonly used classes from the System.IO namespace.

TABLE 4.3   System.IO Classes

Class	Description
File	The File class provides shared methods that allow you to perform actions on physical files on disk.
StreamReader	The StreamReader class allows you to open and read information from a file on disk.
StreamWriter	The StreamWriter class allows you to write to files on disk.

A File object represents a physical file and allows you to perform actions such as copying and deleting files. The File class provides Exists, Open, OpenRead, OpenText, and OpenWrite methods to allow you to perform file I/O. These methods of the File class are defined as Shared, which means you do not need to create an instance of a File class to use them. You will learn more about shared methods in Chapter 7, "Working with ASP.NET and VB .NET."

The two classes you will use most often from the System.IO namespace are StreamReader and StreamWriter, and you'll learn about these two classes in the following example.

A System.IO Example

The code in Listing 4.1, located under the "IO Classes" hyperlink on Main.aspx, uses a StreamWriter object to create a new text file on disk. The code uses the shared

Exists method of the File class to determine whether a file exists on disk. (Although it's perfectly reasonable, and possible, for code to overwrite an existing file, this example doesn't do that.) If the file does not exist, the example creates a new StreamWriter object by invoking the CreateText shared method of the File class. This method creates the file and returns a StreamWriter object that can be used to write information into the file. Once the file is opened, the example uses the WriteLine method to place text into the file on disk. When done using the file, the example closes it to release the handle back to the operating system. Here's the code:

LISTING 4.1   Writing to a File Using the Stream and File Objects

```
Imports System.IO

Private Sub WriteFile()
    Dim strName As String
    Dim sw As StreamWriter

    strName = Server.MapPath("Test.txt")

    If File.Exists(strName) Then
        lblError.Text = "File Already Exists"
    Else
        sw = File.CreateText(strName)
        sw.WriteLine("The current Time is: " & Now())
        sw.Close()
    End If
End Sub
```

The System.Text **Namespace**

Just about every business application you create will eventually require you to work with strings in some manner. String manipulation is a very common activity in most applications, but creating, adding to, and deleting from strings are expensive in terms of processor time and memory.

If you create a variable of type String, you are actually creating a String object; all base data types in .NET inherit from the base Object class, so all data types are actually objects. The contents of a String object cannot be changed once you've placed text into the string—in order to change its contents, you must place the return value of a method call into a new String object. For example, the String class provides a Remove method, which allows you to remove a portion of a string. However, because the contents of a String object are immutable, the Remove method doesn't do its work "in place." Instead, it returns a new string object as its return value, as shown here:

```
Dim strNew As String
Dim strOld As String = "This is a test"
' Remove the first four characters of the string.
strNew = strOld.Remove(0, 4)
```

If you perform many string operations that return strings, you're consuming memory and processor cycles that you might be able to avoid using a handy alternative: the StringBuilder class. This class manages a memory buffer containing your text for you, and it provides methods to modify text "in place," without requiring you to assign the result to a new string each time you make a modification to a string. If you are performing a few simple assignments or concatenations, don't worry about the overhead. However, if you are building a string inside a loop, the StringBuilder provides better performance with less overhead. The System.Text namespace also contains classes for encoding characters into bytes and decoding bytes into characters. Also, encoders and decoders are available for converting to and from ASCII and Unicode.

A System.Text **Example**

This example creates a System.Text.StringBuilder object and provides a string in the object's constructor. The code retrieves the seventh character in the string and displays it in a Label control on the page. The code invokes the Replace method to replace a substring within the string with another string. Finally, the example inserts a new value into a specified location within the string. (In this case, the code adds this new value to the end of the original string.) The example in Listing 4.2 uses the ToString method of the StringBuilder object to retrieve its contents:

LISTING 4.2   Use the StringBuilder for Efficient String Handling

```
Private Sub StringBuilderExample()
   Dim sb As New _
   System.Text.StringBuilder(".NET is cool")

   ' Display the 7th character
   lblMsg.Text = sb.Chars(6)

   ' Replace .NET with Microsoft.NET
   sb.Replace(".NET", "Microsoft .NET")
   lblMsg.Text = sb.ToString()

   sb.Insert(sb.Length, " and fun.")
```

LISTING 4.2   Continued

```
    lblMsg.Text = sb.ToString()

End Sub
```

What makes this more efficient than using a normal String object is that when you create a new StringBuilder object, it automatically manages memory for you by creating a buffer with extra room for growth. If the buffer needs to grow, the StringBuilder object takes care of the memory management for you. If you want, you can pass the initial size of the buffer to the constructor to specify how much space to allocate when a new StringBuilder object is created.

The System.Collections **Namespace**

Use the System.Collections namespace when you need to create a data structure that can hold a group of similar objects. The System.Collections namespace contains all the classes and interfaces needed to define collections of objects. Some of the classes that you might use most often are listed in Table 4.4.

TABLE 4.4   System.Collections Classes

Class	Description
ArrayList	An ArrayList is similar to an array, but the ArrayList class allows you to add items without managing the size of the list yourself (much like a VB Collection object).
CollectionBase	This class is the base for a strongly typed collection, which is critical for creating collection classes.
DictionaryBase	This class is the base for a strongly typed collection utilizing associated keys and values. This is similar to the Dictionary object found in VBScript and used by many ASP developers.
SortedList	This class represents a collection of keys and values that you insert into the list. A SortedList object is always automatically sorted by the key value. You can access the values with either the key value or an index number.

A common use of the System.Collections namespace is to create strongly typed collections. Consider the following scenario:

Assume you create a class called Customer. The Customer class has a number of properties, methods, and events. You now want to create several Customer objects within one structure so you can iterate through the collection and print each customer to the printer. You could just create a variable of type Array, ArrayList, or SortedList, but these standard collections can hold any type of object. In other words, you could add a Customer object as the first item in the collection, but you could then add an Employee object as the second item, a String object as the third, and so on. If you try to iterate over this collection and apply the Update method, it might work on the Customer and Employee objects, but when your loop attempts to call the Update method of a String object, it will certainly fail.

To get around this sticky situation, you can create your own class that looks like a generic collection object but restricts its members to only one data type. This new class will include the standard methods of the collection base type, such as the Add and Remove methods, as well as an Item property, but your class's Add method will only allow you to add Customer objects.

In Visual Basic 6.0, you could provide this functionality, and you generally started by creating an empty class and then creating an Add method, a Remove method, an Item property, a Count property, and so on. This is easier in .NET, thanks to the base classes in the System.Collections namespace.

A System.Collections **Example**

Assume that you need to create a Customer object to hold values from a Customer table in your database. The structure of the Customer object is very simple, containing just a CompanyName property. Imagine that you want to create a collection class named Customers (note the letter *s* on the end) to hold a set of Customer objects. You first need to create the Customer class as shown in the following code snippet:

```
Public Class Customer
    Public CustomerName As String

End Class
```

Next, you create your new Customers collection class. Your class must inherit from the System.Collections.CollectionBase class. (This base class gives you all the functionality of a normal collection but allows you to override any of the base methods, such as Add and Item.) Listing 4.3 provides the new class and its overridden Add and Item members:

LISTING 4.3   Building Collection Classes Is Easy with the .NET Framework Class CollectionBase

```
Public Class Customers
    Inherits System.Collections.CollectionBase

    Public Sub Add(ByVal cust As Customer)
        Me.List.Add(cust)
    End Sub
```

LISTING 4.3   Continued

```
    Public ReadOnly Property Item( _
    ByVal Index As Integer) As Customer
        Get
            If Index > Count - 1 Or Index < 0 Then
                ' Return error message
            Else
                Return CType( _
                Me.List.Item(Index), Customer)
            End If
        End Get
    End Property
End Class
```

In your collection class, you'll need to override the Add method so that instead of accepting a generic Object type, your method accepts only a Customer object. You can then use the internal List property from the base class to add the Customer object to the internal collection of generic objects.

You also need to override the Item method so it returns a Customer object instead of a generic Object data type. Notice the use of the CType function. This function converts the data in the built-in List property from a generic Object data type to a Customer data type.

Using inheritance, you certainly end up writing a lot less code to implement a collection class when compared to the code you had to write in Visual Basic 6.0. To use the collection class you created in Listing 4.3, you could write code like that shown in Listing 4.4.

LISTING 4.4   Collection Classes Are Very Easy to Use

```
Private Sub CustCollection()
    Dim cust As Customer
    Dim colcust As New Customers()
    Dim strMsg As String

    cust = New Customer()
    cust.CustomerName = "Microsoft Corporation"
    colcust.Add(cust)

    cust = New Customer()
    cust.CustomerName = "SAMS Publishing"
    colcust.Add(cust)
```

LISTING 4.4   Continued

```
    strMsg = "Count = " & _
     colcust.Count.ToString() & "<BR>"

    For Each cust In colcust
        strMsg &= cust.CustomerName & "<BR>"
    Next

    lblMsg.Text = strMsg

    colcust.RemoveAt(0)

    lblMsg.Text = strMsg & _
     "After the removal = " & colcust.Count
End Sub
```

This code creates two new `Customer` objects, sets the `CustomerName` property of each to a unique name, and then adds each one to the `Customers` collection class. You can use the `Count` property from the base class to determine the number of items in the collection, even though you did not implement it in your `Customers` class. You can use the `For Each` iterator to loop through each `Customer` object. You can also utilize the base class's `RemoveAt` method to remove a specific item at a specified index in the collection.

The `System.Web.Services` Namespace

XML Web Services provide one of the newest and most exciting technologies for development, as far as we're concerned. Although the .NET platform, and Visual Studio .NET in particular, makes it easy to get started creating XML Web Services, Web Services have been available for some time on the Microsoft platform, thanks to the SOAP Toolkit. (Stop by `http://msdn.microsoft.com/xml` for more information on the SOAP Toolkit and how it can enable you to consume Web Services in non-.NET client applications.)

XML Web Services make it possible to execute method calls provided by objects via the Web. Distributed components have been available for years, in the form of ActiveX components accessed via DCOM, but Web Services make components available over HTTP using SOAP as the underlying messaging protocol. DCOM is a binary standard that doesn't transmit well through firewalls or proxy servers. In addition, DCOM is only supported on platforms running COM, which has basically limited COM/DCOM to Windows platforms.

With Web Services, however, the landscape has changed. The call and response to a Web Service are in XML format and are generally transported over HTTP. This means that the component can be called using simple text and by any client on any platform. The result comes back in XML format, meaning that any client that understands XML can consume the results. Finally, you can code your components using your favorite Microsoft tools and allow those components to be used by people running on Unix or an AS/400—or any other platform that can make HTTP calls and consume XML. Realize that you can consume a Web Service from a Windows application, a Web application, or any other client you can imagine, including the growing set of wireless devices, such as PDAs and Web-enabled phones. This opens up a new world of interoperability and means you can distribute your application on servers around the world and tie them together using just HTTP.

Creating XML Web Services is fairly straightforward, as you will see in the next section. In Part IV of this book, you will learn how to create more fully-functional Web Services. In this chapter, you will just learn to create a simple Web Service, and you'll see a simple way to access that Web Service.

NOTE

We use the term *Web Services* to refer to the technology that allows you to communicate with objects using specially formatted XML streams, usually over HTTP. The term we ought to be using is *XML Web Services*, because there are other emerging technologies that provide services over the Web. This terminology becomes distracting, however, and we'll simply refer to it as Web Services throughout the book.

A System.Web.Services **Example**

In order to create a new Web Service, start by creating a new project in Visual Studio .NET and selecting the ASP.NET Web Service template. Name the new project TestWebService (accepting the default location, http://localhost). Select Service1.asmx in the Solution Explorer window, and select the View, Code menu item to display the associated class. As you can see, Visual Studio .NET has created the shell of the service for you, including commented lines of code showing how to expose public Web methods. Add the following procedure to the sample class:

```
<WebMethod()> _
Public Function Hello( _
 ByVal Name As String) As String
    Return "Hello, " & Name
End Function
```

The one public function here, Hello, simply returns a greeting to the name you pass in as a parameter.

NOTE

What's the <WebMethod()> text you see in the procedure declaration for? This procedure attribute indicates to the compiler that the procedure should be serialized using the SOAP serializer, for use as part of a Web Service. Without this, you'd simply be creating a public method of a class, just like normal.

Choose the Build, Build Solution menu item to rebuild the project. (This step creates a DLL and places it in a location on your Web server within the project folder.)

It's simple to test the Web Service: Open your Web browser and type in the following URL, replacing the server name and project name if necessary:

```
http://localhost/TestWebService/Service1.asmx/
Hello?Name=Paul
```

The result that will appear in your browser is the XML response from the Web Service. It will look like this:

```
<?xml version="1.0" encoding="utf-8" ?>
  <string xmlns="http://tempuri.org/">Hello, Paul</string>
```

If you're not excited yet, think about this: You called a method in a component over standard HTTP and retrieved the result, all over the Internet! (Okay, you're on your local machine, but it could just as easily have been over the Internet!) This is a very powerful technique, and it opens up a whole new way of programming and creating distributed applications.

Normally, you'd call this Web Service from a client application. In Visual Studio .NET, you can simply add a Web reference to your Web Service. This is just like adding a reference to a COM component in previous versions of Visual Studio. After adding the Web reference, you refer to the Web Service as you would any other component.

The System.Xml Namespace

You'll use the System.Xml namespace for processing XML data. This namespace supports an ever-expanding host of XML standards, such as the following:

- XML 1.0
- Namespaces
- Schemas
- XSL/T
- SOAP 1.1

The System.Xml namespace contains classes that represent the various XML elements, similar to the objects provided by the MSXML library for Visual Basic 6.0 developers. For example, you'll find an XmlDocument class, an XmlEntity class, and an XmlNode class. You can also use XmlValidatingReader in order to read XML and validate it against a Document Type Definition (DTD), XML Data Reduced (XDR) schema, or an XML Schema Definition (XSD).

The System.Xml namespace includes reader and writer classes that provide fast, forward-only reading and writing of XML streams. Back in the System.Data discussion, you learned about the DataReader class, which is used for fast forward-only data access. XmlTextReader provides the same basic functionality against an XML stream.

When you use a reader object to read XML, you can use properties of the reader to determine each node type and act accordingly. A writer class has methods such as WriteCData, WriteDocType, and WriteNode in order to create an XML document, element by element.

A System.Xml **Example**

The example in Listing 4.5 combines several of the namespaces covered in this chapter. First, it uses System.Data classes to read data from SQL Server. Next, it uses System.IO classes to output that data into an XML file. Finally, it reopens the original XML file and uses System.Xml to read the contents of the file and copy the data into a text box. Here's the code:

> **NOTE**
>
> More node types are possible when reading in an XML document than are shown in the Select Case statement. However, for brevity, the number of types examined is small.

LISTING 4.5   Use an XmlTextReader Class to Parse an XML Document

```
Imports System.IO
Imports System.XML
Imports System.Text
Imports System.Data.OleDb

Private Sub XMLWrite()
    Dim strConn As String
    Dim strSQL As String
    Dim strName As String
    Dim strXML As String
```

LISTING 4.5 Continued

```vb
Dim sw As StreamWriter
Dim sr As XmlTextReader
Dim sb As New StringBuilder(256)
Dim da As OleDbDataAdapter
Dim ds As DataSet

strConn = "Provider=sqloledb;" & _
  "Data Source=(local);" & _
  "Initial Catalog=Northwind;" & _
  "User ID=sa"
strSQL = "SELECT ProductID, ProductName FROM Products"

da = New OleDbDataAdapter(strSQL, strConn)
ds = New DataSet()
da.Fill(ds)
strName = "c:\test.xml"

sw = File.CreateText(strName)
sw.WriteLine(ds.GetXml)
sw.Close()

sr = New XmlTextReader(strName)
sr.WhitespaceHandling = WhitespaceHandling.None

' Parse the file and display each of the nodes.
While sr.Read()
  Select Case sr.NodeType
    Case XmlNodeType.Element
      sb.AppendFormat("<{0}>", sr.Name)
    Case XmlNodeType.Text
      sb.Append(sr.Value)
    Case XmlNodeType.XmlDeclaration
      sb.Append("<?xml version='1.0'?>")
    Case XmlNodeType.Document
    Case XmlNodeType.DocumentType
      sb.AppendFormat("<!DOCTYPE {0} [{1}]", _
        sr.Name, sr.Value)
    Case XmlNodeType.EndElement
      sb.AppendFormat("</{0}>", sr.Name)
```

LISTING 4.5 Continued

```
    End Select
  End While

  txtXML.Text = sb.ToString()
End Sub
```

Summary

This chapter covered some of the more common namespaces you will use when developing your .NET applications. There are many other namespaces available, and you may find yourself often using a namespace not covered in this chapter. Regardless of which namespace you use, gaining a familiarity with the functionality of the .NET Framework and how to use it in your applications is important. Here are some key points to take from this chapter:

- There are many namespaces in the .NET Framework. You won't need to use them all in order to get started programming in VB .NET.

- The .NET Framework supplies classes for garbage collection, threading, and managing collections, among thousands of others.

- All .NET languages can take advantage of the .NET Framework to create modern, object-oriented, distributed applications.

5

Introduction to Internet Programming

- Review Internet basics
- Learn the difference between HTML and ASP
- Understand what makes ASP.NET better than ASP

The Internet is a wide area network—the widest area network possible, really—that consists of a huge number of computers connected via phone lines, wireless connections, and satellites. When you access the Internet, your computer becomes part of that network.

In order to take advantage of ASP.NET, and to understand how Web pages and data make their way across the Internet, you must first have a basic understanding of how the Internet works. In addition, because requesting an ASP.NET page from within a browser retrieves HTML as the response, it's important that you understand at least the basics of HTML and its various tags. That way, as you investigate the code created by your ASP.NET pages, you'll understand exactly what the controls on your page are creating for the user.

The material in this chapter may seem somewhat basic—that is, you may already have a good understanding of both the Internet and HTML. In that case, you may want to skim ahead to the content specific to the sample application you'll be building, toward the end of the chapter. Don't skip that material, however!

Internet Basics

All computers on the Internet are uniquely identified by an IP address. Just like a phone number uniquely identifies a particular phone, an IP address uniquely identifies a specific server. URLs are resolved to a specific server via domain naming services (DNS). A domain name service translates a URL such as www.microsoft.com into a specific IP address such as 207.46.230.220.

> **NOTE**
>
> The simplistic discussion here about IP addresses and computer names assumes that the computers all have static IP addresses. Most home (and many business) users are assigned dynamic IP addresses by their Internet Service Provider (ISP), and DNS doesn't provide any mapping service for these dynamic addresses.

In order to connect to the Internet (unless your company is a lot larger than most), you'll need an Internet Service Provider (ISP). An ISP supplies basic services and access to the Internet for most users. Many people believe their ISP (AOL, for instance) is the Internet. That's not true, of course. Instead, ISPs are simply service providers. AOL and MSN simply dress up their services with pretty front ends and lots of hand-holding for novice users. Services from an ISP typically include e-mail, URL resolution, and content management.

You might think of an ISP as being similar to a phone company. The ISP manages a large network of computers that provide services, just like the phone service company provides basic services and a dial tone. There are many different ISPs, just as there are many different phone companies. What's more, phone companies are often ISPs, which makes a lot of sense.

Once you're connected to the Internet, you normally enter a Uniform Resource Locator (URL) into a browser to browse the Web. When you type a URL into the address box in a browser and then press the Enter key, your browser uses a TCP/IP connection to send the address to the ISP. Windows also sends the client computer's IP address. An ISP's server resolves the URL as an IP address and sends the request to the IP address (that is, a Web server computer).

The server processes the request and returns whatever information has been requested. The server uses the client computer's IP address to know where to return the information. Windows intercepts the information and provides it to the application (the Web browser).

Increasingly, applications that aren't specifically Web browsers are using Internet communications to do their jobs. For instance, you might build a complete database application that uses data stored remotely on a server computer, taking advantage of XML Web Services to retrieve the data as necessary. You will see examples of this as you work through this book.

HTML Basics

Under the covers, the Web uses the Hypertext Markup Language (HTML) to send information to Web browsers. This common markup language can be used by any browser, on any computer. When you request a response from a Web page, you're getting back an HTML stream, consisting of text "marked up" with HTML elements as tags. If you're going to generate your own Web pages, you need to have at least a basic understanding of HTML and how it renders in the browser.

> **TIP**
>
> Yes, you can get by without really understanding anything about HTML, and our guess is that most readers already have a reasonable grasp of HTML. However, a basic knowledge of HTML can be important, because ASP.NET generates HTML both at design time and at runtime, and your development experience will go more smoothly if you're comfortable with HTML.

HTML has only a handful of basic tags that you need to learn in order to create just about any Web site you want. Most of these tags are very simple to use. The following subsections introduce some of the more common tags you will encounter.

HTML Elements

HTML provides a huge list of elements as well as attributes that describe those elements. We're going to cover a tiny portion of the available HTML functionality here, mostly so you'll recognize the HTML elements used throughout the book. The intent here is definitely *not* to provide an HTML primer, but just to make sure we're all starting at the same place. For more information on HTML, consult the appropriate reference materials on that topic.

> **TIP**
>
> HTML isn't case sensitive. You'll note in the examples that the various elements are sometimes in uppercase letters, and other times in lowercase letters. You'll see HTML formatted both ways. Although HTML accepts mixed-case elements (for example, `<LI></li>`), other similar markup languages (such as XML) do not. Don't mix cases like this, or sooner or later it will bite you back.

Hyperlink

The hyperlink provides the main form of navigation on a typical Web page. A hyperlink typically appears as a highlighted word or group of words. Clicking the hyperlink makes a request to a particular Web server, which responds with the requested page.

To insert a hyperlink, you use text such as this:

```
<a href="Page to load">Text to display</a>
```

Note the matching begin and end tags (`<a>` and `</a>`) and the attribute (`href="Page to load"`) that's included within the opening tag. Any element can contain one or more attributes—in this case, there's only the one `href` attribute.

The following example, `Main.htm`, contains a number of hyperlinks. You'll find this example in the `InternetBasics` folder, and you can either load it into a text editor to see its source, shown in Listing 5.1, or double-click to load it directly into a browser.

LISTING 5.1   The Contents of `Main.htm`

```
<HTML>
<BODY>
<H3>Hyperlink</H3>

<a href="UnorderedList.htm">Unordered List</a><br>
<a href="OrderedList.htm">Ordered List</a><br>
<p>
<a href="Select.htm">Select</a><br>
<a href="Table.htm">Table</a><br>
<a href="Input.htm">Input</a><br>
</p>

</BODY>
</HTML>
```

Line Break

HTML output generally flows from left to right, top to bottom through a page (this is generally called *flow layout*). If you want to insert a line break yourself, you can insert the <br> tag into the document. Unlike most HTML tags, the <br> tag doesn't require an ending tag. You can see the use of this tag in the hyperlink example earlier.

> **NOTE**
>
> In order to insert a paragraph break, add a <p> element to your document. The sample page, `Main.htm`, uses a <p> element to break the information into paragraph groupings.

Bulleted List

To create a bulleted list of items, use the <UL> tag. In between the <UL> and </UL> tags, use the <LI> and </LI> tags to create each individual list item. The <LI> tag automatically adds a line break after each item.

To try out this sample page (see Listing 5.2), which includes an unordered list, locate `UnorderedList.htm` in the `InternetBasics` folder.

LISTING 5.2   Contents of `UnorderedList.htm`

```
<HTML>
<BODY>
<H3>Unordered list</H3>

<UL>
<LI>Arizona</LI>
<LI>California</LI>
<LI>Nevada</LI>
</UL>

</BODY>
</HTML>
```

Numbered List

To create a numbered list of items, use the <OL> tag. In between the <OL> and </OL> tags, use the <LI> and </LI> tags to create each individual list item. The <LI> tag automatically adds a line break after each item. Listing 5.3 includes an example of this technique.

To try out this sample page, which includes an ordered list, locate `OrderedList.htm` in the `InternetBasics` folder:

LISTING 5.3   Contents of `OrderedList.htm`

```
<HTML>
<BODY>
<H3>Ordered list</H3>

<OL>
<LI>Wash the car</LI>
<LI>Feed the cats</LI>
<LI>Take a nap</LI>
</OL>

</BODY>
</HTML>
```

Combo and List Boxes

To create a drop-down list or list box containing list items, use the <SELECT> tag. The element supports a size attribute that allows you to control the behavior of the control. If you set the size attribute to 1, you'll get a drop-down (combo box) control. If you set it to a larger value, you'll get a list box control.

Each list item in a SELECT element can contain both text, which displays in the control itself, and a text value associated with that list item. Listing 5.4 shows an example of this. When you're programmatically interacting with these elements, later in the book, you'll use the values.

To try out this page, load Select.htm in the InternetBasics folder.

LISTING 5.4   Contents of Select.htm

```
<HTML>
<BODY>
<H3>Select</H3>

<SELECT size=1>
<OPTION value="AZ">Arizona</OPTION>
<OPTION value="CA">California</OPTION>
<OPTION value="NV">Nevada</OPTION>
<OPTION value="TX">Texas</OPTION>
</SELECT>

<SELECT size=4>
<OPTION value="AZ">Arizona</OPTION>
<OPTION value="CA">California</OPTION>
<OPTION value="NV">Nevada</OPTION>
<OPTION value="TX">Texas</OPTION>
</SELECT>

</BODY>
</HTML>
```

Table

If you wish to create a grid containing items, use the <TABLE> tag. Within the <TABLE> and </TABLE> tags, use a combination of <TR>, <TH>, and <TD> tags to create each row, header, and detail cell for the table. Listing 5.5 shows an example of this.

The following page, Table.htm, demonstrates the use of a table, with rows, cells, and headers:

LISTING 5.5   Contents of Table.htm

```
<HTML>
<BODY>
```

LISTING 5.5   Continued

```
<H3>Table</H3>

<TABLE Border=1>
<TR>
  <TH>Abbr</TH>
  <TH>State</TH>
</TR>
<TR>
  <TD>AZ</TD>
  <TD>Arizona</TD>
</TR>
<TR>
  <TD>CA</TD>
  <TD>California</TD>
</TR>
<TR>
  <TD>NV</TD>
  <TD>Nevada</TD>
</TR>
</TABLE>

</BODY>
</HTML>
```

Images

To display an image within a Web page, use the `<IMG>` tag. You must supply the `src="FileName"` attribute in order to specify the name of the file that contains the picture you wish to display. Table 5.1 contains a list of the different types of files Internet Explorer 5 and later can display.

TABLE 5.1   Image Types Supported by Internet Explorer

File Extension	Description
.avi	Audio/Visual Interleaved (AVI)
.bmp	Windows Bitmap (BMP)
.emf	Windows Enhanced Metafile (EMF)
.gif	Graphics Interchange Format (GIF)
.jpg, .jpeg	Joint Photographic Experts Group (JPEG)
.mov	Apple QuickTime Movie (MOV)
.mpg, .mpeg	Motion Picture Experts Group (MPEG)

TABLE 5.1   Continued

File Extension	Description
.png	Portable Network Graphics (PNG)
.wmf	Windows Metafile (WMF)
.xbm	X Bitmap (XBM)

NOTE

Your browser might not support all the different image types listed in Table 5.1.

To try out using an image, load the following page, `Image.htm`:

```
<HTML>
<BODY>
<H3>Pictures</H3>

<img src="Northwind.gif">

</BODY>
</HTML>
```

Input Types

You'll need some way to allow users to input data onto your page. You can do this using the <INPUT> tag. You can add several attributes to this tag to control the type of input control you get on the page, as listed in Table 5.2.

TABLE 5.2   These Attributes Control the Behavior of Elements Created Using the SELECT Tag

Type	Description
CheckBox	Displays a box that the user can check or uncheck.
File	Displays a control that will allow the user to browse for a file on the local computer.
Hidden	A value that does not show up on the user's screen but will be submitted when the form is posted to the server.
Image	Displays an image on the page.
Password	Displays an asterisk for each character the user types in.
Radio	Displays a mutually exclusive radio button. Use this in combination with other radio input types to create a list that the user can select one and only one value from.
Reset	Resets all input types to their default states.
Submit	Posts the form with all input values to the server.
Text	An input area in which the user can enter text.
TextArea	A multiline input area in which the user can enter text.

Load Input.htm to try out the sample code shown in Listing 5.6.

LISTING 5.6   Contents of Input.htm

```
<HTML>
<BODY>
<H3>Input</H3>

<form action="Process.asp" method="post">
<table border=0>
<tr>
<td>First Name</td>
<td><input type="text" value="John"
maxlength="20" id=txtFirst></td>
</tr>

<tr>
<td>Last</td>
<td><input type="text" value="Smith"
maxlength="20" id=txtLast></td>
</tr>

<tr>
<td><input id="RadioButton1" name="Gender"
type="radio" value="Female">Female</input></td>
<td><input id="RadioButton2" name="Gender"
type="radio" value="Male">Male</input></td>
</tr>
</table>

<input type="Submit" Value="Submit">
</form>

</BODY>
</HTML>
```

Creating Web Sites Before ASP.NET

Before ASP.NET, developers using Microsoft products had two paths they could take:
Developers could either create simple HTML pages or they could use Active Server
Pages (ASP). Obviously, there were other choices as well, including several techniques
superceded by ASP. The next two sections outline the two existing techniques for
creating Web applications.

Using HTML to Create Sites

You can create a Web site using nothing but HTML if you want. However, when you do this, you do not have the ability to provide any runtime customization. For example, suppose you have a product catalog. If you wish to add or delete items from the catalog, you have to go into the HTML page that has the products and manually add and delete these products. This can be quite laborious.

The following page, Page1.htm, provides simple support for submitting data to another page using a submit button:

```
<HTML>
<BODY>
<H3>Enter Login Information</H3>
<form action="Process.htm" method="post">
Login ID <input type="textbox" value="BJones" name="txtLoginID"><br>
Password <input type="password" name="txtPassword"><BR>
<input type="submit" value="Login" name="btnLogin">

</FORM>

</BODY>
<HTML>
```

This page contains a Form element, which in turn contains all the data you might want to post to a page on your Web server. In this case, when you click Submit, you'll navigate to a page named Process.htm (which doesn't exist, in this little example). This page would need to somehow retrieve the values sent to it via the HTTP request. Luckily, you won't need to use this technique.

Using ASP

Microsoft realized the limitations of creating active Web sites using HTML and created Active Server Pages (ASP). (Microsoft wasn't alone in this—there are other, competing technologies, as well, that provide similar functionality.) This technology allowed some script to run on the server, and the final output of this script was HTML. That is, the request to the page would cause script code to run, which in turn could render HTML for display in any browser. For example, the script could retrieve data from a table in a database and generate a product catalog dynamically.

The following page, Page1.asp, demonstrates how ASP applications might appear. Notice the mixture of HTML and script code—that was the nature of the ASP beast. If you want to run this page, you'll need to set up a virtual root in IIS, load the page into that folder, and then browse to the server from within a browser. (In other words, you can't simply double-click ASP pages and view them in a browser—they require processing by IIS in order to render their output.) Here's the code for the page:

```
<%

Dim strLogin
Dim strPassword

' First time through, no data
strLogin = Request("txtLoginID")
strPassword = Request("txtPassword")

%>

<HTML>
<BODY>
<H3>Enter Login Information</H3>
<FORM action="Page1.asp" method="POST">
Login ID <input type="textbox" value="" name="txtLoginID"><br>
Password <input type="password" value="" name="txtPassword"><BR>

<input type="submit" value="Login" name="btnLogin">

<div><p><%= strLogin %> - <%= strPassword %></div>
</FORM>

</BODY>
<HTML>
```

Web Sites Created Using ASP.NET

ASP seemed great a few years ago, but now ASP.NET provides a simpler, faster, more powerful way to create Web applications. Instead of using a scripting language, you may now create real, fully compiled applications. You can write these applications using any of the .NET-compliant languages available, and you can use the great tools provided by Visual Studio .NET to do your work. Any developer can now create full-featured, powerful Web applications.

Creating a New ASP.NET Application

Enough talking about it—how about actually creating a simple Web application? To get started, you'll create a project with a Web Form that allows users to input first and last names. After entering the data into these two text controls on the Web page, a user clicks a button and sees the entered information appear in a label below the button.

Figure 5.1 shows the sample Web Form you will create.

FIGURE 5.1.   This simple page allows you to enter values, and clicking the button runs code to process those values.

Creating the Login Form

To get started, you'll need to create a new Web Application project in Visual Studio .NET:

1. Start Visual Studio .NET and select the File, New, Project menu item.

2. In the New Project dialog box, select Visual Basic Projects in the Project Types pane.

3. In the Templates pane, select ASP.NET Web Application.

4. In the Location text box, enter `http://localhost/Jumpstart/Northwind` as the location for the project.

5. Click OK to allow Visual Studio .NET to create the virtual root, add the project template, and prepare for you to begin working on the project. This may take a few moments.

6. By default, Visual Studio .NET creates a page named `WebForm1.aspx`. Although you could develop your application using this page, you'll generally want to rename the page, the code file, and the programming class contained within the code file. It's easier to simply delete the whole page and create a new one, using your own name.

7. Select `WebForm1.aspx` in the Solution Explorer window (most likely, the Solution Explorer window will appear in the upper-right corner of the Visual

Studio .NET environment), right-click, and select Delete from the context menu.

8. Select the Project, Add Web Form menu item.

9. Set the name of this new page to Login.aspx and then click Open to add the page.

10. Use the View, Toolbox menu item to ensure that the Toolbox window is visible. Then add controls and set properties as shown here.

Control Type	Property	Value
Label	ID	Label1
	Text	First Name
TextBox	ID	txtFirst
Label	ID	Label2
	Text	Last Name
TextBox	ID	txtLast
Button	ID	btnLogin
	Text	Login
Label	ID	lblName
	BorderStyle	Inset
	Text	(Delete the text, so you see just the label's name.)

11. To view the layout information you've created, choose the View, HTML Source menu item (or click the HTML tab at the bottom of the designer window). You'll see HTML but no programming code—that goes into a separate location.

12. Select the View, Design menu item to get back to the normal design view.

13. Select File, Save All to save your project.

Running the Login Form

At this point, you can run this application and see the Web Form appear in your browser. Although this page does not have any functionality yet, this exercise is a good test to make sure everything is running up to this point. Here are the steps to follow:

1. Select Login.aspx in the Solution Explorer window.

2. Right-click and select Set as Start Page from the context menu.

3. Press F5 to run this sample application.

TIP

If you have trouble running the application, refer back to the instructions in Chapter 1, "Getting Started with the Sample Application." You may need to configure your project to allow debugging.

You should now see the Web Form displayed in your browser, and you can enter data into the two text fields. If you click the button, nothing will happen because you have not told it to do anything yet. You need to add some code in order for the button to have any effect.

TIP

While your page is open in the browser window, right-click and select View Source from the context menu. Although there will be a bunch of stuff in the page that you didn't put there (ASP.NET adds some useful support that you'll learn about later), you should see standard HTML for the controls you did place on the page.

Adding Code to the Button

If you want the button to actually "do" anything, you need to add some code. For this example, you need to add code so that the button posts the data you entered in the text boxes and fills in the appropriate data in the label below the button control. Follow these steps to add the Visual Basic .NET code you need:

1. Stop the program from running by closing down the browser.

2. While the page is open in the Visual Studio .NET page designer, double-click the LogIn button. You will now see a code window appear with the procedure btnLogin_Click already created for you.

3. Modify this procedure, which will run when a user clicks the button, so that it looks like this:

```
Private Sub btnLogin_Click( _
ByVal sender As Object, _
ByVal e As System.EventArgs) _
Handles btnLogin.Click

  lblName.Text = txtLast.Text & ", " & txtFirst.Text
End Sub
```

NOTE

In your editor, the code will look slightly different. The first long line of code, the procedure definition, will appear all on a single line. To make the code fit on the printed page, we've wrapped this one logical line of code into multiple physical lines, ending each line with Visual

Basic .NET's line continuation characters (a space followed by an underscore). You needn't make this same change in your own code, unless you want to. We do this throughout this book to make the code visible within the limited range of printed space.

4. The code you just wrote retrieved the Text property from both the txtLast and txtFirst text boxes, and it places the data into the Label control on the page. If you've ever programmed in any flavor of Visual Basic, this should look awfully familiar. In fact, the whole point of programming in .NET is that you should be able to use familiar techniques, like these, no matter what type of application you're creating.

Finally, it's time to test your masterpiece.

5. Run the application by pressing F5 again.

6. Enter a first and last name and click Login.

7. If you have done everything correctly, you should see the entered name appear in the label below the button.

Where did you put your code? When you created the Web Form, you created a file with an .aspx extension (Login.aspx). This file contains only layout information, generally. When you added code, you modified a corresponding file, the "code-behind" file (believe us, we don't make these things up), named Login.aspx.vb. All the programming code goes into this separate file, as part of a class named Login:

```
Public Class Login
...

  Private Sub btnLogin_Click( _
    ByVal sender As Object, _
    ByVal e As System.EventArgs) _
    Handles btnLogin.Click

      lblName.Text = txtLast.Text & ", " & txtFirst.Text
  End Sub
End Class
```

This class defines the programmatic behavior for this page. When you press F5 to run the project, Visual Studio .NET compiles your class into a DLL. When you browse to the page, ASP.NET loads the layout information from the ASPX page as well as the code from the compiled DLL. This separation provides for all sorts of exciting flexibility (you can update the code on your site, even while users are currently viewing pages on the site, for example) and makes it simpler to create sites.

It's important to consider what happens when you click the button on the sample page:

1. The form posts its data back to the server.

2. The server recomposes the page using the data you typed in and places it back into the page. The server then sends the page back to the browser.

3. The browser renders the page again.

It's interesting (and important) to note that if you were using ASP (rather than ASP.NET), it would be up to you to place the values back into the appropriate HTML tags. In this case, even after you click the button, the first name and last name values you entered still appear in the text box controls. If you were using a standard ASP page, that wouldn't be the case.

Summary

This chapter provided a quick overview of the Internet, HTML, ASP, and ASP.NET. You will find as you go through this book that ASP.NET is much more flexible and powerful than ASP.

In particular, you learned:

- How the Internet works

- About simple HTML tags

- How HTML pages work

- How ASP pages work

- How to get started with ASP.NET

- How to create a simple ASP.NET project

Introduction to ASP.NET

6

OBJECTIVES

- Learn about Web Forms, the basis of ASP.NET applications

- Learn the various types of server controls and determine when to use each

- Build a sample Web Form with some simple VB .NET code attached

Microsoft ASP.NET is the next generation of technology for Web application development. It takes the best from Active Server Pages (ASP), the rich services and features provided by the Common Language Runtime (CLR), and adds many new features. The result is a robust, scalable, and fast Web development experience that will give you great flexibility with little coding.

Overview of ASP.NET

ASP.NET consists of several different technologies, including Web Forms, Web Services, server controls, HTML controls, and validation controls, as shown in Figure 6.1. All these technologies, working together, make it possible (and some might even say "easy") to create robust, maintainable, scalable Web applications. You'll use Web Forms to lay out the user interface of your applications, using server controls as the basis for user interaction. (If you're importing an existing HTML or ASP page, you might use the other set of controls, HTML controls, which don't provide as rich an experience for users, nor are they as easy to work with, programmatically, as server controls. For new pages, you'll most likely want to use the new server controls.) In addition, the set of validation controls (actually, just a subset of the total set of server controls) makes it easy for you to validate user input, either on the client side, on the server side, or both. Web Services provide a platform for creating distributed component-based applications, and ASP.NET makes it easy to create and consume Web Services.

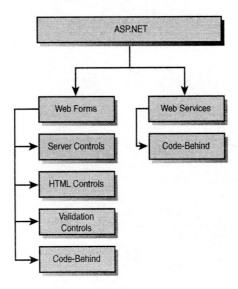

FIGURE 6.1   ASP.NET includes many different technologies.

You will be introduced to each of these different technologies in this chapter, and you'll explore them in further detail in subsequent chapters.

Web Forms

Web Forms are the heart and soul of ASP.NET. Web Forms are the user interface (UI) elements that give your Web application its look and feel. Web Forms are similar to the .NET Framework's Windows Forms (or even VB6's forms) in that they provide properties, methods, and events for the controls that are placed on them. However, these UI elements render themselves in the appropriate markup language required by the request (in this case, HTML). If you use Visual Studio .NET, you also get the familiar drag-and-drop interface for creating the interface for your Web application.

When you create Web applications using Visual Studio .NET, Web Forms are made up of two files: the visual portion (the ASPX file) and the code behind the page, which resides in a separate class file. (Microsoft refers to this separate file containing code as the page's *code-behind file*. We're not kidding.) If you create Web applications outside Visual Studio .NET (yes, it's possible, although it's not terribly productive), you can place the user interface and the code in the same file. The layout information will still be separated from the code, but both parts can exist within the same file.

Web Forms and ASP.NET were created to overcome some of the limitations of ASP.
The new strengths of ASP.NET include the following:

- Separation of the HTML interface from application logic

- A rich set of server-side controls that can detect the browser and send out
  appropriate markup language, such as HTML

- Data binding capabilities of the new server-side .NET controls, which means
  less code to write

- An event-based programming model that is familiar to Visual Basic programmers

- Compiled code and support for multiple languages, as opposed to ASP, which
  supported only interpreted VBScript or JScript

- Allowing third parties to create controls that provide additional functionality

XML Web Services

XML Web Services make up the second portion of ASP.NET's functionality.
Developers have, for several years, required some means of executing methods across
the Internet—that is, some way to programmatically request information or an
action and then retrieve the results. A Web Service is an object that can be called
remotely (normally using HTTP) that solves this need.

ASP.NET makes it easy for you to create Web Services, and any application that
understands how to work with XML data can consume the service.

> **NOTE**
>
> When you use an XML Web Service, under the covers, ASP.NET is using the Simple Object
> Access Protocol (SOAP) standard for its messaging protocol. This standard indicates how a
> Web Service consumer should package up its method requests, and it specifies how a Web
> Service should send back its results. As long as both sides (service and consumer) follow the
> SOAP specification, any Web Service should be able to interact with any Web Service
> consumer.

These Web Services may be written in any .NET language, or any language running
on any platform, as long as the Web Services follow the SOAP specification. Web
Services can also be called from any .NET language or any language that has the
capability to process SOAP envelopes and call HTTP interfaces.

A Web Service created in .NET always returns an XML string. When you use the .NET Framework, you will not need to get your hands "dirty" handling any of the XML manually; any return value you send back will automatically be wrapped into an XML string for you. That is, the .NET Framework handles all the details, packaging and unpackaging the XML necessary for the Web Service to do its job. All you need to do is create the code that performs the work, passing in parameters as necessary, and returning the correct value. The .NET Framework will manage converting XML packets into your parameters and converting the return value back into an XML string for the Web Service consumer.

Figure 6.2 shows, in a simplified fashion, how a client application might consume an XML Web Service. Things don't have to work this way, but if you take all the default options in Visual Studio .NET, this is the path your Web Service data will take.

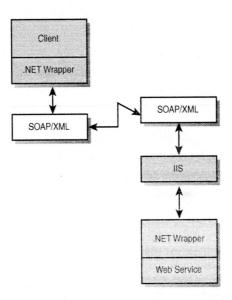

FIGURE 6.2   A Web Service client receives and sends information to and from the Web Service.

When you create a Web Service in .NET, you create a class that has public methods. Each public method may be exposed as a method simply by you adding a procedure attribute to the method as you create the procedure. (By adding the <WebMethod()> attribute, you're telling the .NET Framework that it must expose the procedure as a Web Service method.) The .NET compiler takes care of creating the necessary files that allow another process to call this Web Service across an HTTP interface. Figure 6.3 demonstrates, in a simplified manner, how the translation occurs.

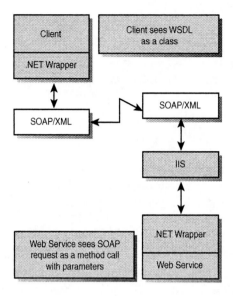

FIGURE 6.3   .NET hides the SOAP implementation.

When you compile a Web Service created in .NET, it will automatically generate a number of files for you. When a Web Service consumer application (either created in .NET, or not) needs to determine information about the Web Service and its available methods, it will use these files:

TIP

It's important to realize that nothing about XML Web Services requires any Microsoft technology. In this book, we'll focus on creating and consuming XML Web Services in the context of Microsoft's tools and servers, but none of these is actually required. If you want to create a Web Service hosted on a Linux server, using Apache, you're welcome to do so. If you want to consume a Web Service using a Lotus Notes application, that works fine, too. That's the beauty of embracing an existing standard. All we can say is that it's a lot easier creating and consuming Web Services using Visual Studio .NET than in any other tool we've seen.

- .VSDISCO. A Visual Studio Discovery file. This file gives a list of Web Services available on a particular Web site.

- .WSDL. A Web Services Description Language file. This file describes the method name(s) available for the selected Web Service. For each method, there is also a list of parameters and a description of the return value.

Introducing Web Form Controls

As mentioned earlier, ASP.NET provides two sets of controls you can choose from when developing Web Forms. We suggest you spend most of your time using the standard Web Forms controls. You might also need to support existing HTML or ASP pages and therefore might need to investigate the HTML controls. The following subsections describe both types of controls.

HTML Controls

HTML controls mimic the actual HTML elements you would use if you were using FrontPage or any other HTML editor to draw your UI. You can use standard HTML elements in Web Forms, too. For example, if you wanted to create a text box, you would write the following:

```
<input type="text" id=txtFirstName size=25>
```

If you are using Visual Studio .NET, you choose a Text Field control from the HTML tab on the Toolbox window and draw the control where you want it on the Web Form.

Any HTML element can be marked to also run as an HTML control when the Web Form is processed on the server by adding the runat attribute to the tag and setting its value to be "server", as shown here:

```
<input type="text" id=txtFirstName size=25 runat="server">
```

If you are using Visual Studio .NET, you can right-click the HTML element in Design View and select Run as Server Control from the context menu. By adding the runat="server" attribute, you allow ASP.NET to process server-side events for the control, thus adding an enormous level of power and flexibility to your page.

HTML controls allow you to handle server events associated with the tag (a button click, for example) as well as manipulate the HTML tag programmatically in the Web Form's code. When the control is rendered to the browser, the tag is rendered just as it is saved in the Web Form, minus the runat="server" part. This gives you precise control over the HTML that is sent to the browser. Table 6.1 lists the HTML controls available in ASP.NET.

TABLE 6.1   HTML Controls Available in ASP.NET

Control	Description	Web Form Code Example
Button	Used to respond to click events.	`<input type=button runat= server>`
Reset Button	Resets all other HTML form elements on a form to their default values.\	`<input type=reset runat=server>`

TABLE 6.1   Continued

Control	Description	Web Form Code Example
Submit Button	Automatically posts the form data to the specified page listed in the `Action=` attribute in the `FORM` tag.	`<input type=submit runat=server>`
Text Field	Gives the user an input area on an HTML form.	`<input type=text runat=server>`
Text Area	Used for multiline input on an HTML form.	`<input type=textarea runat=server>`
File Field	Places a text field and a Browse button on a form and allows the user to select a file name from the local machine after clicking the Browse button.	`<input type=file runat=server>`
Password Field	An input area on an HTML form. Any characters typed into this field are displayed as asterisks.	`<input type=password runat=server>`
Check Box	Gives the user a check button that he can select or clear.	`<input type=checkbox runat=server>`
Radio Button	Always used in groups of two or more. Allows the user to choose one of the options within the group.	`<input type=radio runat=server>`
Table	Allows you to present information in a tabular format.	`<table runat=server></table>`
Image	Displays an image on an HTML form.	`<img src="FileName" runat=server>`
List Box	Displays a list of items to the user. You must set the `size` attribute to a value greater than 1 in order to see the items in a list. (Setting the `size` attribute to 1 or omitting the attribute displays the items in a drop-down list.) You can set the size from two or more to specify how many items you wish to show. If there are more items than will fit within this limit, a scroll bar is automatically added to this control.	`<select size=2 runat=server >` `</select>`

TABLE 6.1   Continued

Control	Description	Web Form Code Example
Dropdown	Displays a list of items to the user, but only one item at a time will appear. The user can click a down arrow from the side of this control and a list of items will be displayed.	`<select><option></option></select>`
Horizontal Rule	Displays a horizontal line across the HTML page.	`<hr>`

All these controls emit standard HTML into the Web Form. You may optionally assign an ID attribute to each control, allowing you to write client-side JavaScript code for any of the events that are common for this particular type of control. Table 6.2 lists some of the more common client-side events.

TABLE 6.2   Common Client-Side Events You Might Handle

Event Name	Description
`OnBlur:`	The control loses focus.
`OnChange:`	The contents of the control are changed.
`OnClick:`	The control is clicked.
`OnFocus:`	The control receives focus.
`OnMouseOver:`	The mouse moves over the control.

Web Form Server Controls

HTML controls allow for compatibility with existing Web pages, but they don't provide a useful object model and aren't simple to program against. Server controls provide a consistent, object-oriented programming model. They provide event handling on the server and render their output as HTML for the requesting browser. For example, if you set the page's `pageLayout` property to `GridLayout` (as opposed to `FlowLayout`), you can place controls at any location on the page. (Normal HTML layout requires a left-to-right, top-to-bottom "flow" layout.) At runtime, ASP.NET must decide how to render this particular page. For example, should it use absolute positioning (not all browsers support this feature) or should it try to render the page in a manner that down-level browsers can support? If ASP.NET determines that the browser can't render absolute positioning, it creates a table on-the-fly and positions the controls as near to their design-time positions as possible. The HTML sent to the browser is far larger, and far more complex, than what's sent if the browser supports absolute positioning, but the page still looks the same. By decoupling the control design and layout from the rendering at runtime, ASP.NET makes it possible to support just about any browser, in any environment.

All Web Form controls inherit from a common base class, namely the `System.Web.UI.WebControls` class. This base class implements a set of common properties that all these controls will have. Here's a list of some of these common properties:

- `BackColor`
- `Enabled`
- `Font`
- `ForeColor`
- `TabIndex`
- `Visible`
- `Width`

The Microsoft .NET Framework supplies a few different categories of server controls. Some controls have an almost one-to-one correspondence with their HTML counterparts. Some controls provide additional information when posted back to the server, and some controls allow you to display data in tabular or list-type format. Table 6.3 provides a list of Web Form server-side controls and the tags you will see within an ASPX page. Each control is represented by a similar tag within the design-time environment. In each case, the tag is prefixed with "asp:", as in `<asp:Hyperlink>`.

TABLE 6.3   Server-Side Controls Used in ASP.NET and Web Forms

Control	Description
Label	Displays text on the HTML page.
TextBox	Gives the user an input area on an HTML form.
Button	A normal button control used to respond to click events on the server. This control posts back to the server when clicked.
LinkButton	This control is like a button in that it posts back to a server, but the button looks like a hyperlink.
ImageButton	This control can display a graphical image, and, when clicked, it posts back to the server command information such as the mouse coordinates within the image.
HyperLink	A normal hyperlink control that responds to a click event.
DropDownList	A normal drop-down list control like the HTML control, but this control can be bound to a data source.
ListBox	A normal list box control like the HTML control, but this control can be bound to a data source.

TABLE 6.3   Continued

Control	Description
DataGrid	A more powerful HTML table. You bind this control to a data source, and the control displays all the column information. You can also perform paging, sorting, and formatting.
DataList	Allows you to create a template-based layout for data, using a table-like layout. You can bind the data to template items or snippets of HTML that repeat for each item.
Repeater	Allows you to create a template-based layout for repeating data as a single column. You can bind the data to template items, which are like bits of HTML put together in a specific repeating format.
CheckBox	Very similar to the normal HTML control that displays a check box for the user to check or uncheck.
CheckBoxList	Displays check boxes that work together as a group.
RadioButton	Similar to the normal HTML control that displays a round button for the user to check or uncheck.
RadioButtonList	Displays a group of radio button controls that all work together. Only one of the group can be selected at a time.
Image	Similar to the normal HTML control that displays an image within the page.
Panel	Groups other controls so that you can refer to the group of controls as a single entity.
PlaceHolder	Acts as a location where you can add new server-side controls dynamically at runtime.
Calendar	Creates an HTML version of a calendar. You can set the default date, move forward and backward through the calendar, and so on.
AdRotator	Allows you to specify a list of ads to display. Each time the user accesses the page, the display rotates through the series of ads.
Table	Similar to the normal HTML table control.
XML	Displays XML information within the rendered HTML. This control can also be used to perform an XSLT transform prior to displaying the XML.
Literal	This control is like a label in that it displays literal HTML, but the output of this control isn't part of the Controls collection of the page. Basically, this control simply allows you to send data directly to the rendered page.

All these controls change their output based on the type of browser detected for the user. If the user's browser is Internet Explorer 4.0 or higher, ASP.NET can take advantage of Dynamic HTML (DHTML) and other more "modern" extensions to HTML. If ASP.NET detects a down-level browser (something other than IE 4.0 or higher), the normal HTML 3.2 standard is sent back to the user's browser.

Field Validator Controls

Often, you'll need to validate user input before the user submits the page back to the server. The rich set of validation controls, described in Table 6.4, perform client-side validation if possible (depending on the browser). ASP requires you either to write complex client-side validation code or to force a roundtrip in order to validate input. ASP.NET creates client-side code for you and can validate on the client side. Each of these controls renders client-side JavaScript code into the HTML page so that the values can be checked without a roundtrip. The JavaScript works on most browsers, but if your browser doesn't support scripting, all the validation can still occur on the server side.

TIP

Even if you can take advantage of client-side validations, ASP.NET always validates the values one last time when the page gets posted to the server.

TABLE 6.4   Field Validator Controls

Control	Description
RequiredFieldValidator	Validates a control against an initial value. If the control contains the `InitialValue` property of the associated RequiredFieldValidator control, the control won't validate. By default, the `InitialValue` property contains an empty string, so unless you modify the behavior, using this control forces users to supply a value in the control.
CompareValidator	Compares the contents of a control against a value or the contents of another control. If the values don't match, the control won't validate.
RangeValidator	Allows you to check to see whether the value you entered in a control is within a specified range. If it isn't, the control won't validate.
RegularExpressionValidator	Allows you to check to see whether a control's contents match the input mask (regular expression) you defined. If they don't, the control won't validate.
CustomValidator	Allows you to specify a server-side and a client-side function to validate the contents of a particular control. Your functions return a Boolean value, indicating the validity of the control's data.

TABLE 6.4   Continued

Control	Description
ValidationSummary	Automatically gathers all the ErrorMessage properties from each of the other validator controls on this form and displays each one in a numbered list, a bulleted list, or a paragraph format.

How Web Forms Work

Just as you'll find when working with Windows Forms, ASP.NET Web Forms raise events in a certain order as the page initializes and loads. ASP.NET also raises events in response to user interaction in the browser. When you think about how a standard ASP or HTML page is created and sent to a browser, you assume that everything is processed in a very linear, top-down fashion. However, for a Web Form, nothing could be further from the truth.

Like a Windows Form, a Web Form goes through the standard Load, Draw (Render), and Unload types of events. Throughout this process, different procedures within the page's class module are called. When a page is requested from a client browser, a DLL that encapsulates the tags in the ASPX page as well as the page code is loaded and then processed.

First, the Init event occurs as ASP.NET sets the page to its initial state, as described by the tags in the ASPX file. If the page is posting back to itself, Init also restores any page state that may have been stored by the page previously.

Next, ASP.NET raises the Load event as the page is loaded. In the event handler for this event, you can use the Page.IsPostback property to determine whether the page has posted back to itself. This might happen because a user has clicked a button or is interacting with some other control that caused a postback to the page. You might perform some initialization only on the first page load—for example, you might bind data into the controls. (You're far more likely to trigger a postback with ASP.NET pages than you are when creating ASP applications. Because ASP.NET makes it so simple to have just about any control passed back to the page and to run event code before the page renders again, you'll find that you end up running code in the Page_Load procedure quite often. Checking the Page.IsPostback property will allow you to only run code the first time the page is loaded, if that makes sense.)

Next, if the page is being posted back, ASP.NET raises control events. (If the page isn't being posted back—that is, being loaded for the first time—event procedures won't run. There's obviously no event that requires handling yet.) First, all the "change" events are fired. These events are batched up in the browser and executed only when the page is sent back to the server. These "change" events include changing the text in a text box and selecting an item in a ListBox or DropDownList control.

TIP

Event procedures only run when you post back to a page. Postback happens immediately, and automatically, when you click a button. You may want to have postback occur automatically when you select an item from a list or when you check a check box. Doing this in ASP requires you to write client-side script. In ASP.NET, it's as simple as setting a control's AutoPostBack property to True. When you do that, ASP.NET inserts the appropriate client-side script for you, so clicking the check box or selecting an item from a list triggers a postback, and the page can run the associated event code immediately.

TIP

You cannot control the order in which the "change" events fire on the server. You are guaranteed only that they will all fire.

Next, and only if the page is posted back, the control event that caused the page to post back is fired. Examples of postback events include a button's Click event or controls for which you've set the AutoPostBack property to True, like a check box's CheckedChanged event.

Next, the page is rendered to the browser. Some state information (the page's view state) is included in a hidden field in the page so that when the page is called again through a postback, ASP.NET can restore the page to its previous state. (You'll learn more about view state and managing state in Chapter 23, "State Management in ASP.NET.")

There is a final page event your code can handle before the page is disposed: the Unload event. Because the page is already rendered, this event is typically used to perform cleanup and logging tasks only. Finally, the class that represents the running page is removed from memory, and the page is unloaded from memory as well.

If you change the ASPX page or its code, the dynamically generated DLL that represents the page will be regenerated the next time the page is requested. This DLL is stored to disk each time it is generated.

Internet Information Server (IIS) Objects

IIS supplies many objects that can be used by hosting platforms such as ASP and ASP.NET. These objects aren't new in ASP.NET—they're the same objects (with a few new properties) that you might have used in an ASP application. You can use these objects to return information about your application and your IIS server. ASP.NET makes all these objects available to you from the code in your Web Form's code-behind file.

The Response **Object**

The Response object allows you to place information into the HTML stream prior to sending a complete HTML page back to the client. For example, you could include code such as this to insert text directly into the rendered output:

```
Response.Write("An invalid password was entered")
```

The Request **Object**

The Request object allows you to receive information from the user. Requests can be input fields on an HTML page or values passed on the URL. The following code retrieves the value from a text box on the requesting page:

```
strLastName = Request("txtLastName").ToString()
```

The Request object can also retrieve information from a URL. For example, given the URL

```
http://www.yoursite.com/YourPage.aspx?Keyname=John
```

as entered from the browser, you could retrieve the Keyname parameter using code like this:

```
Request.QueryString("KeyName")
```

The Session **Object**

IIS creates a Session object globally, once for each user's session. Using this object, you can retrieve and set properties such as Session.TimeOut and Session.SessionID. The TimeOut property indicates how long to wait for a user to respond to a page before IIS kills the session. The SessionID property is a unique long integer value that corresponds to this specific session. The Session object also provides a dictionary-type collection of name/value pairs. You can also add and retrieve your own variables within this object. The following code takes a value from the Request object and stores it as a Session variable for later reuse:

```
Session("LoginID") = Request("txtLoginID")
```

If you run this same line of code again, it will replace the contents in the LoginID session variable with the updated contents of the txtLoginID value. The Session object and all its contents are destroyed when a user leaves a site or when the session times out.

> **TIP**
>
> You may have discovered that using `Session` and `Application` objects—and their associated dictionaries of values—wasn't a good idea in ASP because of scalability issues and because of the need to save data as cookies on the user's computer. These issues have been handled in ASP.NET, and you'll learn more about state management in Chapter 23.

The `Application` Object

IIS supplies another global object, `Application`. IIS creates this object the first time a user comes to a Web site. You might use the `Application` object to store a database connection string. Because the connection information doesn't need to change from user to user, the `Application` object is a perfect place to store this type of information. For example, the following code stores a connection string so that it can be accessed at any time within your site's processing:

```
Application("ConnectString") = _
 "Provider=sqloledb;Initial Catalog=Employees;" & _
 "Data Source=DataServer"
```

The `Server` Object

The `Server` object has some properties that relate to information in the IIS server. You might call the `MapPath` method if you need to return a hyperlink to a file on the server in a virtual directory. Here's an example:

```
strPath = Server.MapPath("EmpMaint")
```

The preceding code might return the following for a specific Web site:

```
d:\inetpub\wwwroot\EmpWeb\EmpMaint
```

The `global.asax` File

The `global.asax` file is similar to the `global.asa` file in ASP, although there are more events available in ASP.NET. Also, just as ASP.NET compiles the code in every page regardless of which language you use to create the code-behind file (as opposed to interpreting the code, as in ASP), the code in `global.asax` is fully compiled as well. ASP.NET allows you to handle a sequence of site-wide events using code in your `global.asax` file. Table 6.5 lists the event procedures available to you within the `global.asax` file.

TABLE 6.5   Event Procedures Available Within `global.asax`

Event Procedure	Description
Application_Start	Raised when the first user hits your Web site.
Application_End	Raised when the last user in the site's session times out.
Application_Error	Raised when an unhandled error occurs in the application.
Session_Start	Raised when any new user hits your Web site.
Session_End	Raised when a user's session times out or ends.
Application_AcquireRequestState	Raised when ASP.NET acquires the current state (for example, session state) associated with the current request.
Application_AuthenticateRequest	Raised when a security module establishes the identity of the user.
Application_AuthorizeRequest	Raised when a security module verifies user authorization.
Application_BeginRequest	Raised when ASP.NET starts to process the request, before other per-request events.
Application_Disposed	Raised when ASP.NET completes the chain of execution when responding to a request.
Application_EndRequest	Raised as the last event during the processing of the request, after other prerequest events.
Application_PostRequestHandlerExecute	Raised right after the ASP.NET handler (such as a page or XML Web Service) finishes execution.
Application_PreRequestHandlerExecute	Raised just before ASP.NET begins executing a handler (such as a page or XML Web Service).
Application_PreSendRequestContent	Raised just before ASP.NET sends content to the client.
Application_PreSendRequestHeaders	Raised just before ASP.NET sends HTTP headers to the client.
Application_ReleaseRequestState	Raised after ASP.NET finishes executing all request handlers. This event causes state modules to save the current state data.
Application_ResolveRequestCache	Raised after ASP.NET completes an authorization event to let the caching modules serve requests from the cache, bypassing execution of the handler (the page or Web Service, for example).
Application_UpdateRequestCache	Raised after ASP.NET finishes executing a handler in order to let caching modules store responses that will be used to serve subsequent requests from the cache.

Creating User Controls

In addition to the built-in server controls in the .NET Framework, you can also build your own controls to be placed on Web Forms. ASP.NET supports two different types of user-created controls: user controls and custom controls. The creation of custom controls is beyond the scope of this book, but it's simple to create user controls. These controls are basically saved pages (or *pagelets*) that act as self-contained controls.

For example, you may wish to create a menu system along the left side of every page in your site, where each menu item is built from a database. You might also want to place a standard logo and header on each page. What you need is some way to include standard pages, or parts of pages, within each of your pages.

User controls provide this functionality and are the replacement for #include files in ASP.NET. Figure 6.4 displays the output you might want to generate. In this example, the image and header "Northwind Traders" are both in one user control. The menu going down the left side is another control.

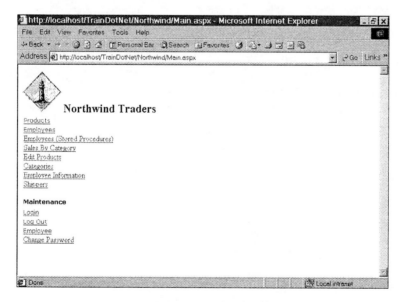

FIGURE 6.4 User controls output HTML on the client side.

Figure 6.5 shows the same Web page in design mode. As you can see, these user controls are simply placeholders. You can see the full UI for such controls by opening the file where you built them within your project.

FIGURE 6.5   User controls do not display any HTML on the server side; they are just placeholders.

Creating the Northwind Solution

To demonstrate working with Web Forms and server controls, in this section you'll add a main page to the Northwind Trading Company application that includes links to pages you'll add in later chapters. In addition, you'll create a login page that you'll use in several later chapters, adding login capabilities to the application.

To get started, load the Northwind.sln solution you have been working on up to this point. Follow these steps to add Main.aspx and controls to the page:

1. Select Project, Add Web Form from the menu bar.

2. Set Name to Main.aspx and click Open.

3. Add the following controls:

Control	Property	Value
Label	ID	Label1
	Text	Northwind Traders
	Font.Bold	True
	Font.Size	Large
Hyperlink	ID	hypProducts
	Text	Products
	NavigateURL	Products.aspx

Control	Property	Value
Label	ID	Label2
	Text	Maintenance
	Font.Bold	True
	Font.Size	Small
Hyperlink	ID	hypLogin
	Text	Login
	NavigateURL	Login.aspx
LinkButton	ID	lnkLogout
	Text	Log Out
	Visible	False
Hyperlink	ID	hypEmpMaint
	Text	Employee
	NavigateURL	EmpMaint.aspx
	Visible	False
Hyperlink	ID	hypPwdChange
	Text	Change Password
	NavigateURL	PWDChange.aspx
	Visible	False

4. To set Main.aspx as the startup page, right-click Main.aspx in the Solution Explorer window and then select Set as Start Page from the context menu.

5. In the Solution Explorer window, right-click Global.asax and select View Code from the context menu. Modify the Session_Start() procedure in the code window, like this:

```
Sub Session_Start(ByVal sender As Object, ByVal e As EventArgs)
    Session("LoginID") = String.Empty
    Session("Password") = String.Empty
End Sub
```

6. In the Solution Explorer window, double-click the Login.aspx page you created in the last chapter to load the page into the page designer.

7. Change the Text property of the First Name label to **Login ID**.

8. Change the Text property of the Last Name label to **Password**.

9. Click the text box named txtFirst.

10. Change the ID property to **txtLoginID**.

11. Click the text box named txtLast.

12. Change the ID property to **txtPassword**.

13. Change the Textmode property to **Password**.

14. Change the lblName label control at the bottom of the form to the name **lblError**. Reset the BorderStyle property to None.

15. Change the Click event procedure to the following code:

```
Private Sub btnLogin_Click( _
 ByVal sender As System.Object, _
 ByVal e As System.EventArgs) Handles btnLogin.Click
    Server.Transfer("Main.aspx")
End Sub
```

Finally, it's time to test your application, just to make sure the login page redirects you correctly to the main page. Follow these steps to verify that things are "hooked up" correctly:

1. Press F5 to run the project.

2. On the main page, click the Log In link to navigate to Login.aspx.

3. On the login page, click the button to navigate back to the main page.

4. Close any open pages when you're done.

Summary

Using HTML pages, ASPX (Web Form) pages, HTML controls, and Web Form controls, you now have a fantastic environment for creating very robust, scalable, and flexible Web applications in ASP.NET. This chapter introduces a lot of concepts, and later chapters will dig into many of these concepts in more detail. You should find that the move from ASP or VB6 to ASP.NET is easier than the move from VB6 to ASP, because you now have the same development environment and the same programming model as you're used to working with.

7

Working with ASP.NET and VB .NET

OBJECTIVES

- Learn event-handling basics
- Learn Visual Basic .NET data types
- Learn to create procedures and classes
- Use the StringBuilder class

When you start coding using the .NET Framework, you will find yourself faced with many new concepts. Even if you are moving to .NET from the Visual Basic 6 programming environment, you will find that many familiar features now behave slightly differently, and these differences all have enough of a twist to them that you will need to take some time to learn how the new and modified features work.

Of course, one of the most important programming concepts in Visual Basic is that of *events*. You need to learn about how events happen, as well as what the parameters that the .NET Framework passes to event-handling procedures are used for. Event handling is probably the most important concept in any .NET application, whether you are writing a desktop application or a Web application. Much of what you do as a developer revolves around writing code in response to the user performing some action. It is up to you to create the code that runs in response to these user actions.

Manipulating data is another key area that you should understand before you get too far along with your .NET programming. There are many different types of data—such as text, numeric values, and objects—that you will need to work with in your code. VB .NET supplies specific data types to help you distinguish between all the different types. It is important you understand what you can store into each data type and how you can convert one data type to another.

Another important concept is that of *classes* and *objects* and their use. Although classes are not new to most Visual

Basic developers, the techniques you employ to create and use them is somewhat different in VB .NET than in Visual Basic 6. In this chapter, you will learn the basics of creating a class, and you'll apply those concepts to the Northwind solution that you have been building so far in this book.

Event-Handling Basics

The process of creating a Web Forms user interface involves placing controls onto a page and then writing code to react to events that occur as users interact with those controls. ASP.NET makes it simple for you to work with pages, controls, and events as if the entire process were taking place on a client computer.

Interacting with the Server

In actuality, almost all event handling takes place on the Web server, and it's important that you understand what happens when you add event code that runs in reaction to user events. More important, code that you write in reaction to control events *always* runs on the server, except in one case: When you write script code that handles events on the client, in JavaScript or VBScript, the code does run on the client. Even the validation controls (covered in Chapter 8, "Validation Controls") run code on the server to validate data, even though the controls also provide client-side script for validating on the client side.

When you place a command button on a page, you can add code to react to that button's Click event. Clicking a command button control always triggers a postback to the server, where the page's Load event occurs. Then, your button's Click event procedure runs, allowing the procedure to react to the user clicking the button.

Each control supplies its own set of events that it can react to. For example, CommandButton controls provide a Click event. ListBox and DropDownList controls supply a SelectedIndexChanged event. RadioButton controls provide a CheckChanged event. It's your job as a developer to learn which controls supply which events and write code reacting to the appropriate events.

> **TIP**
>
> It's important to remember that none of the code you create in reaction to events, in your page's code-behind file, runs on the client. All this code runs on the server and requires a roundtrip to the server in order to run. This is a startling realization for Visual Basic 6.0 developers, who are used to having all event code run immediately in response to triggering an event.

Very few controls automatically trigger a postback to the server (in other words, very few controls' code runs automatically when you interact with the controls). For example, selecting an item in a list box won't automatically trigger a postback to the server and won't run the SelectedIndexChanged event procedure. The next time the page does post back, the code will run. If you want immediate feedback (more like a Visual Basic 6.0 form), you can set the AutoPostBack property for most controls to True. Doing this causes a change to the control's value to trigger a postback to the server.

You'll need to set the AutoPostBack property to True for controls in which you require immediate feedback—perhaps selecting an item from a list requires updating a label on the page. Alternatively, you might want to filter a list of values based on a selection in another list. Several examples in this chapter make use of the AutoPostBack property.

> **WARNING**
>
> There's no "free lunch" here. A roundtrip to the server is, well, a roundtrip to the server, and that takes time. If you have every control on your page initiate a roundtrip, by setting the AutoPostBack property to True for all the controls, you might be sorry due to increased network traffic and the time it takes for the page to respond to the user. With the Web server on your local machine, it's hard to determine the price you'll pay for postbacks, but even there, roundtrips aren't immediate. Consider carefully when you actually need to post back to the server—your users will appreciate it.

How Event Handling Works

In order to demonstrate some of the features of event handling and the VB .NET language, we've provided a simple project named VBLanguage.sln. You'll want to load this sample project so you can follow along with the discussion. This project already includes the layout for the pages, but you'll need to add the appropriate event code. The first page we'll discuss, Events.aspx, is shown in Figure 7.1.

We'll start by investigating the Click event of the CommandButton control on this page. Each server control (such as the CommandButton control) provides a default event procedure, and double-clicking the control in Design view will load the code editor and create the stub of the event procedure for you. Double-clicking the Click Me command button, for example, loads the code editor and writes this code for you:

```
Private Sub btnClickMe_Click( _
 ByVal sender As System.Object, _
 ByVal e As System.EventArgs) Handles btnClickMe.Click

End Sub
```

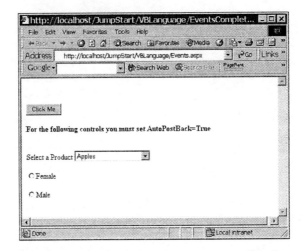

FIGURE 7.1   Clicking a button or changing the selection within a drop-down list can fire an event procedure back on the server.

TIP

Here, and throughout this book, we've reformatted event procedures so that they fit within the requirements of the printed page. We've added line continuation characters (a space, followed by an underscore, and then a carriage return/linefeed) to the end of lines that need to be broken to fit on the printed page. The Visual Studio .NET editor doesn't perform these same line breaks for you, so the code you see on the screen will be formatted slightly different from the code you see printed here.

You should notice some important things about this procedure:

- Visual Studio .NET generates a procedure name for you. In this case, the procedure is named btnClickMe_Click. Unlike in Visual Basic 6.0, the name of the procedure is arbitrary—that is, the name isn't used internally by the event handling in the page framework. Visual Studio .NET generates a name based on the name of the control and the name of the event, but that's only for your convenience—the name could be anything at all. When you double-click the Click Me button, you'll see the following code:

```
Private Sub btnClickMe_Click( _
 ByVal sender As System.Object, _
 ByVal e As System.EventArgs) Handles btnClickMe.Click

End Sub
```

- The event procedure provides two parameters, which you'll learn about in the next sections. These parameters are highlighted here:

```
Private Sub btnClickMe_Click( _
  ByVal sender As System.Object, _
  ByVal e As System.EventArgs) Handles btnClickMe.Click

End Sub
```

- The procedure ends with a Handles clause. This clause indicates to the event handler that the page framework should run this particular procedure in reaction to the specified event (btnClickMe.Click, in this case). This *object.event* name is crucial—if the object and its event name don't match an actual object and event on the page, your code won't compile. We've highlighted the Handles clause here:

```
Private Sub btnClickMe_Click( _
  ByVal sender As System.Object, _
  ByVal e As System.EventArgs) Handles btnClickMe.Click

End Sub
```

The sender **Parameter**

The first parameter passed to every event procedure is a reference to the object that raised the event. In most cases, this will be the control listed in the Handles clause. However, as you'll see later in this chapter, it's possible for one event procedure to handle more than one control's events. In that case, the Handles clause will contain a comma-delimited list of controls, and the sender parameter will indicate which of those controls raised the event.

The e **Parameter**

For some events, the page framework will need to pass information to the event-handling procedure. The page framework passes most controls' events an object of type EventArgs in this parameter. This object has no useful properties itself, but many controls' events use classes that inherit from this base class. For example, if you place an ImageButton control on a page, its Click event receives an object of type ImageClickEventArgs in this parameter. This object has all the standard EventArgs properties, and in addition, supplies X and Y properties so that the event procedure can determine where, within the image, the user clicked.

TIP

Many classes inherit from the base `EventArgs` class. You should always investigate, for any event procedure you write, the e parameter, to see whether the page framework is sending your procedure useful information based on the conditions when the event was raised.

Button Control Events

To test out event handling, you could have a label display some text in reaction to clicking a button. On the sample page, you might have the Label control, lblMessage, display "You clicked on a button" when you click btnClickMe. To make that happen, modify the `btnClick_Click` procedure so that it looks like this:

```
Private Sub btnClickMe_Click(_
 ByVal sender As System.Object, _
 ByVal e As System.EventArgs) Handles btnClickMe.Click
    lblMessage.Text = "You clicked on a button"
End Sub
```

Right-click the `Events.aspx` page in the Solution Explorer window and select Build and Browse from the context menu. When you click the Click Me button, you should see text appear in the Label control on the page.

What happened? Clicking a CommandButton control always triggers an immediate postback to the server. At that point, the page's Load event procedure runs. Then, the btnClickMe_Click event procedure takes its turn, running the code you just added that writes text to the Label control on the page.

The `SelectedIndexChanged` Event

Selecting an item from a DropDownList control triggers that control's `SelectedIndexChanged` event. To test this out, open `Events.aspx` in Design view and double-click the DropDownList control (ddlProducts) on the page. Modify the event procedure stub so that it looks like this:

```
Private Sub ddlProducts_SelectedIndexChanged( _
 ByVal sender As System.Object, _
 ByVal e As System.EventArgs) _
 Handles ddlProducts.SelectedIndexChanged
    lblMessage.Text = "You selected " & _
     ddlProducts.SelectedItem.Text
End Sub
```

Try running Events.aspx and select an item. Nothing happens. Click the Click Me button, and you'll see that the page posts back to the server and that the text is inserted. If you look carefully, you might see the selected item from the DropDownList control before you see the text from the command button.

What's up? Selecting an item in a DropDownList control doesn't trigger an automatic postback, unlike clicking a command button, which does. When you do click a command button, you trigger a postback, and the page framework runs both event procedures (btnClickMe_Click and ddlProducts_SelectedIndexChanged). The order of event handlers isn't clear, but both run.

If you want to trigger an immediate postback when you select an item from the DropDownList control, you'll need to set the control's AutoPostBack property to be True (it's False by default). Try that now. With Events.aspx open in Design view, set the AutoPostBack property of ddlProducts to True.

Try running Events.aspx again, and this time, select an item from the DropDownList control. Now, selecting an item triggers an immediate postback, and the event procedure writes text into the lblMessage control.

The CheckChanged Event

A RadioButton control raises its CheckChanged event when you change the "checked" state of the control. Just like the DropDownList control, the RadioButton control doesn't trigger an automatic postback unless you set the control's AutoPostBack property to True.

In addition, you normally want RadioButton controls to work in a group—that is, if you select one control, you'd like other controls in the same group to be deselected (in other words, the selections in the group are mutually exclusive). In order for this to happen, you must set the GroupName property of associated controls to be the same group name.

It would be nice if you could share the same CheckChanged event handler for both RadioButton controls, because both controls require similar actions when you select them. In order to make that happen, you'll take advantage of the power of the Handles clause. Double-click one of the RadioButton controls, and Visual Studio .NET places you in the CheckChanged event procedure for that control. Modify the procedure so that it looks like Listing 7.1.

LISTING 7.1   You Can Use the sender Parameter to Determine Which Control Was Selected

```
Private Sub Sex_CheckedChanged( _
 ByVal sender As System.Object, _
 ByVal e As System.EventArgs) _
 Handles rdoMale.CheckedChanged, rdoFemale.CheckedChanged
  If sender Is Me.rdoMale Then
    lblMessage.Text = _
     "You clicked on the Male radio button"
  Else
    lblMessage.Text = _
     "You clicked on the Female radio button"
  End If
End Sub
```

Because this procedure lists multiple *object.event* items in its Handles clause, the page framework will run this event procedure in reaction to the events of either control. Because the code runs for either control, you must use the sender parameter to determine which control raised the event.

> **TIP**
>
> The sample code uses the Is operator to determine which RadioButton control raised the event. This operator compares objects (not values). Because the code is attempting to determine which object raised the event and is comparing one object (sender) to another (the controls), the Is operator is required. (The alternative would be to use the = operator, which compares values, not objects.)

The Page's Load Event

Each and every time you request a page, that page's Load event runs the code you've placed in the Page_Load event procedure. You may have some code that you'd like to have run only the first time the page is loaded, and other code for subsequent loads. To make that possible, the Page object provides the IsPostBack property—a Boolean value that indicates whether the page is being loaded because of a postback.

The sample page, Events.aspx, only needs to fill in the drop-down list of products the first time it's loaded. To accomplish this goal, choose the View, Code menu item to display the code-behind file for the page and then find the Page_Load procedure, which looks like Listing 7.2.

LISTING 7.2   You Can Use the Page_Load Procedure to Preload Values into Controls

```
Private Sub Page_Load( _
 ByVal sender As System.Object, _
 ByVal e As System.EventArgs) _
 Handles MyBase.Load
  If Not Page.IsPostBack Then
    With ddlProducts
        .Items.Add("Apples")
        .Items.Add("Pears")
        .Items.Add("Plums")
    End With
  End If
End Sub
```

You'll see that the code only loads the list (ddlProducts) with values if Page.IsPostBack isn't True. You can take advantage of this same mechanism to take different steps, depending on whether your page is posting back to itself.

There are clearly many more controls, many more objects, and many more events to be investigated in ASP.NET. We've selected a small subset to give you the flavor of working with event procedures and controls. When working with any control, investigate its event procedures carefully and take advantage of the event-specific parameters passed to those procedures from the page framework.

Data Types

Visual Basic .NET provides a broad range of data types that you can use when defining variables and working with data. These data types are slightly different from those provided by VB6 or VBScript. Table 7.1 lists the available types, along with the corresponding .NET Framework data types (each .NET language, such as Visual Basic .NET or C# .NET, maps its specific data types to data types provided by the .NET Framework).

> **TIP**
>
> Note that the VB6 Currency data type is gone. Currency was a strange type: In order to avoid some round-off errors, Visual Basic multiplied the data values you entered by 10,000 for storage in memory and then divided by 10,000 again for display. In the .NET Framework, use

the Decimal type instead, if you want floating-point values that don't exhibit round-off errors when you perform calculations on the values.

TABLE 7.1 Visual Basic .NET Supplies a Broad Range of Data Types

VB Type	CLR Type	Storage Size	Value Range
Boolean	System.Boolean	2 bytes	True or False.
Byte	System.Byte	1 byte	0 to 255 (unsigned).
Char	System.Char	2 bytes	0 to 65,535 (unsigned).
Date	System.DateTime	8 bytes	January 1, 0001 to December 31, 9999.
Decimal	System.Decimal	16 bytes	+/-79,228,162,514,264,337,593,543,950,335 with no decimal point; +/- 7.9228162514264337593543950335 with 28 places to the right of the decimal.
Double	System.Double	8 bytes	-1.79769313486231E+308 to -4.94065645841247E-324 for negative values; 4.94065645841247E-324 to 1.79769313486231E+308 for positive values.
Integer	System.Int32	4 bytes	-2,147,483,648 to 2,147,483,647.
Long	System.Int64	8 bytes	-9,223,372,036,854,775,808 to 9,223,372,036,854,775,807.
Object	System.Object	4 bytes	Any type can be stored in a variable of type Object.
Short	System.Int16	2 bytes	-32,768 to 32,767.
Single	System.Single	4 bytes	-3.402823E+38 to -1.401298E-45 for negative values; 1.401298E-45 to 3.402823E+38 for positive values.
String	System.String	Depends on the implementing platform	Zero to approximately 2 billion Unicode characters.
User-defined type (structure)	Sum of the sizes of its members		Each member of the structure has a range determined by its data type and is independent of the ranges of the other members.

Load VBLanguage.aspx in the page designer. This page, shown in Figure 7.2, allows you to try out all the sample code for the remainder of this chapter. Double-click VB.NET Data Types to load the following code. This procedure provides examples of how to declare and assign a value to each of the different data types:

NOTE

You may be wondering why some of the assignments in the sample code require extra method or function calls. For example, to assign a value into a Decimal variable, we must call the CDec function. To print out the value of an Object variable, we had to call the ToString method. It's the Option Strict directive that forces this extra work—see the next section for more information.

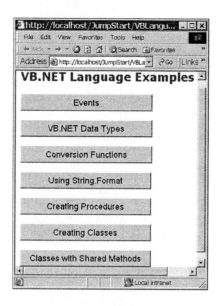

FIGURE 7.2   This sample page allows you to try out all the code.

Listing 7.3 shows code from the sample project that uses many of the basic data types.

LISTING 7.3   This Code Shows Examples of the Types Available in VB .NET

```
Private Sub DataTypesSample()
  Dim blnValue As Boolean
  Dim bytValue As Byte
  Dim chrValue As Char
  Dim dtValue As Date
  Dim decValue As Decimal
  Dim dblValue As Double
  Dim intValue As Integer
  Dim lngValue As Long
  Dim oValue As New Object()
  Dim srtValue As Short
  Dim sngValue As Single
  Dim strValue As String
```

LISTING 7.3   Continued

```
blnValue = True
bytValue = 32
chrValue = CChar("A")
dtValue = #1/1/2002#
decValue = CDec(100.5)
dblValue = 10.25
intValue = 10
lngValue = 1000000
oValue = "A String"
srtValue = 0
sngValue = 1.5
strValue = "This is a string"

With Response
  .Write("blnValue = " & blnValue & "<BR>")
  .Write("bytValue = " & bytValue & "<BR>")
  .Write("chrValue = " & chrValue & "<BR>")
  .Write("dtValue = " & dtValue & "<BR>")
  .Write("decValue = " & decValue & "<BR>")
  .Write("dblValue = " & dblValue & "<BR>")
  .Write("intValue = " & intValue & "<BR>")
  .Write("lngValue = " & lngValue & "<BR>")
  .Write("oValue = " & oValue.ToString() & "<BR>")
  .Write("srtValue = " & srtValue & "<BR>")
  .Write("sngValue = " & sngValue & "<BR>")
  .Write("strValue = " & strValue & "<BR>")
 End With
End Sub
```

Option Strict

Visual Basic has, in its past versions, allowed data type conversions that other
languages never permitted. For example, in Visual Basic 6.0, it was quite possible to
assign an integer into a string and to perform mathematical operations on strings,
like this:

```
Dim x As String
x = 25 + "2"
```

After running this code, the variable x would contain the string "27".

Because this type of programming can lead to errors, when variables can contain data that you might not have intended, Visual Basic .NET supports an option that forces you to explicitly convert from one type to another: Option Strict. You can add this statement to the top of each module to turn on strict conversions for the module:

```
Option Strict On
```

You can also right-click the project in the Solution Explorer window, select Properties from the context menu, and then select the Build tab in the left pane of the window. In the Option Strict drop-down list, select On to turn the option on for the entire project.

With Option Strict set to On, you won't be able to make the type of "loose" conversions you might have made in Visual Basic 6.0. Attempting to compile code that doesn't meet the stringent requirements of Option Strict will fail.

HANDLING OPTION STRICT

In VB .NET, Option Strict is off by default. This is a poor decision, in our eyes, because it allows the same sort of code you might have written in VB6, including potentially dangerous type conversions. With Option Strict turned on, you can catch these errors at compile time, instead of at runtime—basically, there's less to worry about at runtime, with the tradeoff being more to worry about at coding time. It also forces you into a better understanding of the objects you are working with, and it enables code to be reused in a project where Option Strict is on. As it is, you must open the project properties for each new project you create, in order to turn on Option Strict (or you can manually add it to the top of each file, which is certainly an onerous task).

You can set Option Strict on in VB .NET for all new projects you create, but it's a nontrivial task. To do this, find the folder containing all the project templates. For example, this might be a folder such as H:\Program Files\Microsoft Visual Studio.NET\Vb7\VBWizards. Starting in that folder, use Windows Explorer to search for *.vbproj. Load all the files named *.vbproj into a text editor and modify the XML at the top of the file so that it looks something like this (what we're showing here is just the beginning of the vbproj file; leave all the existing tags alone and simply insert the OptionStrict attribute within the Settings element):

```
<VisualStudioProject>
    <VisualBasic>
        <Build>
            <Settings
                OptionStrict = "On"
                -- more attributes and elements follow --
```

Save each file, and the next time you create a project based on one of these templates, Option Strict will be on, by default. Most likely, you want Option Strict on for development in VB .NET, and you'll forget to turn it on manually.

Conversion Functions

Once you've enabled `Option Strict` in Visual Basic .NET, you'll need to take advantage of a group of functions that allow you to convert from one data type to another. You can use either the `CType` function (which can convert any type to any other compatible type) or the individual conversion functions (`CStr`, `CChar`, `CLng`, and so on).

The `CType` function takes two arguments: The first argument is the variable or value you wish to convert, and the second argument is the data type you wish to convert the value to. The general syntax looks like this:

```
var1 = CType(var2, DataType)
```

Visual Basic .NET also provides a group of distinct functions (the names all begin with C) that you can use to convert data types from one type to another. In fact, these functions have not changed much from the similar functions available in Visual Basic 6.0. The list of conversion functions includes `CBool`, `CByte`, `CDate`, `CDbl`, `CDec`, `CInt`, `CLng`, `CSng`, `CShort`, and `CStr`.

The procedure shown in Listing 7.4, from the file `VBLanguage.aspx`, demonstrates using several of the conversion functions:

LISTING 7.4   Converting from One Data Type to Another Is Common in Many Applications

```
Private Sub ConversionSample()
    Dim srtValue As Short = 0
    Dim intValue As Integer = 10
    Dim lngValue As Long = 100
    Dim sngValue As Single = 1.5
    Dim dblValue As Double = 10.25

    ' Convert up using CType
    sngValue = CType(srtValue, Single)
    dblValue = CType(sngValue, Double)
    lngValue = CType(intValue, Long)

    ' Convert up using C* functions
    sngValue = CSng(srtValue)
    dblValue = CDbl(sngValue)
    lngValue = CLng(intValue)
End Sub
```

TIP

This example takes advantage of one of VB .NET's new features: the ability to initialize a variable at the time you declare it. Although we don't recommend overusing this privilege—both in terms of scoping issues and in terms of the errors that can occur when code runs as you declare a variable—it works well for simple constant values.

Constructing Text Using the `String.Format` Method

You'll often find that you need to construct strings—either by concatenating bits and pieces of text or by inserting values into placeholders within an existing string. To make this task simpler, the .NET Framework supplies the `String.Format` method. This method allows you to supply a template string containing numbered placeholders for replacements. You provide the replacements as the rest of the parameters for the `String.Format` method, and at runtime the .NET Framework replaces each placeholder with its value. (You can also supply the replacements as an array of objects rather than as individual values, as we've done here. It's up to you.)

To try out the `String.Format` method, double-click Using String.Format on the sample page. This leads you to this procedure:

```
Private Sub StringFormatSample()
  Response.Write(String.Format( _
    "Customer {0} spent {1:C} in {2}.", _
    12, 14.56, "January"))
End Sub
```

In this example, the template string (`Customer {0} spent {1:C} in {2}.`) provides three placeholders, which must begin numbering at 0. The second one (`{1:C}`) provides additional formatting information (`:C` indicates currency formatting). The documentation lists the complete set of possible formatting options. At runtime, the code replaces each of the placeholders with one of the last three parameters.

Running the code in this example provides the following result:

```
Customer 12 spent $14.56 in January.
```

As you can see, the code replaces each of the placeholders in turn with the corresponding value from the remainder of the parameter list. You'll see another example of using the `String.Format` method in the next section.

Creating Your Own Procedures

As you write Visual Basic .NET applications, you'll want to break your code up into manageable "chunks." This shouldn't be a new concept to you, and it should make sense. The larger the blocks of code you're working with, the harder it is to debug, maintain, and manage the code. You've seen several examples of this throughout this chapter already.

The building block of Visual Basic .NET code is the *procedure*. A procedure has a beginning (a declaration), a middle (the code inside the procedure) and an end (the End Sub statement, for example). As you'll see throughout this book, there are a number of types of procedures, but for now, we'll focus on Sub and Function procedures.

A Sub procedure is a block of code that includes code, takes some action, but doesn't return a value. A Function procedure takes some action but returns a single value. So far, you've seen event procedures—Sub procedures that run in reaction to events on pages.

Why use procedures? Certainly, if you find that you're writing the same lines of code in multiple places, you would want to create a procedure you could call from all the places you would otherwise use the code and copy that code into the new procedure.

If you double-click the Creating Procedures button on the VBLanguage.aspx Web Form, it will lead you to the procedure shown in Listing 7.5.

LISTING 7.5   Procedures Are Useful for Breaking Up Code into More Manageable Chunks

```
Private Sub ProceduresSample()
  Dim strConn As String

  ' Call a procedure that
  ' doesn't return a value.
  InitControls()

  ' Call a Function to Return a Value
  strConn = ConnectStringBuild("BJones", "password")

  Response.Write("strConn = " & strConn & "<BR><BR>")
End Sub
```

The InitControls procedure is a simple Sub that takes an action (hiding a control) and returns no value at all:

```
Private Sub InitControls()
  ' Demonstrate a procedure
  ' that doesn't return a value.
  btnDataTypes.Visible = False
End Sub
```

The `ConnectStringBuild` procedure allows you to pass parameters, making it possible to create generalized functionality. VB6 developers should note that all parameters are passed by value in VB .NET, unless you specify otherwise using the `ByRef` keyword. (This is the exact opposite of the way VB6 works.) In addition, if you don't specify `ByRef` or `ByVal`, Visual Studio .NET inserts the `ByVal` keyword for you. The `ConnectStringBuild` procedure provides an example of this, allowing you to specify two parameters that the procedure uses in creating an appropriate ADO.NET connection string:

```
Private Function ConnectStringBuild( _
 ByVal LoginID As String, _
 ByVal Password As String) As String
  Return String.Format("Provider=sqloledb;" & _
   "Data Source=(local);Initial Catalog=Northwind;" & _
   "User ID={0};Password={1}", LoginID, Password)
End Function
```

Creating Classes

Creating your own classes allows you to encapsulate behavior in a reusable fashion and allows you to provide the templates for creating multiple instances of an object based on the template. That is, using classes, you can create your own additions to the base class library provided by the .NET Framework—every single object you use in your applications is based on some class, created by some developer, describing the behavior of that object.

The techniques for creating classes in VB .NET haven't changed much since VB6, although you can now have more than one class per file. You still need to create properties, methods, and possibly events. Methods and event declarations have not changed much since VB6, but creating properties requires a slightly different syntax.

As an example, we've provided the `LoginInfo` class, which provides `LoginID`, `Password`, and `DataSource` properties, and the `ConnectStringBuild` method.

Double-click Creating Classes on the `VBLanguage.aspx` Web Form to find a procedure that creates an object of the `LoginInfo` type. The definition for this class also resides in the `VBLanguage.aspx` file, just below the end of the Web Form's class. The code for this class is shown in Listing 7.6.

LISTING 7.6   Classes Can Be Used to Group Data with Procedures That Interact with That Data

```
Public Class LoginInfo
  Private mstrLoginID As String
  Private mstrPassword As String
```

LISTING 7.6   Continued

```
Private mstrDataSource As String

Property LoginID() As String
  Get
    Return mstrLoginID
  End Get
  Set(ByVal Value As String)
    mstrLoginID = Value
  End Set
End Property

Property Password() As String
  Get
    Return mstrPassword
  End Get
  Set(ByVal Value As String)
    mstrPassword = Value
  End Set
End Property

Property DataSource() As String
  Get
    Return mstrDataSource
  End Get
  Set(ByVal Value As String)
    mstrDataSource = Value
  End Set
End Property

Public Function ConnectStringBuild() As String
  Return String.Format("Provider=sqloledb;" & _
    "Data Source=(local);Initial Catalog=Northwind;" & _
    "User ID={0};Password={1}", Me.LoginID, Me.Password)
End Function
End Class
```

To use this class, you will declare a new instance of it, set the properties you require, and then invoke the ConnectStringBuild method to have it return the value. Listing 7.7 shows an example of creating and using a class.

LISTING 7.7   Using Your Own Class Is as Simple as Declaring a New Instance of the
Class

```
Private Sub ClassSample()
  Dim oLogin As New LoginInfo()

  With oLogin
    .LoginID = "BJones"
    .Password = "password"
    .DataSource = "(local)"

    Response.Write("ConnectString=" & _
      .ConnectStringBuild() & "<BR>")
  End With
End Sub
```

One problem with the LogInfo class, as it stands, is that you must create a unique
instance of the class each time you want to generate the connection string.
Sometimes, you may want to be able to call a method of a class without needing to
instantiate the object yourself. For example, when you used the String.Format
method, you didn't need to create a String object variable, set it equal to a new
String object, and then work with the object. The String class provides the Format
method (among many of its methods) in a special way that allows the .NET
Framework to instantiate an object for you, as necessary. By adding the Shared
keyword to a method, you won't need to create an instance of the parent object
before calling the method—the .NET Framework will handle this for you.

We've provided a class, in DataHandler.vb, that we'll use throughout many
examples (and we'll expand the class as necessary). This class provides a shared
ConnectStringBuild method—you pass it user ID and password values, and the
method returns the appropriate connection string. The important thing to remember is that because the method is shared, you needn't create an instance of the
DataHandler class—simply call the method, and the .NET Framework will
do the work for you.

The following procedure, called when you click Classes with Shared Methods on
VBLanguage.aspx, calls the ConnectStringBuild method of the DataHandler class.
Note that the code never creates an instance of the DataHandler class because the
ConnectStringBuild method is shared. Here's the code:

```
Private Sub SharedMethodSample()
  Dim strConn As String

  strConn = _
```

```
DataHandler.ConnectStringBuild("Bjones", "Password")

Response.Write(strConn)
End Sub
```

The definition for the DataHandler class can be found in the DataHandler.vb file within the VBLanguage.sln solution. This class looks like this:

```
Public Class DataHandler
  Public Shared Function ConnectStringBuild( _
    ByVal LoginID As String, _
    ByVal Password As String) As String
    Dim strConn As String

    If LoginID = String.Empty Then
      LoginID = "sa"
    End If
    strConn = String.Format("Provider=sqloledb;" & _
      "Data Source=(local);Initial Catalog=Northwind;" & _
      "User ID={0};Password={1}", LoginID, Password)

    Return strConn
  End Function
End Class
```

Applying What You Learned

Let's now take some of the techniques you have learned throughout this chapter and apply them to the Northwind solution you are building. Follow these steps to add a class that will be used throughout the rest of this book:

1. Bring up your Northwind.sln file.

2. Set Option Strict to On.

3. Select the Project, Add Class menu item.

4. Set the class name to DataHandler.vb.

5. Add a shared method named ConnectStringBuild to this DataHandler class. Re-create the code shown in the shared ConnectStringBuild method in this chapter.

6. Bring up Main.aspx in the page designer.

7. Double-click the Logout LinkButton control and modify the `lnkLogout_Click` procedure so it looks like this:

```
Private Sub lnkLogout_Click( _
 ByVal sender As System.Object, _
 ByVal e As System.EventArgs)
  Session.Abandon()

  Response.Redirect("Main.aspx")
End Sub
```

8. Open `Login.aspx` in the page designer.

9. Double-click the Login button and modify the `btnLogin_Click` procedure so that it looks like this:

```
Private Sub btnLogin_Click( _
 ByVal sender As System.Object, _
 ByVal e As System.EventArgs) Handles btnLogin.Click
  Session("LoginID") = "sa"
  Session("Password") = ""

  Server.Transfer("Main.aspx")
End Sub
```

For now, you will just set `LoginID` to `"sa"` so you can log in to your SQL Server database.

10. Change the `Page_Load` procedure of `Main.aspx` to set the `Visible` property, depending on whether `Session("LoginID")` is an empty string, as shown here:

```
Private Sub Page_Load(ByVal sender As System.Object, _
 ByVal e As System.EventArgs) Handles MyBase.Load

  Dim blnShow As Boolean
  blnShow = _
   (Session("LoginID").ToString = String.Empty)

  lnkLogout.Visible = blnShow
  hypEmpMaint.Visible = blnShow
  hypPwdChange.Visible = blnShow
End Sub
```

Summary

In this chapter, you learned about some of the features of ASP.NET event handling and the VB .NET language. These features will help you program effectively in VB .NET and ASP.NET. We focused on features that are different from those you might have used in VBScript or VB6. Although we just barely touched on many of the topics, you'll learn more about these issues as you work through future chapters. To recap, you learned the following key items in this chapter:

- Events run on the server.

- Event procedures are always passed two parameters.

- There are many data types that you can use in VB .NET.

- You should create classes when programming your .NET applications.

8

Validation Controls

OBJECTIVES

- Investigate the validation controls provided by ASP.NET

- Create Web forms that validate data

Before ASP.NET, validating the data users entered onto a Web page either required complex script code that ran in the client browser or a roundtrip to the server to run code on the server side to determine the validity of the data. Things are a lot simpler in ASP.NET. Here, you'll find a series of controls—the validation controls—that make validating data on either the client or server side much simpler.

If your users view your page using an "up-level" browser (that is, IE 4.0 or higher), ASP.NET can render script so that the browser can perform client-side validation. If not, ASP.NET can only validate the controls' data on the server. Even if your users browse to the page using an up-level browser, ASP.NET will always perform a final server-side validation, ensuring that no clever hacker can bypass the validation by replacing code on the client side. Performing client-side validation not only simplifies your development, but also makes the runtime experience more interactive—your users see validation warnings immediately upon leaving a control that handles invalid data.

To add validation support to any control, add an associated validation control to the page and set the properties of the control to indicate the following:

- The control that needs to be validated.

- The set of acceptable values. This information differs depending on the type of validation control you're using.

- The text to be displayed within the validation control if the associated control's value isn't valid.

- The text to be displayed in a validation summary.

You can place the validation control at any location on the page, but most people place the control adjacent to the data-entry control it's validating.

In this chapter, you'll learn about the different types of validation controls, and you'll see examples of working with each.

Requiring Data Entry

You'll often need to ensure that users enter a value into a control on a page. To make this easy, ASP.NET provides its RequiredFieldValidator control. On the sample page, EmpMaint.aspx, users must supply values for the First Name, Last Name, Birth Date, and Hire Date fields. Leaving any of these blank isn't allowed, and you need some way to indicate this to users. Figure 8.1 shows the sample form, after a user has attempted to submit the page by clicking Save without filling in any information. This page displays individual indicators of the fields that must be supplied.

TIP

If you watch carefully as you test this page, you'll see that if you're using an up-level browser, you don't incur a roundtrip to the server when you click Save with no data filled in. Because Internet Explorer supports client-side scripting, ASP.NET emits the correct JavaScript code so that the page can validate the data before being submitted back to the server. This capability offloads some of the processing from the server and reduces network traffic by not requiring a roundtrip just to validate the data.

FIGURE 8.1   The RequiredFieldValidator control makes it easier to avoid data fields left empty.

In order to use a RequiredFieldValidator control, you'll normally need to set the properties of the control listed in Table 8.1.

TABLE 8.1   Set These Properties for RequiredFieldValidator Controls

Property	Description
ControlToValidate	The name of the control you need to validate.
ErrorMessage	The text to be displayed if the associated control's value isn't valid. If you also supply the Text property value, this property's text only appears in a validation summary. That is, the Text property overrides the ErrorMessage property for display within the control.
Text	The text to be displayed within the control if the associated control's value isn't valid. If you don't supply this value, the control displays its ErrorMessage text.

TIP

You'll normally set the properties listed in Table 8.1 for all the validation controls. We won't list them again, but each validation control will need to have these properties specified.

TRY IT OUT   To demonstrate the use of the RequiredFieldValidator control, you will modify the EmpMaint.aspx form, adding the necessary RequiredFieldValidator controls, as shown in Figure 8.1. You'll load this Web Form from the Employee hyperlink under the Maintenance section on the main form. Follow these steps to add the RequiredFieldValidator controls:

1. Select Project, Add Existing Item. Be sure to change the Files of Type combo box to "All Files (*.*)".

2. Add the EmpMaint.* files from the Jumpstart\ValidationControls folder. There should be three files: EmpMaint.aspx, EmpMaint.aspx.resx, and EmpMaint.aspx.vb.

3. Now that you've added the form to your project, double-click the EmpMaint.aspx file to display the form.

4. Place your cursor to the right of the First Name text box.

5. In the Toolbox, double-click the RequiredFieldValidator control to add it adjacent to the text box.

6. Repeat this for the Last Name, Birth Date, and Hire Date text boxes.

7. Set the properties for the new controls as shown in Table 8.2.

TABLE 8.2   Set These RequiredFieldValidator Properties

Control	Property	Value
RequiredFieldValidator1	ControlToValidate	txtFirst
	ErrorMessage	First Name must be filled in
RequiredFieldValidator2	ControlToValidate	txtLast
	ErrorMessage	Last Name must be filled in
RequiredFieldValidator3	ControlToValidate	txtBirthdate
	ErrorMessage	Birth Date must be filled in
RequiredFieldValidator4	ControlToValidate	txtHireDate
	ErrorMessage	Hire Date must be filled in

To test your page, right-click the page in the Solution Explorer window and then select Build and Browse from the context menu. Without entering any data, click Save. You should see the appropriate error messages appear next to each text box. Try it again, this time entering some data into some of the text boxes, and verify that the controls validate correctly.

Although you didn't take advantage of it here, the RequiredFieldValidator control doesn't actually require you to supply a value—that's not how it works. Actually, the RequiredFieldValidator control invalidates its associated control if the value in that control isn't different from the value in the InitialValue property of the RequiredFieldValidator control. For example, you may want to have the text "Enter a value" in a text box, and leaving this text intact isn't valid. Placing "Enter a value" into the InitialValue property of the RequiredFieldValidator control associated with the text box will ensure that users modify the value of the text box. In this case, the validator isn't verifying that the user entered a value but that the user entered a value that is different from the initial value. The default value of the RequiredFieldValidator's InitialValue field is an empty string, so by default, the validator forces users to enter a value that's different from its default—an empty string.

NOTE

Try posting the page back (click Save) with invalid data on the page. You won't be able to—the page simply won't post back when it contains invalid data.

Checking a Range

The RangeValidator control allows you to verify that the value of a control falls within a specified range. For example, you could make sure that a text box's value is between 5 and 10 or between a month ago and the current date.

Normally, you'll need to set the properties shown in Table 8.3, in addition to those listed in Table 8.1.

TABLE 8.3   Set These Properties for RangeValidator Controls

Property	Description
MaximumValue	The maximum allowable value.
MinimumValue	The minimum allowable value.
Type	The type of data to compare, selected from String, Integer, Date, Double, or Currency. This property controls the type of comparison to perform—it wouldn't make sense to perform a text comparison when you're entering numeric values, for example. If you did, "2" would be greater than "11." Select the correct data type to perform the correct type of comparison.

TRY IT OUT In order to try out this control, you will modify the sample page, EmpMaint.aspx, adding a RangeValidator control to ensure that the employee birth date falls between 1/1/1900 and 12/31/1984. Here are the steps to follow:

1. Click to the right of the RequiredFieldValidator control that's associated with the BirthDate field, moving the selection point to that location.

2. In the Toolbox, double-click the RangeValidator control to add it adjacent to the existing RequiredFieldValidator control.

3. Set the properties for the control as shown in Table 8.4.

TABLE 8.4   Set These Properties for the RangeValidation Control

Property	Value
ID	rvalBirthdate
ControlToValidate	txtBirthDate
ErrorMessage	Birth Date must be between 1/1/1900 and 12/31/1984
MaximumValue	12/31/1984
MinimumValue	1/1/1900
Type	Date

4. Right-click the page and select Build and Browse from the context menu.

5. Enter an invalid date for the Birth Date field (perhaps a date after 12/31/1984) and then press Tab to leave the control. You should see an error appear immediately.

6. Close the browser window.

TIP

Although we've used dates formatted correctly for the United States here, you'll need to take into account the current locale when testing your pages. If your date format is different from ours, make sure you attempt to validate dates that are correct for the locale of the browser.

Although you did see the correct error message, you may have noticed that it didn't appear immediately to the right of the associated text box. Because you had already placed another validation control adjacent to the Birth Date text box, that control "consumes" the space where you'd expect to see the out-of-range error message.

To solve this problem, you can use the `Display` property of the validation controls. This property has three values: `None`, `Dynamic`, and `Static`. The default value is `Static`, indicating that the control always takes up the same amount of space on the rendered page. Selecting `None` causes the control to take up no space and never display any text (unless you add a ValidationSummary control to the page). Selecting `Dynamic` allows the control to take up no space if it isn't displaying any text. This choice, then, will fix the problem. Simply follow these steps:

1. Select each of the validation controls on the page and set the `Display` property for each to `Dynamic`.

2. Repeat the previous experiment and prove to yourself that the display works better now.

TIP

If you only want to validate that the user has entered a particular data type (a date, for example) but don't care about the specific value, you can use the CompareValidator control, discussed later in the chapter.

3. If you want to provide a dynamic range for the RangeValidator control (for example, allowing dates to be entered for the Birth Date field between 70 years ago and 17 years ago, figuring that you can't hire anyone older than 70 or younger than 17), you'll need to write a little code. You might want to modify the `EmpMaint.aspx` page so that it adds these restrictions as it loads.

4. Modify the `Page_Load` procedure of `EmpMaint.aspx` so that it looks like this:

```
Private Sub Page_Load( _
  ByVal sender As System.Object, _
  ByVal e As System.EventArgs) Handles MyBase.Load

  If Not Page.IsPostBack Then
    With rvalBirthDate
```

```
      .MinimumValue = CStr(Today.AddYears(-70))
      .MaximumValue = CStr(Today.AddYears(-17))
      .ErrorMessage = String.Format( _
        "Enter a date between {0} and {1}", _
        .MinimumValue, .MaximumValue)
    End With
  End If
End Sub
```

5. Browse the page again and try entering a birth date that's more than 70 years ago or less than 17 years ago. You'll see the error message, indicating the valid range of dates.

The previous example brings up some interesting ideas:

- You can use the AddYears method of a date to add or subtract years.

- The MinimumValue and MaximumValue properties of the RangeValidator control both accept String values—you'll need to convert anything you place in these properties into strings.

- You can dynamically modify the ErrorMessage text of a control.

Validating Expressions

What if you need to verify that text someone has entered is a correctly formatted Canadian postal code? What if you need a user to enter a valid e-mail address? Although you could write the necessary code to validate these types of expressions (and many ASP developers did just that), ASP.NET makes it easy to validate complex expressions.

Using the power of regular expressions, a widely accepted standard for generalizing pattern matching, ASP.NET provides the RegularExpressionValidator control. This control allows you to specify a regular expression to match against text entered into a control. (Regular expressions are templates for matching text—the DOS wildcards, * and ?, allow you to create very simple regular expression-like templates, although real regular expressions are far more complex.)

Although coverage of creating your own regular expressions is beyond the scope of this book (it's a huge topic, with reference books all its own), Visual Studio .NET helps you create common regular expressions by providing a list of the ones you're most likely to need, including U.S., French, German, and Japanese phone numbers and postal codes, Internet e-mail addresses, and Internet URLs.

As an example, the regular expression for U.S. ZIP codes looks like this (remember that U.S. ZIP codes can be either five digits, such as 98765, or five digits followed by a hyphen and four more digits, such as 98765-1234. No other formats are allowed):

```
\d{5}(-\d{4})?
```

Here's an explanation of this example, taken apart bit by bit:

- The \d{5} part of the expression matches against exactly five numeric digits.

- The (-\d{4})? part of the expression allows for the optional four digits.

- The ()? part of the expression creates an optional group—either the whole group appears or it doesn't. The parentheses group the expressions, and the question mark indicates that the group is optional.

- The hyphen (-) in this expression allows a hyphen as the first character in the group.

- The \d{4} part of the expression matches against four numeric digits.

To illustrate the use of this control, let's assume that on the sample page, EmpMaint.aspx, you need to restrict data entry in the Home Phone field to ensure valid U.S. phone numbers. You need to restrict data entry in the Zip Code field as well. Follow these steps to add RegularExpressionValidator controls to manage the input into these controls, as shown in Figure 8.2:

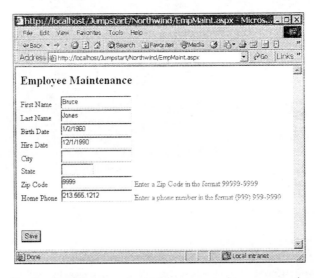

FIGURE 8.2   Use the RegularExpressionValidator control to manage data input for complex values.

1. Click to the right of the Zip Code text box, placing the insertion point at that location.

2. In the Toolbox window, double-click the RegularExpressionValidator control, placing a new instance on the page adjacent to the Zip Code text box.

3. Repeat the previous two steps for the Home Phone text box.

4. Set the properties for the two validation controls as shown in Table 8.5.

TABLE 8.5   Set These Properties for Your RegularExpressionValidator Controls

Control	Property	Value
RegularExpressionValidator1	`ControlToValidate`	txtZipCode
	`Display`	Dynamic
	`ErrorMessage`	Enter a ZIP code in the format 99999-9999
	`ValidationExpression`	Click the ... button and select U.S. Zip Code to insert `\d{5}(-\d{4})?)`
RegularExpressionValidator2	`ControlToValidate`	txtHomePhone
	`Display`	Dynamic
	`ErrorMessage`	Enter a phone number in the format (999) 999-9999
	`ValidationExpression`	Click the ... button and select U.S. Phone Number to insert `((\(\d{3}\))?|(\d{3}-))?\d{3}-\d{4})`

After setting all the properties, view the page in Browse mode again and verify that entering invalid ZIP code and phone number values does indeed display error messages as the page attempts to validate the data.

Creating Your Own Validation

There may be times when you can't find one of the built-in validation controls that handles your specific data. For example, which control could verify that a number the user has entered is an even number (if that was a requirement of your page)? There isn't such a control, but ASP.NET provides the CustomValidator control, which allows you to specify procedures to be run in order to validate the data in the associated input control.

For this example, your goal is to ensure that users enter either CA, NV, or AZ into the State text box on the page. You could use a DropDownList control for this, or you could use a RegularExpressionValidator control (setting the expression to be

CA|NV|AZ). However, for the sake of this example, suppose you want to take advantage of the CustomValidator control.

The CustomValidator control requires you to supply code for the control's ServerValidate event—it calls this code as it attempts to validate the data on the server. No matter what browser has loaded the page, this code will run before the entire page can be validated. If the browser supports client-side script, it is nice to provide the script to run from within the browser, on the client side, to provide the same sort of experience you get when working with the other validation controls.

Therefore, you'll need to write the event procedure, in the page's code-behind file, to provide server-side validation. In addition, in the page itself, you'll need to insert the client-side script that will be sent down to the browser. (In addition, you'll need to set the control's ClientValidationFunction property to indicate the name of the client-side function.) Both procedures receive two parameters: The first parameter contains the object that raised the event (the CustomValidator control itself), and the second parameter is a ServerValidateEventArgs object containing information about the event. You can use the Value property of the second parameter to retrieve the value the user entered, and you'll set the IsValid property of the argument to indicate whether the value is valid.

To add validation for the State text box, follow these steps:

1. Add a CustomValidator control adjacent to the State text box.

2. Set the properties for the control as shown in Table 8.6.

TABLE 8.6   Set the CustomValidator Control's Properties to Match These Items

Property	Value
ID	cvalState
ClientValidationFunction	ValidState
ControlToValidate	txtState
Display	Dynamic
ErrorMessage	Enter CA, NV or AZ

Double-click the CustomValidator control and modify the ServerValidate procedure so that it looks like this:

```
Private Sub cvalState_ServerValidate( _
 ByVal source As System.Object, _
 ByVal args As _
 System.Web.UI.WebControls.ServerValidateEventArgs) _
 Handles cvalState.ServerValidate
```

```
   Select Case args.Value
      Case "CA", "NV", "AZ"
         args.IsValid = True
      Case Else
         args.IsValid = False
   End Select
End Sub
```

TIP

The `ServerValidate` event handler uses the `Value` property of its second parameter to determine the value the user has entered and the `IsValid` property to indicate whether the value is valid.

Close the code-behind file and then press Ctrl+PgDn (or use the View, HTML Source menu item) to view the HTML source for the page.

Immediately below the <BODY> element, near the top of the page, add the following script code, which provides the client-side validation:

```
<SCRIPT language="VBScript">
Sub ValidState(source, arguments)
   Select Case arguments.value
      Case "CA", "NV", "AZ"
         arguments.IsValid = True
      Case Else
         arguments.IsValid = False
   End Select
End Sub
</SCRIPT>
```

Now that you've added both the server-side and the client-side validation procedures, browse to the page and verify that entering an invalid state does trigger the validation code.

Summarizing Validation Messages

As you may have noticed, all the validation messages take up a lot of space on the page—you may not want to sacrifice all that space for your validation messages. ASP.NET provides its ValidationSummary control so that you can display all the validation messages in one place as well as display either nothing at all or a simple indicator next to each invalid control. The sample page, shown in Figure 8.3, displays an asterisk next to each invalid control and full error message text in the summary.

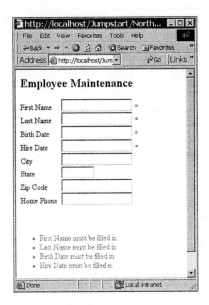

FIGURE 8.3   The ValidationSummary control lists all the ErrorMessage properties for invalid controls in one place.

Adding the ValidationSummary control is simple: All you have to do is place the control on your page. It automatically seeks out all the various validation controls on the page, gathering the ErrorMessage property from each control as necessary.

To set the text to be displayed within the validation controls themselves, set the Text property for each control. This property overrides the ErrorMessage property, and each control uses the Text property to determine what to show within its own display. (If you don't specify the Text property, as has been the case throughout this chapter, the controls display their ErrorMessage property.) To add the ValidationSummary control to your page, follow these steps:

1. Select the first validation control on the page and then Shift+click each of the remaining validation controls, selecting them all.

2. In the Properties window, set the Text property (for all the selected controls) to *.

3. Click directly above the Save button to place the insertion point within the page. In the Toolbox window, double-click the ValidationSummary control to insert an instance of this control.

4. Browse the page and then click Save without entering any data. Try entering invalid data in some of the controls. When you submit the page, you should

see asterisks next to the invalid controls and a summary of the errors at the bottom of the page.

TIP

If you want to modify the layout and behavior of the ValidationSummary control, check out the `DisplayMode` property, which can be set to `List`, `BulletList`, or `Paragraph`. Try them all to see how they affect the display. In addition, you might check out the `ShowMessageBox` property, which allows you to have up-level browsers (such as Internet Explorer) display a message box alert containing the validation information.

Comparing Values

It's sometimes useful to be able to validate one control's data by comparing it to the data in another control or to a specified value. The CompareValidator control allows you to do both. An example familiar to all Web users would be the need to compare two entries of a user's password. In order to confirm that a user has entered the correct password, most sites require the user to enter the same value twice. Figure 8.4 shows a sample page comparing two text box controls' values.

FIGURE 8.4   The CompareValidator control allows you to compare the values in two controls.

Follow these steps to add the Password Change form to your project:

1. Select Project, Add Existing Item. Be sure to change the Files of Type combo box to "All Files (*.*)".

2. Select all `PwdChange.*` files from the Jumpstart\ValidationControls folder. There should be three files: `PwdChange.aspx`, `PwdChange.aspx.resx`, and `PwdChange.aspx.vb`.

3. Bring up the PwdChange.aspx file in design mode.

4. Click immediately to the right of the Confirm Password text box to place the insertion point after the control.

5. In the Toolbox window, double-click the CompareValidator control to place a new instance of the control to the right of the Confirm Password text box.

6. Set the properties of the new control as shown in Table 8.7.

TABLE 8.7   Set These Properties in the CompareValidator Control

Property	Value
ControlToCompare	txtPassword
ControlToValidate	txtConfirm
ErrorMessage	'Password' and 'Confirm Password' must match

Run the application, bring up the Password Change page, and attempt to change the password. Check out what happens when you enter two different passwords on the page—you should see the error message displayed in the CompareValidator control.

OTHER USES FOR THE COMPAREVALIDATOR CONTROL

The CompareValidator control does more than just compare the values of two controls. You can also compare a control to a specific value. In addition, the Operator property of the control allows you to check for other comparisons besides equality. The Operator property can be any of these values: Equal (the default value), NotEqual, GreaterThan, GreaterThanEqual, LessThan, LessThanEqual, or DataTypeCheck. This last option, DataTypeCheck, allows you to simply check that the value entered into the control matches a specific data type. If you select DataTypeCheck for the Operator property and set the Type property to Date, for example, and leave ControlToCompare and ValueToCompare empty, you can allow the user to enter any date, but only a date.

Summary

The .NET Framework supplies a complete set of validation controls that you can use in your ASP.NET applications. From the simple RequiredFieldValidator control to the CustomValidator control, which allows you to supply both client- and server-side validation procedures, you have complete control over exactly what data you'll accept from your users. You no longer have to write complex scripting code, as you did when creating ASP applications! You'll want to dig into regular expressions a little, as well, because the ability to create your own expressions will cut down on the code you must write.

You can use validation controls to do the following:

- Require input or ensure entered data is different from a default value by using the RequiredFieldValidator control

- Force entered data to be within a specified range by using the RangeValidator control

- Validate common text expressions by using the RegularExpressionValidator control

- Supply your own validation rules by using the CustomValidator control

- Display a summary of all invalid controls by using the ValidationSummary control

- Compare the values of two controls by using the CompareValidator control

9

Debugging in Visual Studio .NET

OBJECTIVES

- Learn the three modes of Visual Basic

- Learn to invoke the debugger

- Learn to watch variables and set breakpoints

- Learn to control and view the execution path of your source code in the debugger

- Learn to use the Immediate window

This chapter examines the basics of the source code debugger that is built in to the Visual Studio .NET environment. You will learn about the different modes in which you'll work within Visual Studio, how to step through code, and how to set breakpoints. In addition, you will learn about many of the debugging tools and windows provided by the Visual Studio .NET environment.

> **TIP**
>
> To follow along with the material in this chapter, load the sample project Debugger.sln.

Using the Debugger

Visual Studio .NET provides a useful toolbar you can use while debugging but doesn't display it by default. In this section, you'll see both how to load the Debug toolbar and how to get started debugging.

Three Modes of Existence

While creating applications in Visual Studio .NET, you'll find yourself in one of three "modes." Each mode has a specific function, and knowing which mode you are in is important. The three modes are as follows:

- **Design mode.** In this mode you build your user interface and write your code.

- **Break mode.** In this mode you can single-step through code, view and modify variable values, and inspect memory.

- **Run mode.** In this mode you are, effectively, testing your application within the Visual Studio .NET environment.

You can determine which mode you are in by looking at the Visual Studio .NET title bar. At the end of the other information in the title bar, you will see one of the following: [design], *f*, or [break]. Get used to looking at the title bar for information on what mode you are currently in. There are things you can and can't do in each mode.

TIP

What can't you do in design mode? You can't use the Immediate window to test out code or expressions as you could in VB6. In break mode, you can't modify code, as you could in VB6. If you're coming to VB .NET from VB6, you may find some of these new limitations frustrating and confusing.

It is Break mode we'll focus on in this chapter, because it's in Break mode that you'll be able to single-step through code and debug the code as it runs.

Finding the Debug Toolbar

Visual Studio .NET provides many options for debugging your code, and although you can use menu items or keyboard shortcuts, you may find the Debug toolbar the easiest way to work. To make sure the Debug toolbar is visible, right-click the toolbar area of the Visual Studio .NET IDE and then select the Debug toolbar from the list of available toolbars. Once you've made the selection, you will see the toolbar shown in Figure 9.1.

FIGURE 9.1   The Debug toolbar gives you most of the debugging functionality without needing to dig into keyboard shortcuts or menu items.

From this toolbar, you will be able to run, stop, and pause the application. You will also be able to perform other functions related to debugging your application. From the left, the tools are as follows:

- **Start.** Runs the project.

- **Break All.** Pauses the project.

- **Stop Debugging.**

- **Restart.** Continues running the application from the current location.

- **Show Next Statement.** Jumps to the next statement that will be executed while single-stepping through code.

- **Step Into.** Single-steps into procedures in your code.

- **Step Over.** Single-steps, running procedures full speed.

- **Step Out.** Runs full speed from the current location back to the procedure that called the current procedure.

- **Hexadecimal Display.** Toggles the display of all values in the QuickWatch window between decimal and hexadecimal formats.

- **Breakpoints/Immediate.** Displays and then toggles between displaying the Breakpoints and Immediate windows.

You will learn more about these and other tools in this chapter.

> **TIP**
>
> While in Break mode, you have other tricks up your sleeve, as well. You can select the next line of code you'd like to execute, for example, by simply dragging the current line indicator to a different line (within the same procedure). You'll find debugging in Visual Studio .NET to be a very powerful experience!

Invoking the Debugger

To begin debugging your application, select Debug, Step Into or the Debug, Step Over menu options (or the corresponding toolbar items). The hotkeys for each of these may be different, depending on how you customized your profile when you first ran Visual Studio .NET. For example, if you are set up as a Visual Studio developer, the hotkeys for these two commands will be F11 and F10, respectively. If you are set up as a Visual Basic developer, however, you will use F8 and Shift+F8, respectively.

> **TIP**
>
> No matter how hard you try, debugging from within an ASP.NET application simply doesn't work unless you press F5 (or use the Debug, Start menu item) to begin running your code. (Your application must have a start page in order for this to work. Right-click the correct page, in the Solution Explorer window, and select Set as Start Page from the context menu.) There are other ways to accomplish the same goal, but this is how we've gotten debugging to work. Certainly, selecting a page, right-clicking, and selecting the Build and Browse or View

With... context menu item will not allow you to debug. In addition, before you can debug an ASP.NET project, you must set the project properties correctly. Right-click the project in the Solution Explorer, select Properties from the context menu, and verify that on the Configuration Properties, Debugging page, the ASP.NET Debugging check box is selected. Otherwise, you'll never be able to debug the current project.

Stepping into Code

Single-step mode executes each statement in your code, one at a time. You can step through code by clicking the Step Into button on the Debug toolbar or by selecting Debug, Step Into.

If, while debugging, you encounter a user-defined procedure during single-step execution, you will single-step into each statement within that procedure before returning to the called procedure.

Stepping over Code

Stepping over code is very similar to stepping into code, except that rather than executing every statement within a called procedure, stepping over code executes the entire procedure, while your debugging session never leaves the current procedure. This allows you to quickly step over procedures that you've already determined to be error free.

Use procedure step mode by clicking the Step Over toolbar button or selecting Debug, Step Over.

TIP

We're not going to attempt to describe the keystrokes associated with each debugging toolbar item, because the keystrokes depend on the profile you've selected. Instead, check the Debug menu for each item and determine the keystrokes from the tips provided on the menus.

WARNING

If you are moving from Visual Basic 6.0, you may be used to changing your code while in Break mode and then continuing with these changes in place. Visual Studio .NET doesn't make this possible, at least not in this first release. You must stop your application, make your changes, and then restart your debugging session in order to test your changes.

Entering Break Mode

When your application is running, you may invoke the debugger and enter the Break mode in several ways:

- Press Ctrl+Break while your code is running.

- Place a Stop statement in your code. (Be wary of this technique! We'll have more discussion of this later in the chapter.)

- Set a breakpoint in your code.

- Select Debug, Step Into to run the program.

The Stop Statement

If you want to place a permanent breakpoint into your code, place a Stop statement at the location where you want the breakpoint. You'll want to make sure you remove any Stop statements prior to distributing your application—even when you create the release version of your application, Stop statements drop into Break mode (or they halt the application, if the debugger isn't available).

One good way to make sure any Stop statements are removed from your code at release time is to always surround them with conditional compilation directives that only include the statements if you've built a Debug build, like this:

```
Private Sub BreakPointsSample()
  Dim intValue As Integer

#If DEBUG Then
    Stop
#End If

  intValue = 10

  Proc1()
End Sub
```

Introducing the Debugging Tools

Visual Studio .NET provides many tools you can use to debug your applications. In addition, Visual Basic .NET provides tools you can use, such as the Stop statement, the Debug and Trace objects, and conditional compilation. Table 9.1 provides a brief definition of each of these items.

TABLE 9.1   Tools You Can Use to Debug Your Application

Tool	Description
Breakpoints	Breakpoints allow you to drop into Break mode before a particular line of code executes. Once in Break mode, you can single-step through your code. You can set as many breakpoints as you like, and your breakpoints are preserved with your project.
Debug class	This class provides methods that allow you to interactively debug your application at development time. You can output text to any of a number of listeners as you're debugging your application. The default listener is the Output window, although you can add other listeners as well, such as the Event Log, text files, or the Console window.
Conditional statements	These statements allow you to include or exclude statements at compile time. Excluded statements simply don't exist within your compiled applications.
Debugging tools	Visual Studio .NET provides a host of windows that give you all sorts of information about variables, breakpoints, memory, the call stack, and much more.
Stop statement	A Stop statement acts as a permanent runtime breakpoint. Unlike breakpoints, however, you cannot leave Stop statements in your compiled applications, because your applications will simply stop when the code execution reaches the Stop statement. Stop statements are included mostly for backward compatibility because breakpoints are now persisted with your projects. (In VB6, developers lost their breakpoints when they shut down the development environment, so developers often used Stop statements to preserve their breakpoints.)
Trace class	This class provides runtime tracing support, allowing you to write text to a number of listeners as your application runs on client machines. You can send information to any number of different listeners, such as the Event Log, text files, or the Console window. (This topic is beyond the scope of this chapter. For more information, see the .NET Framework documentation.)

The following subsections introduce you to these various tools.

Using Breakpoints

Often, as you're testing an application on your own machine, you won't want to step through every line of code (using the Step Into or Step Over techniques) in order to arrive at the point where you think an error might be lurking. Instead, you can set a breakpoint in your source code to indicate to Visual Studio .NET where it should stop executing and drop into Break mode. To insert a breakpoint, you can simply click the mouse in the left margin, next to the line of code on which you'd like to drop into Break mode. Figure 9.2 shows a procedure including a breakpoint.

FIGURE 9.2 Click in the margin to insert a breakpoint into your code.

After a breakpoint is set, you can start and run the application normally. When Visual Basic hits the line of code marked with the breakpoint, it automatically puts you in Break mode.

Breakpoints are saved with your project, so after you close Visual Studio .NET and restart it, your breakpoints will still be available to you.

The Breakpoints Window

To make it easier for you to see all your breakpoints, Visual Studio .NET provides the Breakpoints window. Select Debug, Windows, Breakpoints to see the window shown in Figure 9.3.

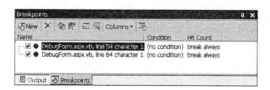

FIGURE 9.3 The Breakpoints window shows all the breakpoints in your solution.

This window provides a list of all the breakpoints you have set in your application. If you double-click a breakpoint, the window will take you directly to that breakpoint within your source code.

Breakpoints Toolbar

The Breakpoints window contains a toolbar that provides a series of buttons you'll find useful while debugging. Table 9.2 lists and describes the buttons, from left to right, for you.

TABLE 9.2   The Breakpoints Window Toolbar Includes These Buttons

Tool	Description
New	Creates a new breakpoint and allows you to configure the conditions under which the program will stop on this breakpoint. See the next section for more information on setting up conditional breakpoints.
Delete	Deletes the currently selected breakpoint.
Clear All Breakpoints	Deletes all breakpoints from the current solution.
Disable All Breakpoints	Disables all breakpoints until you enable them again.
Go To Source Code	Moves your cursor to the line in your source code where the currently selected breakpoint is located.
Go To Disassembly	Opens the disassembly window to the line where the currently selected breakpoint is located.
Columns	Allows you to choose which columns you wish to display in the Breakpoint window. You can display Name, Condition, Hit Count, Language, Function, File, Address, Data, and Program.
Properties	Allows you to configure the conditions under which the program will stop on the currently selected breakpoint. See the next section for information on setting conditional breakpoints.

Conditions on Breakpoints

If you right-click any breakpoint in the Breakpoints window and select Properties from the context menu (or select the Properties button on the window's toolbar), you can set and retrieve attributes about the selected breakpoint. If you want to create a new breakpoint, setting conditional attributes, you can right-click any breakpoint and select New Breakpoint from the context menu or click New on the window's toolbar. (The New Breakpoint dialog box is essentially identical to the Breakpoint Properties dialog box.) Figure 9.4 shows the New Breakpoint dialog box.

The Function tab (shown in Figure 9.4) allows you to determine in which function you want to create the breakpoint. You can specify the line number and even the character number where you want the breakpoint. (Allowing you to set the character number takes into account Visual Basic's ability to have multiple statements on the same line, separated with a colon [:] character.)

The File tab allows you to set a breakpoint within a specific file in your application by line number and character. Figure 9.5 shows the New Breakpoint dialog box with the File tab selected.

The Address tab of the New Breakpoint dialog box lets you set the actual address of the instruction where you wish to set the breakpoint. You're unlikely to use this option, shown in Figure 9.6, from within Visual Basic .NET.

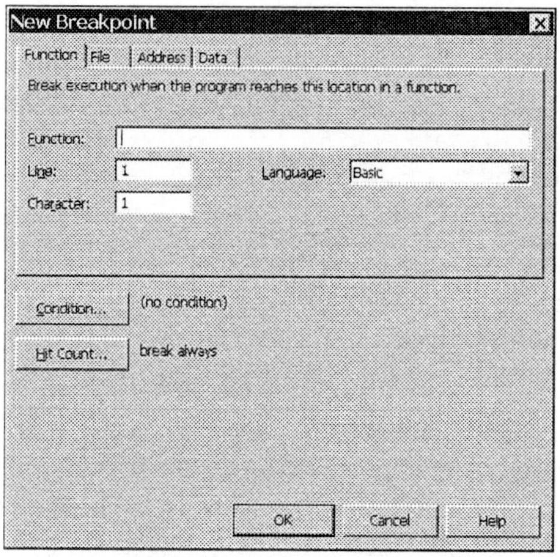

FIGURE 9.4   The New Breakpoint dialog box shows you information about a breakpoint. A similar dialog box allows you to create a new breakpoint.

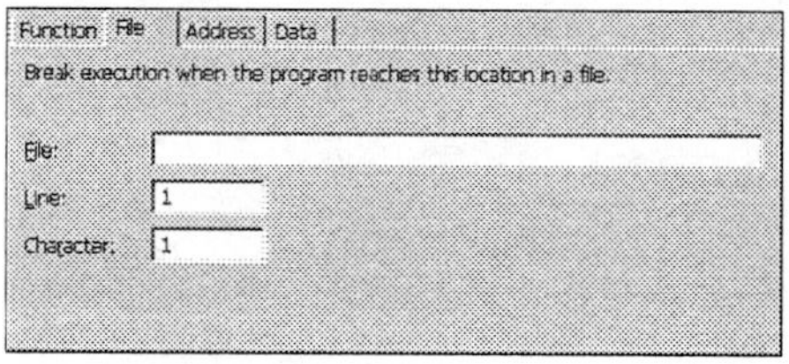

FIGURE 9.5   The File tab of the New Breakpoint dialog box allows you to set the file and line number at which you wish to set a breakpoint.

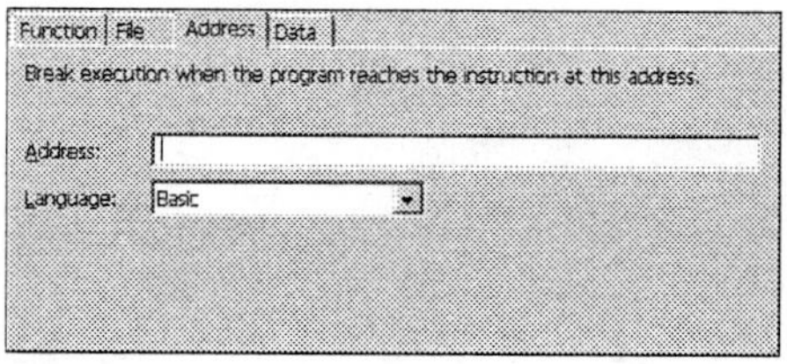

FIGURE 9.6   The Address tab of the New Breakpoint dialog box lets you set the instruction address at which to break.

The Data tab of the New Breakpoint dialog box allows you to enter Break mode when a specified variable changes its value. This can be very useful for tracking down where in your program a global variable changes its value. Figure 9.7 shows the Data tab.

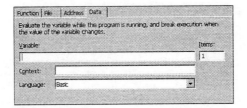

FIGURE 9.7   The Data tab of the New Breakpoint dialog box allows you to break when a specified variable changes its value.

Setting a Condition

Sometimes, you'll want to trigger a breakpoint only if some specific condition is met. You can click the Condition button on the New Breakpoint dialog box (or the same button on the Breakpoint Properties dialog box) to enter a condition. Clicking the button displays the dialog box shown in Figure 9.8.

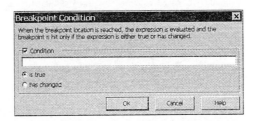

FIGURE 9.8   The Breakpoint Condition dialog box allows you to specify a condition, such as `intNumber = 5` or `boolValue = True`.

In the Breakpoint Condition dialog box, you can enter expressions and force the program to drop into Break mode either when your expression is true or when the expression changes its value. For example, you might specify an expression such as `intNumber = 10` or `boolValue = True`. If you want to track a variable's value changing, you can enter the variable's name and select Has Changed. Anytime the value of that variable changes, Visual Studio .NET will place you into Break mode.

Specifying a Hit Count

Sometimes you may not want to step through a loop 50 times just to find an error on the 50th iteration through the loop. To avoid this drudgery, you can select Hit Count on the New Breakpoint dialog box and enter the hit count on which you'd like to drop into Break mode. When you click this button, you will see the dialog box shown in Figure 9.9.

The Breakpoint Hit Count dialog box supplies four options you can select from the drop-down list on the dialog box. Table 9.3 outlines each of these options.

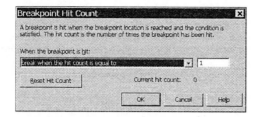

FIGURE 9.9   The Breakpoint Hit Count dialog box lets you control exactly when you enter Break mode.

TABLE 9.3   Choose One of These Options to Determine How and When You Drop into Break Mode

Option	Description
Break always	Like a standard breakpoint, selecting this option will stop execution each time the breakpoint is reached.
Break when the hit count is equal to	Selecting this option indicates that when the breakpoint has been the number of times you've specified, you'll drop into Break mode.
Break when the hit count is a multiple of	Selecting this option indicates that when the breakpoint has been hit a number of times that is an even multiple of the value you've specified, you'll drop into Break mode. For example, if you specify 5, you'll drop into Break mode the 5th, 10th, 15th, and so on, times you hit the breakpoint.
Break when the hit count is greater than or equal to	Selecting this option indicates that when the breakpoint has been hit at least the number of times you've specified, you'll drop into Break mode each time you hit the breakpoint after that. For example, if you specify 5, you'll drop into Break mode on the 5th, 6th, 7th, and so on, times you hit the breakpoint.

Setting the Next Statement to Execute

Sometimes when debugging your application in Break mode, you might need to skip a section of code or back up and execute the same code again. Visual Studio .NET allows this, as long as the line you want to move to is within the current procedure.

While in Break mode, simply click and drag the yellow arrow within the left margin to a new location within the same procedure to set the instruction pointer to the newly selected line of code. Figure 9.10 shows the action of dragging the yellow arrow to select a new line of code to execute.

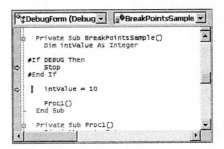

FIGURE 9.10   Click and drag the yellow arrow to set the new instruction pointer.

Useful Versus .NET Debugging Tools

Breakpoints are great, but they're not enough. You need to be able to view and modify data, find out how the execution path got you to the current location, and what's going on in the environment. To help you out, Visual Studio .NET provides many useful tools you can use while debugging. The following subsections show some of the tools you may want to investigate.

Watching Variables Using Your Mouse

If you want to investigate the value of a simple variable while debugging in Break mode, you could use the Immediate window or one of several other windows. The simplest technique, however, is to simply hover the mouse pointer over the variable. Visual Studio .NET will display a tool tip containing the name of the variable and the value contained within the variable. Figure 9.11 shows the tool tip while in Break mode.

FIGURE 9.11   Hover your cursor over a variable in Break mode to see the value of that variable.

Watch Window

You can use the Watch window to view the value of variables and expressions as your code is executing. This can be useful if you want to be able to single-step through code, and for each line of code, investigate the value of one or more variables or expressions. Use the Debug, Windows, Watch menu to display the window shown in Figure 9.12. You can add new variables or expressions just by typing within the Name column. You can also modify the values of your variables (but not expressions, of course) by typing within the Value column.

FIGURE 9.12   The Watch window can display the value of variables or expressions.

TIP

Right-click a specific watch within the Watch window and select Delete Watch from the context menu to delete it.

Adding Watch Values Using QuickWatch

If you are in Break mode and wish to view the contents of a variable or expression in the current procedure, position your cursor on that variable (or select the expression) and select Debug, QuickWatch. You will then see a dialog box like the one in Figure 9.13, showing your watch variable/expression. Click Add Watch to add a watch to the Watch window.

FIGURE 9.13   QuickWatch is great for looking up the value of an expression, and it allows you to easily add a watch to the Watch window.

Call Stack Window

While in Break mode, Visual Studio .NET allows you to display the list of procedures you have executed to get your current location. This is very handy when you are not sure how you got to where you are. You can display the Call Stack window, shown in Figure 9.14, by selecting Debug, Windows, Call Stack.

FIGURE 9.14   The Call Stack window lets you see where you came from as you debug an application.

> **TIP**
>
> The grayed-out procedures in the Call Stack window are procedures you didn't call directly—they were called by the .NET Framework in order to get to your code. You can double-click any of your own procedures in the Call Stack window to have Visual Studio .NET highlight the procedure call within your code.

Using the Command Window

The Command window (also known as the *Immediate window*) allows you to perform simple calculations. Use the Debug, Windows, Immediate menu item to display this window. You can also display or modify the value of a variable. The statements you enter into the Command window may be any valid Visual Basic expression. For example, you can print the results of an operation, print the contents of a variable or property, or even set the value of a variable or property. Use the "?" operator (which stands for "print the value of the expression that follows") to display a value or to run a function. Simply enter an assignment or method call that doesn't return a value into the window to execute the expression. Figure 9.15 shows the Command window in use.

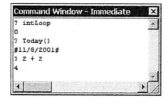

NOTE

Unlike in Visual Basic 6.0, in Visual Studio .NET, you must be in Break mode in order to enter text into the Command window. You'll also find other differences. For example, you cannot delete lines in the Command window. Right-click and use the Clear All context menu item to delete text from the window.

Other Useful Debugging Windows

Visual Studio .NET provides even more windows and tools. Some of these are tools you'll use every day; others are a bit more specialized and won't be used as part of your daily routine.

Locals Window

If you wish to keep an eye on all the local variables in a procedure, you can select Debug, Windows, Locals from the menu bar. This window, shown in Figure 9.16, will display each of the variables in each procedure as you work through the procedures in your debugging session. This window also displays information about controls on the current page.

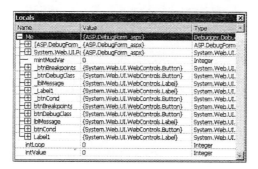

FIGURE 9.16   The Locals window shows you all your local variables.

Autos Window

If you just want to watch local variables, and nothing more, you can use the Autos window (Debug, Windows, Autos). Figure 9.17 shows the Autos window while debugging a simple procedure.

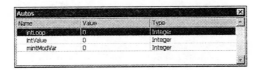

FIGURE 9.17   The Autos window shows all local variables.

> **TIP**
>
> You might be wondering where the name "Autos window" came from. It's one of those C/C++/C# things—in those languages, local variables are often called *auto variables* (hence, the window name).

Me Window

The Me window, accessed via the Debug, Windows, Me menu item, displays all the objects within the current class. Figure 9.18 shows the Me window in use.

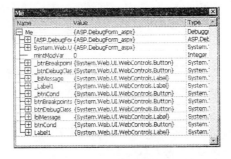

FIGURE 9.18   The Me window shows all objects and variables within the current class.

> **TIP**
>
> The Locals, Autos, and Me windows are related. The Locals window shows a union of the information provided by the Autos and Me windows—that is, local variables and class variables.

Threads Window

The Threads window, accessed via the Debug, Windows, Threads menu item, displays a list of all executing threads in your application. Most of the time, in simple ASP.NET applications, you'll only be working with a single thread. Figure 9.19 shows the Threads window for a simple debugging session.

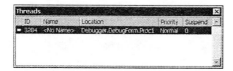

FIGURE 9.19   The Threads window displays all executing threads.

Modules Window

The Modules window will show you all the modules that were loaded in order to run an application. (This information is fun, if you're interested in how things work "under the covers.") Display this window using the Debug, Windows, Modules menu item. Figure 9.20 shows the Modules window for the sample application.

Name	Address	Path	Or...	Version	Pri
mscorlib.dll	61940000-61B...	e:\winnt\microsoft.net\framewor...	1	1.0.2914.16	[2
system.xml.dll	5FA10000-5FB...	e:\winnt\assembly\gac\system.x...	2	1.0.2914.16	[2
microsoft.vi...	53140000-531...	e:\winnt\assembly\gac\microsoft....	3	7.0.9254.0	[2
system.web...	5EEA0000-5EF...	e:\winnt\assembly\gac\system.w...	4	1.0.2914.16	[2
system.web...	5EFC0000-5EF...	e:\winnt\assembly\gac\system.w...	5	1.0.2914.16	[2
system.web...	5EFE0000-5F0...	e:\winnt\assembly\gac\system.w...	6	1.0.2914.16	[2
system.data...	5D680000-5D...	e:\winnt\assembly\gac\system.da...	7	1.0.2914.16	[2
system.web...	03D50000-03...	e:\winnt\assembly\gac\system.w...	8	1.0.1722.2	[2
system.dra...	5EC00000-5EC...	e:\winnt\assembly\gac\system.dr...	9	1.0.2914.16	[2
system.dll	5E4B0000-5E6...	e:\winnt\assembly\gac\system\1...	10	1.0.2914.16	[2
system.ent...	60050000-600...	e:\winnt\assembly\gac\system.e...	11	1.0.2914.16	[2
system.ent...	61540000-615...	e:\winnt\assembly\gac\system.e...	12	1.0.2914.16	[2

FIGURE 9.20   The Modules window shows you all loaded modules.

Disassembly Window

If you like digging into the bits and bytes of your code, check out the Disassembly window by selecting Debug, Windows, Disassembly. This may be more information than you ever wanted to know about your code, but it's all there for your entertainment and education. Should you ever really want to know what Visual Basic .NET is doing under the covers, here's how you can find out! Figure 9.21 shows the disassembly of some simple VB .NET code.

Registers Window

The Registers window, shown in Figure 9.22, will display what is in the registers of the machine after the current instruction in your .NET application. Use the Debug,

Windows, Registers menu item to display this window. (We doubt most Visual Basic .NET developers will ever take advantage of this window—we've included it here for completeness only.)

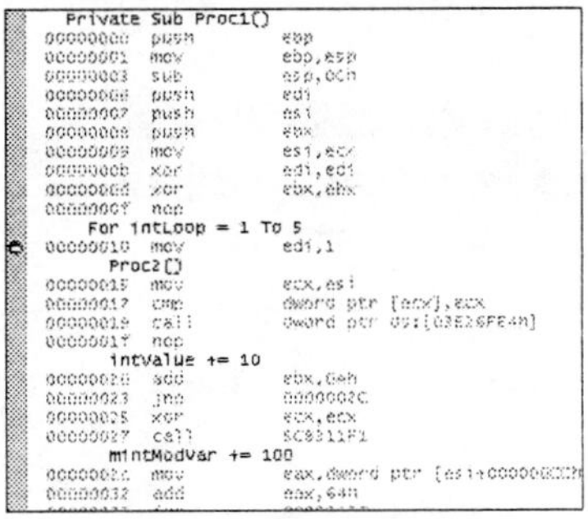

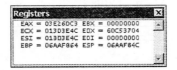

FIGURE 9.21   The Disassembly window shows you the assembly language version of your code.

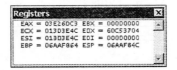

FIGURE 9.22   The Registers window shows you each register of your computer.

Using the Debug Class

During the testing of your application, you may find that when you are stepping through code the application works fine, but when you run the program straight through it does not work the way you expected. The reason for this is that you can change the way your program runs by using the debugger—the fact that you're executing the code extremely slowly can affect the behavior of the application! Instead of using the debugger to test values, you may find it convenient to print those values to the Immediate window.

You may print directly to the Output window (use the View, Other Windows, Output menu item to display this window and select Debug from the drop-down list at the top of the window) from within your application by executing the `Debug.Write` or `Debug.WriteLine` method. The values placed into the Immediate window using either of these methods will still be available in Break or Design mode. It can be useful to see those values without having to enter Break mode and thereby possibly change the execution of your program. You'll most likely use the

WriteLine method of the Debug object, simply sending the method a string to display in the Output window, like this:

```
Debug.WriteLine("Now executing btnStart_Click()")
```

> **TIP**
>
> The Output window can display both Build and Debug information. Make sure you select Debug from the drop-down list at the top of the window in order to see the Debug.WriteLine output.

To illustrate these points, make sure DebugForm.aspx is the start page for the sample project, run the project, and select Debug Class on the Web page. Clicking this button loads a Web Form named DebugEvents.aspx. This form includes several calls to the Debug.WriteLine method in several different event procedures. This page illustrates the use of the Debug.WriteLine method and also gives you an idea of which events are fired when a Web Form loads and unloads. Figure 9.23 shows some of the sample output from these Debug.WriteLine method calls.

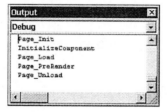

FIGURE 9.23   Sample output from DebugEvents Web Form.

> **NOTE**
>
> If you're a VB6 developer, you may be used to the output from the Debug class going into the Immediate window. Look there all you like in Visual Studio .NET, but you won't find what you're looking for. This content now goes to the Output window instead.

Listing 9.1 shows part of the code that creates the output shown in Figure 9.23.

LISTING 9.1   The Example Uses This Code to Help Demonstrate Debugging Techniques

```
Private Sub Page_Load( _
  ByVal sender As System.Object, _
  ByVal e As System.EventArgs) _
  Handles MyBase.Load
```

LISTING 9.1   Continued

```
 'Put user code to initialize the page here

 Debug.WriteLine("Page_Load")

End Sub

Private Sub Page_PreRender( _
 ByVal sender As Object, _
 ByVal e As System.EventArgs) _
 Handles MyBase.PreRender

  Debug.WriteLine("Page_PreRender")

End Sub

Private Sub Page_Unload( _
 ByVal sender As Object, _
 ByVal e As System.EventArgs) _
 Handles MyBase.Unload

  Debug.WriteLine("Page_Unload")

End Sub
```

The Debug class has several methods you might find useful, in addition to the
WriteLine method. Table 9.4 describes some of the more common ones you
might use.

TABLE 9.4   Methods of the Debug Class

Method	Description
Assert	Stops the program if the condition you pass to this method does not evaluate to True. This method only works in the design mode: All Debug statements are removed from the final compiled program.
Write	Writes a value to the output window without a CRLF.
WriteLine	Writes a value to the output window with a CRLF.
WriteIf	Writes a value to the output window without a CRLF, if a specified condition is true.
WriteLineIf	Writes a value to the output window with a CRLF, if a specified condition is true.

The `Assert` Method

The `Debug.Assert` method allows you to insert assertions in your code—that is, debugging statements that display information into the Output window if a specific condition isn't met. `Debug.Assert` is a powerful debugging tool in that it allows you to ensure that you've passed correct parameters to a procedure or that a variable always contains a specific value or range of values. Some programmers insist that you shouldn't program an application without using the `Debug.Assert` method scattered throughout your whole application anytime you make any type of assumption about the current state of parameters of variables. The following code shows how you might check to see whether a number typed into a text box was typed in correctly:

```
Private Sub AssertSample()
  Dim intNum As Integer

  intNum = CInt(Val(txtNumber.Text))


  Debug.Assert(intNum >= 0 And intNum <= 5, _
    "Number must be between 0 and 5")
End Sub
```

If you run this code and enter **6** into the text box on sample form (`DebugClass.aspx`), the assertion will return `False`. The .NET runtime will display a message into the Output window like the one shown in Figure 9.24.

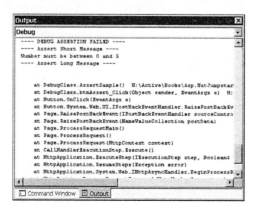

FIGURE 9.24 `Debug.Assert` displays information like this into the Output window when the assertion fails.

> **TIP**
>
> Debug.Assert isn't normally used to validate input, as you've seen here. The validation controls provided by ASP.NET do a better job at that. We've purposefully selected a simple example here, just to demonstrate how you might use Debug.Assert. Normally, you'd use Debug.Assert to verify that the data sent to a procedure meets certain criteria that you just assume—for example, that a string isn't too long or that a value that shouldn't be zero is, in fact, not equal to zero.

The WriteLineIf Method

If you only wish to write a line to the Output window when a specified condition is true, you can use the WriteLineIf method of the Debug class. For example, the sample page uses code like the following to check a condition before writing information to the Output window:

```
Private Sub WriteLineIfSample()
  Dim intNum As Integer

  intNum = CInt(txtNumber.Text)
  Debug.WriteLineIf(intNum >= 0 And intNum <= 5, _
    "You input a correct number")
End Sub
```

> **TIP**
>
> If you want to dig a little deeper, you'll find that the Debug class (and its cousin, the Trace class) are far more powerful than you've seen here. Each of these classes relies on the concept of "listener" objects—that is, objects that "listen" for output and collect the output for display. By default, the only listener for the Debug class is the Output window. Without too much effort, you can create listeners that write output to a text file or to the Windows Event Log. Although doing this work is beyond the scope of this material, you can check out the Debug class in the online help for information on creating other listeners.

Conditional Compilation

Although debugging techniques can help you iron out problems in your code, you may want to simply add chunks of code at compile time (if you're currently in the debugging phase of your project) or remove the same chunks when you release your code. Conditional compilation makes it possible to add and remove chunks from the executable.

Conditional compilation relies on compiler directives in your code that indicate to the compiler, as it's compiling your code, how it should use the code. Compiler directives are #If statements that direct the compiler as to which code it should leave in and which code it should leave out. For example, you might wish to put debugging code in your application, but when you create a final compile, you don't want the debugging code to be there. Or maybe you wish to take out the code for certain features if you are creating a demo version of your product.

To use conditional compilation, you will first need to declare a compiler constant. You declare then using the #Const statement. Each constant is given a unique name and assigned a value. Once these constants are declared, you can use them within an #If... #End If block. As you'll see, there are several ways to define conditional compilation constants.

Declaring a File-Level Compiler Constant

You can declare a compiler constant anywhere within a file in your program. That compiler constant is then available anywhere within that file. It does not matter whether you place the constant declaration at the top of the file, within a defined class, or within a procedure, it will still be available throughout the whole file. For example, the sample page DebugForm.aspx defines the following constant at the top of its code-behind file:

```
#Const DEMO = True
```

Using Conditional Compilation Constants

To create a compiler directive, use the #If... #End If construct. You might, for example, want to include one block of code for demo versions of your application and different code for retail versions, like this:

```
Private Sub ConditionalSample()
#If DEMO Then
  lblMessage.Text = "Demo version"
#Else
  lblMessage.Text = "Retail version"
#End If
End Sub
```

NOTE

You may be wondering why you'd use conditional compilation rather than simple conditional statements in your code. One good reason is that you may have large blocks of code that are different for two versions of your application. There's no reason to load both sets of code when they're mutually exclusive. Instead, you can make the choice as to which block you want to include at compile time (not at runtime) using conditional compilation.

Unlike a normal If statement, the #If statement actually removes the unused code as it compiles. This leads to a reduced application size in memory and prevents unnecessary or unwanted code being deployed as part of the application. For the preceding example, the compiler will actually only see the following code (assuming that the DEMO constant is set to True):

```
Private Sub ConditionalSample()
  lblMessage.Text = "Demo version"
End Sub
```

TIP

Visual Studio .NET provides two built-in compile-time constants: DEBUG and TRACE. By default, they're both defined for you (although you can modify this behavior using the Project Properties dialog box). The DEBUG constant is defined to be True when you are compiling a Debug build of your program. (You can choose what type of build you are making by selecting Build, Configuration Manager from the menu bar and then choosing either the Debug or Release version. Once you set your application to build as Release, the Debug constant is set to False.) The TRACE constant allows you to control runtime tracing of your application.

Declaring a Global Compiler Constant

To declare a compiler constant that can be used throughout your whole application, select the project within the Solution Explorer window, right-click, and select Properties from the context menu. On the Property Pages dialog box, select Configuration Properties, Build. Figure 9.25 shows the Property Pages dialog box.

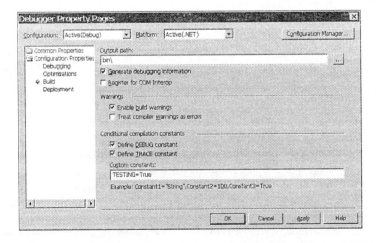

FIGURE 9.25   Use this property page to set compile-time constants.

In the Custom Constants text box, enter the constant name, an equal sign, and the value to assign. (Compile-time constants follow the same naming rules as any other Visual Basic .NET variables.)

Summary

This chapter presented you with the different features of the integrated debugging environment in Visual Studio .NET. These powerful tools help you track down bugs easily. In this chapter, you learned:

- How to set and use breakpoints

- How to step through your code, line by line, as well as how to step over procedures

- How to use the various debugging windows and tools provided by Visual Studio .NET

- How to add conditional compilation constants to your code, allowing you to include or exclude blocks of code based on those constants

Using the powerful tools provided by Visual Studio .NET, you should be able to track down and destroy bugs in your applications, quickly and efficiently.

PART II

Data Handling

IN THIS PART

10

Introduction to ADO.NET

OBJECTIVES

- Learn about the ADO.NET classes

- Compare ADO.NET to ADO

Most applications will need to manage data, sooner or later, and the .NET Framework provides ADO.NET as a data-handling API that's available to all .NET applications. You can think of ADO.NET as the latest evolution of Microsoft's database APIs, and it supplements the existing support for DAO, ADO, and other data-management object models. ADO.NET has been designed to make it possible to support multitiered, distributed applications. In addition, ADO.NET provides strong support for working with XML data.

Basically, ADO.NET is an object model that lets you build sets of data in memory. You can create DataSets from data you hard-code in a program, retrieve them from a text file, an Exchange server, or a database system. ADO.NET does not "care" where the data comes from as long as you can fit it into rows and columns within its objects.

In this chapter, you will learn about the different classes available in ADO.NET. You will learn which classes just deal with data in memory and which classes are used to retrieve data from databases. Two distinct namespaces provide the various ADO.NET objects: One allows you to work with data from any OLE DB data source, and one is solely for working with data from Microsoft SQL Server 7.0 or later.

Using ADO.NET Classes

ADO.NET provides several classes you will need to become familiar with. Table 10.1 provides a short description of each of the classes you will encounter over the next several chapters.

TABLE 10.1   ADO.NET Classes

Class	Description
DataSet	DataSet objects can contain one or more DataTable objects, much like an in-memory database. You have the ability to set relationships between these DataTable objects. You can modify the data in a DataSet, and DataSet objects can hold both the original set of data and any modifications made to this data. You can then use other ADO.NET objects to submit these changes back to the data source. This class does not provide any means to communicate directly with any type of data source—that functionality is provided by the DataAdapter objects.
DataTable	DataTable objects hold rows of data. Each row is made up of columns, and each column can hold some discreet data. The DataTable object provides a collection of DataRow objects and a collection of DataColumn objects. Each DataRow object contains the data stored within a single row in the DataTable, and DataColumn objects provide information about the schema of the DataTable. Like the DataSet object, DataTable objects have no means to communicate with any type of data source. You can add data to the DataTable object programmatically, one row at a time, or you can use the Fill method of a DataAdapter object to fill a DataTable with data from a data source.
DataView	Instances of this class provide a specific view of a DataTable. This object is frequently used to set sort orders or filters on a DataTable object.
Connection*	Use a Connection object to create a connection to a data source. You can open a connection to a data source and keep this connection object open for as long as you need it.
Command*	Use a Command object to submit SQL statements to a back-end data source. You can use SQL or calls to stored procedures for all data retrieval and modification. You can use the ExecuteReader method to return a DataReader object, ExecuteNonQuery to run an update/delete/insert query, or ExecuteScalar to return a single value as the result of the SQL you've provided.
DataAdapter*	The DataAdapter object provides four Command object properties: one each for a Select, Update, Insert, and Delete command. You'll use a DataAdapter object's Fill method (and its SelectCommand property) to populate a DataSet or a DataTable object with data from a database. You can use the Update method of the DataAdapter to save changes you've made to a DataSet back to the original data source(s), and the DataAdapter will determine, based on the changes you've made, which of its commands (Update, Insert, or Delete) to use.

TABLE 10.1   Continued

Class	Description
CommandBuilder*	When you work with a DataAdapter object, you'll need to provide Insert, Update, and Delete commands, in addition to a Select command, if you want to modify data. Although you can supply the SQL expressions yourself, it would be easier if someone else could do the work. That's the job of the CommandBuilder object, which can generate Insert, Update, and Delete commands based on the Select command you supply. A DataAdapter can then use these commands to update the original data source(s). (You should note that the CommandBuilder does build commands for you, but the SQL it creates won't be optimized and will almost always include more fields than you might need.)
DataReader*	The DataReader class provides a forward-only, read-only cursor (sometimes called a fire hose cursor) that reads data from a data source in the most efficient manner available to ADO.NET. This class is excellent for filling DataGrids, list boxes, and combo boxes. Under the covers, the DataAdapter object uses a DataReader to fill the contents of a DataSet.

We're referring to these objects by generic names, but their actual names include information about the namespace that provides them. For example, the .NET Framework provides SqlConnection and OleDbConnection objects, and we're referring to them both, generically, as the Connection class here. The same goes for Command, CommandBuilder, and so on.

Figure 10.1 shows you how some of the different classes in .NET work together to retrieve data, create DataTables within a DataSet, and how those DataSets can be consumed. Datasets can be created by DataAdapters, which read from a data store such as SQL Server, Oracle, or Access. Datasets can also be created by code you write in VB .NET or C#. Once the DataSet is built, it may be consumed by a WinForm, a WebForm, or a Web Service, or it can be sent across an HTTP interface to some other consumer, such as a Web page written in Java running on a Unix server.

ADO.NET Namespaces

The root namespace for working with data in the .NET Framework is System.Data. This namespace provides the DataSet and DataTable objects you'll use to work with any type of data. In addition, the .NET Framework provides two specific namespaces that each provides objects for retrieving data that you'll learn about in this book:

- System.Data.OleDb. Used for working with any OLE DB data source, such as Jet, Oracle, and so on. This namespace supports existing unmanaged (that is, with code written outside the CLR) ADO providers. This namespace includes the OleDbConnection, OleDbCommand, OleDbDataReader, and OleDbDataAdapter objects.

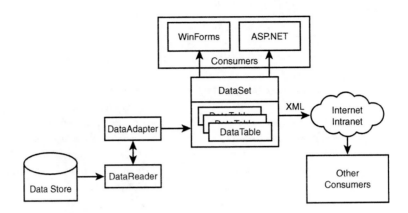

FIGURE 10.1   An overview of the .NET classes.

- `System.Data.SqlClient`. Provides direct support for SQL Server 6.5 and later, using a managed provider. If you know you'll be working only with SQL Server, you'll want to take advantage of the optimized behavior of this set of classes. This namespace includes the `SqlConnection`, `SqlCommand`, `SqlDataReader`, and `SqlDataAdapter` objects.

You can be relatively sure that Microsoft (and other vendors) will release additional assemblies (and namespaces) containing ADO.NET objects. For example, before the Visual Studio .NET shipped, Microsoft had already released the `System.Data.ODBC` namespace, and by the time you read this, it's likely that an Oracle-specific namespace will be available as well. (The Oracle namespace wasn't available at the time we wrote this book.) We'll focus on the `OleDb` and `SqlClient` namespaces throughout the rest of this book.

To get a copy of the `System.Data.Odbc` namespace, visit Microsoft's download site at `http://msdn.microsoft.com/downloads`. Search for `odbc`, and you'll find this useful addition to the .NET Framework.

Visual Basic .NET adds an implicit `Imports` statement for `System.Data` to all your projects for you (unless you change this behavior in the Property Pages dialog box for your project). Although you could refer to ADO.NET objects like this, you can also abbreviate them, as the following code fragment shows:

```
Dim da1 As System.Data.SqlClient.SqlDataAdapter
' This works fine, too
Dim da2 As SqlClient.SqlDataAdapter
```

If you're going to be using the `System.Data.SqlClient` namespace throughout your application, you might consider adding an `Imports` statement for the namespace at the top of each file that uses the objects, like this:

```
' Insert this at the top of a file:
Imports System.Data.SqlClient
```

```
' Now this works, as well:
Dim da3 As SqlDataAdapter
```

You can use the same techniques when working with the System.Data.OleDb namespace as well.

Getting Started with ADO.NET

Now that you've seen the objects provided by the ADO.NET namespaces and classes, you might want to see some simple code that uses these objects. The next two subsections introduce two examples that take advantage of ADO.NET. Don't worry about the details at this point—you'll build several pages using ADO.NET and data access throughout the rest of this book. For now, just take a look at how the various ADO.NET objects work together to accomplish data-access goals.

Using a DataAdapter to Fill a DataSet

If you need to get data into a DataSet, you'll most likely use a DataAdapter object to do the work. You supply the DataAdapter object with the SQL string that describes the data you need, as well as a connection string that describes the connection to the data source. The DataAdapter object provides its Fill method, which you can call in order to add a DataTable to the DataSet, using the SQL string to retrieve the data you need. Listing 10.1 shows how to load a DataSet using the OleDbDataAdapter object.

LISTING 10.1   You Can Fill a DataSet Using a DataAdapter

```
Private Sub DataSetLoad()
  Dim da As OleDb.OleDbDataAdapter
  Dim ds As New DataSet()

  Dim strSQL As String = _
   "SELECT * FROM Products"
  Dim strConn As String = _
   "Provider=sqloledb;Data Source=(local);" & _
   "Initial Catalog=Northwind;User ID=sa"

  ' Create DataAdapter.
  da = New OleDb.OleDbDataAdapter(strSQL, strConn)

  ' Fill the DataSet
  da.Fill(ds, "Products")
```

LISTING 10.1   Continued

```
' Now use the DataSet...
End Sub
```

The code in Listing 10.1 fills a DataSet with all the rows and columns from the Products table in the Northwind sample database from your local SQL Server installation. Once you've filled the DataSet, you could use it in lots of different ways. You could modify its contents or bind it to a DataGrid control, for example. Later chapters show several examples working with data in DataSets.

Using a DataReader Object

If you simply want to iterate through all the rows in some set of data, you're likely to use the DataReader object to retrieve the data for you. In order to create the DataReader, you'll need to first create Connection and Command objects. The Connection object provides properties and methods that allow you to connect to a data source, and the Command object does the work of retrieving the data for you. Before you can retrieve data, you'll need to open the connection and then set up the Command object to use the open connection.

Once you've opened the connection and created a Command object, you can use the ExecuteReader method of the Command object to submit the instructions for retrieving data (the SQL string you've supplied, in this example) on the open connection. This retrieves a server-side, forward-only, read-only cursor. When you first retrieve the DataReader, the current row is a "phantom" row just prior to the first row in the result set. You can use the Read method of the DataReader to move to the next row (the first row), and you can use the Item method to retrieve any column (or columns) you need within the current row. As long as the Read method returns True, you can loop through all the rows in a forward-only fashion. (After you move to a new row, the previous row is no longer available to your code.) Once the Read method returns False, you know there aren't any more rows, and your loop ends. The example in Listing 10.2 loops through a DataReader object and adds the values in the ProductName column from the Northwind Products table to a ListBox control on a page. (There are better ways to accomplish this goal, as you'll see in later chapters.)

LISTING 10.2   You Use Command and Connection Objects to Create a DataReader Object

```
Private Sub DataReaderList()
    Dim cmd As OleDb.OleDbCommand
    Dim dr As OleDb.OleDbDataReader
    Dim cnn As OleDb.OleDbConnection
```

LISTING 10.2   Continued

```
Dim strSQL As String = _
 "SELECT ProductName FROM Products"
Dim strConn As String = _
 "Provider=sqloledb;Data Source=(local);" & _
 "Initial Catalog=Northwind;User ID=sa"

 ' Create Command and Connection Objects
 cnn = New OleDb.OleDbConnection(strConn)
 cnn.Open()

 ' Create the Command, and retrieve the DataReader.
 cmd = New OleDb.OleDbCommand(strSQL, cnn)
 dr = cmd.ExecuteReader()

 ' Loop through DataReader
 Do While dr.Read
   lstProducts.Items.Add(dr.Item("ProductName"))
 Loop

 ' Close DataReader and Connection.
 dr.Close()
 cnn.Close()
End Sub
```

Benefits of ADO.NET

You may wonder why Microsoft felt it necessary to start over again, putting ADO "out to pasture" and moving on to ADO.NET. Wasn't ADO good enough? It isn't that ADO was not good enough; rather, developer's needs have changed.

The biggest difference between ADO.NET and ADO is that ADO.NET was constructed, from the ground up, to support disconnected manipulation of data. With ADO.NET, you read through the data using a forward-only, read-only stream. If you need to work with a set of data, you retrieve a cached version of the data you need, work with it in a disconnected environment, and then send updates back when you're done.

Certainly, ADO's connected model requires less thought on the part of the developer. You connect to data, do your work, and disconnect when you're done. It may take a while to "get the hang" of the new object model and how it all fits together. However, we've been convinced, and we hope that over the course of the next few chapters you buy into it as well.

The following list describes some of the areas where ADO.NET excels over ADO:

- **Performance.** ADO.NET uses a disconnected architecture, allowing static data to be stored in memory and requiring fewer roundtrips to the database. (Of course, ADO supported disconnected recordsets as well, but the support was limited, and this wasn't the way most developers used ADO.) In addition, COM developers always had to pay the price of marshalling ADO recordsets from tier to tier in a multitiered application. In ADO.NET, data is normally transported as XML, thus reducing the need for translations.

- **Scalability.** A disconnected scenario is often superior, in terms of scalability, because you never have users maintaining lengthy connections to the database and using up valuable resources. Instead of tying up database connections and locks, ADO.NET clients retrieve the data, disconnect, and release their resources.

- **Interoperability.** ADO.NET transports data as XML. This means that it is easy to pass data from one component to another, because XML is pure text. Components can be on the same machine, different machines, or separated by the Internet, and they can even be on different operating systems. This makes interoperating between these various components easy and flexible. XML is supported by every modern operating system and platform, and even non-.NET clients can consume the data provided by ADO.NET.

- **Programmability.** Visual Studio .NET provides tools to create classes that "wrap up" DataSets, providing methods and properties for working with a specific schema. These classes, named *typed DataSets*, make it easier to interact programmatically with the DataSet. If you choose to use typed DataSets, you get extra design-time benefits. Typed DataSets provide strong data typing when working with columns within your DataSets. In addition, they also provide properties that represent the columns within your data.

  For example, if you had created a DataSet containing a DataTable named Customers and you wanted to retrieve the AvailableCredit column from row 3, you might write code like this:

  ```
  credit = _
    ds.Tables("Customers").Rows(3)("AvailableCredit")
  ```

  Using a typed DataSet, you could rewrite the same code as this:

  ```
  credit = ds.Customers(3).AvailableCredit
  ```

The code for the typed DataSet is both easier to read and easier to write, because Visual Studio can provide IntelliSense as you enter column names. The code for the typed DataSet is safer, as well, because it provides for compile-time checking of types. For example, suppose that AvailableCredit is a `Decimal` type. If the programmer erroneously assigns the AvailableCredit column to a `String` variable, Visual Studio .NET would report the error to the programmer at compile time. When working with a standard DataSet, the programmer wouldn't learn of the error until runtime.

TIP

When you work with a typed DataSet, you're creating an instance of a particular class that inherits from the `DataSet` object. This class provides properties that have the same name as the columns within the underlying DataSet, and these properties supply the data you're working with. When you refer to a column, such as `ds.Customers`, you're actually referring to a property of the typed `DataSet` class, not a real column within the DataSet. It's a subtle distinction, but it's important to understand that you're interacting with a class that Visual Studio .NET generated for you, not with the actual DataSet itself. All the source code is available—there's no hidden magic. You can investigate and study the typed DataSet source code that's available as part of your project once you create the class.

Summary

Ostensibly, ADO.NET and ADO provide similar functionality: Each provides an object model for retrieving and manipulating data. In addition, the object models provide some similar objects: `Connection`, `Command`, and `DataSet` objects, for example. Under the covers, however, the two object models are really quite different, with ADO.NET directly focused on creating distributed, multitier applications.

In this chapter, you were introduced to the following subjects:

- The many different ADO.NET classes

- Namespaces used to work with data from data sources

- Examples of how to use some of the ADO.NET classes

- The benefits of using ADO.NET

11

Data Binding on Web Forms

Although you could write all the code necessary to open a data source, retrieve the data, and fill in controls on an ASPX page, you needn't do this. Web Forms can use ADO.NET under the covers to handle all the "plumbing" for you. Using data binding, you do not need to explicitly write the code that instantiates a connection and creates a DataSet (as you would if you were creating an unbound form). Visual Studio .NET includes tools to create the necessary Connection and Command objects for you, and ASP.NET controls include code that allows them to bind to these data objects with very little code. Web Forms allow you to bind easily to almost any structure that contains data. You can bind Web Forms to traditional data stores, such as data stored in a Microsoft SQL Server or Oracle database, or you can bind to the result of data read from text files, data within other controls, or data stored in an array. In this chapter, you will learn to bind to a SQL Server table.

You're most likely going to want to be able to bind the DataGrid, ListBox, and DropDownList controls to data sources. We'll focus on these controls, then, in this chapter, and show how you can display data from a SQL Server table in each of these controls.

Creating a Sample Page

The simplest way to get started with data binding is to display the contents of a single table in a DataGrid control. As you'll see, this requires very little effort on your part, at least, if your only goal is to simply display the data.

(Adding, editing, and deleting data require a bit more effort, and these topics are covered in Chapter 17, "Editing Data Using the DataGrid Control.")

To get started, in this section you'll walk through building the sample page shown in Figure 11.1.

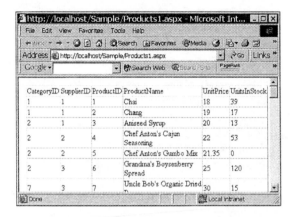

FIGURE 11.1   You'll build this page in the first part of this chapter.

The example involves these basic steps (all described in detail in the following sections):

- Building a Web Form.
- Creating and configuring the DataSet to which you wish to bind a control on the form.
- Adding a DataGrid control to the page.
- Binding the DataGrid control to the data source.

Before digging into the details of setting up the bound DataGrid control, you'll need to add a new page to your project. Follow these steps to add the new page:

1. Select Project, Add Web Form from the menu bar.

2. Set the name of this form to Products.aspx.

3. Click Open to add this new Web Form to your project.

Creating and Configuring a DataSet

Once you've created the Products page, you're ready to create and configure the DataSet you'll use on this page. In this example, you'll retrieve data from the

Products table that's part of SQL Server's Northwind sample database. Because a DataSet is an in-memory cache consisting of tables, relations, and constraints, it acts as an "in-memory" database, and you'll bind controls on your page to DataSet objects. You need to start by filling a DataSet using a DataAdapter object.

NOTE

Although we had a choice, when designing the examples in this chapter (and throughout the book) of using either the System.Data.OleDb or System.Data.SqlClient namespaces, we opted for the OleDb namespace because of its flexibility. That is, had we chosen the SqlClient namespace, and then you decided to modify the examples to work with a DB2 database back end, you would have to modify every object in every example. Using the OleDb namespace, all you need to do is modify the connection information and field names. It was a difficult choice, and if you're only working with SQL Server 7.0 or higher, it's not the correct one for you. For this book, however, this choice provides for simpler modifications. Note that we'll often refer to namespace-specific objects (such as the OleDbDataAdapter object) using namespace-agnostic names, such as DataAdapter. There isn't a DataAdapter object out there, but referring to it generically sure beats saying OleDbDataAdapter or SqlDataAdapter each time! If you have time, it would be a worthwhile exercise to try repeating the page created in this chapter using the SqlClient namespace. The issues aren't very different, and you should be able to take the same steps using the different namespace.

Using the Data Adapter Configuration Wizard

The first step in retrieving data is to create a Connection object that contains information on the location and type of your data source. Although you can write code to handle this task, for the purposes of this chapter, you'll use the user-interface tools provided by Visual Studio .NET to create the necessary connection. To do that, you'll use the OleDbDataAdapter component on the Data tab of the Toolbox. Once you've placed this component on your page, Visual Studio .NET walks you through the steps of supplying connection information and building a SELECT command to retrieve the data you need. Once you've built the DataAdapter, you'll still need to write a tiny bit of code to fill a DataSet and bind a grid to the DataSet.

TIP

You could write code that solves all the tasks in this chapter. To keep things simple, however, in this first exploration of ADO.NET, we've elected to use the tools provided by Visual Studio .NET. That way, you don't need to write much code. Later chapters work through the details of creating Connection objects, DataAdapter objects, and so on, all using Visual Basic .NET code.

Follow these steps to set up the OleDbDataAdapter object on your new page:

1. Make sure the Toolbox window is visible (select View, Toolbox, if it's not).

2. Select the Data tab on the Toolbox window.

3. Click and drag the OleDbDataAdapter component onto your page. This starts the Data Adapter Configuration Wizard.

4. The first page of the wizard, shown in Figure 11.2, gives you basic information. Select Next to move on.

FIGURE 11.2   The first page of the Data Adapter Configuration Wizard gives you basic information about what's going to happen.

5. On the Choose Your Data Connection page, shown in Figure 11.3, you have the option to use an existing connection or to create a new one. Because you're unlikely to have an existing connection at this point, select New Connection to create a new one. (Even if you have existing connections, follow along with creating a new one, for now.)

6. Clicking New Connection brings up the Data Link Properties dialog box. (This should be a familiar sight to anyone who has used ADO and OLE DB in the past.) Assuming that you can use the Northwind SQL Server sample database on your local computer, log in as "sa" with no password (not a good idea, in general) and fill in the dialog box as shown in Figure 11.4. Click OK when you're done to dismiss the dialog box; then click Next to move to the next page.

NOTE

If you can't connect to the Northwind SQL Server sample database, you may need to talk with a network administrator, who can supply information about how to connect to the sample database.

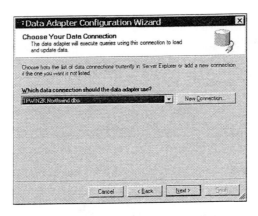

FIGURE 11.3   Choose your data connection.

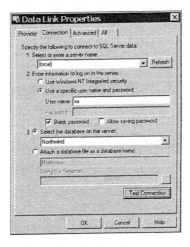

FIGURE 11.4   Supply data link properties.

7. The Choose a Query Type page, shown in Figure 11.5, allows you to designate the type of query you want to use when the DataAdapter fills a DataSet. Select Use SQL Statements (in order to have the wizard create local SQL statements, as opposed to using existing or new stored procedures) and click Next.

8. On the Generate the SQL Statements page, you must either enter a SQL statement manually or click Query Builder to use a visual tool to create the query. In this simple example, it's easy enough to simply type in the required SQL. Enter the following text into the text box, so that the page looks like Figure 11.6:

```
SELECT CategoryID, SupplierID, ProductID, ProductName,
UnitPrice, UnitsInStock
FROM Products
```

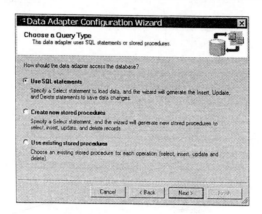

FIGURE 11.5   Designate the type of query the wizard should use.

FIGURE 11.6   Enter a SQL expression to be used by the `DataAdapter`.

9. Click Next to proceed to the final page. Then click Finish to complete the process. Notice that `OleDbConnection` and `OleDbDataAdapter` objects named `OleDbConnection1` and `OleDbDataAdapter1` appear in the tray area of the form.

10. Select `OleDbConnection1` and, in the Properties window, set the `Name` property to `cnNorthwind`.

11. Select `OleDbDataAdapter1` and, in the Properties window, set the `Name` property to `daProducts`.

At this point, the cnNorthwind object contains information about how to access the selected database. The daProducts object contains a query defining the tables and columns in the database that you want to access. You'll use both those objects in order to retrieve the data you need.

> **TIP**
>
> If you'd rather use the slightly more efficient SqlClient namespace objects, you can follow the same steps listed here, using the SqlConnection and SqlDataAdapter objects. The steps are identical, although you may need to modify the code later on in order to complete the chapter.

Retrieving Data

You can't bind controls to a DataAdapter object because a DataAdapter object doesn't contain any data—you need a DataSet to bind data to controls. At this point, you have two choices: You can have Visual Studio .NET generate a typed DataSet for you, or you can write code to create a standard DataSet yourself. For the purposes of this chapter, it doesn't matter which technique you choose—the code you have to write is similar in either case. If you're going to interact programmatically with the DataSet or want the extra functionality provided by the typed DataSet, you might go that route. If you simply want to get the DataGrid filled with data, you might want to create the DataSet yourself. In this section, we'll use a typed DataSet. When it comes time to bind a DropDownList control, you'll write all the code yourself—that is, bind to data without using the design-time components provided by Visual Studio .NET.

Using a Typed DataSet

In order to generate the typed DataSet, follow these steps:

1. Select Data, Generate DataSet to display the Generate DataSet dialog box.

2. Select the New radio button. Next to the New radio button, enter **dsProducts** as the name for your DataSet, as shown in Figure 11.7.

3. Click OK to dismiss the dialog box and generate the DataSet schema definition and class files.

4. After this step completes, you will see a new component, DsProducts1, in the tray area for the page. This new component represents the schema definition file, dsProducts.xsd, that Visual Studio .NET added to your project. This file contains the complete definition for the table and columns of the SQL statement you entered earlier, described as an XML Schema Definition (or XSD) file. Visual Studio .NET also provides a code-behind file for this schema. You won't see the code-behind file unless you select Project, Show All Files.

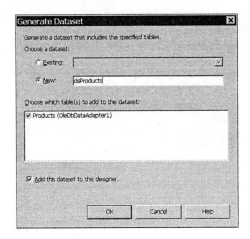

FIGURE 11.7   The Generate DataSet dialog box allows you to specify the name for the DataSet you're generating.

5. Once you've shown all files, you can expand the `dsProducts.xsd` node to see the `dsProducts.vb` file, as shown in Figure 11.8. The `dsProducts.vb` file contains a class that "wraps up" the behavior of the DataSet, providing an object that inherits from the standard `DataSet` class, adding properties that map to the columns from the underlying table and methods that allow you to work with the data.

FIGURE 11.8   An XML Schema Definition (XSD) file has a class module that contains the code that loads the DataSet into memory.

> **TIP**
>
> You won't use any of the features of the typed DataSet in this chapter, although it's nice to know how easy it is to create the class, should you ever need the functionality.

Displaying Your Data

Everything you've done so far is invisible at runtime. You've set up a `DataAdapter` object, a `Connection` object, and a `DataSet` object, but you can't see any of these things. In order to actually see the data you're working with, you'll need to add controls to the page. ASP.NET makes this simple.

Adding the Grid

Now that you've set up all the data-handling components, it's time to add the DataGrid control to the page and hook it up. Follow these steps to display the data retrieved by the DataAdapter in a grid:

1. In the Solution Explorer window, select Products.aspx and select View, Designer (or simply double-click) to view the page in the designer.

2. From the Web Forms tag of the Toolbox window, drag a DataGrid control from the Toolbox window onto the page.

3. Set properties for the grid as shown in Table 11.1.

TABLE 11.1   Set These Properties for the Sample Grid

Property	Value	Description
ID	grdProducts	You're going to need to interact with this control programmatically, so you should set its name to something that indicates its purpose.
DataSource	dsProducts1	The DataSource property of the grid indicates where it should look in order to retrieve its data.
DataMember	Products	The DataMember property of the grid allows you to specify which table within the data source to use to fill the grid. In this case, there's only one table in there, so you don't really have to specify this value. There may be multiple tables in the DataSet, however, and in that case, you'd need to indicate the specific table you want to use. (Note that the programmer filling the DataSet specifies the table name—this normally isn't tied directly to the name of the table from which the data was retrieved. In this case, the wizard set the name for you. You simply choose the name from the list provided in the Properties window.)

4. In the Solution Explorer, right-click the Products.aspx page, select Build and Browse from the context menu, and load the page. (You expect to see data, don't you?)

As you can see, setting the DataGrid control's properties isn't all you need to do. It takes a few lines of code to fill the DataSet and bind the grid. The next section walks you through the final steps necessary to display data in the grid.

NOTE

The DataGrid control, as you're using it here, isn't terribly attractive. If you want to make it look "prettier," right-click the control and select Auto Format from the context menu. You're on your own, for now. You'll find information on formatting the DataGrid control in Chapter 16, "Using the DataGrid Control."

Populating the DataGrid with Data

Although you've set properties that would appear to bind the DataGrid control to a DataSet, the page doesn't automatically populate the DataSet when you load the page. You'll need to use the page's Page_Load event procedure to populate the DataGrid control with data as the page is loaded.

To display the data in the grid, follow these steps:

1. If the page is still loaded in a browser window, close the browser window.

2. Back in the page designer, double-click the page (not on a specific control) to load the code-behind file, which is ready for you to enter the contents of the Page_Load procedure.

3. Modify the Page_Load procedure so that it looks like this:

```
Private Sub Page_Load( _
 ByVal sender As System.Object, _
 ByVal e As System.EventArgs) _
 Handles MyBase.Load

  daProducts.Fill(DsProducts1)
  grdProducts.DataBind()
End Sub
```

TIP

The Fill method of the DataAdapter object accepts a DataSet or DataTable object as its parameter, and it fills its parameter with data. The DataBind method of the DataGrid object tells the control to bind itself to its data source, effectively filling the grid from the DataSet you specified as its data source.

4. In the Solution Explorer window, right-click the sample page, select Build and Browse from the context menu, and verify that the page looks like Figure 11.1. You've now managed to load the data from the SQL Server table using only two lines of code!

Filling a DropDownList Control with Data

Using the design-time components that create `Connection`, `DataAdapter`, and `DataSet` objects is fine, but it is hard to see everything that is going on behind the scenes. In fact, the wizards actually build a complete class that handles adding, editing, deleting, and retrieving data. This is generally overkill when all you need to do is load a list full of data. In these cases, it may make more sense to write the code yourself.

Extending the example you built in the first half of this chapter, in this second part, you'll add a drop-down list of available categories and filter the displayed products based on the category you select. In this case, you'll write all the code required to bind the DropDownList control to a DataSet, instead of using the design-time components.

TIP

Once you've worked through this section, you may find it useful to go back and revise the previous example so that it uses a similar technique—that is, modify the example so that you fill the DataGrid control by hand, as well.

Follow these steps to set up the DropDownList control:

1. With the `Products.aspx` page open in the designer, add a Label control and a DropDownList control to the page. Modify the properties of the controls as shown in Table 11.2. When you're done, the page should look like Figure 11.9.

TABLE 11.2 Set Properties of the Controls Using These Values

Control	Property	Value
Label1	`Text`	Categories
DropDownList1	`ID`	ddlCategories
	AutoPostBack	True

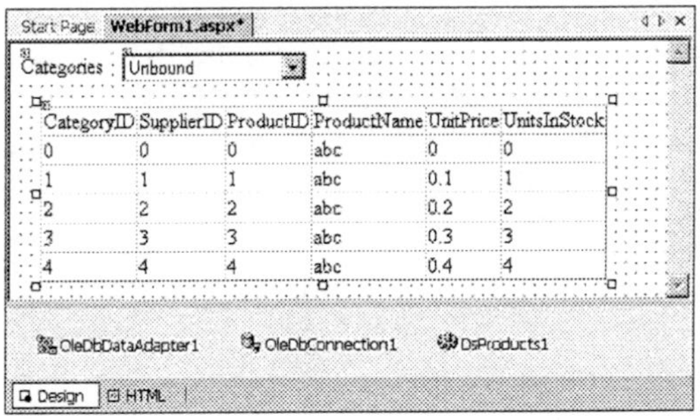

FIGURE 11.9 How the finished page should look in Design view.

2. Select View, Code to load the code-behind file in the code editor and then find the Page_Load procedure. Modify the Page_Load procedure so that it looks like this:

```
Private Sub Page_Load( _
 ByVal sender As System.Object, _
 ByVal e As System.EventArgs) _
 Handles MyBase.Load

   If Not Page.IsPostBack Then
     CategoryLoad()
   End If
End Sub
```

3. Add the following statement at the very top of the code-behind file (adding this allows you to refer to classes within the OleDb namespace without having to explicitly include the OleDb name each time):

```
Imports System.Data.OleDb
```

4. Add the procedure in Listing 11.1 below the Page_Load procedure (but above the End Class statement).

LISTING 11.1   Load the Category Drop-Down List with Category Information

```
Private Sub CategoryLoad()
  Dim ds As DataSet
  Dim da As OleDbDataAdapter

  Dim strSQL As String = _
   "SELECT CategoryID, CategoryName " & _
   "FROM Categories"

  ds = New DataSet()
  da = New OleDbDataAdapter(strSQL, cnNorthwind)
  da.Fill(ds)

  With ddlCategories
    .DataTextField = "CategoryName"
    .DataValueField = "CategoryID"
    .DataSource = ds
    .DataBind()
  End With
End Sub
```

5. In the Solution Explorer window, right-click Products.aspx and select Build and Browse from the context menu. The page should contain a drop-down list containing all the available categories. (Of course, you're no longer filling the grid—that comes back in the next section.)

Before going further, you should investigate what happened in the CategoryLoad procedure. This procedure first declares the two ADO.NET variables it will need— DataSet and OleDbDataAdapter:

```
Dim ds As DataSet
Dim da As OleDbDataAdapter
```

The code then creates the SQL string it will need in order to retrieve just the columns it requires for the drop-down list:

```
Dim strSQL As String = _
 "SELECT CategoryID, CategoryName " & _
 "FROM Categories"
```

> **TIP**
>
> Although Visual Basic .NET allows you to initialize variables on the same line of code on which they're declared, we generally shy away from this technique. There is a good reason for not doing this: error handling. If an error could occur as you're declaring the variable, you'll need to place the declaration in a `Try`/`End Try` block. But placing the declaration in a `Try`/`End Try` block scopes the variable so that it's only available within that block—it's not even available in the `Catch` block! This makes it impossible to use the variable throughout the procedure, so we tend to declare the variable outside the error-handling block and supply its value within the error handling. Our rule of thumb: We only take advantage of this new feature for assigning constant values, where it's not possible that a runtime error could occur. This is just a personal preference, and you may do what you like. However, that's the style you'll see throughout this book.

The code then instantiates the `DataAdapter` object, passing in a SQL string (which supplies the `SELECT` command for this `DataAdapter` object) and an `OleDbConnection` object, supplied at design time on the form. Next, the code calls the `Fill` method of the `DataAdapter` object, filling the data in the DataSet:

```
ds = New DataSet()
da = New OleDbDataAdapter(strSQL, cnNorthwind)
da.Fill(ds)
```

We had a number of options in the preceding code fragment. We could have created a new `OleDbConnection` object and supplied the connection information in the code. Because we had the available connection object already created, there didn't seem much sense in doing that. We had no command information (that is, information on retrieving the data) already prepared, so this example sets up its own SQL string and its own `OleDbDataAdapter` object.

Finally, the code sets up the DropDownList control so that it fills itself with data. This requires setting three properties and calling a method:

```
With ddlCategories
  .DataTextField = "CategoryName"
  .DataValueField = "CategoryID"
  .DataSource = ds
  .DataBind()
End With
```

The `DataTextField` property contains the name of the field from the data source that provides the content to be displayed within the drop-down portion of the control. This is the information you see on the screen. The `DataValueField` property contains the name of the field from the data source that provides the value of each list item. Although this could be the same field as the `DataTextField` property, most of time it won't be. Most often, you want to display one item but have the option of retrieving a different value when the user makes a choice. In this case, you're displaying the category name and retrieving the category ID when the user selects a category. You must set the `DataSource` property, telling the control which DataSet or DataTable it should use to provide its data. Finally, when you're ready to display the data, call the `DataBind` method, which binds the control to its data source.

It's interesting to see the HTML created by the .NET page framework. If you view the page in a browser and then right-click and select the View Source option, you'll see code like Listing 11.2 for the drop-down list control (we've removed extraneous attributes).

LISTING 11.2   In the Browser, You'll See HTML Like This, Rendered by ASP.NET

```
<select name="ddlCategories">
  <option value="1">Beverages</option>
  <option value="2">Condiments</option>
  <option value="3">Confections</option>
  <option value="4">Dairy Products</option>
  <option value="5">Grains/Cereals</option>
  <option value="6">Meat/Poultry</option>
  <option value="7">Produce</option>
  <option value="8">Seafood</option>
</select>
```

As you can see, the page framework retrieved the `CategoryName` field and set it as the displayed text of each list item and set the `CategoryID` field as the value for each item.

Using the DropDownList Control to Filter by Categories

As the final step in this demonstration, you need to hook up the code that will display a list of products within the selected category. To do that, follow these steps:

1. Make sure you've closed any browser windows displaying `Products.aspx`.

2. In the page designer, double-click the DropDownList control, loading the code editor with the `ddlCategories_SelectedIndexChanged` procedure selected.

3. Modify the procedure so that it looks like this:

```
Private Sub ddlCategories_SelectedIndexChanged( _
  ByVal sender As System.Object, _
  ByVal e As System.EventArgs) _
```

```
    Handles ddlCategories.SelectedIndexChanged
      ProductsLoad
    End Sub
```

4. Add the code in Listing 11.3 to the page's class:

LISTING 11.3   Filter the DataGrid Control Based on the Selected Category

```
Private Sub ProductsLoad()
  Dim ds As DataSet
  Dim strSQL As String

  strSQL = daProducts.SelectCommand.CommandText & _
    " WHERE CategoryID = " & _
    ddlCategories.SelectedItem.Value

  ds = New DataSet()

  With daProducts
    .SelectCommand.CommandText = strSQL
    .Fill(ds)
  End With

  With grdProducts
    .DataSource = ds
    .DataBind()
  End With
End Sub
```

5. Modify the Page_Load procedure once again, adding a call to the ProductsLoad procedure:

```
Private Sub Page_Load( _
  ByVal sender As System.Object, _
  ByVal e As System.EventArgs) _
  Handles MyBase.Load

  If Not Page.IsPostBack Then
    CategoryLoad()
    ProductsLoad()
```

```
   End If
End Sub
```

6. In the page designer, select the DataGrid control. In the Properties window, remove the text from the `DataSource` and `DataMember` properties—because you're setting the `DataSource` property in code, you don't need these values.

7. Build and browse the page once again. This time, you should be able to select a category from the drop-down list and see the associated products displayed in the grid.

8. When you're done, close the browser window and save your project.

The code in the `ProductsLoad` procedure does the work of loading the grid with products from the selected category. It starts by retrieving the SQL string from the `DataAdapter` object you set up on the page, in the first half of the chapter. The code uses the `CommandText` property of the `SelectCommand` property and then concatenates a `WHERE` clause to the SQL:

```
strSQL = daProducts.SelectCommand.CommandText & _
  " WHERE CategoryID = " & _
  ddlCategories.SelectedItem.Value
```

This new SQL expression pulls in all the fields you set up originally but limits the rows to only those whose `CategoryID` field matches the selected item in the drop-down list.

The code then instantiates a new `DataSet` object, resets the `CommandText` property of the DataAdapter's `SelectCommand` object, and fills the DataSet with the newly filtered rows:

```
ds = New DataSet()

With daProducts
  .SelectCommand.CommandText = strSQL
  .Fill(ds)
End With
```

The code finishes up by setting the DataGrid control's `DataSource` property to be the new DataSet (instead of `dsProducts1`, which it used in the earlier example), and then binds the grid to its new data source.

Summary

In this chapter, you got a good start working with data and data binding in ASP.NET. Specifically, here's what you accomplished:

- You created a `Connection` object that contains information on the location and type of data.

- You created a `DataAdapter` object that handles retrieving the data using the `Connection` object.

- You generated a typed `DataSet`, a class that handles providing the data to data-bound controls.

- You bound a DataGrid control to the typed `DataSet`, displaying data on the page.

- You added a bound DropDownList control and filtered the data in the DataGrid based on the selection in the drop-down list.

- Although you didn't investigate creating `OleDbConnection` objects in this chapter, you'll see how you can do all the work without any of the design-time components in Chapter 13, "ADO.NET `Connection` and `Command` Objects."

12

Error Handling

The .NET Framework provides structured exception handling using the `Try`, `Catch`, `Finally`, and `Throw` keywords in VB .NET. This type of error handling has been available, in some fashion, in C++ for a number of years. With the release of the .NET Common Language Runtime (CLR), this type of error handling is available to all the .NET languages, including VB .NET.

The Promise of Structured Exception Handling

Many ASP.NET developers using VB .NET will be coming to this environment with some VB6, VBA, or VBScript development experience. Although Visual Basic in its various "flavors" has supported its own mechanism for handling errors for as long as "Visual" has been attached to the title, the techniques available to VB developers have never seemed fully fleshed out. In planning for exception handling in .NET, it's useful to contrast the new features with those many developing in ASP.NET are accustomed to using. (Listing 12.1 demonstrates a simple VB6 procedure with standard error-handling code in place.) Several issues surrounding VB's error handling have caused much complaining among VB developers, both experienced and novice:

OBJECTIVES

- Compare error handling in Visual Basic .NET to that found in VB6

- Learn to use `Try`/`Catch` blocks to handle runtime errors

- Find out how to use `Exception` objects to determine what error has occurred

- See how to throw exceptions back to procedure callers

- VB6 requires you to jump around within procedures in order to handle errors. The On Error Goto, Resume, and Resume Next statements all involve jumping either forward or backward in code. The standard VB6 error-handling techniques involve at least two jumps within a procedure (one forward to the error-handling block, and a second back to a common procedure exit point).

- If you follow good programming practices in VB6, including ensuring that your procedures have only a single exit point, the most convenient place to put that exit point is in the middle of your procedures (before the error-handling block). It is all too easy to forget the important Exit Sub or Exit Function.

- VB6 provides no way to "push" and "pop" error handlers. If you want to preserve the current error trap, set up a different one, and later return back to the first, you must remember to include the correct On Error Goto… statement every time you want to change handlers.

- VB6 includes only a single Err object. If an error occurs and you don't handle it immediately, you may permanently lose the error information before you get a chance to handle the error.

- VB6's documentation includes almost no coverage of the types of errors (that is, the error numbers) you might receive due to an action you've taken in your code. Your only recourse is to experiment, see what error numbers you can generate by triggering errors while testing, and then trap those specific errors in your code.

LISTING 12.1   Error Handling in VB6 Required at Least One Jump, and Often More

```
Sub TestVB6()
    On Error GoTo HandleErrors

    ' Do something in here that
    ' might raise an error.

ExitHere:
    ' Perform cleanup code here.
    ' Disregard errors in this
    ' cleanup code.
    On Error Resume Next
    ' Perform cleanup code.
```

LISTING 12.1   Continued

```
    Exit Sub

HandleErrors:
    Select Case Err.Number
        ' Add cases for each
        ' error number you want to trap.
        Case Else
            ' Add "last-ditch" error handler.
            MsgBox "Error: " & Err.Description
    End Select
    Resume ExitHere
End Sub
```

In addition, although VB developers are perfectly capable of using the `Err.Raise` method to raise errors back to calling procedures, this technique has never become a standard. Many developers creating code that is called by others simply return an error value to indicate success or failure, instead of raising an error upon failure. Because it's possible (and easy) to simply disregard error values returned from procedures you call, in too many cases, code that fails for any reason at runtime never raises the appropriate errors back to its callers.

Structured exception handling is a standard technique of managing faults that occur within applications. In general, this technique allows you to create blocks of code that work together to manage runtime error trapping, error detection, and error propagation within applications. With the addition of structured exception handling in VB .NET, it's easier for developers to manage error notification, raise errors, and determine the cause of a runtime error. Structured exception handling provides several advantages over the previous error-handling techniques used in VB6:

- Error handling in .NET is based on the `Exception` class, which means you can obtain from it information about the current error as well as a linked list of errors that may have triggered it.

- You can inherit from the `Exception` class, creating your own exceptions that have the same functionality as the base class, or extended functionality, as necessary. Because your code can trap for specific exceptions, creating your own exception class gives you a lot of flexibility.

- Because every class in the .NET Framework throws exceptions when it encounters runtime errors, developers will get in the habit of trapping for exceptions and handling them. This makes it more likely that exceptions you throw from within your components will be successfully handled.

- You can nest Try/Catch blocks within the Try, Catch, and Finally blocks. This gives you the capability of managing exception handling to any level of granularity that you require.

Listing 12.2 shows the layout of a simple exception handler in VB .NET. The following sections describe, in detail, how to use each of the keywords shown in Listing 12.2, and how to make use of the Exception class in tracking and raising errors.

LISTING 12.2   Error Handling in VB .NET Doesn't Require Jumping Around

```
Sub TestVBNET()
  Try
    ' Do something in here that
    ' might raise an error.
  Catch
    ' Handle exceptions that occur within
    ' the Try block, here.
  Finally
    ' Perform cleanup code in here.
  End Try
End Sub
```

TIP

You can mix old-style VB6 error handling with .NET structured exception handling in the same project, but not within the same procedure. On Error and Try can't exist within the same procedure.

Using Exception Handling

The following sections work through a series of examples, adding increasingly complex error-handling features to the sample code you've seen already. Starting with a scenario in which you've added no exception handling code at all, these examples introduce the concepts of trapping and identifying exceptions.

TIP

We'll use the terms *exception handling* and *error handling* to mean the same thing—that is, code you add to a procedure so that it can manage runtime errors as they occur.

All the examples use the same basic premise: Your goal is to open a file, retrieve its length, and then close the file. Each example uses this code to do its job, retrieving the filename from a text box (txtFileName) on the sample form named Errors.aspx:

```
Dim lngSize As Long
Dim s As FileStream

s = File.Open(txtFileName.Text, FileMode.Open)
lngSize = s.Length
s.Close()
```

Of course, it's possible (for many reasons) that the code might fail. For example, the code will raise an exception if any of the following are true:

- The file isn't found.

- The path doesn't exist.

- The drive containing the file isn't ready (perhaps you've requested the size of a file on a floppy drive that doesn't contain media).

- You don't have permissions to access the file or folder.

- You've specified an invalid filename.

The list could go on and on. All the following examples use some variation of this code in order to demonstrate features of structured exception handling.

NOTE

In order to follow along with the discussion in this chapter, you'll need to open the sample project, Jumpstart\ErrorHandling\ErrorHandling.sln.

The sample application corresponding to this material, ErrorHandling.sln, includes a Web Form, Errors.aspx, that allows you to try out the various techniques described here (see Figure 12.1). For each case, try entering the path to a file that doesn't exist, a drive that doesn't exist, a drive that doesn't contain any media, or any other path that might trigger a file system error.

The Base Case: No Error Handling at All

What happens if your code includes no exception handling at all? In that case, any errors that occur at runtime bubble back up to the .NET runtime, and the runtime will greet your users with a confusing and hard-to-read Web page, as shown in Figure 12.2. In order to avoid this page, should a runtime error occur, you'll need to add exception handling to at least your top-level procedures and to lower-level procedures as necessary.

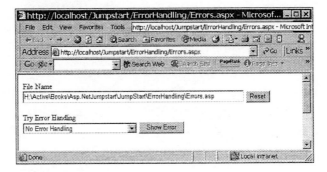

FIGURE 12.1   Use this sample Web Form to demonstrate all the different features discussed in this chapter.

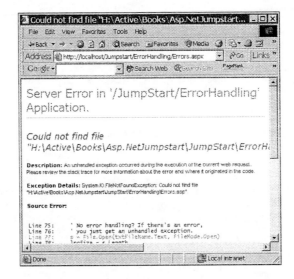

FIGURE 12.2   Although this Web page may make sense to a programmer, an end user should never see it.

TIP

Just as in VB6, if you don't add exception handling to a procedure, and an error occurs within that procedure, the .NET runtime will pop the current procedure off the call stack and will return to the previous procedure. If that procedure includes error handling, the runtime will use that code. If not, the runtime continues to pop procedures off the stack until it backs out to a procedure that does include error handling. If no procedures include error handling, all the way back to the first-called procedure, the .NET runtime handles the error itself, as you saw in Figure 12.2.

Adding a Simple Try/Catch Block

In order to gracefully handle runtime errors, add a Try/Catch/End Try block around any code that you want to protect. If a runtime error occurs in the code within the Try block, execution will immediately continue with the code within the Catch block, as demonstrated in Listing 12.3.

LISTING 12.3 The Simplest Structured Exception Handling Includes Try and Catch Blocks

```
Private Sub SimpleCatch()
    Dim lngSize As Long
    Dim s As FileStream

    ' This is better, but not much. You
    ' don't really have any idea what
    ' went wrong!
    Try
        s = File.Open(txtFileName.Text, FileMode.Open)
        lngSize = s.Length
        s.Close()
    Catch
        lblError.Text = "Error occurred!"
    End Try
End Sub
```

When this code runs, rather than the application displaying the error page and halting, you'll see a simple "Error occurred" message appear in a label control on the page. To test this yourself, choose the Simple Catch option in the Error Handling combo box on the sample form.

TIP

If you add a Try/End Try block to your procedure, you'll need to include at least a single Catch block (you'll find more on including multiple Catch blocks later). If you want to disregard errors that occur, simply put nothing at all in the Catch block. This isn't a great idea, because simply disregarding errors can hide serious flaws in your application, but it will quietly disregard any errors that occur.

Determining What Happened

Once a runtime error occurs, how can you determine what error it is and how to deal with it? You can create a variable, declared As Exception, to retrieve error information for you. The Exception class provides information about the runtime error, as shown in Table 12.1.

TABLE 12.1   Useful Members of the Exception Class

Member	Description
HelpLink	Links to the help file associated with this exception.
InnerException	References the inner exception (the exception that originally occurred) if this exception is based on a previous exception. Exceptions can be nested. That is, when a procedure throws an exception, it can nest another exception inside the exception it's raising, passing both exceptions out to the caller. The InnerException property gives access to the inner exception.
Message	Error message text.
StackTrace	The stack trace, returned to you as a single string containing all the information about how you got to where you are in the code, at the point the error occurred.
TargetSite	The name of the method that raised the exception.
ToString	Converts the exception name, description, and the current stack dump into a single string.
Message	Returns a description of the error that occurred.

The Catch block includes the reference to the variable, like this:

```
Try
    ' Code that might trigger an exception.
Catch exp As Exception
    ' Handle the exception, using exp, in here.
End Try
```

You can also declare the Exception variable outside the Catch block:

```
Dim exp As Exception
Try
```

```
    ' Code that might trigger an exception.
Catch exp
    ' Handle the exception, using exp, in here.
End Try
```

You might use code like what's shown in Listing 12.4 to trap an exception and display text indicating the problem that has occurred.

LISTING 12.4   Use the `ToString` Method of the `Exception` Object to Display Error Information

```
' Simple Exception option on the sample form.
Private Sub SimpleException()
  Dim lngSize As Long
  Dim s As FileStream

  ' Display the entire contents of the Exception object.
  Try
    s = File.Open(txtFileName.Text, FileMode.Open)
    lngSize = s.Length
    s.Close()
  Catch exp As Exception
    Error.Text=exp.ToString
  End Try
End Sub
```

NOTE

The name of the `Exception` variable isn't important. The sample code uses `exp` as the variable name, but that choice was arbitrary. If you find this name inconvenient in your own procedures, you may prefer to choose a different one.

If you simply want to display an error message, indicating the particular error that you've trapped, you can use the `Message` property of the `Exception` class, like this:

```
lblError.Text = e.Message
```

So far, you've seen how to trap an exception when it occurs and how to indicate to the user what went wrong. Most of the time, you'll also need to be able to take distinct action depending on the specific error that occurred. In VB6, this meant adding a `Select Case` block based on the active error number. In VB .NET, this involves adding additional `Catch` blocks for each error you'd like to trap individually. The next section digs into how you can add this functionality to your procedures.

Working with Specific Exceptions

The .NET Framework provides a significant number of specific exception classes, all inheriting from the base Exception class. In the .NET Framework documentation, you'll find tables listing all the possible exceptions that might occur when you call any method. For example, Table 12.2, taken from the .NET Framework documentation, makes it easy to determine what might go wrong when calling the File.Open method.

TABLE 12.2 Exception Types That Can Be Generated When You're Attempting to Open a File

Exception Type	Condition
SecurityException	The caller to this routine does not have sufficient permissions.
ArgumentException	The path is empty, contains invalid characters, or contains only whitespace.
FileNotFoundException	The file cannot be found in the location specified.
ArgumentNullException	The path or mode was not passed.
UnauthorizedAccessException	The path requested is marked as read-only or is only a folder name with no filename.
DirectoryNotFoundException	The requested directory cannot be found.

Your procedures can include as many Catch blocks as necessary in order for you to handle individual exceptions differently. The procedure in Listing 12.5, from the sample project, tests for several different exceptions and handles each individually.

LISTING 12.5 Use Hierarchical Exceptions, Arranged in a Logical Order, to Determine Exactly Which Error Occurred

```
Private Sub MultipleExceptions()
    Dim lngSize As Long
    Dim s As FileStream

    ' Use the most specific exception that you can.
    ' To test this, change the file name to be:

    ' 1.) In a good location, but the file doesn't exist.
    ' 2.) On a drive that doesn't exist.
    ' 3.) In a path that doesn't exist.
    ' 4.) On a drive that isn't ready.

    Try
        s = File.Open(txtFileName.Text, FileMode.Open)
        lngSize = s.Length
        s.Close()
```

LISTING 12.5   Continued

```
            ' The code will match against the most specific
            ' error it can. Both FileNotFoundException and
            ' DirectoryNotFoundException inherit from
            ' IOException, and the code will use those first.
            ' If they weren't here, the code would always fall
            ' into(IOException) for those errors.
        Catch exp As ArgumentException
            lblError.Text = _
            "You specified an invalid filename. " & _
            "Make sure you enter something besides spaces."
        Catch exp As FileNotFoundException
            lblError.Text = _
            "The file you specified can't be found. " & _
            "Please try again."
        Catch exp As ArgumentNullException
            lblError.Text = "You passed in a Null argument."
        Catch exp As UnauthorizedAccessException
            lblError.Text = _
            "You specified a folder name, not a file name."
        Catch exp As DirectoryNotFoundException
            lblError.Text = _
            "You specified a folder that doesn't exist " & _
            "or can't be found."
        Catch exp As SecurityException
            lblError.Text = "You don't have sufficient " & _
            "rights to open the selected file."
        Catch exp As IOException
            ' A generic exception handler, for any IO error
            ' that hasn't been caught yet. Here, it ought
            ' to just be that the drive isn't ready.
            lblError.Text = "Drive selected is not ready" & _
            " Make sure the drive contains valid media."
        Catch exp As Exception
            lblError.Text = "An unknown error occurred."
        End Try
    End Sub
End Sub
```

To test this procedure, try a number of specific exceptions. For example, change the filename to be in one of the following locations:

- In a good path (but select a file that doesn't exist)

- On a drive that doesn't exist

- In a path that doesn't exist

- On a drive that isn't ready

The Exception Hierarchy

Following any of the links in the Exceptions table shown in Table 12.2 takes you to documentation on the individual `Exception` object. This documentation includes the following inheritance hierarchy (you'll need to understand this hierarchy of objects when you add multiple `Catch` blocks):

```
Object
    Exception
        SystemException
            ArgumentException
                ArgumentNullException
                ArgumentOutOfRangeException
                InvalidEnumArgumentException
                DuplicateWaitObjectException
```

Because each level inherits from the class defined above it, each lower level is an instance of the type specified above it. `ArgumentNullException` "is a" `ArgumentException`, which "is a" `SystemException`, which "is an" `Exception`. Here, "is a" appears in quotes because it's a meaningful operator—when you have multiple `Catch` blocks, those blocks match against the current exception using an "is a" rule. In other words, the order of the `Catch` blocks is significant, based on this "is a" relationship. When you're processing multiple `Catch` blocks and the runtime first finds a match where the current exception meets the "is a" rule for the exception trapped by the `Catch` block, the runtime uses that `Catch` block to process the exception and doesn't look any further. All exceptions inherit from the base `Exception` class, so you'll always want to include a `Catch` block to handle the base `Exception` class last, if you include it at all.

Throwing Exceptions

You may want to raise errors out of your procedures to indicate to callers that some exception has occurred. You might want to simply pass back a standard runtime exception provided by the .NET Framework, or you might want to create your own exception condition. In either case, you'll use the `Throw` keyword to raise the exception out of the current block.

NOTE

The `Throw` keyword works in much the same manner as the `Err.Raise` method in VB6.

Error-Handling Options

You can determine which exceptions you want to handle and which ones you want to raise back to your callers. When an exception occurs, your options include the following:

- **Do nothing at all.** In this case, the .NET runtime will automatically raise the exception back out to the procedure that called your code.

- **Catch specific errors.** In this case, exceptions you do handle won't be passed back out, but those you don't handle will be thrown back to the calling procedure.

- **Handle all errors.** Add a `Catch e as Exception` block to your set of `Catch` blocks, and no error will ever pass through your exception handling, unless you specifically throw an error yourself.

- **Throw errors.** You have the option to throw any error back out to the caller, explicitly. Using the `Throw` statement, you can raise the current error, or any other error, to the caller's exception handler.

TIP

It might not be obvious why you would want to throw an error yourself. There are times, however, when you might want to accept any type of error, but present it to the caller of your procedure as a more generic error. Perhaps you want to "hide" the details of the error and simply indicate that some disk error occurred, for example, when the user attempts to open a file. In that case, no matter which exception has occurred, you might raise a generic disk-handling exception. You'll see an example of this in the next section.

Using the Throw Keyword

You can use the `Throw` keyword in two ways:

- You can rethrow an error from within a `Catch` block:

```
Catch exp As Exception
   Throw
```

- You can throw an error from within any code, including a `Try` block:

```
Throw New FileNotFoundException()
```

NOTE

The first technique, rethrowing an exception, only works from within a `Catch` block. The second technique, throwing a new error, works anywhere.

Searching for Handlers

When you throw an exception, the .NET runtime works its way up the procedure call stack, looking for an appropriate exception handler. (If you're in a Try block when you throw your exception, the runtime will use the local Catch blocks, if any, to handle the exception first.) As soon as the runtime finds a Catch block for the exception you've thrown, it executes the code it finds there. If it can't find any appropriate Catch block all the way up the call stack, the runtime handles the exception itself (as shown earlier in Figure 12.2).

> **TIP**
>
> If you throw an exception using the Throw keyword, VB6-style On Error Goto error handling can trap the error as well. That is, the .NET runtime uses the same plumbing for all exceptions, whether you use the old or new error-handling conventions.

Passing Error Information

If you want to intercept different exceptions and raise them all back out to the caller as a single exception type, Throw makes it easy. In the next example, the code catches all exceptions, and regardless of what caused these exceptions, it throws a FileNotFoundException object back to the caller. In some cases, like this one, the calling procedure may not care exactly what happened or why the file couldn't be found. The caller may only care that the file wasn't available and needs to discern that particular exception from other, different exceptions.

> **NOTE**
>
> The Exception object's constructor is overloaded in several ways. You can pass in no parameters (you'll get a generic Exception object, with default values for its properties), a string indicating the error message you want sent back to the caller, or a string and an Exception object indicating the error message and the original exception that occurred (filling in the InnerException property of the exception you pass back to the caller). The example here uses the final constructor, passing back the inner exception.

You may also wish to make the original exception information available to the caller, in addition to the exception your code raises. In that case, you'll find that the constructor for the Exception class provides an overloaded version that allows you to specify the inner exception. That is, you can pass the Exception object that originally raised the error. The caller can investigate this exception, if it needs to.

TIP

The InnerException property of an exception is itself an Exception object, and it may also have an InnerException property that isn't Nothing. Therefore, you may end up following a linked list of exceptions when you start digging into the InnerException property. You may need to continue retrieving the InnerException property repeatedly until the property returns Nothing, in order to dig through all the errors that may have occurred.

In the following example, the TestThrow procedure throws a FileNotFoundException back to its caller, no matter what error it receives. In addition, it fills in the exception's InnerException property with the original Exception object. The example in Listing 12.6 displays the fabricated error message, along with the text associated with the original exception:

LISTING 12.6   You Can Throw an Exception, Wrapping Up the Original Exception in the InnerException Property

```
Private Sub ThrowException()
    Dim lngSize As Long
    Dim s As FileStream

    ' Catch an exception thrown by the called procedure.
    Try
        TestThrow()
    Catch exp As FileNotFoundException
        lblError.Text = "Error occurred: " & exp.Message
        ' Use exp.InnerException to get to error
        ' that triggered this one.
        Try
            lblError.Text = exp.InnerException.Message
        Catch
            ' Do nothing at all!
        End Try
    Catch exp As Exception

    End Try
End Sub

Private Sub TestThrow()
    Dim lngSize As Long
    Dim s As FileStream
```

LISTING 12.6   Continued

```
    ' No matter what happens, throw back
    ' a File Not Found exception.
    Try
        s = File.Open(txtFileName.Text, FileMode.Open)
        lngSize = s.Length
        s.Close()
    Catch exp As Exception
        Throw (New FileNotFoundException( _
            "Unable to open the specified file." exp))
    End Try
End Sub
```

Running Code Unconditionally

You may find that, in addition to code in the `Try` and `Catch` blocks, you want to add code that runs whether or not an error occurs. You may need to release resources, close files, or handle other issues that need to take place under any circumstances. In order to run code unconditionally, you'll need to use the `Finally` block.

To run code unconditionally, add a `Finally` block after any `Catch` blocks. The code in this block will run even if your code throws an exception, and even if you add an explicit `Exit Function` (or `Exit Sub`) statement within a `Catch` block.

You may decide, for example, that your code needs to set the `FileStream` object variable to `Nothing`, whether or not any error occurs when working with the file. You can modify the procedure to look like Listing 12.7, calling the finalization code regardless of whether an error occurs.

LISTING 12.7   Use the `Finally` Block to Run Code Unconditionally

```
Private Function TestFinally() As Integer
    Dim lngSize As Long
    Dim s As FileStream

    ' Use Finally to run code no matter what else happens.
    ' A somewhat meaningless example, but you get the
    ' idea.

    Try
        s = File.Open(txtFileName.Text, FileMode.Open)
        lngSize = s.Length
```

LISTING 12.7   Continued

```
        s.Close()
    Catch exp As Exception
        lblError.Text = exp.Message
    Finally
        ' Run this code no matter what happens.
        s = Nothing
    End Try
End Function
```

TIP

Although your Try/End Try block must contain either one or more Catch blocks or a
Finally block, it needn't contain both. That is, a Finally block without Catch blocks is fine.
Why include a Finally block if you don't include a Catch block? If an exception occurs
within your procedure, the .NET runtime will look for an appropriate exception handler, and
that may mean it leaves your procedure (if there's no Catch block, this will certainly happen),
looking up the call stack for that exception handler. If you want to run code before the
runtime leaves your procedure, you need to include a Finally block.

Creating an Error Page

If you want to add application-wide error handling so that any unhandled error
takes you to a page of your choosing (as opposed to the scary page shown in Figure
12.2), you can make a simple modification in the Web.Config file to add your
settings. Open Web.Config and modify the customErrors element, which normally
looks like the following:

```
<customErrors mode="RemoteOnly" />
```

You can change it so any error that occurs will redirect to a specific page using the
defaultRedirect attribute:

```
<customErrors mode="RemoteOnly" defaultRedirect="ErrorPage.aspx" />
```

You must create the page you're redirecting users to; that is, ErrorPage.aspx must be
a page you've created in your application. To test this out in the sample application,
you'll also need to modify the mode attribute—by default, this attribute indicates
that your error page only takes effect for remote requests (requests coming in from
outside the current machine). Because you're browsing to this page locally, set this
attribute to On and then try the No Error Handling option on the sample page.

You'll be directed to a very simple page indicating that an error occurred.

Once you've set the attributes correctly, triggering an unhandled exception will redirect you to the error-handling page. (Handled exceptions, of course, don't redirect users—that's the point of having exception handling in the first place.)

TIP

The three options allowed for the mode attribute are On, Off, and RemoteOnly. If you set this attribute to On, all requests that generate unhandled errors redirect to the specified page. If you set it to Off, you'll only see the default page if an unhandled error occurs (as you saw in Figure 12.2). If you set it to RemoteOnly (the default value), only remote requests will be redirected to the error page.

Summary

In this chapter you learned how to use the new structured exception handling that is pervasive through the .NET Framework. You will find this type of error handling much more powerful than the On Error GoTo structure you were forced to use in VB. And of course, it is much better than the On Error Resume Next of ASP. In this chapter, you learned the following:

- How to use a Try block to add exception handling to a block of code.

- How to add Catch blocks, as necessary, to trap individual exceptions.

- The .NET runtime handles Catch blocks in order, looking for an "is a" match against the current exception. It uses the first block it finds that matches.

- How to nest Try blocks, making it easy to effectively "push" and "pop" exception-handling states.

- How to add a Finally block to your Try block to run code unconditionally, whether an error occurs or not.

13

ADO.NET Connection and Command Objects

OBJECTIVES

- Learn to create an ADO.NET Connection object

- Learn to submit SQL through an ADO.NET Command object

In order to work with data, your application needs to be able to supply some important information. Among other things, you might need to provide answers to the following questions:

- What data source do you want to use (SQL Server, Access/Jet, Oracle, DB2, and so on)?

- Where is the data located (physical path or server name)?

- How do you log in if security is involved?

Without this information, your application can't even *find* the data, much less use it. ADO.NET's Connection objects (specifically, OleDbConnection or SqlConnection) manage this information for you.

Before you can retrieve or manipulate data, you'll need to supply connection information. You can either create a Connection object explicitly or simply supply connection information in the form of a connection string and have ADO.NET generate a Connection object for you, as necessary. You can use the design-time ADO.NET components provided by Visual Studio .NET to create a Connection object for you, as well.

In this chapter, you'll investigate creating your own Connection object and also look into how and when you should create and destroy your Connection object. You'll also learn how to use the Command object provided by ADO.NET, in conjunction with the Connection object, to retrieve data.

> **TIP**
>
> As a reminder, when we refer to a Connection object, we're just simplifying matters. There are at least two different Connection objects available as part of ADO.NET: OleDbConnection and SqlConnection (basically, one for each ADO.NET namespace). If there are differences between the two types, we'll note them. If not, we'll refer to both objects generically as Connection. The same thing applies to Command objects, later in the chapter.

> **TIP**
>
> You'll need a Connection object in order to work with data. There's no way around it. Whether you create the connection implicitly or explicitly, it's there. You should think about keeping the connection open for as short a period of time as possible, every time you work with data.

Providing ADO.NET Connection Information

In order to create a connection to a data source, you'll need to supply a string containing a series of name/value pairs, providing the information that ADO.NET requires in order to locate and use the data. For example, if you want to connect to a SQL Server database using the System.Data.OleDb namespace, you might use a connection string like this:

```
Provider=sqloledb;Data Source=(local);
Initial Catalog=Northwind;User ID=sa;Password=;
```

Alternatively, to connect to a Microsoft Access (Jet) database, you might use a connection string like this:

```
Provider=Microsoft.Jet.OleDb.4.0;
Data Source=C:\Northwind.mdb
```

If you're using SQL Server with integrated security, you won't want to pass in the user ID and password in the connection string. Instead, you can modify the connection string so that it indicates to SQL Server that you want to use its integrated security:

```
Provider=sqloledb;Data Source=(local);
Initial Catalog=Northwind;Integrated Security=SSPI;
```

Connection strings you might use when accessing SQL Server directly, using the System.Data.SqlClient namespace, are slightly different. See the online help for the SqlConnection object for more information on creating the appropriate connection string.

In an earlier chapter, you created a class named `DataHandler` that included a `ConnectStringBuilder` procedure, shown in Listing 13.1.

LISTING 13.1   You'll Use This Procedure in Many Examples, Creating a Connection String Based on the Supplied User ID and Password

```
Public Shared Function ConnectStringBuild( _
 ByVal LoginID As String, _
 ByVal Password As String) As String
  Dim strConn As String

  If LoginID = String.Empty Then
    LoginID = "sa"
  End If
  strConn = String.Format("Provider=sqloledb;" & _
   "Data Source=(local);Initial Catalog=Northwind;" & _
   "User ID={0};Password={1}", LoginID, Password)

  Return strConn
End Function
```

This procedure accepts as parameters a login ID and a password, and it generates a valid string that you can use with an `OleDbConnection` object in order to retrieve data from the Northwind sample database in SQL Server.

You could call the `ConnectStringBuild` procedure from your code every time you need a connection to the data source, but there's no need—most likely, the connection information won't change within a given session. You might find it more useful to create the connection string as each session starts and store it in a `Session` variable from then on. In this sample application, you'll place the connection information into a `Session` variable named `ConnectString`.

NOTE

In Chapter 11, "Data Binding on Web Forms," you used the user-interface data tools provided by Visual Studio .NET in order to bind a DataGrid control to a SQL Server table. Although you can use these tools, we think it's important to work carefully through the steps involved in writing all this code manually. This chapter and future chapters all use code to bind data to controls rather than using the components provided by Visual Studio .NET.

WARNING

Be careful using Session variables to store important information such as the connection string. Unless you understand the limitations of storing stateful information this way, you may be limiting your application's scalability. You'll find coverage of state management in Chapter 23, "State Management in ASP.NET." Make sure you investigate that information, as well, before using a Session variable in a real application. There are many options for managing state, and one of them will certainly fit your needs.

To modify your application and add support for the session-wide connection information, follow these steps:

1. In the Solution Explorer window, select Global.asax.

2. Right-click and select View Code from the context menu.

3. In the code-behind file, locate the Session_Start procedure. Modify the procedure so that it looks like Listing 13.2.

LISTING 13.2   Session_Start Runs Each Time a User Begins a Session

```
Sub Session_Start( _
 ByVal sender As Object, ByVal e As EventArgs)
  Session("LoginID") = String.Empty
  Session("Password") = String.Empty
  Session("ConnectString") = _
   DataHandler.ConnectStringBuild("sa", "")
End Sub
```

This procedure calls the ConnectStringBuild procedure that you created in an earlier chapter, passing in hard-coded values for the user ID and password. Later chapters will show how you can use a login page to gather this information and validate users before allowing them into your application.

Using ADO.NET Connection Objects

As you work through the steps in this chapter, you will create and open a connection to a SQL Server database using an OleDbConnection object and then retrieve information using an OleDbCommand object. In addition, in the second half of the chapter, you will submit SELECT and UPDATE statements to the same SQL Server database using the OleDbCommand object. These are the steps you'll often use—anytime you want to retrieve information and display it in a control, you'll write code like the code you'll see here.

Adding Code to Retrieve and Display Data

For this example, you'll open a connection to a SQL Server database and return the average price of products within a product category. Figure 13.1 shows what your Products.aspx page will look like when you have completed this section.

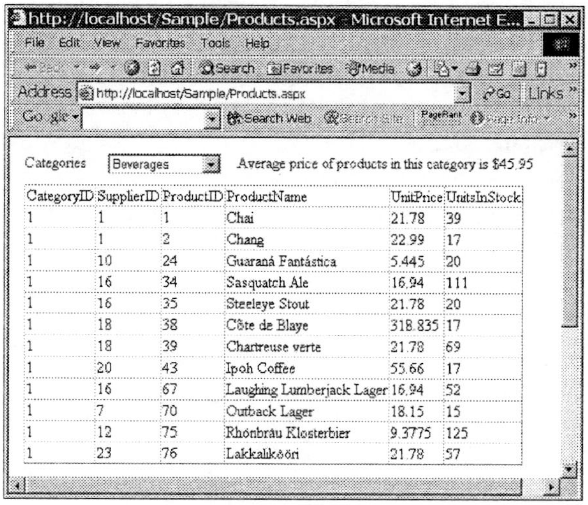

FIGURE 13.1   You'll create this page as you work through this section.

Follow these steps to add a label and retrieve the calculated average:

1. Open Products.aspx in the page designer.

2. Add a Label control to the page, to the right of the DropDownList control. Set the new control's ID property to lblAverage and its Text property to an empty string.

3. Double-click the DropDownList control to load the ddlCategories_SelectedIndexChange procedure in the code editor.

    Not only do you need to load the products using the ProductsLoad procedure, but you will also need to call another procedure, CategoryAvgPrice, that will calculate the average price.

4. Modify the procedure so that it looks like this (because the CategoryAvgPrice procedure doesn't yet exist in the class, you'll see a blue squiggle in the code—don't worry, you'll fix that soon):

```
Private Sub ddlCategories_SelectedIndexChanged( _
 ByVal sender As System.Object, _
 ByVal e As System.EventArgs) _
```

```
Handles ddlCategories.SelectedIndexChanged

  ProductsLoad()
  CategoryAvgPrice()
End Sub
```

5. Add the procedure shown in Listing 13.3 to the class.

LISTING 13.3   Display the Average Price for a Category in a Label

```
Private Sub CategoryAvgPrice()
  Dim cmd As OleDbCommand
  Dim cnn As OleDbConnection
  Dim strSQL As String

  strSQL = _
    "SELECT Avg(UnitPrice) " & _
    "FROM Products " & _
    "WHERE CategoryID = " & _
    ddlCategories.SelectedItem.Value

  Try
    ' Create and open a new Connection
    cnn = New OleDbConnection()
    With cnn
      .ConnectionString = _
        Session("ConnectString").ToString
      .Open()
    End With

    cmd = New OleDbCommand()
    With cmd
      .Connection = cnn
      .CommandText = strSQL
      lblAverage.Text = _
        String.Format("Average price of products " & _
        "in this category is {0:C}", .ExecuteScalar)
    End With

  Catch exp As Exception
    lblAverage.Text = exp.Message
```

LISTING 13.3   Continued

```
Finally
  cnn.Close()
End Try
End Sub
```

TIP

The code in the CategoryAvgPrice procedure counts on you having added the appropriate Imports statement to your file. If you don't see Imports System.Data.OleDb at the top of your code-behind file, add it now.

6. Modify the Page_Load procedure, adding a call to the CategoryAvgPrice procedure as well, as shown in Listing 13.4.

LISTING 13.4   Add a Call to CategoryAvgPrice to the Page_Load Procedure

```
Private Sub Page_Load( _
ByVal sender As System.Object, _
ByVal e As System.EventArgs) _
Handles MyBase.Load

  If Not Page.IsPostBack Then
    CategoryLoad()
    ProductsLoad()
    CategoryAvgPrice()
  End If
End Sub
```

7. Build and browse the Products.aspx page and then select a category. You should see the label at the top of the page change to reflect the newly selected category.

Investigating the CategoryAvgPrice **Procedure's Code**

Obviously, it's the CategoryAvgPrice procedure that's doing all the work here. It's worth taking the time to figure out what the procedure is doing by reviewing each step carefully. The procedure takes these actions:

- It creates a SQL string that it will use to retrieve just the data it needs from SQL Server. The procedure needs to calculate the average price for a particular category (the category supplied by the Value property of the selected item in the drop-down list):

```
strSQL = _
 "SELECT Avg(UnitPrice) " & _
 "FROM Products " & _
 "WHERE CategoryID = " & _
 ddlCategories.SelectedItem.Value
```

• It sets up exception handling and instantiates an OleDbConnection object. The error handling ensures that if anything goes wrong, you'll see a description in the label on the page. No matter what happens, the open Connection object gets closed in the Finally block:

```
Try
    ' Create and open a new Connection
    cnn = New OleDbConnection()

    ' code removed here...

Catch exp As Exception
    lblAverage.Text = exp.Message

Finally
    cnn.Close()
End Try
```

• It uses the Session variable, ConnectString, to set up the Connection object and then calls its Open method to open the connection:

```
With cnn
 .ConnectionString = _
    Session("ConnectString").ToString
 .Open()
End With
```

• It instantiates a new OleDbCommand object and sets its Connection and CommandText properties appropriately. The Command object needs a connection in order to retrieve its data, and it uses the object you just created. In addition, the `Command` object needs a `CommandText` property, which indicates what you want the `Command` to do:

```
cmd = New OleDbCommand()
With cmd
  .Connection = cnn
  .CommandText = strSQL

  ' code removed here...

End With
```

- Finally, it fills the Label control with the results of executing the command text you specified:

```
With cmd

  ' code removed here...

  lblAverage.Text = _
    String.Format("Average price of products " & _
    "in this category is {0:C}", .ExecuteScalar)
End With
```

In this case, the code uses the `ExecuteScalar` method of the `Command` object. In the next section, you'll learn how to use the `ExecuteNonQuery` method. In Chapter 14, "Working with Data," you'll learn about the other method you might use to retrieve data using a `Command` object: the `ExecuteReader` method.

The `ExecuteScalar` method executes the SQL statement you've supplied (in this case, calculating the average price for a given category of products) and then returns the value from the first column in the first row of the set of rows created by executing the command. This method makes it simple to request a single value back from a database, given a criteria and a calculation.

TIP

The example uses the `String.Format` method and the replaceable parameter `{0:C}` to convert the results of the `ExecuteScalar` method into currency formatting. Although there are other ways to format an object into a currency value, this is one of the simplest. `String.Format` supplies a large group of formatting values, such as the "C" used here, to format numbers and dates.

Updating Data Using a `Command` Object

Command objects can retrieve data, as you saw in the previous example. You can also use them to update, delete, and insert data—that is, you can use them to take action with the data. In this example, you'll add code that can update the prices of items in the Products table, using a Command object. After you add the required controls and code to the page, it should look like Figure 13.2.

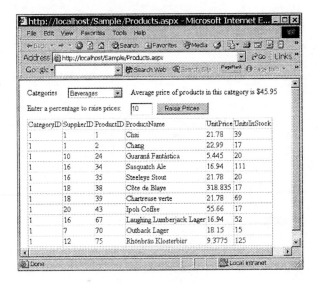

FIGURE 13.2   Raising prices can be accomplished with just a few controls and a little code.

Follow these steps to modify the layout of Products.aspx and to add the code necessary to update prices:

1. Immediately above the DataGrid control, add Label, TextBox, and Button controls (to match the layout shown in Figure 13.2).

2. Set the properties of the controls as shown in Table 13.1.

TABLE 13.1   Set Properties of the New Controls to Match These Values

Control	Property	Value
Label	Text	Enter a percentage to raise prices:
TextBox	ID	txtPercent
	Text	10
Button	ID	btnRaise
	Text	Raise Prices

3. Double-click the btnRaise button to load the code-behind file and modify the btnRaise_Click procedure so that it looks like Listing 13.5.

LISTING 13.5   Add a Call to the `RaisePrices` Method

```
Private Sub btnRaise_Click( _
 ByVal sender As System.Object, _
 ByVal e As System.EventArgs) _
 Handles btnRaise.Click

  RaisePrices()
End Sub
```

4. Add the `RaisePrices` procedure shown in Listing 13.6.

LISTING 13.6   Use a Command Object to Raise All Prices

```
Private Sub RaisePrices()
 Dim cmd As New OleDbCommand()
 Dim strSQL As String
 Dim strConn As String

 strSQL = _
  "UPDATE Products " & _
  "SET UnitPrice = UnitPrice * {0} " & _
  "WHERE CategoryID = {1}"

 strSQL = String.Format(strSQL, _
  1 + (CDec(txtPercent.Text) / 100), _
  ddlCategories.SelectedItem.Value)

 strConn = Session("ConnectString").ToString
 With cmd
   .Connection = New OleDbConnection(strConn)
   .Connection.Open()
   .CommandText = strSQL
   .CommandType = CommandType.Text

   .ExecuteNonQuery()

   .Connection.Close()
 End With
```

LISTING 13.6   Continued

```
' Redisplay the grid
ProductsLoad()
CategoryAvgPrice()
End Sub
```

5. Build and browse the page once more. This time, verify that clicking Raise Prices does indeed raise the prices by the amount you've specified in the text box.

RaisePrices does its work by taking these actions:

- It creates a new OleDbCommand object:

```
Dim cmd As New OleDbCommand()
```

- It sets up a SQL string template, with placeholders for the amount to raise prices and the category. In this case, the SQL statement is an UPDATE statement, specifying the field(s) to be updated and the value(s) to be inserted. The code then uses the String.Format method to insert the appropriate amount and category:

```
strSQL = _
"UPDATE Products " & _
"SET UnitPrice = UnitPrice * {0} " & _
"WHERE CategoryID = {1}"

strSQL = String.Format(strSQL, _
1 + (CDec(txtPercent.Text) / 100), _
ddlCategories.SelectedItem.Value)
```

- It retrieves the connection string from the Session variable, sets the necessary properties of the Command object, and calls the ExecuteNonQuery method of the Command object:

```
With cmd
    .Connection = New OleDbConnection(strConn)
    .Connection.Open()
    .CommandText = strSQL
    .CommandType = CommandType.Text

    .ExecuteNonQuery()
```

```
   .Connection.Close()
End With
```

- It redisplays the data:

```
' Redisplay the grid
ProductsLoad()
```

This example uses the `ExecuteNonQuery` method of the `OleDbCommand` object. This method requires that you supply, in the `CommandText` property, either the name of a stored procedure that doesn't return any rows or an `UPDATE`, `INSERT`, or `DELETE` SQL statement. Because you're not using a DataSet here, you needn't create and fill a DataAdapter—you simply need to execute the SQL you've supplied.

TIP

In case you need to retrieve the number of rows your SQL statement has modified, use the `ExecuteNonQuery` method. In this case, it doesn't matter, but if you should need the information, it's available.

To Close or Not to Close?

Here's something to consider: You can, if you want, open a connection to a data source and keep that connection open. Doing this makes it easier for you as a developer. You open the connection once, perhaps store the `Connection` object somewhere you can always use it, and then close it when your application has completed. The problem with this solution is that it's difficult, in an ASP.NET application, to really know when the application is done. In addition, `Connection` objects tie up valuable resources. You may, for example, pay for your connections individually—you might not be able to have more than a fixed number of concurrent connections to your data source, for example. Opening a connection and leaving it open would tie up your resources quickly. In the interests of scalability, you generally want to use a connection for as short a period of time as possible. Generally, you want to open a connection, get the information you need, and then close the connection. This is how all the examples in this chapter (as well as those in later chapters) work.

Should you explicitly close `Connection` objects that you open? When the `Command` object you created goes out of scope, it will be destroyed (when the memory is required and when the garbage collector gets to it). When that happens, the connection used by the `Command` object will be destroyed as well. So why bother explicitly closing the `Connection` object? Calling the `Close` method explicitly releases the connection back to the connection pool (if connection pooling is available and enabled), and it rolls back any pending transactions.

TIP

In general, close connections when you're done with them. This leaves your data in a known state, at a known time. If you allow the garbage collector to close your connections for you, you won't be able to determine when the connection is closed and released.

SETTING CONNECTION PROPERTIES

In ADO, you could set several connection-related properties, such as the `ConnectionTimeOut`, `DataSource`, and `Database` properties. In ADO.NET, you can only set these values as part of a connection string. For example, to set the connection timeout, you'll need to include the `Connect Timeout=n` clause as part of your connection string. All these properties of the `Connection` object are still available—they're just read-only in ADO.NET.

Summary

Although you can use Visual Studio .NET's data components, it's important to understand what's going on under the covers. This chapter walked you through managing data in your own code. Along the way, you learned how to do the following:

- Create connection strings

- Use ADO.NET Connection objects to connect to a data source

- Use ADO.NET Command objects to retrieve data from a data source

- Use Command objects to update data using a bulk update SQL statement

- Close Connection objects when you're done working with the data

14

Working with Data

OBJECTIVES

- Learn to use the ADO.NET DataReader class

- Learn to create a function to return a DataSet, given a SQL string

- Learn to set relationships between DataTables

Once you've managed to connect to a data source and retrieve data (see Chapter 13, "ADO.NET Connection and Command Objects"), you'll need to work with the data. ADO.NET provides two completely separate sets of objects for manipulating data. The Connection and Command objects you've already seen must be aware of the specific data source in order to do their work, and the same applies to the DataAdapter object you'll learn about in this chapter. Other objects, such as the DataSet, DataTable, DataView, and DataRow objects, work in a disconnected manner—once you've loaded them with data, they don't know or care where the data originated.

In this chapter, you'll learn to work with both types of objects. You'll fill disconnected DataSet objects with data, and you'll work with DataTable objects within DataSets. To get started, you'll work with a connected data access object: the DataReader.

Using the DataReader Object

ADO provided a Recordset object, and this object allowed for both connected and disconnected as well as cursored and cursorless data access. There were so many options that many developers never really figured out all that an ADO recordset could do. To avoid this overloading nightmare, ADO.NET provides separate objects, based on functionality. The DataAdapter object (SqlDataAdapter or OleDbDataAdapter) contains SQL command information and connection information, and it can go out and retrieve or manipulate data for you. The DataSet object provides a client-side cache for working with data.

Under the covers, there must be some read-only, forward-only, highly optimized means of retrieving data as quickly as possible from a data source—the DataSet has to have some way to retrieve data to fill its cache, right? And so it does. The DataReader object (actually, the SqlDataReader or OleDbDataReader object) is a distinct class that includes methods, properties, and events all focused on retrieving data much like a forward-only, read-only recordset in ADO. Of course, while a DataReader is retrieving its data, it must be connected to its data source. There's no caching involved in a DataReader's activity—it simply reads a row and provides the row to your code; then it moves on to the next row.

Using a DataReader is simple: You use the ExecuteReader method of a Command object to retrieve the DataReader; then you call the Read method of the DataReader to retrieve each row in turn. When the Read method returns False, you know you're done. In the simplest form, your code that works with a DataReader might look like this (assuming that cmd is an OleDbCommand object, already opened and poised for action):

```
Dim dr As OleDbDataReader
dr = cmd.ExecuteReader()
Do While dr.Read
   ' Do something with columns within the current row
Loop
```

NOTE

There are other issues, of course. For example, when you call the ExecuteReader method, you can pass in values indicating how you want the DataReader to behave. If you only want to retrieve a single row, using the CommandBehavior.SingleRow value will optimize for that situation. If you know you'll only want to retrieve data in column order, you can optimize for that situation by passing the CommandBehavior.SequentialAccess value. See the online help for the OleDbDataReader object for more information.

Why use the DataReader? If your goal is to fill a ListBox or DropDownList control programmatically, you can't beat it—it's the fastest way to get your job done. Given that the DataSet object uses a DataReader under the covers to fill its own cache, you have to believe that you'll get better performance by using it yourself, in situations where you can live with forward-only, read-only access.

Using a DataReader to Fill a DropDownList Control

To demonstrate using a DataReader in an application, this section will walk through the steps involved in filling a DropDownList control with data from a DataReader. You've already seen how to accomplish this same goal by setting properties of the control to read its data from a DataSet. If your data is static, however, and you only need to fill the list once, you may decide to use a DataReader to accomplish the same goal.

In this section, you'll add a DropDownList control containing a list of suppliers. When you select a supplier, you'll filter the grid to display only products from the selected supplier. (Selecting a category will also filter the grid, to only show products from the selected category.) When you're done, the page will look like Figure 14.1.

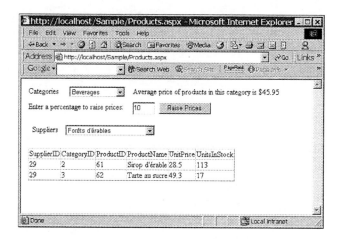

FIGURE 14.1   Add the Suppliers drop-down list to filter products by the SupplierID field.

Adding the `GetDataReader` Method

Although you could add code to your page to retrieve a `DataReader` object, it's a task you're likely to need to accomplish in more than one place in your application. Therefore, it makes sense to add a generic `GetDataReader` method to your `DataHandler` class. Given a connection string and a SQL string, this method will create an `OleDbDataReader` object and will return the DataReader back to your calling code.

Follow these steps to add the `GetDataReader` method:

1. Make sure your `Northwind.sln` solution is open in Visual Studio .NET.

2. In the Solution Explorer window, select `DataHandler.vb`.

3. Double-click to open the code editor window.

4. Scroll to the top of the file and add the following `Imports` statement:

```
Imports System.Data.OleDb
```

5. Add the procedure shown in Listing 14.1 to the class.

LISTING 14.1   Given a SQL Statement and a Connection String, Create a DataReader Object

```
Public Shared Function GetDataReader( _
ByVal SQLStatement As String, _
ByVal ConnectionString As String) As OleDbDataReader

 Dim dr As OleDbDataReader
 Dim cmd As New OleDbCommand()

 With cmd
   .Connection = _
     New OleDbConnection(ConnectionString)
   .Connection.Open()

   .CommandText = SQLStatement
   dr = .ExecuteReader(CommandBehavior.CloseConnection)
 End With

 Return dr
End Function
```

TIP

Because the GetDataReader procedure uses the Shared modifier, you needn't instantiate a DataHandler object before using the GetDataReader method.

To do its job, GetDataReader takes these actions:

- Declares an OleDbDataReader variable and creates an OleDbCommand object:

```
Dim dr As OleDbDataReader
Dim cmd As New OleDbCommand()
```

- Sets the Connection property of the Command object and opens the Command's connection:

```
With cmd
  .Connection = _
    New OleDbConnection(ConnectionString)
  .Connection.Open()
  ...
End With
```

- Sets the CommandText property of the Command object and then calls the ExecuteReader method of the Command object to retrieve the DataReader object:

```
With cmd
    ...
    .CommandText = SQLStatement
    dr = .ExecuteReader(CommandBehavior.CloseConnection)
End With
```

- Returns the DataReader object as the return value of the function:

```
Return dr
```

WARNING

It's important for you to close any connections that you've opened when you're done working with them. Normally, you can simply call the Close method of the Connection object when you're done with an object. In this case, however, you're passing the DataReader object back as the return value of the function, and the connection is still in use. Therefore, you can't close the connection! To solve this problem, ADO.NET allows you to pass the CommandBehavior.CloseConnection value when you call the ExecuteReader method. This value indicates to ADO.NET that it should close the connection for you, when you close the associated DataReader object. That's the approach we've taken here—it's up to your code, however, to close the DataReader when you're done with it.

Loading Suppliers Using a DataReader

Now that you have a method that can build a DataReader for you, follow these steps to fill a drop-down list with supplier information (you'll use the CompanyName field as the text displayed in the list and the SupplierID field as the value for each item in the list):

1. Add Label and DropDownList controls for suppliers, as shown in Figure 14.1.

2. Set the properties for the new controls as shown in Table 14.1.

TABLE 14.1   Set These Properties for the New Controls

Control	Property	Value
Label	Text	Suppliers
DropDownList	ID	ddlSuppliers
	AutoPostBack	True

3. Double-click the page to display the Page_Load procedure and then modify the procedure so that it looks like this:

```
Private Sub Page_Load( _
 ByVal sender As System.Object, _
 ByVal e As System.EventArgs) _
 Handles MyBase.Load

 If Not Page.IsPostBack Then
   CategoryLoad()
   ProductsLoad()
   CategoryAvgPrice()
   SupplierLoad()
 End If
End Sub
```

4. Add the SupplierLoad procedure:

```
Private Sub SupplierLoad()
  Dim oItem As ListItem
  Dim dr As OleDbDataReader
  Dim strSQL As String
  Dim strConn As String

  strSQL = _
   "SELECT SupplierID, CompanyName " & _
   "FROM Suppliers ORDER BY CompanyName"

  strConn = Session("ConnectString").ToString

  Try
    dr = DataHandler.GetDataReader(strSQL, strConn)

    Do While dr.Read
      oItem = New ListItem( _
        dr("CompanyName").ToString, _
        dr("SupplierID").ToString)

      ddlSuppliers.Items.Add(oItem)
    Loop
    dr.Close()
  Catch
```

```
    End Try
End Sub
```

The SupplierLoad procedure fills in the DropDownList control with all the suppliers, using these actions:

- It builds the appropriate SQL and connection strings:

```
strSQL = _
 "SELECT SupplierID, CompanyName " & _
 "FROM Suppliers ORDER BY CompanyName"

strConn = Session("ConnectString").ToString
```

- It retrieves the DataReader object, supplying the SQL and connection strings:

```
dr = DataHandler.GetDataReader(strSQL, strConn)
```

- It loops through all the rows provided by the DataReader and then closes the DataReader (which also closes the connection):

```
Do While dr.Read
   ...
Loop
dr.Close()
```

- For each row provided by the DataReader, the SupplierLoad procedure creates a new ListItem object, supplies the ListItem object with the text and value to be added to the DropDownList control, and then adds the new ListItem object to the DropDownList control:

```
oItem = New ListItem( _
 dr("CompanyName").ToString, _
 dr("SupplierID").ToString)

ddlSuppliers.Items.Add(oItem)
```

One more interesting side note: How can you retrieve field values from the DataReader? You have a number of choices here:

- You can retrieve the columns by their ordinal position (for example, dr.Item(3) or dr(3)).

- You can retrieve the columns by name (for example, dr.Item("CompanyName") or dr("CompanyName")). This is the technique we used in the example.

- You can retrieve the columns by calling a function that returns a specific data type. For example, `dr.GetString(0)` returns a string containing the value in column 0. You'll find `Get…` methods for all the basic data types. This is the most efficient technique, because it requires no data conversion. The other techniques require you to convert from an object to the appropriate data type—we used the `ToString` method in the example to accomplish this conversion.

To keep things simple, this example uses the field name to retrieve the field value. Although this is the simplest technique, in terms of development and maintenance, it's also the least efficient. If speed is your goal, look into the `Get…` methods.

TRY IT OUT To try out all the changes you've added to the page, follow these steps:

1. In the Solution Explorer window, right-click `Products.aspx` and select Build and Browse from the context menu.

2. Verify that the list of suppliers has been filled in and that you can select a supplier from the list.

You don't need to loop through the rows in a DataReader to fill a DropDownList control with data. You can get the benefits of using a DataReader using the same type of data binding you've already seen—ASP.NET allows you to bind a DropDownList control to a DataReader, just as you can bind it to a DataSet. We included the previous example to show how you can work with a DataReader, because it's important that you see how to loop through the rows of the DataReader explicitly.

Actually, you could rewrite the code in the `SupplierLoad` procedure so that it simply binds the control to the DataReader, as shown in Listing 14.2.

LISTING 14.2   Rewrite of the Previous Version, Binding the DropDownList Control

```
Private Sub SupplierLoad()
  Dim oItem As ListItem
  Dim dr As OleDbDataReader
  Dim strSQL As String
  Dim strConn As String

  strSQL = _
    "SELECT SupplierID, CompanyName " & _
    "FROM Suppliers ORDER BY CompanyName"

  strConn = Session("ConnectString").ToString
```

LISTING 14.2   Continued

```
Try
    dr = DataHandler.GetDataReader(strSQL, strConn)

    With ddlSuppliers
        .DataSource = dr
        .DataTextField = "CompanyName"
        .DataValueField = "SupplierID"
        .DataBind()
    End With
    dr.Close()
Catch

End Try
End Sub
```

If you like, try it out—you get the exact same results, and the code may run the slightest bit faster, as well. In production code, most likely we'd use this technique.

When would you loop through the rows of a DataReader? If you needed to run some code for each row, as you loaded the DropDownList control, for example, it might be necessary to visit each row in turn before adding content to the list. It's up to you—it requires just about the same amount of code either way.

Filtering the Grid Based on Supplier ID

Now that your page includes a list of suppliers, it only makes sense that you would want to be able to filter the grid to show all products from a given supplier or all products from a given category, depending on which drop-down list you select.

The ProductsLoad procedure currently takes only the CategoryID value into account when building the SQL string it uses to create the DataSet that fills the grid. You can modify the procedure so that if you pass an optional supplier ID, it will use that value instead. To add this functionality, follow these steps:

1. With Products.aspx open in the designer, double-click ddlSuppliers to load the ddlSuppliers_SelectedIndexChanged procedure. Modify the procedure so that it looks like this:

```
Private Sub ddlSuppliers_SelectedIndexChanged( _
 ByVal sender As System.Object, _
 ByVal e As System.EventArgs) _
 Handles ddlSuppliers.SelectedIndexChanged
```

```
ProductsLoad(ddlSuppliers.SelectedItem.Value)
End Sub
```

2. Modify the ProductsLoad procedure, adding code to support the SupplierID parameter:

```
Private Sub ProductsLoad( _
 Optional ByVal SupplierID As String = "")
  Dim ds As DataSet
  Dim strSQL As String

  strSQL = daProducts.SelectCommand.CommandText
  If SupplierID = String.Empty Then
    ' No supplier ID? Use the value in the
    ' Category dropdown list.
    strSQL &= " WHERE CategoryID = " & _
     ddlCategories.SelectedItem.Value
  Else
    ' If you got a SupplierID value, use
    ' that to filter the data.
    strSQL &= " WHERE SupplierID = " & _
     SupplierID
  End If

  ds = New DataSet()

  With daProducts
    .SelectCommand.CommandText = strSQL
    .Fill(ds)
  End With

  With grdProducts
    .DataSource = ds
    .DataBind()
  End With
End Sub
```

TIP

In Visual Basic .NET, you can add optional parameters to procedures, as we've done here. If you don't pass a value for the SupplierID parameter, the code will assign it a default value (""). If you do pass a value, the parameter will take on that value.

3. Browse the page, verifying that selecting either a category or a supplier correctly filters the grid.

Retrieving Datasets Generically

Because you're likely to need `DataSet` objects as part of your applications, and the typed DataSet created by the user-interface components may be more than you need, it makes sense to provide a generic "get me a DataSet" procedure. You pass in the SQL string and the connection string, and the `GetDataSet` procedure does the rest.

The sample form, `Products.aspx`, uses DataSets in the `CategoryLoad` and `ProductsLoad` procedures. In both cases, the code is quite similar: You supply the SQL string and the connection string and then create a DataAdapter that uses this information. You call the `Fill` method of the DataAdapter, filling up the DataSet you need. You can have the user-interface components provided by Visual Studio .NET do this same work for you, but either way, if all you want is a DataSet to work with, the same concepts apply.

To add `GetDataSet` to your arsenal of tools, follow these steps:

1. In the Solution Explorer window, select `DataHandler.vb`. Double-click to open the class in the code designer window.

2. Add the following procedure to the module:

```
Public Shared Function GetDataSet( _
 ByVal SQLString As String, _
 ByVal ConnectionString As String) As DataSet

  Dim da As OleDbDataAdapter
  Dim ds As DataSet

  Try
    ' Create new DataAdapter
    da = New OleDbDataAdapter( _
     SQLString, ConnectionString)

    ' Fill DataSet from DataAdapter
    ds = New DataSet()
    da.Fill(ds)

  Catch
    Throw
```

```
        End Try

        Return ds
    End Function
```

It's not that this procedure does anything miraculous—it simply encapsulates code that you'll call often, if you decide not to use the user-interface components for creating DataSet objects.

Using the GetDataSet Procedure

Now that you've got a generic procedure for creating a DataSet, you really don't need the user-interface objects you placed onto Products.aspx in an earlier chapter, nor do you need the blocks of code you've previously written. To clean things up, you'll need to modify the ProductsLoad and CategoryLoad procedures you created earlier.

To fix up the procedures, follow these steps:

1. With Products.aspx loaded in the page designer, press F7 to view the code designer (or choose the View, Code menu item).

2. Modify the CategoryLoad procedure so that it looks like this (removing the extra code):

```
Private Sub CategoryLoad()
    Dim ds As DataSet
    Dim strSQL As String
    Dim strConn As String

    strSQL = _
        "SELECT CategoryID, CategoryName " & _
        "FROM Categories"

    strConn = Session("ConnectString").ToString()

    ' Build DataSet
    ds = DataHandler.GetDataSet(strSQL, strConn)

    With ddlCategories
        .DataTextField = "CategoryName"
        .DataValueField = "CategoryID"
        .DataSource = ds
        .DataBind()
    End With
End Sub
```

3. Modify the `ProductsLoad` procedure so that it looks like this:

```
Private Sub ProductsLoad( _
 Optional ByVal SupplierID As String = "")

  Dim ds As DataSet
  Dim strSQL As String
  Dim strConn As String

  strSQL = "SELECT SupplierID, CategoryID, " & _
    "ProductID, ProductName, UnitPrice, UnitsInStock " & _
    "FROM Products"

  If SupplierID = String.Empty Then
    ' No supplier ID? Use the value in the
    ' Category dropdown list.
    strSQL &= " WHERE CategoryID = " & _
      ddlCategories.SelectedItem.Value
  Else
    ' If you got a SupplierID value, use
    ' that to filter the data.
    strSQL &= " WHERE SupplierID = " & _
      SupplierID
  End If

  strConn = Session("ConnectString").ToString()

  ' Build DataSet
  ds = DataHandler.GetDataSet(strSQL, strConn)

  grdProducts.DataSource = ds
  grdProducts.DataBind()
End Sub
```

4. Press Shift+F7 (or use the View, Designer menu item) to load the page designer and then delete all the items from the tray area of the page (daProducts, cnNorthwind, and DsProducts1). You can also delete dsProducts.xsd from the Solution Explorer window, because you won't be needing it any longer.

5. Browse the page once again and verify that everything works the way it did originally.

As you can see, using the generic GetDataSet procedure makes your code simpler, more readable, and removes your reliance on the data tools provided by Visual Studio .NET.

Working with Relations in a Dataset

An ADO.NET `DataSet` object is much like an in-memory database. This object can contain `DataTable` objects, where each of these is a representation of the data that was retrieved via a `SELECT` statement. (The source of data in the DataTable might include data from multiple tables, but that's not a concern once that data's stored in the `DataTable` object.) Datasets can also store schema information as well as constraints and relationships between multiple `DataTable` objects.

You may need to represent and work with relationships between `DataTable` objects in your DataSets. For example, you might want to examine both employees and their orders as well as be able to view orders for any employee on a page without having to take a roundtrip back to the database server in order to retrieve the information for each different employee.

Suppose you'd like to create a DataSet—a client-side data cache (this time, the page itself is a client to the database server)—that contains information on all the employees and all the orders for all employees, related by the EmployeeID field. You'd like to be able to select an employee and see that employee's orders in a grid and then select another employee and see that employee's orders—all without requesting more data from the SQL Server!

You can accomplish your goal using ADO.NET, but it does require some features you haven't yet investigated. In this section, you'll create a new page and add code that supports these relational features. Along the way, we'll explain how the code works so that you can expand and reuse it in your own applications. Figure 14.2 shows the finished page, which allows you to select an employee and see the orders for that employee.

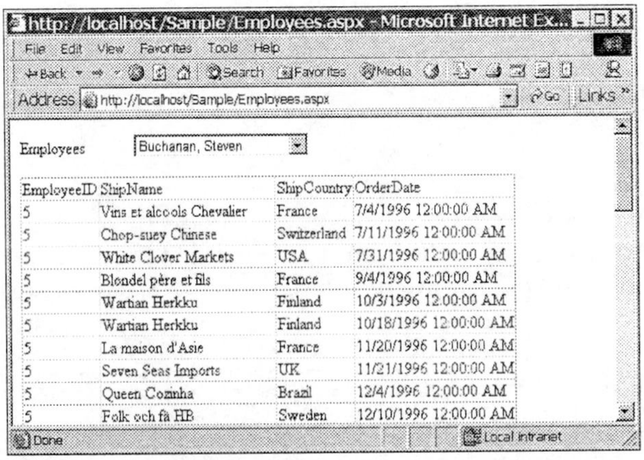

FIGURE 14.2   The finished Employees page allows you to view orders by employee.

To be able to navigate to the new page from the finished application, you need to add a new hyperlink on Main.aspx to call this new page. To do so, follow these steps:

1. Load Main.aspx in the page designer window.

2. Drag a new hyperlink control to the Web page just underneath the Products hyperlink.

3. Set the properties for the control as shown in Table 14.2.

TABLE 14.2   Use These Property Settings for the New Hyperlink

Property	Value
ID	hypEmployees
NavigateURL	Employees.aspx
Text	Employees

4. Select Project, Add Existing Item. Be sure to change the Files of Type combo box to "All Files (*.*)."

5. Add the Employees.* files from the Jumpstart\WorkingWithData folder. There should be three files: Employees.aspx, Employees.aspx.resx, and Employees.aspx.vb.

Investigating the Relation-Handling Code

In order to modularize the code required to support the relational DataSet, we've separated out two useful, reusable procedures: AddRelation and AddPrimaryKey.

Adding Relations

The AddRelation procedure allows you to take a DataSet that contains two tables and add a relationship between the tables. You supply a number of values as parameters, including the following:

- **The DataSet.** You pass in an open DataSet, filled with the tables you want to relate.

- **The name of the new DataRelation object.** By supplying a name, you can refer to the DataRelation object by name, later on. We didn't have the code supply a name in the sample code, so you could only refer to the relation by its position within the collection of DataRelation objects in the DataSet object.

- **ParentTable and ParentField names.** The code uses the ParentTable and ParentField names to create the "parent" side of the relationship.

- **ChildTable and ChildField names.** The code uses these names to create the "child" side of the relationship.

Once the code has run, the DataSet contains a defined relationship between the two `DataTable` objects. Once you have the data relation, you can use it to iterate through all the parent rows, and for each parent row, retrieve all the associated child rows—that's how the Employees page will display orders for a selected employee.

Locate the `AddRelation` code shown in Listing 14.3 to investigate how it works.

LISTING 14.3   The `AddRelation` Method Takes Care of Relating Two `DataTable` Objects

```
Private Sub AddRelation( _
 ByVal ds As DataSet, _
 ByVal Name As String, _
 ByVal ParentTable As String, _
 ByVal ParentField As String, _
 ByVal ChildTable As String, _
 ByVal ChildField As String)

  Dim dcParent As DataColumn
  Dim dcChild As DataColumn
  Dim drn As DataRelation

  dcParent = ds.Tables(ParentTable).Columns(ParentField)
  dcChild = ds.Tables(ChildTable).Columns(ChildField)
  drn = New DataRelation(Name, dcParent, dcChild)
  ds.Relations.Add(drn)
End Sub
```

To create a `DataRelation` object, ADO.NET requires a name and two `DataColumn` objects—one from each of the DataTables to be related. This code first retrieves the two columns, given the table and column names:

```
dcParent = ds.Tables(ParentTable).Columns(ParentField)
dcChild = ds.Tables(ChildTable).Columns(ChildField)
```

Next, the code creates a new `DataRelation` object, based on the name you supplied, and the two `DataColumn` objects it just retrieved:

```
drn = New DataRelation(Name, dcParent, dcChild)
```

Finally, the procedure adds the `DataRelation` object to the DataSet's collection of `DataRelation` objects:

```
ds.Relations.Add(drn)
```

Adding Primary Keys

You'll also need to be able to add primary key information to the `DataTable` objects within your DataSet—many operations require them. A primary key is a set of one or more columns whose values are required to be both unique, and nonempty. By supplying a primary key value for a `DataTable` object, you have a quick and easy way to locate any specific row, because each row has some unique, existing value that identifies it. The code in Listing 14.4 shows the `AddPrimaryKey` procedure that makes it easy to add primary keys to your `DataTable` objects.

LISTING 14.4   Add Primary Keys to `DataTable` Objects

```
Private Sub AddPrimaryKey( _
ByVal ds As DataSet, _
ByVal TableName As String, _
ByVal FieldName As String)

  ' The PrimaryKey property of a DataTable
  ' object contains an array of DataColumn
  ' objects.

  ' Create an array that can contain a single item.
  ' The index here (0) indicates that the array
  ' goes from 0 to 0 (containing a single item).
  Dim dcs(0) As DataColumn

  ' Given a table within the dataset,
  ' retrieve a DataColumn object, stuff
  ' it into the array, and assign that array
  ' to the PrimaryKey property. Seems roundabout
  ' but that's how it works!
  With ds.Tables(TableName)
    dcs(0) = .Columns(FieldName)
    .PrimaryKey = dcs
  End With
End Sub
```

The `AddPrimaryKey` procedure handles the simple case where you provide a DataSet, a table name, and a field name. The procedure adds a primary key to the specified table within the DataSet, adding only the single specified field. (You could modify the procedure to accept multiple field names and add the grouping of all the fields as the primary key, but we'll leave that exercise for your spare time.) The `PrimaryKey` property of a `DataTable` object expects to receive an array of `DataColumn` objects, and even though this procedure will never have more than a single `DataColumn` to add, it still must work with an array.

The procedure starts by setting up an array of `DataColumn` objects, allowing only a single value (the array is indexed from 0 to 0, allowing just that element in column 0):

```
Dim dcs(0) As DataColumn
```

Next, the code adds the specified `DataColumn` object to the array:

```
With ds.Tables(TableName)
  dcs(0) = .Columns(FieldName)
  ...
End With
```

Finally, the code sets the `PrimaryKey` property of the `DataTable` object to be the array it just created:

```
With ds.Tables(TableName)
  ...
  .PrimaryKey = dcs
End With
```

Building the Relational DataSet

Now that you've got the two important and complex procedures out of the way, look at the code that builds the relational DataSet. Follow these steps to investigate the code:

1. Find the `Page_Load` procedure, which calls the `LoadEmps` and `LoadOrders` procedures:

    ```
    Private Sub Page_Load( _
      ByVal sender As System.Object, _
      ByVal e As System.EventArgs) _
      Handles MyBase.Load

      If Not Page.IsPostBack Then
        LoadEmps()
        LoadOrders(CInt(ddlEmps.SelectedItem.Value))
      End If
    End Sub
    ```

2. Find the `LoadEmps` procedure. This procedure calls `GetRelationalDataSet` (which you'll add soon) and then binds the DropDownList control to the Employees table within the DataSet:

```
Private Sub LoadEmps()
  Dim ds As DataSet

  ds = GetRelationalDataSet()

  With ddlEmps
    .DataTextField = "EmpName"
    .DataValueField = "EmployeeID"
    .DataSource = ds.Tables("Employees")
    .DataBind()
  End With
End Sub
```

3. Now take a look at the `GetRelationalDataSet` procedure, shown in Listing 14.5. This procedure fills a DataSet with two DataTables (named `EmployeeInfo` and `OrderInfo`), sets up a relation between the two tables, and adds primary keys to both `DataTable` objects. Finally, the procedure stores the DataSet in a Session variable for later in the use of this page.

LISTING 14.5   Retrieve a Relational `DataSet` Object

```
Private Function GetRelationalDataSet() As DataSet
  ' Build a DataSet containing two related tables:
  ' Employees->Orders, related on EmployeeID.
  ' This requires calling the Fill method of the
  ' DataAdapter twice, once for each table.

  ' This method both returns the filled DataSet,
  ' and stuffs the DataSet into a Session variable
  ' for use on postback.

  Dim ds As DataSet
  Dim da As OleDbDataAdapter

  Dim strSQLEmp As String
  Dim strSQLOrders As String
  Dim strConn As String

  ' Build Employee and Orders SQL
  strSQLEmp = "SELECT EmployeeID, " & _
    "LastName + ', ' + FirstName As EmpName " & _
    "FROM Employees"
```

LISTING 14.5   Continued

```
strSQLOrders = "SELECT EmployeeID, " & _
 "ShipName, ShipCountry, OrderDate " & _
 "FROM Orders"

strConn = Session("ConnectString").ToString()
da = New OleDbDataAdapter(strSQLEmp, strConn)


Try
  ' Add the Employees to the DataSet
  ds = New DataSet()
  da.Fill(ds, "EmployeeInfo")

  ' Change the SQL text to the Orders table
  ' Add the Orders to the DataSet. You could
  ' also simply reinstantiate the DataAdapter,
  ' but this is faster, we assume.
  da.SelectCommand.CommandText = strSQLOrders
  da.Fill(ds, "OrderInfo")

  ' Build a relation, and add it to the DataSet.
  AddRelation(ds, "EmpOrders", _
   "EmployeeInfo", "EmployeeID", _
   "OrderInfo", "EmployeeID")

  ' Set the Customers table primary key field
  AddPrimaryKey(ds, "EmployeeInfo", "EmployeeID")

  ' Set the Orders table primary key field
  AddPrimaryKey(ds, "OrderInfo", "OrderID")

  ' Store DataSet in Session Variable
  Session("DS") = ds


  Return ds

Catch
  Throw

End Try
End Function
```

The `GetRelationalDataSet` does a lot of work. It takes these actions as it sets up the two `DataTable` objects:

- It sets up the two SQL strings it needs in order to retrieve its two `DataTable` objects:

```
strSQLEmp = "SELECT EmployeeID, " & _
 "LastName + ', ' + FirstName As EmpName " & _
 "FROM Employees"

strSQLOrders = "SELECT EmployeeID, " & _
 "ShipName, ShipCountry, OrderDate " & _
 "FROM Orders"
```

- It retrieves the application's connection string and creates a new DataAdapter:

```
strConn = Session("ConnectString").ToString()
da = New OleDbDataAdapter(strSQLEmp, strConn)
```

- It creates the new DataSet and fills the first DataTable (named EmployeeInfo) with information from the Employees table:

```
' Add the Employees to the DataSet
ds = New DataSet()
da.Fill(ds, "EmployeeInfo")
```

- It changes the DataAdapter's `CommandText` property and then fills the second DataTable (named OrderInfo) with information from the Orders table:

```
da.SelectCommand.CommandText = strSQLOrders
da.Fill(ds, "OrderInfo")
```

- It adds the relationship between the two tables:

```
AddRelation(ds, "EmpOrders", _
 "EmployeeInfo", "EmployeeID", _
 "OrderInfo", "EmployeeID")
```

- It adds the two primary keys:

```
AddPrimaryKey(ds, "EmployeeInfo", "EmployeeID")
AddPrimaryKey(ds, "OrderInfo", "OrderID")
```

- It stores the DataSet in a `Session` variable for later use and returns the DataSet as its return value:

```
Session("DS") = ds
Return ds
```

TIP

We haven't talked much about using Session variables to maintain the status of data between pages or postbacks to the same page—you'll find this information in Chapter 23, "State Management in ASP.NET." For now, all you need to understand is that we're using a global "bag" in which to store the DataSet so that it's available the next time we need it without having to re-create it.

Filtering the Grid Based on the Relation

When you select an employee from the DropDownList control, you need to be able to filter the grid to show only orders taken by that employee. Follow these steps to accomplish that goal:

1. Find the ddlEmps_SelectedIndexChanged procedure in the code editor:

```
Private Sub ddlEmps_SelectedIndexChanged( _
ByVal sender As System.Object, _
ByVal e As System.EventArgs) _
Handles ddlEmps.SelectedIndexChanged

    LoadOrders(CInt(ddlEmps.SelectedItem.Value))
End Sub
```

2. Note that the DropDownList control calls the LoadOrders procedure when you change the selected index:

```
Private Sub LoadOrders(ByVal EmpID As Integer)
    Dim ds As DataSet
    Dim dt As DataTable

    Dim drwEmp As DataRow
    Dim drwOrder As DataRow
    Dim drw As DataRow

    ' Rehydrate the DataSet
    ds = CType(Session("DS"), DataSet)

    ' Clone the structure of the old table
    dt = ds.Tables("OrderInfo").Clone

    ' Find the row selected
    drwEmp = ds.Tables("EmployeeInfo").Rows.Find(EmpID)
```

```
' Copy all rows from the child relation
' Into a new data table
For Each drwOrder In drwEmp.GetChildRows("EmpOrders")
  dt.ImportRow(drwOrder)
Next

  grdOrders.DataSource = dt
  grdOrders.DataBind()
End Sub
```

The LoadOrders procedure uses a few techniques you've not previously seen. The procedure does its work by executing these actions:

- Besides declaring DataSet and DataTable variables, the LoadOrders procedure declares three DataRow variables to keep track of the various rows of data it will manage:

```
Dim ds As DataSet
Dim dt As DataTable

Dim drwEmp As DataRow
Dim drwOrder As DataRow
Dim drw As DataRow
```

- It retrieves the DataSet object from the Session variable. In an earlier procedure, you stored the saved DataSet object in a Session variable, and now it's time to retrieve it so that the code can display the appropriate rows from the OrderInfo DataTable in the grid. The following code "rehydrates" a DataSet from the value stored in the Session variable. Note that the code must use the CType function to convert from Object (which is what the Session variable returns) to a DataSet type:

```
' Rehydrate the DataSet
ds = CType(Session("DS"), DataSet)
```

- It clones the structure of the OrderInfo table. Because the code will need to add rows to a new table but will need to use the same schema as the OrderInfo DataTable, the procedure uses the Clone method to retrieve a clone of the schema. You can't simply copy the entire DataTable—it contains all the rows, and all you want is a subset that contains just the rows corresponding to the selected employee:

```
' Clone the structure of the old table
dt = ds.Tables("OrderInfo").Clone
```

- It finds the employee you selected. The code uses the `Find` method of the `Rows` property of a DataTable to find a particular row, given the primary key value for the DataTable. The `Find` method returns a `DataRow` object:

```
' Find the row selected
drwEmp = ds.Tables("EmployeeInfo").Rows.Find(EmpID)
```

- It copies the orders for the employee to the new, cloned table. In order to bind the grid, you need to copy the orders for the selected employee to the new DataTable. To make this simple, ADO.NET provides the `GetChildRows` method of a `DataRow` object. This method only works if you've set up a relation between DataTables, as you did here. The `GetChildRows` method returns a collection of `DataRow` objects, and you can call the `ImportRow` method of the new DataTable to import each `DataRow` object you find:

```
For Each drwOrder In drwEmp.GetChildRows("EmpOrders")
  dt.ImportRow(drwOrder)
Next
```

- It binds the grid to the new DataTable. Because you've just laboriously filled a new DataTable with all the orders for the selected employee, it's simple to bind the grid to the new DataTable and display the selected rows:

```
grdOrders.DataSource = dt
grdOrders.DataBind()
```

At this point, run the sample project and verify the behavior of this page. Although there's a ton of code involved (that's why we didn't have you type it yourself), the sample page does show off some interesting techniques involving relational data.

This seems like a lot of code, and it does introduce a large number of new concepts. One thing's for certain: The .NET Framework is incredibly rich, and it provides solutions to most standard programming tasks. We weren't sure, when we started this exercise, exactly how we would accomplish our goals. We approached the challenge by trying one thing after another, digging deep into the methods provided by various objects, until we hit upon what seemed an optimal solution to the problem. It was a fun learning experience. The point here is that you'll learn a lot by picking a particular goal and then spending a few hours trying to accomplish that goal, looking for the best means to get the results you need using methods provided by the .NET Framework.

Summary

In this chapter, you began your exploration of ADO.NET's data-management objects. Here's what you learned:

- The DataReader (OleDbDataReader or SqlDataReader) is great at retrieving data quickly and efficiently. Because it only provides forward-only, read-only access to data (and in many cases, you must retrieve columns in a particular order), it can make your work a little harder when coding. But you will find that the performance benefits are well worth the extra coding you may have to do. A DataSet is made up of one or many DataTable objects, and you can set relationships between these data tables. You may also want to add primary keys to each data table so that you can search within the tables later on.

- You can use a DataRelation object to allow you to retrieve multiple related data tables and look up child rows based on a selected parent row. This allows you to make one request for data to the database server but show specific data from the data tables on request.

15

Using Stored Procedures with ADO.NET

OBJECTIVES

- Learn to execute stored procedures that return data

- Learn to pass parameters to a stored procedure

- Learn to use OUTPUT parameters

It's likely that any reasonably sized database application will need to execute stored procedures at some point. You might use stored procedures to return data or to execute action queries. There are many reasons why you might want to use stored procedures as part of an ASP.NET application. We can't list them all, and you may have your own reasons. However, here are some of the more common reasons:

- You have no choice—you need to retrieve or manipulate data, and you don't control the database server. Your DBA told you that you must use stored procedures.

- Stored procedures are generally more efficient than using dynamic SQL strings as part of your code. Because the database server can precompile and preoptimize the query's execution plan, your applications run more efficiently.

- Stored procedures put the database-handling code where it ought to be—on the database server. There are many reasons to include data-manipulation code in your application, but duplicating the same queries throughout your code is a maintenance nightmare. Placing data-manipulation and retrieval code all in one place makes it much easier to maintain your application.

- Stored procedures allow you to pass parameters that can control the runtime activity. Although you can mimic this behavior in code, by simply building a different SQL string for each way you might use the stored procedure, you lose the precompiled execution plan when you use that technique. Stored procedures can accept parameters as input parameters, output parameters, or both.

We feel quite strongly that you'll do better by placing most, if not all, your data-manipulation and retrieval code in stored procedures, if at all possible. Although we won't spend time in this book discussing the details of creating stored procedures, it's a topic you should at least be conversant in. In addition, because we don't want to meddle with your installation of SQL Server too very much, we'll only use stored procedures in this single chapter.

TIP

Of course, stored procedures are only available on database server applications, such as SQL Server, Oracle, Sybase, and so on. If you're working with data stored in an Access/Jet data-base, you won't be using stored procedures. However, you'll still need to be able to pass parameters into the query (Access queries don't allow output parameters), and you'll need some way to execute the query and retrieve its results. Certainly, running an Access query is far more limited than using a stored procedure, but many of the same concepts apply.

In this chapter, you'll use stored procedures to manipulate data in SQL Server tables. You'll add stored procedures to the Northwind database in SQL Server and use these procedures to add, edit, and delete rows from the tables in the sample database.

Setting Up the Sample Stored Procedures

In this chapter, you'll import a new page, shown in Figure 15.1, that allows you to work with the Employees table in the Northwind sample database. (There's too much code here to ask you to create it yourself—this time, you'll just inspect it.) You'll list all employees, add a new employee, and delete an employee. In each case, you'll use a stored procedure to do your work. In addition, to demonstrate the similarities (and the differences), you'll look at the code that calls the "add" stored procedure twice—first using the `OleDb` namespace and then using the `SqlClient` namespace.

In order to work with `EmployeeSP.aspx`, you'll need to add it to your project. Follow these steps to add the page:

1. Open your `Northwind.sln` solution in Visual Studio .NET.

2. Select Project, Add Existing Item. Be sure to select "All Files (*.*)" from the Files of Type combo box.

3. Find the `EmployeeSP.*` files in the `Jumpstart\StoredProcs` folder and load them into the project.

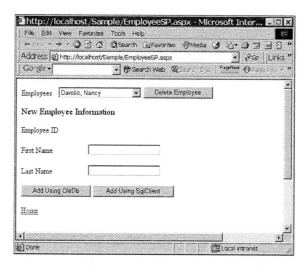

FIGURE 15.1   Use this Web page to input a new employee, list employees, and delete employees using stored procedures.

You should now be able to load the EmployeeSP.aspx page in the page designer and see a Web page that looks similar to the one shown in Figure 15.1.

You'll need to add another hyperlink to the Main page of your Northwind Web site so it can call this new EmployeeSP.aspx page. Follow these steps to add the link:

1. Open Main.aspx in the page designer.

2. Add a new Hyperlink control just below the Employees hyperlink.

3. Set the properties for the control as shown in Table 15.1.

TABLE 15.1   Set These Properties for the New Hyperlink Control

Property	Name
ID	hypEmpSP
Text	Employee (Stored Procedures)
NavigateURL	EmployeeSP.aspx

Adding Stored Procedures to the Database

In order for EmployeeSP.aspx to do its work, you'll need to add three stored procedures to the Northwind sample database. To add the stored procedures to your database, follow these steps:

1. From the Windows Start menu, locate and run the SQL Server Query Analyzer application.

2. In SQL Query Analyzer, use the File, Open menu to locate and select the `JumpStart\StoredProcs\EmpSP.sql` file, which contains the scripts you need to create the new stored procedures.

3. Press F5 to run the script. (If you run the script more than once, you'll see errors on subsequent passes, but you can disregard those errors.)

4. When you're done, shut down the SQL Query Analyzer application.

> **WARNING**
>
> As in the rest of this book, all the steps listed in this section assume that you're running SQL Server on your own local machine and that you have complete rights to modify it. If that's not the case, you'll need to check with your system administrator to see about modifying the schema of the Northwind sample database. The steps listed here also assume that the SQL Server service is running.

The three stored procedures allow you to list, add, and delete employees. The first, `EmployeeList` (see Listing 15.1), retrieves full name and ID information for each employee and returns a set of rows containing the results:

LISTING 15.1   Retrieve a Set of Rows Using a Stored Procedure

```
CREATE PROCEDURE EmployeeList
AS
 SELECT LastName + ', ' + FirstName As Name, EmployeeID
 FROM Employees
GO
```

The second procedure, `EmployeeDelete` (see Listing 15.2), is simple. You pass in an employee ID value, and this procedure deletes that employee:

LISTING 15.2   Delete a Row Using a Stored Procedure

```
CREATE PROCEDURE EmployeeDelete
      @EmpID int
AS
 DELETE FROM Employees WHERE EmployeeID = @EmpID
GO
```

The third procedure, `EmployeeAdd` (see Listing 15.3), is the complex one. This procedure expects you to supply first name and last name values as input parameters. The stored procedure uses an `INSERT` statement to insert the new employee, and it returns the new employee ID in the output parameter, `@EmpID`. The procedure returns the error value, if any, as the return value of the procedure.

LISTING 15.3   Add a Row Using a Stored Procedure

```
CREATE PROCEDURE EmployeeAdd
        @EmpID int OUTPUT,
        @FirstName Char(10),
        @LastName Char(20)
AS
 INSERT INTO Employees( FirstName, LastName)
 VALUES(@FirstName, @LastName)
 SELECT @EmpID = @@IDENTITY
 RETURN @@ERROR
GO
```

Loading the `DataHandlerSqlClient` Class

Throughout this book, you've been building the `DataHandler` class, which provides generic procedures for working with data using the `OleDb` namespace. In this chapter, we've provided examples that also use the `SqlClient` namespace. This namespace includes objects that are specific to SQL Server, and using them can be more efficient if you know you'll only be working with SQL Server. In addition, working with the `SqlClient` namespace alters the way you call stored procedures a bit, and it's important to compare the `OleDb` and `SqlClient` namespaces in this regard. If you dig into the `DataHandlerSqlClient` class, you'll find the same procedures you've seen in the `DataHandler` class, except in this class the procedures interact with the `SqlClient` namespace's objects.

To load the `DataHandlerSqlClient` class into your project, follow these steps:

1. Select Project, Add Existing Item from the menu bar.

2. Find the `DataHandlerSqlClient.vb` file in the `Jumpstart\Northwind` folder and load this file into this solution.

If you investigate the code, you'll find that these procedures are almost identical to their cousins in the `DataHandler` class. One difference is the `Imports` statement at the top. `DataHandler` imports `System.Data.OleDb`, and `DataHandlerSqlClient` imports `System.Data.SqlClient`. Take a few moments and compare the two classes—you'll see that they're almost identical.

> **TIP**
>
> If it bothers you that you have two classes that are nearly identical, you're not alone! Because this book doesn't focus on object-oriented techniques, following through on this tip is beyond the scope of the book. If you're interested, look into the `IDbCommand`, `IDbConnection`, and `IDbDataAdapter` interfaces. You can take advantage of these types to create a generic class that will work with any ADO.NET namespace.

Modifying `Global.asax`

Because you'll need a connection string that works with the `SqlClient` namespace, you'll need to modify `Global.asax` to call the `ConnectStringBuild` procedure in the class you've just added. Follow these steps to add the necessary call:

1. In the Solution Explorer window, select `Global.asax`.

2. Right-click and select View Code from the context menu.

3. Modify the `Session_Start` procedure so that it looks like this:

```
Sub Session_Start( _
 ByVal sender As Object, _
 ByVal e As EventArgs)
  Session("LoginID") = String.Empty
  Session("Password") = String.Empty
  Session("ConnectString") = _
   DataHandler.ConnectStringBuild("sa", "")
  Session("ConnectStringSql") = _
   DataHandlerSqlClient.ConnectStringBuild("sa", "")
End Sub
```

The `OleDb` Namespace and Stored Procedures

In this section, you'll investigate the three stored procedures that use the `OleDb` namespace. You'll use the three stored procedures you added to the Northwind database from a demonstration page. You'll see how to supply parameter values, as well.

Retrieving a List of All Employees

To demonstrate calling stored procedures from your ASP.NET applications, start out by investigating the `EmpLoad` procedure (in `EmployeeSP.aspx.vb`), which calls the `EmployeeList` stored procedure. Listing 15.4 shows the complete `EmpLoad` procedure.

LISTING 15.4 Call a Stored Procedure to Fill a DataSet

```
Private Sub EmpLoad()
  Dim ds As DataSet
  Dim da As OleDbDataAdapter
  Dim strSQL As String
  Dim strConn As String

  strConn = Session("ConnectString").ToString()

  strSQL = "EmployeeList"

  Try
    ds = New DataSet()
    da = New OleDbDataAdapter(strSQL, strConn)

    da.Fill(ds, "Employees")

    With ddlEmps
      .DataTextField = "Name"
      .DataValueField = "EmployeeID"
      .DataSource = ds
      .DataBind()
    End With
```

LISTING 15.4   Continued

```
Catch exp As Exception
   lblError.Text = exp.Message

End Try
End Sub
```

Not much new here! This procedure looks exactly like procedures you've seen in other chapters, except for one big difference: Rather than specifying a SELECT statement as the SQL expression to be evaluated, this procedure uses the name of a stored procedure. It's that simple—pass the DataAdapter object a stored procedure that returns rows, and it can fill a DataSet using the stored procedure just as easily as it did using a SQL SELECT statement directly.

The Page_Load procedure for the page calls the EmpLoad procedure so that the DropDownList control gets filled as you load the page:

```
Private Sub Page_Load( _
 ByVal sender As System.Object, _
 ByVal e As System.EventArgs) _
 Handles MyBase.Load

  If Not Page.IsPostBack Then
    EmpLoad()
  End If
End Sub
```

 It's time to test calling a stored procedure. Follow these steps to verify that things are working as planned:

1. In the Solution Explorer window, right-click EmployeeSP.aspx and select Build and Browse from the context menu.

2. Verify that the DropDownList control contains the list of employees. Remember, you obtained that list by calling a stored procedure.

Adding an Employee

The sample page provides text boxes where you can enter a new employee's first and last names. If you enter values and then click Add Using OleDb (we'll come back to Add Using SqlClient later), you'll run a stored procedure that adds the new employee and passes back the new employee's ID. Clicking the button runs the code in Listing 15.5.

LISTING 15.5   Add a New Row Using a Stored Procedure

```
Private Sub EmpAddOleDb()
  Dim cmd As OleDbCommand
  Dim strSQL As String
  Dim strConn As String
  Dim intRows As Integer

  ' Retrieve connection string
  strConn = Session("ConnectString").ToString

  ' The stored procedure name
  strSQL = "EmployeeAdd"
  Try
    cmd = New OleDbCommand()
    With cmd
      ' Create a Connection object
      .Connection = _
        New OleDbConnection(strConn)

      ' Set the SQL
      .CommandText = strSQL
      .CommandType = CommandType.StoredProcedure

      ' Create return value parameter
      ' Must be the first parameter added
      With .Parameters.Add("ReturnValue", _
        OleDbType.Integer)
          .Direction = ParameterDirection.ReturnValue
      End With

      ' Create OUTPUT Parameter for
      ' EmployeeID which will be
      ' fetched using @@IDENTITY
      With .Parameters.Add("EmpID", OleDbType.Integer)
          .Direction = ParameterDirection.Output
      End With

      ' Add input parameters.
      With .Parameters.Add("FirstName", _
        OleDbType.Char, 10)
          .Value = txtFirst.Text
      End With
```

LISTING 15.5   Continued

```
    With .Parameters.Add("LastName", _
      OleDbType.Char, 20)
        .Value = txtLast.Text
    End With

      ' Open the connection
      .Connection.Open()

      ' Execute the stored procedure
      intRows = .ExecuteNonQuery()

      ' Get the output parameter
      lblEmpID.Text = _
        CStr(.Parameters("EmpID").Value)

      ' Get the return value parameter
      lblError.Text = "ReturnValue = " & _
        CStr(.Parameters("ReturnValue").Value) & _
        "<BR>Rows Affected=" & intRows.ToString()
    End With

    ' Reload DropDownList control
    EmpLoad()

  Catch exp As Exception
    lblError.Text = exp.Message

  Finally
    ' Close the Connection
    With cmd.Connection
      If .State = ConnectionState.Open Then
        .Close()
      End If
    End With
  End Try
End Sub
```

Overall, this procedure doesn't do much (although it does contain what appears to be a lot of code). For the most part, it creates `Parameter` objects (actually, `OleDbParameter` or `SqlParameter` objects) representing each of the parameters you must send the stored procedure, and it appends the parameters to the `Parameters` property of the `Command` object. Once it has done that, it calls the stored procedure. Finally, it retrieves the output parameter (the `EmpID` parameter) and the return value (the error code).

Step by step, the procedure takes these actions:

- It retrieves the connection string and sets up the SQL for the `Command` object:

```
' Set up the connection and SQL strings.
strConn = Session("ConnectString").ToString
strSQL = "EmployeeAdd"
```

- It creates a new `Command` object and sets its properties, as you've seen before:

```
cmd = New OleDbCommand()
With cmd
  ' Create a Connection object
  .Connection = _
    New OleDbConnection(strConn)

  ' Set the SQL
  .CommandText = strSQL
  .CommandType = CommandType.StoredProcedure
  ...
End With
```

TIP

The `CommandType` parameter indicates to ADO.NET what type of value you've placed in the `CommandText` property. In this case, you've given the `CommandText` property the name of a stored procedure and therefore have set the `CommandType` property accordingly. Although ADO.NET can "guess" what you've sent it, it's best to be explicit.

- It creates a new `Parameter` object, indicating that it's to be an `Integer` type and that it's the return value:

```
' Create return value parameter
' Must be the first parameter added
With .Parameters.Add("ReturnValue", _
  OleDbType.Integer)
    .Direction = ParameterDirection.ReturnValue
End With
```

TIP

When you're using the `OleDb` namespace, it's important that you add the "return value" parameter first. (That is, if you set the `Direction` property to be `ParameterDirection.ReturnValue`, it must be the first parameter added.) When using the `SqlClient` namespace, the order doesn't matter. Also, the name of the parameter doesn't matter. We've named this `ReturnValue`, but it could have been named anything. The important issue is that the `Direction` property has been set to `ParameterDirection.ReturnValue`.

- It creates the output parameter object, named `EmpID` (see the definition of the stored procedure, earlier in the chapter, to match up the parameter name). The code indicates that this is an output parameter by setting the `Direction` property:

```
' Create OUTPUT Parameter for
' EmployeeID which will be
' fetched using @@IDENTITY
With .Parameters.Add("EmpID", OleDbType.Integer)
   .Direction = ParameterDirection.Output
End With
```

- It creates the two standard input parameters: `FirstName` and `LastName`. The code sets the value for each (remember, you're sending these values into the stored procedure, so you need to indicate the value of the parameters before calling it):

```
' Add input parameters.
With .Parameters.Add("FirstName", _
 OleDbType.Char, 10)
   .Value = txtFirst.Text
End With

With .Parameters.Add("LastName", _
 OleDbType.Char, 20)
   .Value = txtLast.Text
End With
```

- It opens the connection and calls the procedure. Executing the procedure returns the number of rows it affected:

```
' Open the connection
.Connection.Open()

' Execute the stored procedure
intRows = .ExecuteNonQuery()
```

- The stored procedure filled in its output parameter with the new employee ID value, so the code needs to retrieve that and display it:

```
' Get the output parameter
lblEmpID.Text = _
  CStr(.Parameters("EmpID").Value)
```

- The code retrieves the return value and displays this value and the number of rows affected in the label on the page:

```
' Get the return value parameter
lblError.Text = "ReturnValue = " & _
  CStr(.Parameters("ReturnValue").Value) & _
  "<BR>Rows Affected=" & intRows.ToString()
```

- It reloads the list of employees, because there's now a new one in the list:

```
' Reload DropDownList control
EmpLoad()
```

- Whether the procedure succeeds or fails, it closes the connection. Attempting to close a connection that isn't open triggers a runtime error, so the code checks the state of the connection first and only closes it if necessary:

```
' Close the Connection
With cmd.Connection
  If .State = ConnectionState.Open Then
    .Close()
  End If
End With
```

Deleting an Employee

After the page loads the list of employees, you can select an employee from the list. If you click Delete Employee, you'll run code that executes a stored procedure to delete the selected employee.

> **NOTE**
>
> Due to constraints in SQL Server, not every employee will be able to be deleted. If an employee has taken orders, referential integrity will make it impossible for you to delete the employee—this is a good thing! If you receive an error, that means the chosen employee has sales information that stops the employee from being deleted. Actually, your best bet is to attempt to delete only employees you've added.

When you click the Delete Employee button, the `Click` event procedure will call the `EmpDelete` procedure, as shown in the following code:

```
Private Sub EmpDelete()
  Dim cmd As OleDbCommand
  Dim intRows As Integer
  Dim strSQL As String
  Dim strConn As String

  ' Build Connection String
  strConn = Session("ConnectString").ToString
  strSQL = "EmployeeDelete"

  Try
    cmd = New OleDbCommand()
    With cmd
      ' Create a Connection object
      .Connection = New OleDbConnection(strConn)

      ' Set the SQL
      .CommandText = strSQL
      .CommandType = CommandType.StoredProcedure

      ' Create Parameter for EmployeeID
      With .Parameters.Add("EmpID", OleDbType.Integer)
        .Value = ddlEmps.SelectedItem.Value
      End With

      ' Open the connection
      .Connection.Open()

      ' Execute the stored procedure
      intRows = .ExecuteNonQuery()

      ' Get the return value
      lblError.Text = "# of rows deleted = " & _
        intRows.ToString()

      ' Reload DropDownList control
      EmpLoad()
    End With
```

```
  Catch exp As Exception
    lblError.Text = exp.Message

  Finally
    ' Close the Connection
    With cmd.Connection
      If .State = ConnectionState.Open Then
        .Close()
      End If
    End With
  End Try
End Sub
```

This code is nearly identical to the EmpAddOleDb procedure in all its "moving parts." The only real difference is in the parameters: This procedure includes only a single parameter, and because it's an input parameter (the default type), you needn't specify the direction:

```
With .Parameters.Add("EmpID", OleDbType.Integer)
  .Value = ddlEmps.SelectedItem.Value
End With
```

You do need to specify the type (OleDbType.Integer) and the value (ddlEmps.SelectedItem.Value). Otherwise, the two procedures work nearly identically.

TIP

The order of the parameters you pass to the stored procedure is significant when you use the OleDb namespace. The first parameter must be the return value, if any. After that, you must add parameters to the Parameters collection in the same order in which they appear in the stored procedure (in this case, EmpId, FirstName, and LastName).

The SqlClient Namespace and Stored Procedures

Now that you've seen how to call stored procedures using the OleDb namespace, it's interesting to compare the same tasks using the SqlClient namespace. Remember that when you use the SqlClient namespace, you're using code that's written to interact specifically with SQL Server, and this code can take advantage of specific SQL Server features. The code you'll see, EmpAddSqlClient, works almost identically to the EmpAddOleDb procedure you saw earlier, but there are some subtle differences.

Listing 15.6 shows the entire procedure.

LISTING 15.6   Using the `SqlClient` Namespace to Call a Stored Procedure

```
Private Sub EmpAddSqlClient()
 Dim cmd As SqlClient.SqlCommand
 Dim strSQL As String
 Dim strConn As String
 Dim intRows As Integer

 ' Set up the connection and SQL strings.
 strConn = Session("ConnectStringSQL").ToString
 strSQL = "EmployeeAdd"

 Try
   cmd = New SqlClient.SqlCommand()
   With cmd
     ' Create a Connection object
     .Connection = _
       New SqlClient.SqlConnection(strConn)

     ' Set the SQL
     .CommandText = strSQL
     .CommandType = CommandType.StoredProcedure

     ' Create OUTPUT Parameter for
     ' EmployeeID which will be
     ' fetched using @@IDENTITY
     With .Parameters.Add("@EmpID", _
      SqlDbType.Int)
       .Direction = ParameterDirection.Output
     End With

     ' Create input parameters
     With .Parameters.Add("@FirstName", _
      SqlDbType.Char, 10)
       .Value = txtFirst.Text
     End With

     ' Create input parameter for LastName
     With .Parameters.Add("@LastName", _
      SqlDbType.Char, 20)
       .Value = txtLast.Text
```

LISTING 15.6   Continued

```
      End With

        ' Create Return Value parameter
        ' Doesn't need to be the first parameter added!
        With .Parameters.Add("ReturnValue", _
         SqlDbType.Int)
          .Direction = ParameterDirection.ReturnValue
        End With

        ' Open the connection
        .Connection.Open()

        ' Execute the stored procedure
        intRows = .ExecuteNonQuery()

        ' Get the output parameter
        lblEmpID.Text = _
         CStr(.Parameters("@EmpID").Value)

        ' Get the return value parameter
        lblError.Text = "Return Value = " & _
         CStr(.Parameters("ReturnValue").Value) & _
          "<BR>Rows Affected=" & intRows.ToString()
      End With

      ' Reload DropDownList control
      EmpLoad()

    Catch exp As Exception
      lblError.Text = exp.Message

    Finally
      ' Close the Connection
      With cmd.Connection
        If .State = ConnectionState.Open Then
          .Close()
        End If
      End With
    End Try
  End Sub
```

If you look carefully, you'll note some subtle differences:

- The parameter types use a different enumeration (SqlDbType as opposed to OleDbType).

- The parameter names must match the exact names used in the stored procedure. That is, the parameters you create in your code must include "@," which is part of the stored procedure names:

```
With .Parameters.Add("@EmpID", SqlDbType.Int)
   .Direction = ParameterDirection.Output
End With

' Create input parameters
With .Parameters.Add("@FirstName", SqlDbType.Char, 10)
   .Value = txtFirst.Text
End With

' Create input parameter for LastName
With .Parameters.Add("@LastName", SqlDbType.Char, 20)
   .Value = txtLast.Text
End With
```

- The order of the parameters doesn't matter—given the names you supply, SQL Server can figure out which parameters go where. This is distinctly different from using the OleDb namespace, in which parameter order is significant.

Summary

Using stored procedures is an efficient way to submit SQL to a back-end database. However, one of the downsides is that the code is not as readable, because you must look in two places to really see all the code. In this chapter, you learned:

- How to call a stored procedure to insert, delete, and retrieve data into/from a table in SQL Server from ADO.NET.

- How to retrieve data from an output parameter provided by a stored procedure.

- How to use both the SqlClient and OleDb namespaces when working with stored procedures.

TIP

This chapter, and the book in general, focuses on using Microsoft tools and technologies. If you're interested in working with other data sources, you'll be forced to use the `OleDb` namespace (at least, until a managed provider for your data source becomes available), and you'll use techniques similar to those you used with ADO in order to connect to the data and to call stored procedures. If you're working with Oracle, you can start by studying Microsoft's Knowledge Base articles on the topic. You can find one article at `http://support.` `microsoft.com/default.aspx?scid=kb;EN-US;q229919`.

16

Using the DataGrid Control

One of the important features of ASP.NET and the whole Microsoft .NET platform is that you can create rich, full-featured Web applications quickly and easily. To make this goal possible, Microsoft has provided a large group of server controls, all providing server-side functionality and events. Many of these server controls provide data-binding capabilities, as well. These controls run on the server yet send HTML code out to the client's browser. If you need to display a table of information on an HTML page, one of the best tools for this job is the DataGrid control.

If you need to display tabular data, and you want the maximum flexibility, the DataGrid control is the control you want. (You'll also find the DataList and Repeater controls, covered in other chapters, useful. But these controls provide less functionality than the DataGrid control.) Using the DataGrid control, you can add these features to your display:

- Sorting by column
- Editing
- Deleting rows
- Selecting rows
- Hyperlinked columns
- Automatic paging
- Alternate row formatting
- Templated columns

OBJECTIVES

- Learn to use the DataGrid control on a Web Form
- Format the data in a DataGrid control
- Page data within a DataGrid control
- Sort columns within a DataGrid control
- Select a row within a DataGrid control

And there's more, of course—we're just introducing the control here. In this chapter, you'll learn about formatting the DataGrid control. You'll learn more about editing and managing data using the DataGrid control in a later chapter.

Adding Features to the DataGrid Control

In this chapter, you'll place a DataGrid control on a page and add features. Specifically, you will perform the following tasks:

- Bind a DataGrid control to an ADO.NET DataSet
- Add numeric formatting to a currency field
- Add paging so users can move through subsets of the data
- Select an individual row
- Sort the data by clicking a column header

Figure 16.1 shows the finished page you'll be building as you work through this chapter.

FIGURE 16.1   It's easy to create a bound table using the DataGrid control. To the browser, it's simply an HTML table with code added in for interactivity.

You will need to add a hyperlink to the main page to call the new page you build in this chapter. Follow these steps to add the link:

1. Open `Main.aspx` in design mode.

2. Add a new HyperLink control just below the Employees hyperlink.

3. Set the properties for this new HyperLink control as shown in Table 16.1.

TABLE 16.1   Set the New HyperLink Control's Properties Using These Values

Property	Value
ID	hypCatSales
Text	Sales by Category
NavigateURL	CategorySales.aspx

Loading the DataGrid Control with Data

In a previous chapter, you saw how to use the user-interface data components to bind a grid to a data source. You created `OleDbDataAdapter` and `OleDbConnection` objects and then used the menus to have the `OleDbAdapter` generate a typed DataSet for you. Although you can use these steps, you might want to bypass the overhead of the typed DataSet and bind the DataGrid to a simple DataSet that you create in code. As a matter of fact, you can bind a DataGrid to at least four different data objects:

- `DataSet`
- `DataTable`
- `DataView`
- `DataReader`

The only one of these that you haven't encountered yet is the `DataView` object. This object "wraps" itself around a DataTable and provides a sortable, filterable view of the data in the DataTable. When you want to work with a DataView, you have two choices. You can retrieve the `DefaultView` property of a DataTable (every DataTable provides a single default `DataView` object), like this:

```
Dim dv As DataView
' Assuming that ds is a DataSet containing at
' least one table
dv = ds.Tables(0).DefaultView
```

If you want to create a new `DataView` object, you can write code like this:

```
Dim dv As DataView
' Assuming that ds is a DataSet containing at
' least one table
dv = New DataView(ds.Tables(0))
```

If you want to sort the data in your DataGrid, you'll need to interact with a `DataView` object—that's the object that allows you to sort the data in the DataTable that's providing the data to the DataGrid.

To get started, create the page shown in Figure 16.1 by following these steps:

1. Select Project, Add Web Form.

2. Set the name of this form to `CategorySales.aspx`.

3. Add controls and set properties as shown in Table 16.2.

TABLE 16.2   Add These Controls (and Properties) to Your `CategorySales.aspx` Page

Control Type	Property	Value
Label	ID	Label1
	Text	Sales By Category
	Font.Bold	True
	Font.Size	Large
DataGrid	ID	grdCatSales
	AllowPaging	True
	AllowSorting	True
	AutoGenerateColumns	False
Label	ID	lblCategory
	Text	(Delete the text in the property value.)
Hyperlink	ID	hypHome
	Text	Home
	NavigateURL	Main.aspx

Three of these properties bear some discussion:

- `AllowPaging` (set to True) turns on paging for the DataGrid control and, by default, adds paging indicators in the control's footer. Paging requires adding some code, however, so you'll still need to write some code to make the paging happen.

- `AllowSorting` (set to True) allows you to sort the data in the grid by clicking column headers. Turning this on adds links to the column headers, but you still have to write the code yourself to sort the data filling the grid. It's important to note that in order to sort the data displayed, you don't sort the grid; instead, you sort the data filling the grid and then rebind the grid to its data source.

- AutoGenerateColumns (set to False) turns off the DataGrid control's feature that retrieves the schema for your data from its data source. In this example, you'll want to explicitly control this behavior, so you're turning this feature off.

TIP

Throughout this chapter, you'll use tools provided by Visual Studio .NET to alter the layout and formatting of your grid. Under the covers, all these tools are doing for you is adding HTML to the page designer. At any point, you can switch to HTML view and check out what the design-time tools have done for you. There's no magic here—you could accomplish all the same goals yourself, simply by typing into the HTML editor.

Formatting the DataGrid Control

On its own, the layout of the DataGrid control is awfully drab. You can easily format the control, using predefined layouts, by taking advantage of the Auto Format option on the control's context menu. To set the formatting for your DataGrid control, follow these steps:

1. Right-click the DataGrid control.

2. Select Auto Format from the context menu.

3. From the Auto Format dialog box, select a format that you like (see Figure 16.2).

4. Click OK to apply the format to your DataGrid control.

Once you've finished, your page should look something like Figure 16.3.

TIP

If you check out properties for the DataGrid control in the Properties window, you'll notice that using Auto Format set a number of properties for you. You can always override the formatting you've just applied, changing any individual property value. You'll also find tools to change individual formatting settings in the Property Builder, which you'll see in the next section.

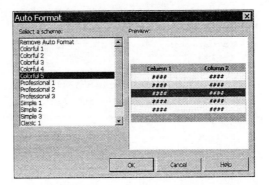

FIGURE 16.2   Select from the supplied formats or set properties individually to provide your own.

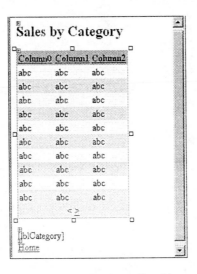

FIGURE 16.3   Your layout should look something like this.

Creating the Columns

You'll need to add columns to your grid, of course, to show data from the DataGrid control's data source. You've seen, in an earlier chapter, how to bind the DataGrid control to a typed DataSet. In this chapter, you'll do the work manually, and you'll work through the steps of adding all the functionality that's required.

To get started adding columns, follow these steps:

1. Right-click the DataGrid control and select Property Builder from the context menu. This dialog box enables you to modify the behavior of the DataGrid control.

2. On the first page, as shown in Figure 16.4, make sure that the Show Header and Allow Sorting options are selected.

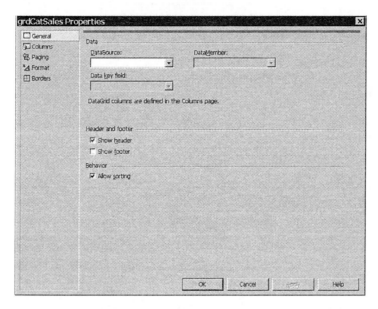

FIGURE 16.4 The grdCatSales Properties dialog box allows you to modify the behavior of the DataGrid control without having to write code.

3. Select the Columns page in the left pane of the dialog box.

4. In the Available Columns list, expand the Button Column node. Click the Select item and then click the > button to add the Select column to the DataGrid control. When you're done, the page should look like Figure 16.5. (You can alter most of the ButtonColumn properties on this page, if you want to experiment, but you should not change the Command Name property— code later on in the chapter expects this name to be Select.)

   Next, you'll add the three bound columns.

5. In the Available Columns list, select Bound Column. Click the > button three times to add three bound columns to the grid.

6. In turn, select each of the three new Bound Column items in the Selected Columns list and modify properties as shown in Table 16.3. When you're done, the dialog box should look like Figure 16.6.

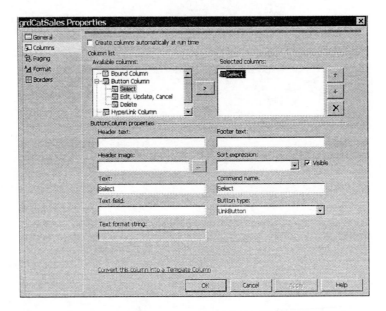

FIGURE 16.5   Add the Select column to your grid.

TABLE 16.3   Add These Properties for the Three Bound Columns

Bound Column Number	Property	Value
1	Header Text	Category ID
	Sort Expression	CategoryID
	Data Field	CategoryID
2	Header Text	Product Name
	Sort Expression	ProductName
	Data Field	ProductName
3	Header Text	Product Sales
	Sort Expression	ProductSales
	Data Field	ProductSales

7. Click OK when you're done to close the dialog box and apply your changes.

8. Note that the DataGrid control now displays the Select column as well as three DataBound columns with the correct headings.

Although you only used two column types, in the Available Columns list, you'll find four different types of columns, as described in Table 16.4.

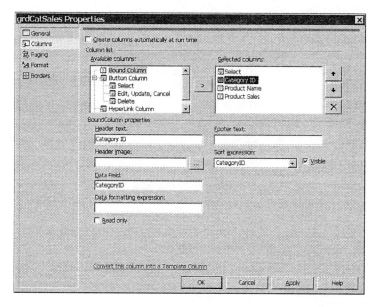

FIGURE 16.6   After adding the four columns, you're ready to bind the data.

TABLE 16.4   You Can Add Four Different Types of Columns to the DataGrid Control

Column Type	Description
Bound	Each of these columns is bound to the data source filling the DataGrid control.
Button	Button columns can look like normal buttons or like hyperlinks. When you use one of the button types listed here, the DataGrid control will raise an event (and you can add code to handle this event) on which type of button you've clicked. The Select type raises the `SelectCommand` event. The Edit, Update, and Cancel types raise the `EditCommand`, `UpdateCommand`, and `CancelCommand` events, respectively. Finally, the Delete type raises the `DeleteCommand` event.
Hyperlink	Creates a hyperlink column. It is up to you to fill in the `NavigateURL` property to indicate to where you wish to navigate when the user clicks this hyperlink.
Template	Allows you to supply your own HTML template that controls the behavior for this column. You could, for example, display each item in the column as a DropDownList control. Using a Template column requires modifying HTML by hand, and you'll see more of this technique in the chapter describing the Repeater control.

Hooking Up the Data

In order to display data in your control, you'll need to write the code that retrieves the data and binds the DataGrid control to that data.

Modifying the `Page_Load` Procedure

The `Page_Load` procedure runs every time the page loads—both the first time and on subsequent postbacks to the page. As you've seen previously, you can use the `IsPostback` property of the page to determine whether the page is in a postback situation and then take different actions if so. In this case, you only need to load the DataGrid control with data on the first "pass." After that, requests for data can retrieve the DataSet from a `Session` variable.

> **TIP**
>
> Although the optimization of storing the DataSet into a `Session` variable isn't required—and perhaps isn't even always desired—in some cases it works well. If your data is relatively static and is unlikely to change while you're working with the page, storing the DataSet in a `Session` variable can save on network traffic and on roundtrips to the database server. For this particular example, it's debatable whether storing the DataSet is ideal. However, it does show off the possibilities and how to use this technique.

To modify the `Page_Load` procedure, follow these steps:

1. Double-click your page, on the page itself (not on any control). This loads the code editor with the `Page_Load` procedure ready to edit.

2. Modify the procedure so that it looks like this:

```
Private Sub Page_Load( _
ByVal sender As System.Object, _
ByVal e As System.EventArgs) _
Handles MyBase.Load

  If Not Page.IsPostBack Then
    CategoryLoad()
    GridLoad()
  End If
End Sub
```

This procedure requires the `CategoryLoad` and `GridLoad` procedures, and you'll add those in the following sections.

Loading the Category Data

The `CategoryLoad` procedure does the work of loading the data from the data source and stores the data in a `Session` variable. (Storing the DataSet means that you don't have to go back to the database server to retrieve it each time you post back to the page.)

Beneath the Page_Load procedure, add the following procedure:

```
Private Sub CategoryLoad()
  Dim strSQL As String
  Dim strConn As String

  ' Set up SQL and Connection strings.
  strSQL = "SELECT * FROM [Sales By Category]"
  strConn = Session("ConnectString").ToString

  ' Create DataSet and
  ' store DataSet into Session variable
  Session("DS") = DataHandler.GetDataSet(strSQL, strConn)
End Sub
```

This procedure uses the Sales By Category view provided by SQL Server to retrieve summary information about sales, by category. Once the code has set up the SQL and connection strings, it calls the GetDataSet method of the DataHandler class (you've seen this method and this class in previous chapters). Then, this code is to place the DataSet object in a Session variable:

```
Session("DS") = DataHandler.GetDataSet(strSQL, strConn)
```

TIP

A Session variable can be any object, referenced by a name ("DS", in this case). Here, you've placed a DataSet object in the Session state and managed by the ASP.NET page framework. You can retrieve the DataSet object later in your code, but because the Session variable comes back to you as an object, you'll need to cast it back to being a DataSet using the CType function.

Loading the DataGrid Control

In order to display data in the DataGrid control, you must take three steps:

1. Retrieve the data.

2. Set the control's DataSource property.

3. Call the control's DataBind method.

The GridLoad procedure handles all three of these tasks. Add the following procedure immediately below the CategoryLoad procedure:

```
Private Sub GridLoad()
  Dim dv As DataView
```

```
' Get default view from stored DataSet
 dv = CType(Session("DS"), DataSet). _
  Tables(0).DefaultView

  ' Fill in DataSource and bind to data.
  grdCatSales.DataSource = dv
  grdCatSales.DataBind()
End Sub
```

Before we begin digging into this procedure, it's important to remember that you can bind a DataGrid control to a number of different types of objects. In this example, the code binds the DataGrid control to a DataView object—this may seem like overkill, because you could just as easily bind the control to the DataSet object you placed into a Session variable earlier. Because you're going to add sorting capabilities later, you'll need to bind the DataGrid control to a DataView object.

GridLoad first retrieves the Session variable, DS, and converts it back to a DataSet object. Then, the code retrieves the DefaultView property of the first table within the DataSet object:

```
dv = CType(Session("DS"), DataSet). _
 Tables(0).DefaultView
```

Then, as promised, the code sets the DataSource property and calls the DataBind method of the DataGrid control:

```
grdCatSales.DataSource = dv
grdCatSales.DataBind()
```

 If you've followed the steps carefully up to now, you should be able to test out your page:

1. In the Solution Explorer, select CategorySales.aspx.

2. Right-click and select Build and Browse from the context menu.

You should see the grid, displaying formatted rows of data from the SQL Server view. (Close the browser window when you're done.)

The remainder of the chapter focuses on adding functionality to the DataGrid control, including column formatting, paging, and sorting.

Formatting Numeric Columns

The DataGrid control allows you to format individual columns, and the Property Builder dialog box makes it easy to add this functionality. You might, for example, want to format the Product Sales column so that the numbers are right aligned and formatted as currency.

To add this functionality, follow these steps:

1. With `CategorySales.aspx` open in the page designer, right-click the DataGrid control.

2. Select Property Builder from the context menu.

3. On the grdCatSales Properties dialog box, select the Format tab and then expand the Columns node. Expand the "Columns[3]—Product Sales" node and select Items. (Effectively, you'll drill down into the various members of the grid until you get to the column you'd like to format.)

4. In the Horizontal Alignment drop-down list, select Right. When you're done, the page should look like Figure 16.7.

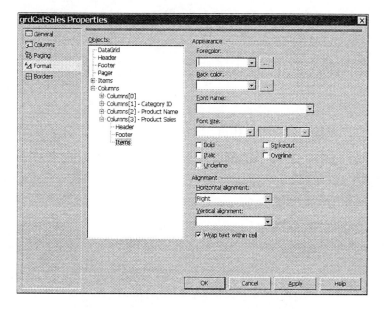

FIGURE 16.7   Set alignment using the Property Builder.

5. Select the Columns tab and then select Product Sales in the Selected columns list.

6. In the Data Formatting Expression text box, enter {0:C}. When you're done, the page should look like Figure 16.8.

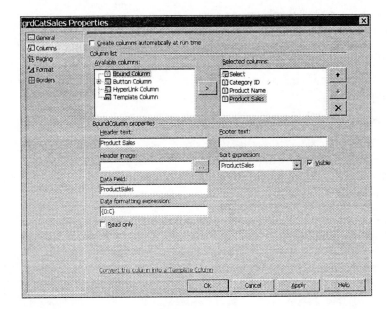

FIGURE 16.8   Enter formatting expressions on the Columns page.

What's going on with the formatting expression? Under the covers, the DataGrid control uses formatting code much like the String.Format method, applying a replaceable parameter, with formatting, to the data that's being displayed in a column. In this case, you want to replace the data with a formatted version, using currency formatting. In this case, {0} acts as the placeholder for the value, and C indicates the particular formatting you want to apply. Table 16.5 contains a list of possible formatting constants.

TABLE 16.5   Select from These Formatting Constants

Format Character	Description	Example
C	Currency	$12.75
D	Decimal	12.75
E	Scientific (Exponential)	1.275000E+001
F	Fixed	12.75
N	Number	12.75
X	Hex	0xC

At this point, browsing the page again contains the correct formatting on the Product Sales column, as shown in Figure 16.9.

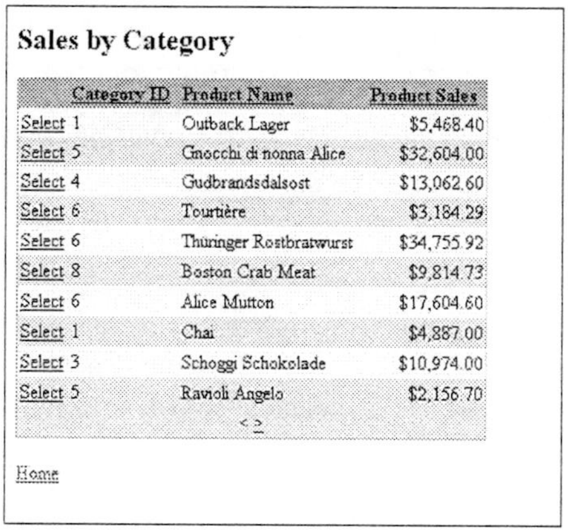

Sales by Category

	Category ID	Product Name	Product Sales
Select	1	Outback Lager	$5,468.40
Select	5	Gnocchi di nonna Alice	$32,604.00
Select	4	Gudbrandsdalsost	$13,062.60
Select	6	Tourtière	$3,184.29
Select	6	Thüringer Rostbratwurst	$34,755.92
Select	8	Boston Crab Meat	$9,814.73
Select	6	Alice Mutton	$17,604.60
Select	1	Chai	$4,887.00
Select	3	Schoggi Schokolade	$10,974.00
Select	5	Ravioli Angelo	$2,156.70
		< >	

Home

FIGURE 16.9   The formatting works, but you'll need code for the interactivity that's required.

At this point you have the grid looking the way you want, but you do not have all the functionality yet. The next sections will walk you through adding paging, selection of data, and sorting.

Enabling Paging

The Sales By Category view in the Northwind sample database returns over 80 rows of data—far too many to display on one page. When you initially set up the DataGrid control, you changed the AllowPaging property to True. This causes, by default, 10 rows of data to be sent out for each page. At the bottom of the grid you see paging links (by default, < and >). Once you've added a little code, you can use these links to page through the data, 10 rows at a time. You can also change the number of rows per page by setting the PageSize property of the DataGrid control. In addition, you can change the style of the paging indicators (adding page numbers rather than simple Next and Previous links). If you want to allow users to page using Next and Previous links, you can also use your own images in place of the text links.

Basically, there are three types of paging mechanisms you can use to help your users browse through the data:

- Next and Previous links (the default behavior)

- Numeric links, displaying page number links

- A custom pager, where you take complete control over how the paging links appear to the user

In order to use any of these techniques, you'll need to add a bit of code. In the control's `PageIndexChanged` event, you must do the following:

- Indicate to the control what its new `CurrentPage` property should be

- Rebind the control to its data source

The first requirement is easy: The `PageIndexChanged` event procedure passes to you an object whose `NewPageIndex` property indicates the value you need to place in the `CurrentPage` property of the grid. The second part is simple, too. You've already added the `GridLoad` procedure to the page. Now you simply need to call that procedure again.

To add support for paging to your DataGrid control, follow these steps:

1. With `CategorySales.aspx` open in the page designer, select the View, Code menu item to view the page's code-behind file.

2. At the top of the code editor window, from the drop-down list on the left, select grdCatSales.

3. From the drop-down list on the right, select PageIndexChanged. This inserts the appropriate event-handling procedure in the class for you.

4. Modify the grdCatSales_PageIndexChanged procedure so that it looks like this:

```
Private Sub grdCatSales_PageIndexChanged( _
ByVal source As System.Object, _
ByVal e As System.Web.UI.WebControls. _
DataGridPageChangedEventArgs) _
Handles grdCatSales.PageIndexChanged

  grdCatSales.CurrentPageIndex = e.NewPageIndex
  GridLoad()
End Sub
```

Note that the second parameter, e, is a `DataGridPageChangedEventArgs` object. This object provides the `NewPageIndex` property, and setting the grid's `CurrentPageIndex` property to e.`NewPageIndex` causes the DataGrid control to only display data from the selected page the next time it redraws. (The grid's `PageSize` property, 10 by default, controls the number of rows displayed per page. Given the page number and the page size, the grid can retrieve exactly the rows it needs from its data source and display just those rows.)

TRY IT OUT With this code in place, you should now be able to browse to the page and select the < and > links to display subsets of the data. Follow these steps to try out the paging capability you've added to the DataGrid control:

1. In the Solution Explorer, right-click CategorySales.aspx and select Build and Browse from the context menu.

2. Use the links at the bottom of the grid to page through the data. By clicking the right angle bracket, you can move forward through the pages. By clicking the left angle bracket, you can move backward through the pages.

TIP

By default, the Pager hyperlink appears at the bottom of the DataGrid control. By modifying the Position property, you can set the pager to the top instead or both the top and bottom.

Customizing the Pager

If you want to modify the "look" of your pager, you can use the Properties dialog box, as you saw earlier. Imagine that you'd like to display the following:

- Numeric paging

- Ten page numbers

- Numbers at bottom of the grid

- Numbers centered

To add these effects, follow these steps:

1. With CategorySales.aspx open in the page designer, right-click the DataGrid control.

2. Select Property Builder from the context menu.

3. Select the Paging tab and then modify the properties as shown in Table 16.6.

TABLE 16.6   Set These Paging Properties

Property	Value
Position	Bottom
Mode	Page numbers
Numeric buttons	10

4. Select the Format tab, select Pager from the Objects list, and set the Horizontal Alignment property to Center.

5. Click OK to dismiss the dialog box.

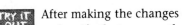 After making the changes outlined in the previous section, browse to the page and verify that you see the paging indicators, as shown in Figure 16.10.

Sales by Category

	Category ID	Product Name	Product Sales
Select	1	Outback Lager	$5,468.40
Select	5	Gnocchi di nonna Alice	$32,604.00
Select	4	Gudbrandsdalsost	$13,062.60
Select	6	Tourtière	$3,184.29
Select	6	Thüringer Rostbratwurst	$34,755.92
Select	8	Boston Crab Meat	$9,814.73
Select	6	Alice Mutton	$17,604.60
Select	1	Chai	$4,887.00
Select	3	Schoggi Schokolade	$10,974.00
Select	5	Ravioli Angelo	$2,156.70
		1 2 3 4 5 6 7 8	

Home

FIGURE 16.10   You can format the paging indicators to match your own needs.

Selecting a Row

Up until now, the Select column in the grid hasn't done anything useful. You might want to allow users to select a row and display information about the selected row. For example, you might want to display the category name associated with the selected item in the grid. Displaying this information requires a little bit of code, as you might imagine.

Actually, selecting an item in the DataGrid control takes no code at all—simply clicking the Select link highlights the row for you, based on the formatting you applied to the grid. Retrieving the information, however, requires that you react to the ItemCommand event of the grid. Clicking any link on the DataGrid control filters through the same event procedure: grdCatSales_ItemCommand, in this case.

How can you differentiate between the various items? When you created the column, you set the CommandName property of the column to be Select, and you can check the CommandName property of the second parameter sent to the event procedure—if it's not Select, you simply don't run any code.

In order to display the category name in the label on the page, follow these steps:

1. With CategorySales.aspx open in the page designer, select the View, Code menu item to view the page's code-behind file.

2. At the top of the code editor window, from the drop-down list on the left, select grdCatSales.

3. From the drop-down list on the right, select ItemCommand. This inserts the appropriate event-handling procedure into the class for you.

4. Modify grdCatSales_ItemCommand so that it looks like this:

```
Private Sub grdCatSales_ItemCommand( _
ByVal source As Object, _
ByVal e As System.Web.UI.WebControls. _
DataGridCommandEventArgs) _
Handles grdCatSales.ItemCommand

   Dim ds As DataSet
   Dim dr As DataRow

   Select Case e.CommandName
     Case "Select"
       ' Get stored DataSet
       ds = CType(Session("DS"), DataSet)

       ' Get the Row from the DataSet
       dr = ds.Tables(0).Rows(e.Item.DataSetIndex)

       ' Display the Category Name column
       lblCategory.Text = "Category: " & _
         dr("CategoryName").ToString
     Case Else
       ' No others, right now.
   End Select
End Sub
```

5. Build and browse the page, select a row, and verify that you see the category name displayed in the label on the page.

The procedure does its work by taking these actions:

- It checks the CommandName value. The code looks at the CommandName property of the second parameter (e) passed to the procedure. If the value is Select, the procedure can react to the user clicking the Select column on the page:

```
Select Case e.CommandName
  Case "Select"
    ...
End Select
```

- It retrieves the DataSet from the Session state and converts the Object to a DataSet:

```
' Get stored DataSet
ds = CType(Session("DS"), DataSet)
```

- It retrieves the row from the DataSet, in the first DataTable, corresponding to the DataSetIndex property of the currently selected item (DataSetIndex returns the row number of the selected row):

```
' Get the Row from the DataSet
dr = ds.Tables(0).Rows(e.Item.DataSetIndex)
```

- It displays the CategoryName column value in the label:

```
' Display the Category Name column
lblCategory.Text = "Category: " & _
  dr("CategoryName").ToString
```

NOTE

Because you'll trigger the ItemCommand event if you select any link within the DataGrid control, you must check the CommandName property of the second parameter (e.CommandName) before running your code. This example used a Select Case statement, so it's easy to add other cases. (For example, if you click any of the pager links, the CommandName property would be Page.)

Sorting Columns

It would be nice if your table could sort its data when you click a column within the table. It would be even better if the data could toggle between sorting in ascending order and sorting in descending order when you click the column header multiple times. You can accomplish this goal, but you'll need to write some code to make it happen.

No sorting can occur in the DataGrid control unless you handle two issues:

- The control's AllowSorting property must be set to True.

- Each column for which you want to allow sorting must have its SortExpression property set to reflect the expression you'd like to use for sorting when that column is selected.

You handled both of these issues when you created the DataGrid control earlier in the chapter. Now, when a user clicks one of the links in the DataGrid control's column headers, the control raises its SortCommand event, and you can include code to sort the underlying data and rebind the grid.

The SortCommand event procedure passes to you, as a property of its second parameter, the sort expression you selected. It doesn't, however, indicate the direction you want to sort—it leaves handling sort direction up to your own code. To accomplish sorting, you will need some way to track the column that's currently sorted as well as the direction it's sorted in. (You need to keep track of both pieces of information so that if a user clicks a column other than the currently sorted column, you know to use an ascending sort. If the user clicks the same column that's currently sorted, you need to toggle the sort order.) To keep track of the sort column and sort order, you can use two Session variables, initialized in the Page_Load procedure.

To add sorting support to your page, you'll need to take these actions:

- Modify the Page_Load procedure to initialize the Session variables Sort and SortDirection.

- Add a procedure, HandleSort, that can rebuild the page's DataSet, taking into account the selected sorting order.

- Modify the CategoryLoad procedure so that it sorts the data correctly.

- Modify the GridLoad procedure to take the sorting into account, as it loads the data into the grid.

- Add the grdCatSales_SortCommand event handler to run the appropriate code when the user clicks a column header.

Follow these steps to add sorting functionality to your page:

1. In the Solution Explorer window, select CategorySales.aspx, right-click, and select View Code from the context menu.

2. Modify the Page_Load procedure so that it looks like this:

```
Private Sub Page_Load( _
  ByVal sender As System.Object, _
  ByVal e As System.EventArgs) _
  Handles MyBase.Load

    If Not Page.IsPostBack Then
      Session("Sort") = String.Empty
      Session("SortDirection") = String.Empty

      CategoryLoad()
      GridLoad()
    End If
End Sub
```

3. Add the HandleSort procedure, shown in Listing 16.1, to the class. This procedure compares the passed-in sort expression to the current sort expression, and
   it sets the sort direction accordingly (toggles between ASC and DESC if the sort
   expression hasn't changed or sets it to ASC if the sort expression has changed).
   The procedure also sets the Sort and SortDirection session variables.

LISTING 16.1   Handle Ascending and Descending Data Sorting

```
Public Sub HandleSort(ByVal SortExpression As String)
  Dim strDirection As String

  If SortExpression = String.Empty Then
    SortExpression = "ProductName"
    strDirection = "ASC"
  End If

  ' Is the current SortExpression the same
  ' as the last time? If so, alter the
  ' direction.
  If SortExpression = CStr(Session("Sort")) Then
    ' Was it sorted ascending or descending
    ' last time? Session("SortDirection") will
    ' tell you.
    If CStr(Session("SortDirection")) = "ASC" Then
      strDirection = "DESC"
    Else
      strDirection = "ASC"
```

LISTING 16.1 Continued

```
    End If
  Else
    strDirection = "ASC"
  End If

  Session("Sort") = SortExpression
  Session("SortDirection") = strDirection
End Sub
```

4. Modify the CategoryLoad procedure, adding support for sorting. You need to add an optional parameter and a call to the HandleSort procedure:

```
Private Sub CategoryLoad( _
 Optional ByVal SortExpression As String = "ProductName")
  Dim ds As DataSet
  Dim strSQL As String
  Dim strConn As String

  ' Set up SQL and Connection strings.
  strSQL = "SELECT * FROM [Sales By Category]"
  strConn = Session("ConnectString").ToString

  ' Create DataSet and
  ' store DataSet into Session variable
  Session("DS") = DataHandler.GetDataSet(strSQL, strConn)

  ' Set Sort Expressions into Session Vars
  HandleSort(SortExpression)
End Sub
```

5. Modify the GridLoad procedure, adding code to sort the DataView object to which you're binding the DataGrid control. If, for example, you selected the ProductName field for the second time, the Sort property value would be ProductName DESC:

```
Private Sub GridLoad()
  Dim dv As DataView

  ' Get default view from stored DataSet
  dv = CType(Session("DS"), _
    DataSet).Tables(0).DefaultView
```

```
' Set Sort property of DataView
dv.Sort = Session("Sort").ToString & " " & _
    Session("SortDirection").ToString

' Fill in DataSource and bind to data.
grdCatSales.DataSource = dv
grdCatSales.DataBind()
End Sub
```

6. Finally, select grdCatSales from the drop-down list at the top left of the code editor window. Select SortCommand from the list of events in the right drop-down list. Modify the event procedure so that it looks like this:

```
Private Sub grdCatSales_SortCommand( _
 ByVal source As System.Object, _
 ByVal e As System.Web.UI.WebControls. _
 DataGridSortCommandEventArgs) _
 Handles grdCatSales.SortCommand

    HandleSort(e.SortExpression)
    GridLoad()
End Sub
```

This step hooks up the event that occurs when a user clicks a column. This event procedure first takes the SortExpression property of the parameter sent to the procedure, which contains the SortExpression property of the column that was clicked. The HandleSort procedure sets up the Session variables Sort and SortDirection, and the GridLoad procedure uses those variables to sort the data correctly as it loads the grid. Because clicking the link reposts the page, as the page renders the DataGrid control's contents, the new sorting takes effect and you see the data sorted correctly.

7. Modify the ItemCommand event procedure to use the DataView in a sorted order. This ensures you are selecting the correct category ID. Listing 16.2 shows the complete procedure.

LISTING 16.2   The ItemCommand Event Handler Runs Whenever You Click Any Clickable Item in the DataGrid Control

```
Private Sub grdCatSales_ItemCommand( _
 ByVal source As Object, _
 ByVal e As System.Web.UI.WebControls. _
 DataGridCommandEventArgs) _
```

LISTING 16.2   Continued

```
      Handles grdCatSales.ItemCommand

    Dim dr As DataRowView
    Dim dv As DataView

    Select Case e.CommandName
      Case "Select"
        ' Convert stored DataSet into DataView
        dv = CType(Session("DS"), _
          DataSet).Tables(0).DefaultView

        dv.Sort = Session("Sort").ToString & _
          " " & Session("SortDirection").ToString

        ' Get the Row from the DataView
        dr = dv.Item(e.Item.DataSetIndex)

        ' Display the Category Name column
        lblCategory.Text = "Category: " & _
          dr("CategoryName").ToString
      Case Else
        ' No others, right now.
    End Select
End Sub
```

TIP

Just as a DataTable object provides a collection of DataRow objects, the DataView object provides a collection of DataRowView objects. The grdCatSales_ItemCommand procedure uses a DataRowView object, which you've not needed previously. This object corresponds to the standard DataRow object but works as part of a DataView rather than a DataTable. You work with a DataRowView object in just the same way you work with a DataRow object, as far as this procedure is concerned.

TRY IT OUT   As a final test, try browsing the page once again. This time, click a column header and verify that it sorts correctly. Click again, and the column sorts in the opposite order.

Summary

The DataGrid control is a powerful server control. As you learned in this chapter, it can do the following:

- Display data from any number of data sources.

- Provide flexible formatting capabilities.

- Sort columns, both ascending and descending, based on the sorting in the underlying data source.

- Provide paging with indicators in various formats.

- Select a row.

- Add, edit, and delete rows. (You'll learn how to add this functionality in Chapter 17, "Editing Data Using the DataGrid Control.")

All this leads to a control that you are sure to take advantage of in your Web Form applications.

17

Editing Data Using the DataGrid Control

Y ou've already seen how to allow users to view data using the ASP.NET DataGrid control. You've also learned how to bind the control to data using the user-interface components provided by Visual Studio .NET and by writing code to bind the grid to a `DataSet`, `DataTable`, `DataView`, or `DataReader` object.

It's likely that you'll also want to allow users to be able to edit data using the DataGrid control. As in most other areas of ASP.NET, you have complete control over how you want the user to interact with the DataGrid control, and you can allow the ASP.NET page framework to do most of the work, if you like.

Project Setup

In this chapter, you'll learn a number of new techniques. Along the way, you will:

- Add a hyperlink column to an existing DataGrid control.

- Edit data on the `ProductDetail.aspx` page.

- Add Edit, Save, and Cancel buttons.

- Add a template column.

- Add a new row using the DataGrid control.

- Delete data using the DataGrid control.

In this chapter, you'll add all these features to the `ProductsEdit.aspx` page. Figure 17.1 shows the finished page.

OBJECTIVES

- Add Edit, Save, and Cancel buttons to the DataGrid control

- Add a Hyperlink column to the DataGrid control

- Add editing support to the DataGrid control

- Edit data on a separate details page

- Add a template column to the DataGrid control

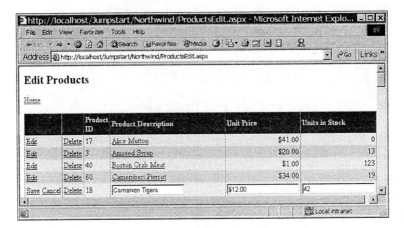

FIGURE 17.1   The finished page allows you to edit data in place, within the DataGrid control.

In order to work through the steps in this chapter, you'll need to add a few prebuilt pages to your application. (We've built them for you because there's a significant amount of code. Don't worry, however, because we'll walk through all the code that's different from the code you've already seen.)

Follow these steps to add the chapter examples to your project:

1. Select the Project, Add Existing Item menu item.

2. At the bottom of the Add Existing Item dialog box, change the Files of Type drop-down list to "All Files (*.*)."

3. Browse to the Jumpstart\DataGridEditing folder and add ProductDetail.* and ProductsEdit.* to your project.

You will also need to add a hyperlink to the main page in order to call the new page you will build in this chapter:

1. Open Main.aspx in the page designer.

2. Add a new HyperLink control just below the Sales By Category hyperlink.

3. Set the properties for this new HyperLink control as shown in Table 17.1.

TABLE 17.1   Set the New Hyperlink's Properties Using These Values

Property	Value
ID	hypProductsEdit
Text	Edit Products
NavigateURL	ProductsEdit.aspx

In the code that you'll use later in this chapter, and in other chapters, you need to add apostrophes around a text value and pass that value back to SQL Server. In order to allow for embedded apostrophes within the text passed back to SQL Server, you must "double up" the apostrophes inside the text; otherwise, Visual Basic .NET will trigger a runtime error.

To make this simple and reusable, add the `QuoteString` method to the `DataHandler` class:

1. Open the `DataHandler` class in the Visual Studio .NET code editor.

2. Add the following procedure:

```
Public Shared Function QuoteString( _
 ByVal Value As String) As String

  Return String.Format("'{0}'", Value.Replace("'", "''"))
End Function
```

This method accepts a string as a parameter and returns that same string, with internal apostrophes doubled, surrounded by apostrophes. For example, if you called `QuoteString` and passed it the value `Eat at O'Neill's`, it would return `'Eat at O''Neill''s'`. Those extra apostrophes are required by the VB .NET parser.

You're likely going to want to execute raw SQL statements more often than you might imagine. It makes sense to create a generic procedure to which you can pass a SQL statement that doesn't return any rows and then have the procedure do all the work for you. Therefore, we've created the `ExecuteSQL` function, which takes a SQL statement as its parameter and returns the number of rows it modified.

Add the procedure shown in Listing 17.1 to your `DataHandler` class.

LISTING 17.1   The ExecuteSQL Procedure Allows You to Execute SQL Statements Without Having to Do All the Setup Work Each Time

```
Public Shared Function ExecuteSQL( _
 ByVal SQLStatement As String, _
 ByVal ConnectionString As String) As Integer
  Dim cmd As OleDbCommand
  Dim intRows As Integer

  Try
    cmd = New OleDbCommand()
    With cmd
      ' Create a Connection object
      .Connection = _
```

LISTING 17.1   Continued

```
        New OleDbConnection(ConnectionString)

        ' Fill in Command Text, set type
        .CommandText = SQLStatement
        .CommandType = CommandType.Text

        ' Open the Connection
        .Connection.Open()

        ' Execute SQL
        intRows = .ExecuteNonQuery()
    End With
Catch
    Throw

Finally
    ' Close the Connection
    With cmd.Connection
        If .State = ConnectionState.Open Then
            .Close()
        End If
    End With
End Try

    Return intRows
End Function
```

Investigating the ProductsEdit Page

The page you've imported, ProductsEdit.aspx, includes a simple DataGrid control. This page has been set up to retrieve its data from the Products table in the Northwind sample database, using techniques you've seen in previous chapters. The page's Page_Load procedure calls the GridLoad procedure, shown here:

```
Private Sub GridLoad()
    Dim ds As DataSet
    Dim strSQL As String
    Dim strConn As String

    ' Get SQL and Connection strings.
    strSQL = "SELECT ProductID, ProductName, " & _
```

```
   "UnitPrice, UnitsInStock " & _
   "FROM Products " & _
   "ORDER BY ProductName "
  strConn = Session("ConnectString").ToString

   ' Get DataSet based on SQL
  ds = DataHandler.GetDataSet(strSQL, strConn)

   ' Put DataSet into session variable
  Session("DS") = ds

   ' Set DataSource and draw grid
   grdProducts.DataSource = ds
   grdProducts.DataBind()
End Sub
```

The DataGrid control, as it's currently set up, contains just three columns (ProductID, UnitPrice, and UnitsInStock). In the next section, you'll learn to add a hyperlink column that you can use to link your DataGrid control to another page—in this case, a page showing detail information about the selected product.

Editing Data Using Links

In order to allow users to edit all the information about a particular product, you might like them to be able to click a link containing the product name and have the link navigate the users to an editing page (ProductEdit.aspx, in this case), with the correct item selected. Adding this functionality will require solving a few problems. You'll need to be able to do the following:

- Add a column to the DataGrid control, containing a link to another page

- Add information to each link, indicating the correct product to display on the detail page

Adding a Hyperlink Column

Visual Studio .NET makes both these problems simple to solve via the Property Builder dialog box you saw in an earlier chapter. To add the hyperlink column, follow these steps.

1. Load ProductsEdit.aspx in the Visual Studio .NET page designer.

2. Right-click the DataGrid control and select Property Builder from the context menu.

3. Select the Columns tab to display information about the columns displayed in the DataGrid control.

4. From the Available columns list, select HyperLink Column and then click the > button to add a new Hyperlink column to the Selected Columns list.

5. Click the up-arrow button twice to place the new column as the second column in the Selected Columns list.

6. Set the properties of the column as shown in Table 17.2. Figure 17.2 shows how the Properties dialog box should look once you're done.

TABLE 17.2   Set These Properties for the Hyperlink Column

Property	Value	Description
Header Text	Product Description	This text appears at the top of the column in the DataGrid control as a column header.
Text Field	ProductName	Each link in the grid displays the value of this field from the grid's data source. Make sure you don't fill in the Text property, which would just insert static text.
URL Field	ProductID	Each link uses this field from the data source as a replacement value in the URL associated with the link. (See the URL format string description.)
URL Format String	ProductDetail.aspx?ID={0}	This value becomes the URL associated with the link, after the grid replaces the placeholder ({0}) with the value in the URL Field property for the current row.

7. In the Solution Explorer window, right-click ProductsEdit.aspx and then select Build and Browse from the context menu.

8. Move your mouse pointer over the links that appear in the grid and note that the URLs that appear in the status bar correctly include the ProductID value associated with each product. Figure 17.3 shows the page with a URL in the status bar.

9. Click one of the links, noting the product name. When ProductDetail.aspx appears, verify that you've navigated to the correct page. Make a change to the unit price or units in stock; then click Save. Note that the value updates correctly on the original page once you dismiss the detail page.

10. Close the browser window and save your project.

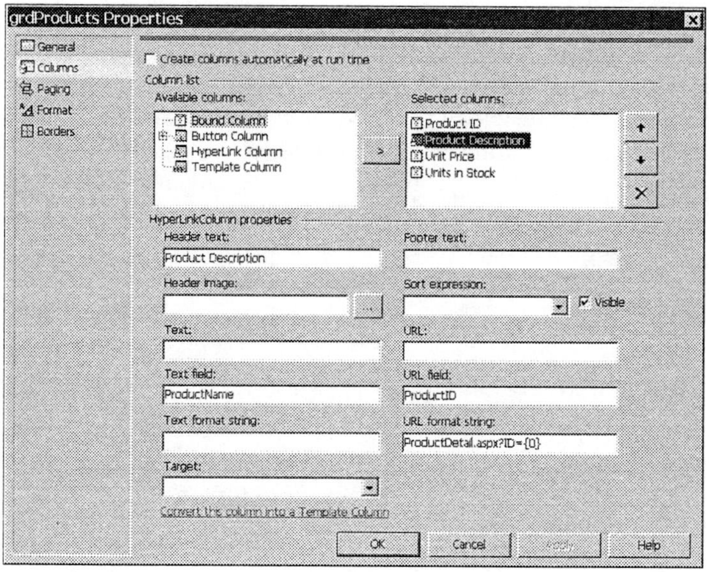

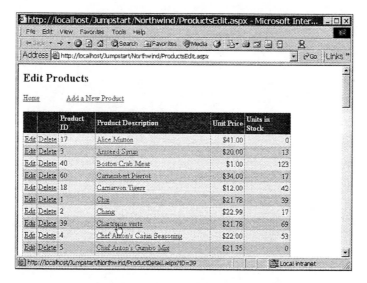

FIGURE 17.2   The finished hyperlink column's properties.

FIGURE 17.3   The DataGrid control formats hyperlink URLs for you.

There's not much magic involved in the Hyperlink column within the DataGrid control. When you add the Hyperlink column, at design time, the ASP.NET page framework renders the column as a hyperlink within an HTML table, at runtime.

The only "magic" occurs in the rendering of the URL for the hyperlink. Because you want each link to navigate to the same page, with a different value in the query string, you might think you have to create some programming code to set up the different links. To make this simple for you, the page framework uses the URLFormatString property of the column, combined with the URLField property, and generates the correct URL for you. Using a replaceable parameter (in the same style as if you were calling String.Format), the grid generates a URL like this one for a product whose ProductID field contains 17:

```
ProductDetail.aspx?ID=17
```

Editing Data on the Detail Page

If you select a link on ProductsEdit.aspx, you'll be taken to the ProductDetail.aspx page, with the data matching the product you selected. This page uses no new techniques, so we won't focus on it here. Instead, this section demonstrates a few specific lines of code that the page uses in order to do its job. The ProductDetail.aspx page, shown in Figure 17.4, contains all the code needed to display and edit a single row of data.

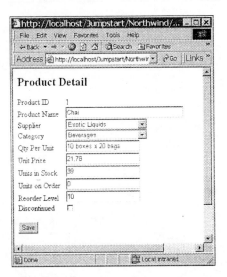

FIGURE 17.4   The ProductDetail.aspx page allows you to edit a single row of data.

Most importantly, how does this page retrieve just the single row of data that you need? In the ProductDisplay method, called from the Page_Load procedure, the code builds a SELECT statement that includes the results of retrieving the ID value from

the query string. If you remember from the previous section, the links on
ProductsEdit.aspx include text such as ID=17 in the query string, and the code in
ProductDisplay.aspx can retrieve that value. Specifically, you'll find the code shown
in Listing 17.2.

LISTING 17.2   Display Product Detail, Given the ProductID Value

```
Private Sub ProductDisplay()
  Dim strSQL As String
  Dim strConn As String
  Dim dr As OleDbDataReader

   ' Get connection and SQL strings
  strConn = Session("ConnectString").ToString
  strSQL = _
   "SELECT ProductID, ProductName, " & _
   "SupplierID, CategoryID, QuantityPerUnit, " & _
   "UnitPrice, UnitsInStock, UnitsOnOrder, " & _
   "ReorderLevel, Discontinued " & _
   "FROM Products " & _
   "WHERE ProductID = " & Request.QueryString("ID")

   ' Load the data.
  Try
    dr = DataHandler.GetDataReader(strSQL, strConn)

    If dr.Read Then
      lblProductID.Text = dr("ProductID").ToString
      txtProductName.Text = dr("ProductName").ToString
      txtQtyPerUnit.Text = dr("QuantityPerUnit").ToString
      txtUnitPrice.Text = dr("UnitPrice").ToString
      txtUnitsInStock.Text = dr("UnitsInStock").ToString
      txtUnitsOnOrder.Text = dr("UnitsOnOrder").ToString
      txtReorderLevel.Text = dr("ReorderLevel").ToString
      chkDiscontinued.Checked = CBool(dr("Discontinued"))

       ' Position to the correct supplier and category
      SelectItem(ddlSupplier, dr("SupplierID").ToString)
      SelectItem(ddlCategory, dr("CategoryID").ToString)
    End If

  Catch exp As Exception
```

LISTING 17.2   Continued

```
    lblError.Text = exp.Message

    End Try
End Sub
```

This procedure builds a SQL string that only retrieves the one row matching the passed-in product ID. Then, once it has retrieved a `DataReader` object, it copies data out of the DataReader's row into the controls on the page.

One interesting side note: The data retrieved from the Products table includes SupplierID and CategoryID fields, and the page needs to convert these ID values into the corresponding text values. The ddlSupplier and ddlCategory controls' items have their `Text` property containing the text to display and their `Value` properties containing the corresponding ID values from their tables. (See the `CategoryLoad` and `SupplierLoad` procedures in the page's code-behind file for the details, but there's nothing new there.) In order to convert from ID values into the corresponding text, the code calls the `SelectItem` procedure:

```
Private Sub SelectItem( _
ByVal Control As ListControl, _
ByVal Value As String)

    ' Given a ListBox or DropDownList control
    ' and a value, select the item containing
    ' the value.
    Dim li As ListItem
    li = Control.Items.FindByValue(Value)
    If Not li Is Nothing Then
        Control.SelectedIndex = Control.Items.IndexOf(li)
    End If
End Sub
```

The `SelectItem` procedure first calls the `FindByValue` method of the `Items` collection of the control in order to retrieve the `ListItem` object matching the value you supplied. It then uses the `IndexOf` method to find the ordinal position of the item in the list and sets the `SelectedIndex` property to match the selected index. It's a rather roundabout technique for setting the value of a DropDownList control, but it's the best we've seen.

In order to save your changes, when you click the Save button, the event handler calls the `ProductSave` procedure, shown in Listing 17.3. Note the use of the

`QuoteString` procedure you added earlier within this code. This procedure adds the necessary apostrophes when building up the SQL string.

LISTING 17.3   Save Changes Made to the Products Information

```
Private Sub ProductSave()

  Dim strSQL As String
  Dim strConn As String

  ' Build SQL and connection strings
  strConn = Session("ConnectString").ToString
  strSQL = String.Format("UPDATE Products SET " & _
   "ProductName = {0}," & _
   "CategoryID = {1}, " & _
   "SupplierID = {2}, " & _
   "QuantityPerUnit = {3}, " & _
   "UnitPrice = {4}, " & _
   "UnitsInStock = {5}, " & _
   "UnitsOnOrder = {6}," & _
   "ReorderLevel = {7}," & _
   "Discontinued = {8}" & _
   " WHERE ProductID = " & Request.QueryString("ID"), _
    DataHandler.QuoteString(txtProductName.Text), _
    ddlCategory.SelectedItem.Value, _
    ddlSupplier.SelectedItem.Value, _
    DataHandler.QuoteString(txtQtyPerUnit.Text), _
    txtUnitPrice.Text, _
    txtUnitsInStock.Text, _
    txtUnitsOnOrder.Text, _
    txtReorderLevel.Text, _
    CInt(chkDiscontinued.Checked))

  Try
    DataHandler.ExecuteSQL(strSQL, strConn)
    Response.Redirect("ProductsEdit.aspx")

  Catch exp As Exception
    lblError.Text = exp.Message

  End Try
End Sub
```

The `ProductSave` procedure simply creates an `UPDATE` statement, uses the `ExecuteSQL` method to send the data back to SQL Server, and uses the `Response.Redirect` method to go back to the previous page.

TIP

The `ProductSave` procedure calls the `QuoteString` method you added to the `DataHandler` class, earlier in the chapter. This method formats strings, including surrounding apostrophes and doubled embedded apostrophes. It's also interesting to note that although the `Checked` property of a check box returns True or False (Boolean values), and the `CInt` function converts these values to -1 and 0, respectively, SQL Server interprets the -1 correctly and stores a 1 in the *bit* data type within the Products table.

Editing Data on the Grid

It's useful to be able to navigate to a new page to edit a full row, but what if you would rather edit data right in the grid? The DataGrid control makes this possible, and, if you're happy with the default layout, extremely easy. By setting a few properties, you can allow users to edit data right in the grid. By writing a little code, you can save the data back out to the original data source.

To add the Edit button to each row (and the associated Cancel and Update buttons, which only display while you're editing a row), you follow the same sorts of steps you used in order to add the Hyperlink column—the Property Builder makes it simple. To add the Edit button, follow these steps:

1. Open `ProductsEdit.aspx` in the page designer.

2. Right-click the DataGrid control and select Property Builder from the context menu.

3. Select the Columns tab to display information about the columns displayed in the DataGrid control.

4. From the Available Columns list, expand the Button Column node. Select Edit/Update/Cancel and then click the > button to add a new column to the Selected Columns list.

5. Click the up-arrow button repeatedly until the new column is first in the list of available columns.

6. Even though you won't use the Delete link until later in the chapter, select the Delete item in the Available Columns list, add it to the Selected Columns list, and move it up until it's the second item in the list.

7. When you're done, click OK to dismiss the dialog box.

TIP

If you'd rather display a standard button instead of a link, you can change the `ButtonType` property to PushButton, rather than LinkButton, before you dismiss the Properties dialog box.

Once you're done, you should immediately see a new column on the left side of the DataGrid control—the Edit column. Unfortunately, editing comes at a price—you must add some code to your page in order to activate editing as well as more code to handle the Cancel and Update buttons that appear while you're editing.

Beginning the Editing

When you click the Edit link on the DataGrid control, the control posts the page back and raises the `EditCommand` event on the server. In order to render the DataGrid control so that you can edit the selected row, you must set the control's `EditItemIndex` property, indicating which row it should be editing. (If no row is being edited, the `EditItemIndex` property is -1.) How can you determine which row you clicked? The `EditCommand` event handler receives, as its second parameter, a `DataGridCommandEventArgs` object. This object provides an `Item` property corresponding to the item (or row of data) that you selected. The `Item` property, an object itself, provides an `ItemIndex` property that contains the row number you need. Therefore, your `EditCommand` property will include at least this line of code (assuming that grdProducts is the name of your DataGrid control):

```
grdProducts.EditItemIndex = e.Item.ItemIndex
```

If you try out the sample page, you'll see that clicking the Edit link on a row places you in editing mode and replaces the Edit link with Save and Cancel links. Any modifiable cell in the grid displays as an editable control, and you can modify the data.

Listing 17.4 shows the sample page's `EditCommand` code.

LISTING 17.4   The `EditCommand` Event Code Runs When You Click the Edit Link on the DataGrid Control

```
Private Sub grdProducts_EditCommand( _
 ByVal source As Object, _
 ByVal e As System.Web.UI.WebControls. _
 DataGridCommandEventArgs) _
 Handles grdProducts.EditCommand

 Dim ds As DataSet
 Dim dv As DataView
```

LISTING 17.4   Continued

```
' Rehydrate the DataSet into a DataView
' You must use a DataView in order to
' use the RowFilter property.
ds = CType(Session("DS"), DataSet)
dv = ds.Tables(0).DefaultView

If IsIE5() Then
  ' If this is IE5 or higher,
  ' smart navigation will display the
  ' edited row in the same place
  ' as on the original page.
  grdProducts.EditItemIndex = e.Item.ItemIndex
Else
  ' If this isn't IE5 or higher, you need
  ' to only show the one row being
  ' edited. Otherwise, users would have
  ' to scroll down to the row.
  grdProducts.EditItemIndex = 0
  dv.RowFilter = "ProductID = " & e.Item.Cells(2).Text
End If

grdProducts.DataSource = dv
grdProducts.DataBind()

Session("AddMode") = False
lnkAdd.Visible = False
End Sub
```

Rather than looking at the procedure sequentially, the following sections break the code up by functionality, describing each chunk of code in detail. There are quite a few new issues covered here, and it's worth discussing each in some depth.

Handling the Data

The EditCommand event handler runs after you've clicked the Edit link for a row in the DataGrid control. You must tell the grid which row it should be editing, and you must rebind the DataGrid control to its data source. (Remember, you're rendering the page and its contents because clicking the Edit link forced a roundtrip to the server. If you don't bind the control to its data source, it simply won't display any data!) The procedure uses this code to "rehydrate" the DataSet object that the page previously stored in a `Session` variable, and it uses the `DefaultView` property to retrieve a `DataView` object based on the only table in the DataSet:

```
Dim ds As DataSet
Dim dv As DataView
...
ds = CType(Session("DS"), DataSet)
dv = ds.Tables(0).DefaultView
```

Why do you need a `DataView` object here? Normally, you could simply bind the DataGrid control to a DataSet and be done with it. In this case, however, depending on the browser that requested the page, you may need a `DataView` object to find the row you need. (The next section solves this mystery—for now, just believe us.)

Given the `DataView` object, the code sets up the data source and rebinds the DataGrid control:

```
grdProducts.DataSource = dv
grdProducts.DataBind()
```

Managing the Grid

If you're testing the sample page using Internet Explorer 5.01 or later (and chances are good that this is a safe assumption), you probably noticed how nicely the browser maintains your position on the page when it rerenders after you click the Edit button. Perhaps you didn't even think about it, forgetting that you've posted back to the same page, making a roundtrip to the Web server. This isn't behavior you would normally expect when rendering a page, yet IE 5.01 (or later) and the ASP.NET page framework make it happen.

The magic in use here is a feature named SmartNavigation. This is a server-side feature provided by the ASP.NET page framework, and it makes postbacks to a page look better, if the request comes from IE5 or later. Specifically, SmartNavigation makes postbacks look better by performing these tasks:

- Eliminating the flash/flickering caused by page navigation

- Saving your position on the page so that when the browser displays the same page, you're at the same location on the page

- Persisting the focus across postbacks so that you're in the same control before and after a postback

NOTE

SmartNavigation only saves information for a single page. As soon as you navigate elsewhere, all "smart" information is lost for the page.

This technology works great if the page request comes from a sufficiently enabled browser—all you need to do is set the SmartNavigation property for your page to True, and you're all set. As a matter of fact, the Page_Load procedure in the sample page sets this property for you:

```
Private Sub Page_Load( _
 ByVal Sender As System.Object, _
 ByVal e As System.EventArgs) Handles MyBase.Load

  If Not Page.IsPostBack Then
    Session("AddMode") = False
    GridLoad()
  End If
  Page.SmartNavigation = True
End Sub
```

If SmartNavigation is enabled, you can simply send the user back to the originally selected row. To do that, your code must set the EditItemIndex property to be the selected row, like this:

```
grdProducts.EditItemIndex = e.Item.ItemIndex
```

What about users who can't use the SmartNavigation feature? You can't really start editing the same row, because that row might be far down the page. Imagine what the user sees: After scrolling down the final row, for example, and clicking the Edit link, the page refreshes back at the top—the user has to scroll down to the bottom again to edit the row that was just clicked! Not good. We suggest you avoid this situation by displaying only the single row the user has selected for editing. To do that, the sample page's EditCommand procedure uses this code:

```
dv.RowFilter = "ProductID = " & e.Item.Cells(2).Text
grdProducts.EditItemIndex = 0
```

This code first retrieves the Text property from the cell within the selected row that contains the product ID (e.Item.Cells(2).Text) and builds up a filter expression. The code assigns the filter to the RowFilter property of the DataView object that contains the grid's data. This code effectively filters the DataView object so that it contains only a single row. The next line of code sets the EditItemIndex property of the grid to 0. Because the grid will only be showing a single filtered row, this is the index you need.

In order to determine which path through the code to take, the sample page includes a function, IsIE5, that determines the capabilities of the browser that made the request to the page:

```
Private Function IsIE5() As Boolean
  ' Check to see if the browser causing the
  ' request was IE5 or higher.
  With Request.Browser
    IsIE5 = ((.Browser = "IE" And .MajorVersion >= 5) _
    And Not FORCEDOWNLEVEL)
  End With
End Function
```

This function uses the `Browser` property of the `Request` object, checking the `Browser` and `MajorVersion` properties. In addition, the page includes the constant `FORCEDOWN-LEVEL`, which is by default set to False. If you set this to True, you'll force the `IsIE5` function to return False, allowing you to test the behavior on down-level browsers.

If you want to test out this behavior, and you only have a browser that supports SmartNavigation, set the `FORCEDOWNLEVEL` constant to True in the code:

```
Private Const FORCEDOWNLEVEL As Boolean = True
```

Then, display `ProductsEdit.aspx` in your browser, click the Edit link for a row, and you should see only that one row displayed in the posted page. Figure 17.5 shows how the page might look after clicking the Edit link, once you've set the `FORCEDOWN-LEVEL` constant to True (or if you've browsed to the page from a down-level browser).

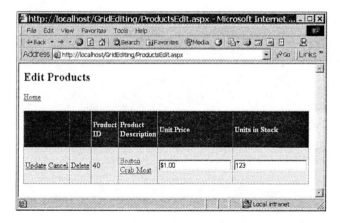

FIGURE 17.5   With a down-level browser, you'll most likely only want to display a single row for editing—it's less confusing to the user.

The whole chunk of code that handles the grid looks like this:

```
If IsIE5() Then
  ' If this is IE5 or higher,
```

```
' smart navigation will display the
' edited row in the same place
' as on the original page.
grdProducts.EditItemIndex = e.Item.ItemIndex
Else
' If this isn't IE5 or higher, you need
' to only show the one row being
' edited. Otherwise, users would have
' to scroll down to the row.
grdProducts.EditItemIndex = 0
dv.RowFilter = "ProductID = " & e.Item.Cells(2).Text
End If
```

TIP

Obviously, we didn't dwell on either of the topics introduced here: the Cells property of the current row or the RowFilter method of a DataView object. You can certainly research both of these topics in the online help. For now, it's important to understand that the DataGrid control provides the selected row to your event procedure as the Item property (e.Item) and that row provides a collection of cells (e.Item.Cells(2), for example). If the cell contains controls (while you're editing, some cells contain TextBox controls, for example), each Cell object provides a Controls collection that allows you to access the controls inside each cell.

Adding Versus Editing

The ProductsEdit.aspx page treats adding a new row and editing an existing row in almost the same way, and even sharing some of the same code. (When you think about it, aren't these really similar operations? Once you add a blank row to contain the new data, editing and adding are the same, from then on, for the most part.) The real differences come when it's time to update the data—when adding, the code must create an INSERT SQL statement; when updating, the code uses an UPDATE SQL statement instead. The sample code keeps track of two different items, based on whether you're adding or editing:

- The Add a New Product link at the top of the page disappears if you're currently editing a row, and it reappears when you're done.

- The Session variable AddMode keeps track of whether you're in Add mode.

The grdProducts_EditCommand procedure handles both of these before it finishes, using this code:

```
Session("AddMode") = False
lnkAdd.Visible = False
```

Because this code only executes when you're entering edit mode, it must set the Session variable so that the code that saves the data knows you weren't in Add mode, and it also must hide the link that allows you to add a new row.

Saving the Data

When you click the Update link on the current row, you trigger a postback to the server, and the page runs the DataGrid control's UpdateCommand event handler. This procedure must perform the following tasks:

- Retrieve the modified items from the grid

- Update the data in the data store

- Reset the DataGrid control's EditItemIndex property so that it doesn't attempt to display any row in edit mode

- Rebind the DataGrid control to its data source

In addition, the sample page must handle saving the data differently if you are editing a row, as opposed to adding a new row. You'll learn more about adding a new row in a later section, but for now, as you peruse the code, just remember that AddMode will be True if you select the link to add a new row, and it will be False otherwise.

The procedure shown in Listing 17.5 runs after you select the Update link for a row in edit mode.

LISTING 17.5 Updating Data Requires a Bit of Code

```
Private Sub grdProducts_UpdateCommand( _
 ByVal source As Object, _
 ByVal e As System.Web.UI.WebControls. _
 DataGridCommandEventArgs) _
 Handles grdProducts.UpdateCommand

  Dim strProductID As String
  Dim strName As String
  Dim strUnitPrice As String
  Dim strUnitsInStock As String
  Dim strSQL As String
  Dim strConn As String

  Try
    ' Retrieve edited items from grid
    With e.Item
```

LISTING 17.5   Continued

```
    strProductID = .Cells(2).Text
    strName = _
     CType(.Cells(3).Controls(0), HyperLink).Text
    strUnitPrice = _
     CType(.Cells(4).Controls(0), TextBox).Text
    strUnitsInStock = _
     CType(.Cells(5).Controls(0), TextBox).Text
  End With

  ' Check to see if we are editing or adding
  If CBool(Session("AddMode")) Then
    strSQL = String.Format( _
     "INSERT INTO Products(ProductName, " & _
     "UnitPrice, UnitsInStock) " & _
     "VALUES( {0}, {1}, {2}) ", _
     DataHandler.QuoteString(strName), _
     strUnitPrice, strUnitsInStock)
  Else
    strSQL = String.Format( _
     "UPDATE Products " & _
     "SET ProductName = {0}, " & _
     "UnitPrice = {1}, " & _
     "UnitsInStock = {2} " & _
     "WHERE ProductID = {3}", _
     DataHandler.QuoteString(strName), _
     strUnitPrice, _
     strUnitsInStock, strProductID)
  End If

    ' Submit SQL
  strConn = Session("ConnectString").ToString
  DataHandler.ExecuteSQL(strSQL, strConn)

Catch oException As Exception
  lblError.Text = oException.Message
  lblError.Visible = True

End Try

' Reset Add flag, and reset the label.
Session("AddMode") = False
```

LISTING 17.5   Continued

```
  lnkAdd.Visible = True

  ' Turn off editing, and re-bind the grid.
  grdProducts.EditItemIndex = -1
  Call GridLoad()
End Sub
```

The grdProducts_UpdateCommand requires some detailed explanation.

The procedure starts by retrieving values from the grid. This issue is somewhat complicated, because you must use both the Cells property of the item provided by the event procedure's parameter, and you must use the Controls collection provided by the individual cell. In order to understand the Cells collection, take a look at Figure 17.5. The Item property represents the entire row in the table, and the Cells collection starts numbering with 0. In this example, Cells(0) contains two controls (the Update and Cancel links), Cells(1) contains one control (the Delete link), and Cells(2) contains the ProductID value. The procedure retrieves the value of the ProductID using this statement:

```
strProductID = .Cells(2).Text
```

Cells(3) contains a HyperLink control, and the procedure retrieves its value using this code:

```
strName = _
CType(.Cells(3).Controls(0), HyperLink).Text
```

Because the Cells collection contains objects, and you need to retrieve the Text property of the hyperlink contained within the collection, you must use the CType function to convert the object into a HyperLink control so that you can retrieve the control's Text property.

The procedure continues, retrieving the value of the rest of the necessary controls, using this code:

```
strUnitPrice = _
CType(.Cells(4).Controls(0), TextBox).Text
strUnitsInStock = _
CType(.Cells(5).Controls(0), TextBox).Text
```

If a cell contains more than a single control (you'll see an example of this later in the chapter), your code would need to take that into account, using Controls(1), for example, to retrieve the second control within a cell.

Once the procedure has retrieved the values from the grid, it takes one of two paths, depending on whether you're adding a new row or editing an existing one. (You'll see more on adding a new row later in this chapter.) If you're adding, the procedure builds a SQL INSERT statement; otherwise, it builds a SQL UPDATE statement:

```
If CBool(Session("AddMode")) Then
  strSQL = String.Format( _
    "INSERT INTO Products(ProductName, " & _
    "UnitPrice, UnitsInStock) " & _
    "VALUES( {0}, {1}, {2}) ", _
    DataHandler.QuoteString(strName), _
    strUnitPrice, strUnitsInStock)
Else
  strSQL = String.Format( _
    "UPDATE Products " & _
    "SET ProductName = {0}, " & _
    "UnitPrice = {1}, " & _
    "UnitsInStock = {2} " & _
    "WHERE ProductID = {3}", _
    DataHandler.QuoteString(strName), _
    strUnitPrice, _
    strUnitsInStock, strProductID)
End If
```

Given the SQL statement appropriate to the action, the code retrieves the connection information and executes the SQL:

```
strConn = Session("ConnectString").ToString
DataHandler.ExecuteSQL(strSQL, strConn)
```

Before the procedure finishes up, it resets the Add a New Product label and the Session variable AddMode:

```
' Reset Add flag, and reset the label.
Session("AddMode") = False
lnkAdd.Visible = True
```

Finally, the procedure resets the DataGrid control's editing (indicating that no row is currently being edited) and rebinds the grid to its data:

```
' Turn off editing, and re-bind the grid.
grdProducts.EditItemIndex = -1
Call GridLoad()
```

Cancelling the Edit

If you're in the middle of editing a row and decide to cancel, you can select the Cancel link on the row (see Figure 17.5). When you do, you trigger a postback to the server, where the page runs the `CancelCommand` event handler for the control. All you need to do in this procedure is indicate to the control that you're no longer editing and then rebind the data to the grid.

To reset the edit mode, you simply set the `EditItemIndex` property of the DataGrid control to -1. The `CancelCommand` event handler in the sample page looks like this:

```
Private Sub grdProducts_CancelCommand( _
  ByVal source As Object, _
  ByVal e As System.Web.UI.WebControls. _
  DataGridCommandEventArgs) _
  Handles grdProducts.CancelCommand

  grdProducts.EditItemIndex = -1
  Call GridLoad()
  lnkAdd.Visible = True
End Sub
```

Adding a Template Column

When you click the Edit link for a row, by default, the DataGrid control provides editing controls for all the columns within the control that can be edited. As you can see in Figure 17.5, hyperlink values can't be edited. You've seen how to add a detail page and link to that page in order to edit all the columns within a row. What if you'd like to be able to view the ProductName field as a link, but when editing a row, be able to edit the ProductName field on the grid? By default, that's not possible.

The DataGrid control allows you to replace the layout of any column with your own content. That is, you can supply the exact layout information for the content you'd like in the header and footer for the column as well as the standard display and editing display for the column. You could add any control (or controls) to be used in the standard display (this is how you might add a DropDownList as a control within a DataGrid control, for example) and perhaps a different control when editing the column.

In this example, to add editing support for a Hyperlink column, you'll need to first convert the column to a Template column (that's the type of column that allows you to supply the layout information). Then, you'll need to lay out the edit template and the item template. Finally, you'll need to set up the data binding so that the correct

information will display within both controls, and you'll need to modify the
grdProducts_UpdateCommand procedure so that it retrieves the value from the correct
control within the cell when it's time to save the changes.

Setting Up the Template Column

To add the template column, follow these steps:

1. Open ProductsEdit.aspx in the Visual Studio .NET page designer.

2. Right-click the DataGrid control and select Property Builder from the context
   menu.

3. Select the Columns tab.

4. Select the Product Description entry in the Selected Columns list.

5. At the bottom of the dialog box, click Convert This Column into a Template
   Column. (Once you do, several options on the page disappear.) Click OK to
   dismiss the dialog box.

6. Right-click the DataGrid control again, and this time select from the context
   menu Edit Template, Columns[3]—Product Description.

7. At this point, you'll see a template editor, like the one shown in Figure 17.6.
   (The figure contains the finished template—you haven't added the text box
   yet.)

FIGURE 17.6   After creating your template column, you'll have both a hyperlink and a
text box.

8. Select the HyperLink control that's already been added to the ItemTemplate
   section. Set the ID property for the control to hypProductDetails.

9. From the Toolbox window, drag a TextBox control into the EditItemTemplate
   section of the designer.

10. Set the new TextBox's ID property to txtProductDetails. At this point, your templates should look just like Figure 17.6.

At this point, you've created the content that will display for the normal rows (the HyperLink control) and the content that will display when editing (the TextBox control). The final issue to handle is the data binding. By default, when you converted the column into a Template column, Visual Studio .NET handled the data binding for the HyperLink control, because that control was already on the grid. For the TextBox control, however, you'll need to do the work yourself.

Follow these steps to add data binding to the TextBox control:

1. In the template designer, select the HyperLink control hypProductDetails.

2. In the Properties window, scroll to the top and select the DataBindings property.

3. At the right of the window, click the ... button to bring up the hypProductDetails DataBindings dialog box.

4. In the Bindable Properties list, select the Text property.

5. In the Custom Binding Expression box, select the entire contents and then press Ctrl+C to copy the contents to the Windows Clipboard. Click OK to dismiss the dialog box without modifying anything.

TIP

The declarative binding for the HyperLink control uses a DataBinder object and its Eval method to perform the binding at runtime. In addition, the Eval method uses the Container and DataItem objects. Although these are important concepts, we'll put off discussion of what they're doing and how they work until the next chapter. For now, accept that the expression you've selected somehow provides runtime data binding, and let it go until the next chapter.

6. Select the TextBox control txtProductDetails. In the Properties window, select the DataBindings property and click the ... button to display the txtProductDetails DataBindings dialog box, just as you did previously.

7. From the Bindable Properties list, select the Text property.

8. Select the Custom Binding Expression option button and press Ctrl+V to paste in the binding expression you copied from the HyperLink control. When you're done, the dialog box should look like Figure 17.7. Click OK to dismiss the dialog box.

9. Right-click the template editor and then select End Template Editing from the context menu.

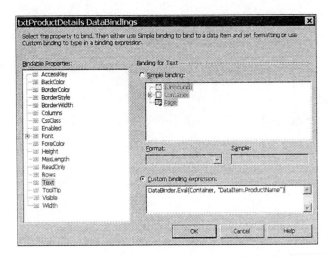

FIGURE 17.7   Paste the data-binding expression into the DataBindings dialog box.

In the past few steps, you've set up data binding so that the DataGrid control "knows" how to display data in both the HyperLink control and in the TextBox control. The HyperLink control only appears while in normal view, and the TextBox control only appears when you're editing a row—that flexibility is the point of creating a template column.

Modifying the UpdateCommand Procedure

The original grdProducts_UpdateCommand procedure expected to find the ProductName field embedded in the HyperLink control (that is, Controls(0)) within its cell. After modifying the column so that it contains two controls (a HyperLink control and a TextBox control), you must modify grdProducts_UpdateCommand so that it now retrieves this value from Controls(1) (the text box) within the column.

To finish grdProducts_UpdateCommand, follow these steps:

1. With ProductsEdit.aspx selected, use the View, Code menu item to display the page's code-behind file.

2. Find the grdProducts_UpdateCommand procedure.

3. Replace text as shown in the following code fragment:

```
' Replace this:

strName = _
```

Adding and Deleting Rows

```
CType(.Cells(3).Controls(0), HyperLink).Text

' with this:

strName = _
    CType(.Cells(3).Controls(1), TextBox).Text
```

4. Test out your newly modified DataGrid control by browsing to the page and clicking the Edit link on a row. Compare this nearly completed version (see Figure 17.1) with the version that didn't include the template column (see Figure 17.5).

Adding and Deleting Rows

To complete this demonstration, you'll need to add functionality that allows you to add and delete rows from your DataGrid control. Neither of these tasks is as difficult as updating data because you're working with an entire row rather than with individual fields.

Adding a New Row

Adding a row using the DataGrid control seems almost simple now, in comparison to some of the other code you've seen in this chapter. There are a few wrinkles, however.

First of all, there's no change to the DataGrid control required in order to allow you to add a row using the control—as far as the DataGrid control is concerned, adding a row is the same as editing a row. Managing the differences between the two is up to your own code. To add a row using the DataGrid control, you must simply bind the control to a data source that consists of a blank row, make the edits, and then save the changes back to the data source.

Saving the data has already been discussed—the grdProducts_UpdateCommand procedure showed how you could make a choice, when saving the data, based on the Session("AddMode") value. If the code determined that you were in "add" mode, it created a SQL INSERT statement (as opposed to a SQL UPDATE statement, otherwise).

When you click the Add a New Product link on the sample page, you run the code shown in Listing 17.6.

LISTING 17.6   Adding a Row to the DataGrid Control Uses Some New Tricks

```
Private Sub ProductAdd()
  Dim ds As DataSet
  Dim dt As DataTable
```

LISTING 17.6   Adding a Row to the DataGrid Control Uses Some New Tricks

```
Dim dr As DataRow

ds = CType(Session("DS"), DataSet)

' Copy the structure of the DataTable
dt = ds.Tables(0).Clone

' Create new row
dr = dt.NewRow()

' Add new blank row to DataTable
dt.Rows.Add(dr)

With grdProducts
  .EditItemIndex = 0
  .DataSource = dt
  .DataBind()
End With

Session("AddMode") = True
lnkAdd.Visible = False
End Sub
```

The sample code isn't lengthy, but it does handle some tricks you might not have seen before. The code takes these actions:

- It rehydrates the DataSet object stored in the Session variable, so the code doesn't need to go out and requery the data source:

```
ds = CType(Session("DS"), DataSet)
```

- It clones the structure of table in the DataSet object, creating, in effect, a new table with no rows with the same exact structure as the real table:

```
' Copy the structure of the DataTable
dt = ds.Tables(0).Clone
```

- It creates a new, blank row and adds the row to the new table:

```
' Create new row
dr = dt.NewRow()
```

```
' Add new blank row to DataTable
dt.Rows.Add(dr)
```

- It sets the EditItemIndex property of the grid, indicating that it should edit row 0 (the first row in the table—the empty row) and that its data source should be the table the code just created. The procedure calls the DataBind method of the grid to bind it to its data source, creating a single blank row in edit mode on the page:

```
With grdProducts
    ' Set editing on first row
    .EditItemIndex = 0

    ' Assign one blank row to data source
    .DataSource = dt

    ' Draw the DataGrid
    .DataBind()
End With
```

- It sets the Session variable AddMode to True so that the updating code knows that you are in "add" mode, and then it hides the Add a New Product link:

```
Session("AddMode") = True
lnkAdd.Visible = False
```

Once you add your data and click the Update link, you'll find yourself back in the grdProducts_UpdateCommand procedure, described earlier in the chapter.

Deleting a Row

Deleting the selected row takes almost no effort at all, in comparison to editing a row. When you click the Delete link in the grid (you added the Delete link at the same time you added the Edit link, earlier in the chapter), the DataGrid control posts back to the server and runs the DeleteCommand event handler you provide. In the DeleteCommand code for the sample page, the code must perform the following tasks:

- Retrieve the selected product ID from the page

- Build a SQL DELETE statement that will delete the row

- Execute the SQL, deleting the row

- Indicate to the DataGrid control that if it is displaying a row for editing, the edit mode has been cancelled

- Rebind the DataGrid control to the data source (minus the deleted row)

WARNING

Because of referential integrity rules applied to the sample database, you won't be able to delete products that have orders associated with them. If you want to test deleting a row, you'll need to add a new product first.

Listing 17.7 shows the DeleteCommand event handler in the sample form.

LISTING 17.7   Deleting a Row Is the Simplest Task of All

```
Private Sub grdProducts_DeleteCommand( _
 ByVal source As Object, _
 ByVal e As System.Web.UI.WebControls. _
 DataGridCommandEventArgs) _
 Handles grdProducts.DeleteCommand

  Dim strProductID As String
  Dim strSQL As String
  Dim strConn As String

  Try
    strProductID = e.Item.Cells(2).Text

    ' Build SQL and Connection strings.
    strSQL = _
     "DELETE FROM Products " & _
     "WHERE ProductID = " & strProductID
    strConn = Session("ConnectString").ToString

    ' Execute SQL
    DataHandler.ExecuteSQL(strSQL, strConn)

  Catch exp As Exception
    lblError.Text = exp.Message
    lblError.Visible = True

  End Try

  lnkAdd.Visible = True
  grdProducts.EditItemIndex = -1
  Call GridLoad()
End Sub
```

This procedure executes these actions:

- It retrieves the product ID. The code uses the `Cells` property of the current item, looking in `Cells(2)` to retrieve its value:

```
strProductID = e.Item.Cells(2).Text
```

- It builds up SQL and connection strings. The SQL string is a SQL DELETE statement, using the product ID retrieved previously:

```
strSQL = _
 "DELETE FROM Products " & _
 "WHERE ProductID = " & strProductID
strConn = Session("ConnectString").ToString
```

- It executes the SQL statement, deleting the selected row:

```
DataHandler.ExecuteSQL(strSQL, strConn)
```

- It resets the editing mode of the grid and rebinds the data:

```
grdProducts.EditItemIndex = -1
Call GridLoad()
```

TRY IT OUT Now that you've worked through all the details involved in the `ProductsEdit.aspx` and `ProductDetail.aspx` pages, give them a complete workout. Try editing, adding, and deleting rows. Try setting the `FORCEDOWNLEVEL` constant to `True` and then `False`, and see how it affects editing.

Summary

In this chapter, you learned:

- How to add, edit, and delete data directly in the DataGrid control. As you've seen, you get a lot of functionality with just a little bit of code using the ASP.NET DataGrid control.

- How to create and navigate to a detail page that will allow you to edit information.

- How to create Hyperlink columns and Template columns.

- How to search for values within a DropDownList control.

18

Using the Repeater Control

OBJECTIVES

- Learn how list-bound controls work

- Add templates to control the behavior of the Repeater control

- Bind data to templates within the Repeater control

- React to events of items in the Repeater control

ASP.NET provides three controls—Repeater, DataList, and DataGrid—that display data, either from ADO.NET or from any data source that supports the IEnumerable interface. Each of these controls provides a template-based display of the data, meaning that you separate the data binding from the display of the data. Each of these controls renders the contents of its data source according to the HTML templates you supply for the header, items, footer, and so on.

The basic concept behind all these controls is that you've provided some data source and, at the time the page framework renders the page, ASP.NET visits each row in the data source and uses templates you supply to fashion the HTML output for the page, one row at a time. It's obvious what the DataGrid control does—you've seen it in action already. The DataList control can present data in any number of ways, using the templates you'll supply for each item. You can set properties of the DataList control that determine the layout of the data displayed on the page, such as the number of columns and whether you want to display rows down the page first or across the page first. The Repeater control gets its name because it can only do one thing: You provide it with a template for displaying items, and it repeatedly fills the template with data and displays that data on the page, from top to bottom, as it navigates through the input data source.

In addition, the DataGrid and DataList controls allow you to select, edit, and delete data as well as provide support for style and appearance properties. The Repeater control, however, has one basic purpose in life: It can display data, using HTML templates, in a flow layout. You can embed server controls within the Repeater so that you can react to navigation requests from within the Repeater control's data. Table 18.1 lists important features of the three different list-bound controls so that you can compare your needs against the available capabilities of the controls to decide which one to use.

TABLE 18.1   Each of the List-Bound Server Controls in ASP.NET Work Slightly Differently

Functionality	Repeater	DataList	DataGrid
Templates	Yes (required)	Yes (Required)	Within columns (optional)
Tabular layout	No	No	Yes
Flow layout	Yes	Yes	No
Columnar/newspaper-style layout	No	Yes	No
Style/appearance properties	No	Yes	Yes
Selection	No	Yes	Yes
Editing	No	Yes	Yes
Deleting	No	Yes	Yes
Paging	No	No	Yes
Sorting	No	No	Yes

The previous chapters dealt with the DataGrid control, in some detail. In this chapter, you'll see how to create a simple Repeater control containing hyperlinks as well as how to create a tabular Repeater that reacts to events triggered as you click links within the control. In the next chapter, you'll try out the DataList control.

How Does the Repeater Control Work?

In order for the Repeater control to display data, you must provide two things: a DataSource property value (indicating the source of the data), and at least one HTML template (indicating how the control should display data from its data source).

Displaying Data

So that the Repeater can display data (its only reason for existence), you must set the control's DataSource property. You can use a DataTable object (as you'll see in the example later in the chapter) or any other object that supports the IEnumerable interface, including Array, ArrayList, DataView, HashTable, Queue, and more.

The Repeater control provides no built-in support for displaying data. You must tell the control what you want it to do with your data by supplying one or more templates for the control's Items collection. Each item in the Items collection renders its data, as you request, and the Repeater iterates through its complete data source using the templates you supply to display data, one row at a time. Table 18.2 lists the data-associated template types that the Repeater control supports. Table 18.3 lists the template types that aren't associated with data.

TABLE 18.2 Data-Associated Item Types Supported by the Repeater Control

Item Type	Description
Item	Created for all rows in the data source, unless you've specified an AlternatingItem template. In that case, it's created for even-numbered, zero-based items.
AlternatingItem	Created for odd-numbered, zero-based items within the data source.

TABLE 18.3 Item Types Supported by the Repeater Control That Aren't Associated with Data

Item Type	Description
Header	Created for the control header
Footer	Created for the control footer
Separator	Created to separate rows of data

As ASP.NET renders the Repeater control, the control follows these steps:

1. The control first looks for a HeaderTemplate element within its body. If it finds one, it outputs the HTML that you've supplied.

2. The control finds the ItemTemplate element and renders the first row of data using the template it finds.

3. If the control finds a SeparatorTemplate element, it uses that element's contents to display a separator between rows.

4. If the control finds an AlternatingItemTemplate element, it uses that template to display the second row of data.

5. The control repeats the previous three steps for all the rows of data in the data source.

6. If the control finds a FooterTemplate element, it uses the template to format the footer for the control.

The Repeater control requires at least an ItemTemplate element. It's the only required template for the Repeater control, but the control won't work without this template.

TIP

Unlike the DataGrid control, the Repeater control provides absolutely no user interface for laying out its templates. You'll need to venture into the HTML view in order to work with the Repeater control. It's a simple control, but it does require some hand-coding in HTML.

Binding Data in Templates

Using ASP.NET's data binding syntax (that is, surrounding data items with <%# ... %> symbols), you can indicate that you want to display data from the Repeater's data source within a template. As ASP.NET renders each template, it provides a logical object, Container, that refers to the RepeaterItem object that represents the template item being displayed. The Container object provides the DataItem property, which refers to the row of data currently being rendered by the control.

The DataBinder object allows ASP.NET to provide data binding as it renders the page, and you'll use the Eval method of the object to perform the data lookup, within the current row, as ASP.NET renders each row of the Repeater's data.

Putting this all together, you'll find expressions such as this one throughout the Repeater's HTML, asking ASP.NET to look up the correct row and column as it renders the page:

```
<%# Databinder.Eval(Container.DataItem, "CategoryName") %>
```

Within the body of your page, this expression tells ASP.NET to retrieve the CategoryName field from the data provided in the current row and to output its value into the HTML stream ASP.NET sends to the browser client.

The DataBinder object's Eval method allows you to specify field names as strings, and at runtime, the DataBinder object retrieves the data from the Container.DataItem object (the current row of data) using the field name you've specified as its source.

Hooking Up the Data

When ASP.NET loads your ASPX file, it won't automatically bind the data to your Repeater control. Because you may need control over exactly when and how the data binding occurs, ASP.NET doesn't make assumptions about when you want to retrieve the data.

In order to fill the Repeater, you must take two steps:

1. Set the DataSource property of the control, as described earlier.

2. Call the DataBind method of the control. This actually causes ASP.NET to render the control and its data.

NOTE

You may decide to call the DataBind method only once—in the event procedure called when the page loads. You may also want to call DataBind when the data itself has changed, or perhaps you'll want to call it each time you post back to the page.

TIP

If you've enabled state management for your page, the Repeater control saves all the required information to re-create its items during postback. You won't need to reset its data source in this case, and the demonstration page takes advantage of this, only binding on the first rendering of the page.

Creating a Repeater

TRY IT OUT The following set of steps walks you through creating a simple demonstration of using the Repeater control. For this demonstration, you'll create a page that reads product category information from the Northwind SQL Server sample database, and creates a list, as shown in Figure 18.1.

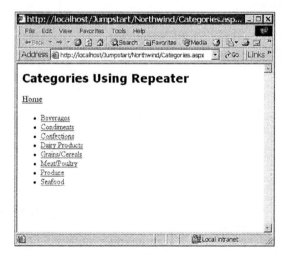

FIGURE 18.1   Creating a list of data items using the Repeater control.

To get started working with the Repeater control, you'll need to both create a new demonstration page and add a link to Main.aspx that navigates to the new page. To get started, follow these steps to modify Main.aspx:

1. Open Main.aspx in the page designer.

2. Add a new Hyperlink control just below the Edit Products hyperlink.

3. Set properties for this new HyperLink control as shown in Table 18.4.

TABLE 18.4   Set the New Hyperlink's Properties Using These Values

Property	Value
ID	hypCategories
Text	Categories
NavigateURL	Categories.aspx

Now, you can create the Categories page that will show you how to use the Repeater control. Follow these steps to create the sample page:

1. Select Project, Add Web Form from the menu bar.

2. Name this new Web Form Categories.aspx.

3. Set the pageLayout property to FlowLayout.

> **NOTE**
>
> Although you could just as easily use GridLayout for the pageLayout property, none of the controls in this example require it, and it just complicates matters. We find using FlowLayout adequate for most demonstration purposes, and it makes the generated code much simpler.

4. Add Label, HyperLink, and Repeater controls to the page and set the properties of each as shown in Table 18.5. When you're done, the page should lay out as shown in Figure 18.1. As you can see in Figure 18.2, you'll need to switch to HTML view in order to do any work with this control—there's no interface within the page designer.

TABLE 18.5   Set Properties for the Page's Controls Using These Suggestions

Control	Property	Value
Label	Text	Categories Using Repeater
	Font.Bold	True
	Font.Size	Large
HyperLink	Text	Home
	Font.Bold	True
	Font.Size	Medium
	NavigateURL	Main.aspx
Repeater	ID	repCat

5. Click the HTML tab at the bottom of the designer window to switch to HTML view.

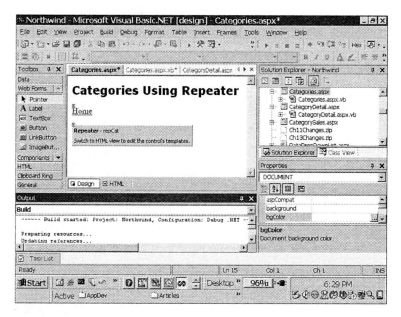

FIGURE 18.2   You can't edit the Repeater control's templates without using HTML view.

Adding the Header and Footer Templates

Because bulleted lists in HTML start with <ul> and end with </ul>, you can put those tags in the HeaderTemplate and FooterTemplate elements, respectively. Follow these steps to set up the header and footer templates:

1. Find the following element within the page's HTML:

```
<asp:Repeater id="repCat" runat="server"></asp:Repeater>
```

2. Between the start and end <asp:Repeater> tags, insert the following HTML, which defines the header and footer templates:

```
<HeaderTemplate>
 <ul>
</HeaderTemplate>
<FooterTemplate>
 </ul>
</FooterTemplate>
```

Adding the Data-Retrieval Code

Follow these steps in order to provide the code that's required to retrieve the data from SQL Server:

1. Press F7 (or use the View, Code menu item) to bring up the code-behind file for the page.

2. Add the following procedure within the page's class to retrieve the data, set the Repeater control's DataSource property, and then bind the data:

```
Private Sub RepeaterBind()
  Dim ds As DataSet
  Dim strSQL As String
  Dim strConn As String

  strConn = Session("ConnectString").ToString
  strSQL = "SELECT CategoryID, CategoryName " & _
    "FROM Categories ORDER BY CategoryName"

  ds = DataHandler.GetDataSet(strSQL, strConn)

  repCat.DataSource = ds
  repCat.DataBind()
End Sub
```

3. Modify the Page_Load procedure so that it calls the RepeaterBind procedure you've just added:

```
Private Sub Page_Load( _
ByVal sender As System.Object, _
ByVal e As System.EventArgs) Handles MyBase.Load

    If Not Page.IsPostBack Then
        RepeaterBind()
    End If
End Sub
```

Adding the `ItemTemplate` Element

The next goal is to add the `ItemTemplate` element to the Repeater control. This template causes the control to display data, one row at a time, from the control's data source.

Follow these steps to add the template and to test out the page:

1. In the Solution Explorer, select the `Categories.aspx` page. Double-click to load the page.

2. Select the View, HTML Source menu item to view the page's source.

3. Find the `HeaderTemplate` and `FooterTemplate` elements you inserted previously. Between the two templates, insert the following element (note the bound expression). This template will simply display the CategoryName from the Categories table in a bulleted list:

```
<ITEMTEMPLATE>
 <LI>
   <%# Databinder.Eval(Container.DataItem, _
   "CategoryName") %>
 </LI>
</ITEMTEMPLATE>
```

4. In the Solution Explorer window, right-click `Categories.aspx` and select Build and Browse from the context menu. Verify that the page displays a bulleted list of categories.

5. Close the browser and save the project.

The HTML you added can be confusing, so take the time to review again:

- The `DataBinder` object provides support for evaluating data binding expressions at runtime.

- The `DataBinder.Eval` method evaluates its parameters, at runtime, and retrieves a value from the control's data source.

- The `Container` class represents the control that's currently being rendered (the Repeater control, in this case).

- The `Container.DataItem` property returns the current row of data from the data source.

- The field name, CategoryName, indicates which field to retrieve from the data source.

Combining all these concepts together provides a somewhat complex expression that retrieves a value from the data source at runtime, based on the expression you create at design time.

You've now seen just about all the Repeater control can do—it displays a repeated list of values from a data source. There's more to the control, of course, and the rest of the chapter digs into some of the details. But the basics are all here—you create templates describing the various parts of the display, and the Repeater control repeats the layout for each row in the input data source.

Adding a Hyperlink

You've created a simple bulleted list, but that wasn't the goal—you need to add links to each of the bullets so that you can use them to navigate to a page that displays category detail information. To finish the page, you'll need to add a HyperLink control (using the `<asp:hyperlink>` tag) between each `<LI></LI>` pair. To add this feature, follow these steps (we've provided the text for this step in a text file, so that you don't need to type it yourself):

1. Open `Jumpstart\Repeater\RepeaterHTML.txt` in Notepad or any text editor.

2. In `Categories.aspx`, replace the existing `<ItemTemplate>` element (including both the beginning and ending `<ItemTemplate>` tags) with the contents of the text file.

3. Once you're done, the Repeater control's HTML should look like this:

```
<asp:repeater id="repCat" runat="server">
  <HEADERTEMPLATE>
    <UL>
  </HEADERTEMPLATE>
  <ITEMTEMPLATE>
    <LI>
      <asp:HyperLink id="Hyperlink1"
        NavigateUrl='<%# "CategoryDetail.aspx?ID=" &
          Databinder.Eval(
            Container.DataItem, "CategoryID")%>'
        Text='<%# Databinder.Eval(
          Container.DataItem, "CategoryName") %>'
        Runat="server">
      </asp:HyperLink>
    </LI>
  </ITEMTEMPLATE>
  <FOOTERTEMPLATE>
```

```
    </UL>
   </FOOTERTEMPLATE>
</asp:repeater>
```

4. Press F5 to run the project, click the Categories hyperlink, and verify that you see the list of category names in the browser window. You can select the links but they'll fail at this point. (You haven't yet supplied the CategoryDetail.aspx page, so the links can't work.)

5. Close the browser, and save the project.

You've just added a HyperLink control, with its NavigateURL and Text properties set to include values from the control's data source. The NavigateURL attribute should contain, at runtime, an expression like this:

```
CategoryDetail.aspx?ID=17
```

The CategoryID value (17) needs to be supplied for each row, as the control renders its display. Therefore, the NavigateURL attribute contains this expression, which retrieves the CategoryID value at runtime for each row and appends it to the URL:

```
NavigateUrl='<%# "CategoryDetail.aspx?ID=" &
  Databinder.Eval(Container.DataItem, "CategoryID")%>'
```

The Text attribute should contain a category name at runtime, and the control's HTML therefore contains this expression:

```
Text='<%# Databinder.Eval(
  Container.DataItem, "CategoryName") %>'
```

This expression retrieves the row's CategoryName field and displays it as the text of the hyperlink.

So far, you've created a simple Repeater control and had it render Header, Footer, and Item templates. The Item template contains information pulled from a SQL Server database, including CategoryName and CategoryID fields.

More Advanced Repeater Features

In the previous section, you created a simple page with links to a page displaying category details. In this section, you'll see how to provide an AlternatingItem template, how to add embedded controls, and how to react to events of those controls. Along the way, you'll create the category detail page shown in Figure 18.3.

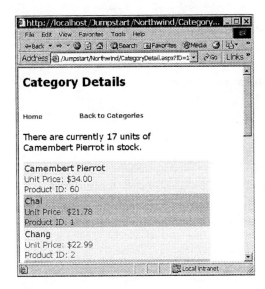

FIGURE 18.3 Clicking a link on this page retrieves the units in stock for the selected item.

Creating the Detail Page

To get started investigating more advanced features, you'll need to create the detail page. Follow these steps to create the base page you'll need:

1. Select the Project, Add Web Form menu item and name the new page `CategoryDetail.aspx`.

2. Set the page's `pageLayout` property to `FlowLayout`.

3. Add controls and set their properties as described in Table 18.6. When you're done, the page should look like Figure 18.4.

TABLE 18.6 Add Controls and Set Their Properties

Control	Property	Value
Label	Text	Category Details
HyperLink	Text	Home
	NavigateURL	Main.aspx
HyperLink	Text	Back to Categories
	NavigateURL	Categories.aspx
Label	ID	lblInventory
	Text	(Delete the text in this property)
Repeater	ID	repCat

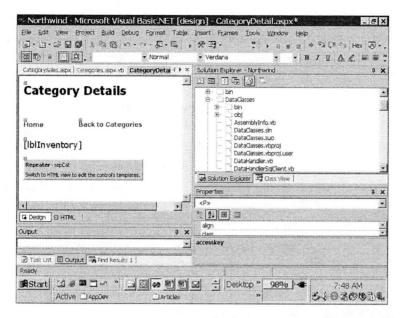

FIGURE 18.4   The `CategoryDetails.aspx` page should look something like this when you're done laying out the controls.

4. Press F7 to load the page's code-behind file.

5. Add this procedure to the page's class:

```
Private Sub RepeaterBind()
  Dim ds As DataSet
  Dim strSQL As String
  Dim strConn As String

  ' Build Connect String
  strConn = Session("ConnectString").ToString

  ' Build SQL and Connection strings
  strSQL = String.Format( _
   "SELECT ProductID, ProductName, " & _
   "UnitPrice, UnitsInStock " & _
   "FROM Products " & _
   "WHERE CategoryID = {0} " & _
   "ORDER BY ProductName", _
   Request.QueryString("ID"))
  ds = DataHandler.GetDataSet(strSQL, strConn)
```

```
' Set DataSource and display data
repCat.DataSource = ds
repCat.DataBind()
End Sub
```

In this case, the `RepeaterBind` procedure retrieves the connection string and then builds a SQL string indicating the rows to retrieve from SQL Server. Because this page receives an `ID` value in the query string sent from the previous page, the code uses `Request.QueryString` to retrieve the `ID` value and inserts it into the SQL string. The code then calls the `DataHandler.GetDataSet` method to create the data set based on the SQL string. The Repeater control's `DataSource` property is then bound to that data set. Finally, the code calls the `DataBind` method in order to fill the Repeater.

6. Modify the `Page_Load` procedure so that it calls the `RepeaterBind` procedure you've just added:

```
Private Sub Page_Load( _
ByVal sender As System.Object, _
ByVal e As System.EventArgs) Handles MyBase.Load

  If Not Page.IsPostBack Then
    RepeaterBind()
  End If
End Sub
```

7. Press Shift+F7 to load the page's designer and then click the HTML tab at the bottom of the window to switch to HTML view.

8. Find the `</asp:Repeater>` tag that ends the Repeater control's definition and insert the following `HeaderItem` and `FooterItem` elements before the `Repeater` control's ending tag:

```
<HEADERTEMPLATE>
  <TABLE border="0">
</HEADERTEMPLATE>

<FOOTERTEMPLATE>
  </TABLE>
</FOOTERTEMPLATE>
```

NOTE

The header and footer templates you've just added constitute the beginning and ending tags for a table. All that's left to add is the contents for each row.

Creating the `ItemTemplate` Element

To create the item template, follow these steps:

1.Between the `HeaderItem` and `FooterItem` elements you've just added, insert the following `ItemTemplate` element:

NOTE

Rather than typing the following large block of HTML, load `Jumpstart\Repeater\RepeaterDtlHTML.txt` into any text editor. Copy and paste the contents of the file into the HTML designer between the `HeaderItem` and `FooterItem` elements.

```
<ITEMTEMPLATE>
  <TABLE style="WIDTH: 400px; HEIGHT: 63px"
cellSpacing="1" cellPadding="1" width="600"
bgColor="papayawhip" border="0">
    <TR>
      <TD colSpan="3">
      <FONT face="Verdana" size="4">
        <asp:LinkButton id="Button3"
        Runat="server"
        Text='<%# Databinder.Eval(
          Container.DataItem, "ProductName") %>'
        CommandName='<%# Databinder.Eval(
          Container.DataItem, "ProductName") %>'>
        CommandArgument='<%#Databinder.Eval(
          Container.DataItem,"UnitsInStock")%>'
        </asp:LinkButton>
      </FONT>
      </TD>
    </TR>
    <TR>
      <TD>
        <FONT face="Verdana">Unit Price:
        <%# FormatCurrency(Databinder.Eval(
          Container.DataItem, "UnitPrice")) %>
        </FONT>
      </TD>
    </TR>
    <TR>
      <TD>
        <FONT face="Verdana">Product ID:
        <%# Databinder.Eval(
```

```
        Container.DataItem, "ProductID") %>
        </FONT>
      </TD>
    </TR>
  </TABLE>
</ITEMTEMPLATE>
```

2. Press F5 to run the project. Verify that you can select the categories on the first page and see the products selected on the second page.

3. Close the browser and save your project.

What's going on here? If you look carefully, you'll see that the `ItemTemplate` element consists of a table with three rows. The first row contains a LinkButton control, with three bound attributes:

```
Text='<%# Databinder.Eval(
  Container.DataItem, "ProductName") %>'
CommandName='<%# Databinder.Eval(
  Container.DataItem, "ProductName") %>'>
CommandArgument='<%#Databinder.Eval(
  Container.DataItem,"UnitsInStock")%>'
```

The `Text` attribute describes what appears in the display of the control. (In this case, the code retrieves the ProductName field from the Repeater's data source.) The `CommandName` and `CommandArgument` attributes contain the ProductName and UnitsInStock fields, respectively. These attributes won't come into play until the next section, but for now, just realize that when you select a LinkButton control within the Repeater, you trigger the Repeater control's `ItemCommand` event. The LinkButton control allows you to specify any text you like in its `CommandName` and `CommandArgument` attributes, and you can retrieve these values from the procedure that handles the `ItemCommand` event.

The other two rows within the table display the UnitPrice and ProductID fields from the data source, using the `DataBinder.Eval` method to retrieve the value at runtime.

The AlternatingItem Template

So far, you've created a table containing items within a category, but you might like to have alternating items displayed in different colors. To do that, you must add an `AlternatingItemTemplate` element to the page. Follow these steps to add the AlternatingItem template:

1. With the `CategoryDetail.aspx` designer open in HTML view, select the entire `ItemTemplate` element, including its tags. Press Ctrl+C to copy the element to the Clipboard.

2. Move the insertion point immediately following the closing `</ItemTemplate>` tag and press Ctrl+V to paste the copied element into the document.

3. Modify the beginning and ending tags of the new element, changing the name from `ItemTemplate` to `AlternatingItemTemplate`.

4. Change the `bgColor` attribute of the row's `style` attribute to a different color. You can try Thistle or any other color of your choice.

TIP

For help selecting colors, you can use tools provided by Visual Studio. Delete the `bgColor` attribute and its value and type **bgColor =**. Visual Studio will provide a "Pick Color" tip, and you can then select from the colors in the dialog box shown in Figure 18.5.

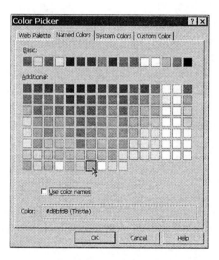

FIGURE 18.5   Choose colors using this helpful dialog box.

NOTE

Although you've only changed the background color for the alternating items in this example, you could change other attributes as well.

5. Run the project, as before, and verify that you now see alternating colors on the CategoryDetail.aspx page.

6. When you're done, close the browser and save your project.

Adding the ItemCommand Event Procedure

It would be great if you could click an item and have its current availability (units in stock) displayed. Although the Repeater control raises several events as ASP.NET renders and destroys the page containing the control, the only event you're likely to react to is the control's ItemCommand event. The control raises this event when you click a button (or link) within the control. In this demonstration, you've created a hyperlink within the Repeater control. To finish the project, you need to add code to display the inventory amount for the selected item.

Besides the standard source As System.Object parameter, the procedure for handling the ItemCommand event receives a parameter defined As RepeaterCommandEventArgs. This object provides four properties, as described in Table 18.7.

TABLE 18.7   The RepeaterCommandEventArgs Object Provides These Useful Properties

Property	Description
CommandArgument	Retrieves the value placed into the CommandArgument attribute in the Repeater control
CommandName	Retrieves the value placed into the CommandName attribute in the Repeater control
CommandSource	Retrieves the source of the command
Item	Retrieves a reference to the RepeaterItem associated with the event

Although you might normally set the CommandName attribute in the Repeater control to represent the name of a command (such as "Sort") and the CommandArgument to contain a subcommand (such as "Descending"), in this example the CommandName attribute contains the ProductName field, and the CommandArgument attribute contains the UnitsInStock field. Because you filled in these attributes (see the previous listing) in the Repeater control, you can retrieve them from within the code-behind file in the ItemCommand event handler.

Follow these steps to add event handling to your sample page:

1. Make sure that CategoryDetail.aspx is open in the designer window.

2. Press F7 to view the code-behind file for the page.

3. In the Class Name combo box, at the left top of the window, select repCat.

4. In the Method Name combo box, at the right top of the window (see Figure 18.6), select ItemCommand. (At this point, the editor inserts the stub of the event handler.)

5. Modify the repCat_ItemCommand procedure so that it looks like this:

```
Private Sub repCat_ItemCommand( _
ByVal source As System.Object, _
ByVal e As _
System.Web.UI.WebControls.RepeaterCommandEventArgs) _
Handles repCat.ItemCommand


    lblInventory.Text = _
     String.Format("There are currently {0} units " & _
     "of {1} in stock.", _
     e.CommandArgument, e.CommandName)
End Sub
```

6. Run the project again, select a category, and then select an item by clicking its link. You should see the available inventory in the label control on the Category Details page.

7. Close the browser and save your project.

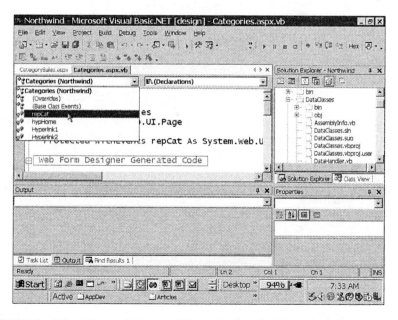

FIGURE 18.6   Select the repCat control from the list of objects that raise events.

Summary

The Repeater control is the simplest of the list-bound controls in that it doesn't do much. However, it can loop through a set of data, and it can display information from each row, without you writing much code or doing much work. Here are some key items you should take away from this chapter:

- The Repeater control is one of three list-bound controls provided by ASP.NET: Repeater, DataList, and DataGrid. Each of the three list-bound controls provides different features, with different uses.

- You must set the Repeater's `DataSource` property to bind it to any object that supports the `IEnumerable` interface. In this example, you bound the control to a `DataTable` object.

- In order for the Repeater control to display its data, you must supply at least one HTML template: the `ItemTemplate` element. You can also supply `HeaderTemplate`, `FooterTemplate`, `SeparatorTemplate`, and `AlternatingItemTemplate` elements.

- You must call the `DataBind` method of the Repeater control in order to load the data into the control.

- You can react to the `ItemCommand` event in your code-behind file, which is raised when a user clicks a button or link within the Repeater control.

- You can pass information from the Repeater to the event handler using the `CommandArgument` and `CommandName` attributes.

Using the DataList Control

OBJECTIVES

- Learn to use the DataList control
- Use DataList control templates
- Display images within a DataList control
- Edit data within a DataList control

The third of the list-bound controls provided by ASP.NET, the DataList control, provides some of the best features of the other two, the Repeater and DataGrid controls. If you want the template-based layout features provided by the Repeater, but you want to be able to edit data in place, the DataList control is for you.

The DataList control allows you to lay out separate templates for normal and alternating items, edited and selected items, headers and footers, and separators. In addition, the DataList control provides a designer where you can lay out the templates (as opposed to the Repeater, which doesn't).

Although the DataList control won't replace the DataGrid control if you need to display tabular data, and there's no reason carrying around the complexities of the DataGrid control if your only goal is to display a simple list of bound data (the Repeater handles this just fine), we think you'll find the DataList control has a solid place right in the middle. It allows you flexible layout that you won't get with the DataGrid control as well as editing that you won't get with the Repeater.

Project Setup

In this chapter, you'll create the page shown in Figure 19.1. This page includes a DataList control that retrieves its data from the Employees table in the SQL Server Northwind sample database.

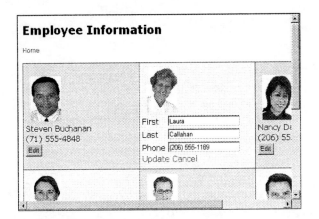

FIGURE 19.1   The DataList control allows you to lay out the items to be displayed, as well as the edited item, using HTML templates.

In this chapter, you'll tackle the following tasks using the DataList control:

- Bind the DataList control to a data source.
- Set up the item template, displaying each row of data.
- Implement data editing within the DataList control.
- Use the DataList control's Property Builder dialog box to set the control's properties.
- Handle events that occur while editing items within the DataList control.

In order to work through this chapter, you'll need to create the EmployeeInfo.aspx page. Follow these steps to get started:

1. Select the Project, Add Web Form menu item.

2. Set the name of the page to EmployeeInfo.aspx.

3. Add the controls to the new page using Table 19.1 as your guide. Once you're done, the page should look like Figure 19.2.

TABLE 19.1   Set the Properties of the Controls on Your Page Using This Table as Your Guide

Control	Property	Value
Label	Font.Bold	True
	Font.Size	Large
	Text	Employee Information

TABLE 19.1   Continued

Control	Property	Value
HyperLink	ID	hypHome
	NavigateURL	Main.aspx
	Text	Home
DataList	ID	datEmps
Label	ID	lblError
	Text	(Delete the text from this property.)

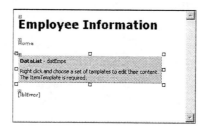

FIGURE 19.2   Your page should look like this in the page designer.

You will also need to add a hyperlink to the main page in order to call the new page you will build in this chapter:

1. Open Main.aspx in the page designer.

2. Add a new HyperLink control just below the Employees hyperlink.

3. Set the properties for this new HyperLink control as shown in Table 19.2.

TABLE 19.2   Set the New Hyperlink's Properties Using These Values

Property	Value
ID	hypEmpInfo
Text	Employee Information
NavigateURL	EmployeeInfo.aspx

Adding the Control's Data Source

In order to display data within the control, you'll need to set up the data source and retrieve the columns you'll want displayed within the control. The following paragraphs walk you through this process. In this case, in order to display the fields as shown in Figure 19.1, you'll need a SQL string like this:

```
SELECT EmployeeID, FirstName, LastName,
(FirstName + ' ' + LastName) As Name,
('Images\' + LastName + '.jpg') As PhotoURL, HomePhone
 FROM Employees ORDER BY LastName
```

This expression retrieves several fields and several expressions based on fields from the Employees table. You'll also need to retrieve the images we've supplied and copy them into the Images folder within your project. Once you've got everything set up, you'll need to set the DataSource property of the DataList control and call its DataBind method in order to display data. (Of course, you'll also need to place controls within the DataList in order to actually see data on the page—that's a job for a later section, however.)

Follow these steps to hook up the data binding:

1. Using Windows Explorer, browse to the Jumpstart\DataList folder. Select the subfolder named Images and press Ctrl+C to copy the folder to the Windows Clipboard.

2. Use Alt+Tab to switch back to Visual Studio .NET. In the Solution Explorer window, select your sample project (Northwind). Press Ctrl+V to paste the folder from the Clipboard, adding the images to your project.

NOTE

The names of the images match the last names of the employees in the sample database. If you change the names in the Employees table or change the names of the files, this example won't work correctly.

3. Make sure that EmployeeInfo.aspx is loaded in the page designer. Double-click the page to load the code designer and modify the Page_Load procedure so that it looks like this:

```
Private Sub Page_Load( _
 ByVal sender As System.Object, _
 ByVal e As System.EventArgs) Handles MyBase.Load

   If Not IsPostBack Then
     DataListLoad()
     DataListBind()
   End If
End Sub
```

4. Add the DataListBind procedure, which will be called from several locations in this book. This procedure handles retrieving the saved DataSet object from a

Session variable, setting the control's `DataSource` property, and calling the
control's `DataBind` method:

```
Private Sub DataListBind()
    ' Bind the DataList control to the
    ' Session variable containing the
    ' data.
    datEmps.DataSource = Session("DS")
    datEmps.DataBind()
End Sub
```

5. Add the `DataListLoad` procedure (see Listing 19.1), which handles retrieving
   the data and placing the `DataSet` object into a `Session` variable for later use.

LISTING 19.1   Load the DataList Control Using This Code

```
Private Sub DataListLoad()
 Dim ds As DataSet
 Dim strSQL As String
 Dim strConn As String

 ' Build SQL and Connection strings
 strSQL = "SELECT EmployeeID, " & _
  "FirstName, LastName, " & _
  "(FirstName + ' ' + LastName) As Name, " & _
  "('Images\' + LastName + '.jpg') As PhotoURL, " & _
  "HomePhone " & _
  "FROM Employees ORDER BY LastName"

 strConn = Session("ConnectString").ToString

 Try
   ds = DataHandler.GetDataSet(strSQL, strConn)

   ' Store the DataSet for later use.
   Session("DS") = ds

 Catch exp As Exception
   lblError.Text = exp.Message

 End Try
End Sub
```

Now that you've added all the code, you might like to verify that the DataList control is working correctly. To do that, you'll need to add a simple ItemTemplate to the control. (The next section discusses the templates and the template editor in more detail.) Follow these steps to display the Name field for each row of data:

1. Use the View, Designer menu item to load the page designer.

2. Right-click the DataList control and select Edit Templates, Item Templates from the context menu. You should see the designer shown in Figure 19.3. (Unlike the Repeater control, which has no user interface for working with templates, the DataList control provides a little bit of help, in the form of this designer.)

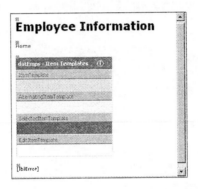

FIGURE 19.3   Use this designer to edit the Item, AlternatingItem, and EditItem templates.

3. From the Toolbox window, drag a Label control into the section of the template editor named ItemTemplate.

4. In the Properties window, set the ID property for your Label control to lblName.

5. Scroll up in the Properties window and locate the DataBindings property. Click the ... button to load the lblName DataBindings dialog box.

6. In the Bindable Properties list, select the Text property.

7. Select the Custom Binding Expression text box and enter the following expression (when you're done, the dialog box should look like Figure 19.4):

```
DataBinder.Eval(Container.DataItem, "Name")
```

8. Click OK to dismiss the dialog box.

9. Right-click the DataList control and select End Template Editing from the context menu.

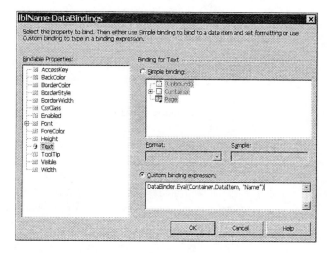

FIGURE 19.4   Set the data-binding properties here.

10. In the Solution Explorer, right-click EmployeeInfo.aspx, select Build and Browse from the context menu, and verify that the DataList control displays each employee's name within the DataList. Close the browser window when you're done.

Adding the Full ItemTemplate

Unlike the DataGrid control (but more like the Repeater), you must supply at least a single HTML template in order to use the DataList control. As you saw in the previous section, you must supply layout information in the ItemTemplate. Creating templates for the DataList control is much like creating templates for the DataGrid control—it's up to you to supply the appropriate HTML within each DataList template to render the correct user interface. Although you only have to supply a single template, the DataList control supports all the templates shown in Table 19.3.

TABLE 19.3   You Can Define All These Templates for the DataList Control

Template Name	Description
AlternatingItemTemplate	If defined, this template provides the content and layout for alternating items in the DataList control. If it's not defined, ItemTemplate is used.
EditItemTemplate	If defined, this template provides the content and layout for the item currently being edited in the DataList control. If it's not defined, ItemTemplate is used.
FooterTemplate	If defined, this template provides the content and layout for the footer section of the DataList control. If it's not defined, a footer section will not be displayed.

TABLE 19.3   Continued

Template Name	Description
HeaderTemplate	If defined, this template provides the content and layout for the header section of the DataList control. If it's not defined, a header section will not be displayed.
ItemTemplate	A required template that provides the content and layout for items in the DataList control.
SelectedItemTemplate	If defined, this template provides the content and layout for the currently selected item in the DataList control. If it's not defined, ItemTemplate is used.
SeparatorTemplate	If defined, this template provides the content and layout for the separator between items in the DataList control. If it's not defined, a separator will not be displayed.

TIP

Creating the ItemTemplate requires a bit of care as well as some time. If you don't wish to follow these steps, you can simply copy and paste the appropriate HTML from the file `Jumpstart\DataList\ItemTemplate.txt`. Paste the contents of the file within the `asp:DataList` element in HTML view.

In this section, you'll finish the ItemTemplate section. In a later section, you'll add the EditItemTemplate. To get started, follow these steps:

1. With `EmployeeInfo.aspx` open in the page designer, right-click the DataList control.

2. From the context menu, select Edit Template, Item Templates. You should see a designer like the one shown in Figure 19.5, including the Label control you added in the previous section.

3. Add the controls to the ItemTemplate section and set their properties using Table 19.4 as your guide. When you're done, the section should look like Figure 19.6.

TABLE 19.4   Set Control Properties Using These Values

Control	Property	Value
Image	ID	imgPhoto
	Height	93px
	Width	66px
Label	ID	lblName
	Text	(Delete the text from this property.)

TABLE 19.4   Continued

Control	Property	Value
Label	ID	lblPhone
	Text	(Delete the text from this property.)
Button	ID	btnEdit
	Text	Edit
	CommandName	Edit

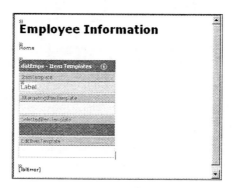

FIGURE 19.5   Use this designer to edit the Item, AlternatingItem, and EditItem templates.

TIP

To get the controls "close together" (inserting a `<br>` tag, rather than a `<p>` tag, into the page's HTML), press Shift+Enter rather than Enter to insert a new line in the designer.

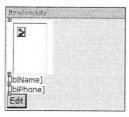

FIGURE 19.6   Your finished ItemTemplate section should look like this.

4. You also must set the data-binding properties for each control. One by one, select each control, find the DataBindings property in the Properties window, click the ... button to display the dialog box, and bind the properties as shown in Table 19.5. (You already set up the binding for lblName; the information is included here for completeness.)

TABLE 19.5   Set Data-Binding Properties for Each Control

Control	Property	Custom Binding Expression
imgPhoto	ImageURL	DataBinder.Eval(Container.DataItem, "PhotoURL")
lblName	Text	DataBinder.Eval(Container.DataItem, "Name")
lblPhone	Text	DataBinder.Eval(Container.DataItem, "HomePhone")
btnEdit	CommandArgument	DataBinder.Eval(Container.DataItem, "EmployeeID")

TIP

Because the custom binding expression values for all the controls are so similar, you may want to type one, copy and paste the others, and then modify each field name. For a refresher on the DataBinder and Container objects, see Chapter 18, "Using the Repeater Control."

5. When you're done, right-click the DataList control and select End Template Editing from the context menu.

6. Test your page in a browser and verify that you now see the image and all the data for each row in the data source.

Using the DataList Control's Properties

You'll want to format the contents of your DataList control, setting fonts, colors, and borders; to make that easier, the DataGrid control supports a named style for each template. (For example, the ItemStyle element in the page's HTML contains the formatting information for the ItemTemplate element; the AlternatingItemStyle element corresponds to the AlternatingItemTemplate element, and so on.) Although you can set each individual property for each template, that can get tedious. Instead, you'll most likely want to start with the automatic formatting provided by the control.

In this section, you'll add these features to your DataList control:

- Format the DataList control, setting up different colors for items and alternating items.

- Add a visible border around the cells.

- Display multiple columns of cells.

To get started, follow these steps:

1. With EmployeeInfo.aspx open in the page designer, right-click the DataList control.

2. Select Auto Format from the context menu. From the dialog box shown in Figure 19.7, select one of the predefined formats. We've selected Colorful 4, but you can select whichever you like. Click OK when you're done, to dismiss the dialog box.

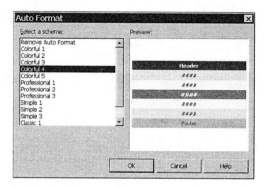

FIGURE 19.7   Select a predefined format from the Auto Format dialog box.

3. Right-click on the DataList control again and then select Property Builder from the context menu.

4. On the General tab of the datEmps Properties dialog box, find the Repeat Layout section. Set the `Columns` property to 3 and the `Direction` property to Horizontal. Figure 19.8 shows the dialog box after you've set the properties.

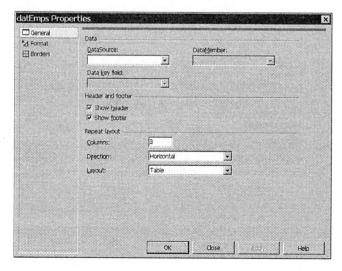

FIGURE 19.8   Select the repeat layout on the General page.

5. On the Format tab, you can peruse (and perhaps change) formatting settings for each of the items within the DataList control. You don't need to change any of the settings now, but Figure 19.9 shows how you can modify colors, fonts, and other formatting settings.

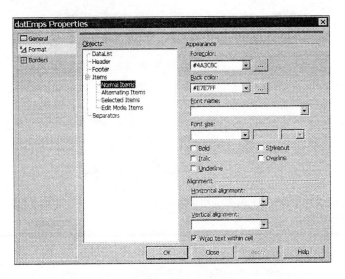

FIGURE 19.9   Use the Format page to modify colors, fonts, and so on.

6. On the Borders tab, you can set borders (or grid lines) for each of the cells within the DataList control. You might set values as shown in Figure 19.10.

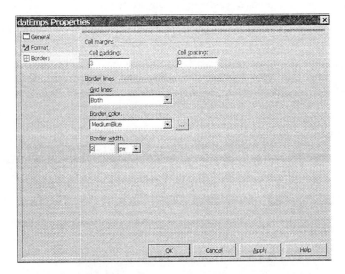

FIGURE 19.10   Try adding borders, both horizontal and vertical.

7. Click OK to dismiss the dialog box. You may need to resize the DataList control, both horizontally and vertically, to make it fit the contents the cells. When you're done formatting the control, it should look like Figure 19.11.

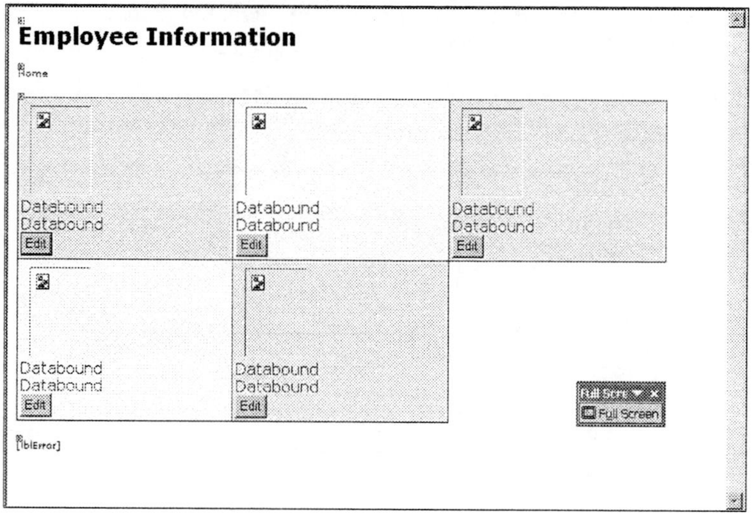

FIGURE 19.11   The finished page should look like this in the page designer.

8. Save your project.

9. Test the page, verifying that you see the data in a "snaking" format, laid out something like Figure 19.1.

Adding the EditItemTemplate Section

You've created the required ItemTemplate so that you can display data, but you'll need to add the EditItemTemplate section if you want to handle editing. This template allows you to supply layout information, used only when you're editing a row of data within the DataList control. You can have completely separate layouts for displaying and for editing data.

TIP

Creating the EditItemTemplate requires a bit of care as well as some time. If you don't wish to follow these steps, you can simply copy and paste the appropriate HTML from the file `Jumpstart\DataList\EditItemTemplate.txt`. Paste the contents of the file within the `asp:DataList` element, in HTML view. We suggest that, for this template, you copy the HTML rather than creating each control individually.

To add the template, follow these steps:

1. With `EmployeeInfo.aspx` open in the page designer, right-click the DataList control.

2. From the context menu, select Edit Template, Item Templates. At the bottom of the design area, you'll find the EditItemTemplate area.

3. Add controls to the ItemTemplate section and set the controls' properties, using Table 19.6 as your guide. When you're done, the section should look like Figure 19.12.

TABLE 19.6   Set the EditItemTemplate Controls' Properties Using This Guide

Control	Property	Value
Image	ID	imgPhoto1
	Height	93px
	Width	66px
Label	Text	First
	Width	50
TextBox	ID	txtFirstName
Label	Text	Last
	Width	50
TextBox	ID	txtLastName
Label	Text	Phone
	Width	50
TextBox	ID	txtPhone
LinkButton	ID	btnUpdate
	CommandName	update
	Height	16px
	Text	Update
	Width	58px
LinkButton	ID	btnCancel
	CommandName	cancel
	Height	16px
	Text	Cancel
	Width	58px

TIP

To get the controls laid out similar to the way they appear in Figure 19.12, press Enter to insert a <p> tag into the HTML after the Image control and after the Phone text box. Press Shift+Enter between the other controls to insert a <br> tag into the HTML.

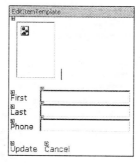

FIGURE 19.12   The finished EditItemTemplate looks like this.

4. One by one, select each control, find the `DataBindings` property in the
   Properties window, click the ... button to display the dialog box, and bind the
   properties as shown in Table 19.7. (If you've pasted the content from the
   `EditItemTemplate.txt` file, you've already added these properties.)

TABLE 19.7   Set Data-Binding Properties for Each Control

Control	Property	Custom Binding Expression
imgPhoto2	ImageURL	DataBinder.Eval(Container.DataItem, "PhotoURL")
txtFirstName	Text	DataBinder.Eval(Container.DataItem, "FirstName")
txtLastName	Text	DataBinder.Eval(Container.DataItem, "LastName")
txtPhone	Text	DataBinder.Eval(Container.DataItem, "HomePhone")
btnUpdate	CommandArgument	DataBinder.Eval(Container.DataItem, "EmployeeID")

TIP

As we mentioned before, because the custom binding expression values for all the controls
are so similar, you may want to type one, copy and paste the others, and then modify each
field name.

5. Right-click the DataList control and select End Template Editing from the
   context menu.

6. Save your project.

Using the LinkButton Control Properties

In this section, you set the `CommandName` and `CommandArgument` properties of
LinkButton controls. Why use these properties? When you click the button, the
DataList control looks at the `CommandName` property. If it finds "edit", "update",

"delete", or "cancel" in that property, it raises the corresponding event back on the server: EditCommand, UpdateCommand, DeleteCommand, or CancelCommand.

TIP

Rather than writing separate event handlers, you could take advantage of the fact that the DataList control raises its ItemCommand event when you click any button or link within the control. You can place all the event-handling code in that one procedure, if you like. (You'll still need to set the CommandName property for each button or link within the control; otherwise, you'll have no way of knowing which control was clicked. We find it easier to use separate event handlers.)

The CommandArgument property allows you to specify data that you want sent to the event-handling procedure. In each case, in this example, if you've set the CommandArgument property, you've bound it to the EmployeeID value for the current row of data. Using this technique, from within the event-handling code, you can take action against the selected employee's data.

How does the event handler retrieve this information? The ASP.NET page framework passes your event handler, as its second parameter, an object of type DataListCommandEventArgs. This object type provides, among its other properties, a CommandArgument property. This property contains the value placed into the CommandArgument property of the control that triggered the event.

For example, in the UpdateCommand event handler, which you'll add in the next section, the code uses the CommandArgument property to retrieve the employee ID for the row you're updating:

```
strSQL = String.Format( _
 "UPDATE Employees " & _
 "SET FirstName = {0}, LastName = {1}, " & _
 "HomePhone = {2} " & _
 "WHERE EmployeeID = {3}", _
 DataHandler.QuoteString(strFirstName), _
 DataHandler.QuoteString(strLastName), _
 DataHandler.QuoteString(strPhone), _
 e.CommandArgument.ToString)
```

Adding Event-Handling Code

Your page is all laid out, and the DataGrid control contains both its ItemTemplate and EditItemTemplate sections, but you won't be able to edit or update data yet—

you must add code to handle the EditCommand, UpdateCommand, and CancelCommand events raised by the control. When you click the Edit button on the page, the DataList control raises its EditCommand event (and your code can react to that event). The same applies to the Update and Cancel buttons, triggering the UpdateCommand and CancelCommand events, respectively.

When you click the Edit button, you trigger a postback to the page. Back on the server, you need to somehow indicate to the DataList control that it's now in "edit" mode and it should display its EditItemTemplate for the selected row.

With the EditItemTemplate displayed, if you click Update, you need to have the data saved back to its source. If you click Cancel, you need to abandon the edit. In either case, you need to post back to the page and somehow indicate to the control that it should display the current row using its ItemTemplate (or AlternatingItemTemplate, if you supplied this template).

TIP

To specify that you want to display a row using the EditItemTemplate, all you need to do is set the EditItemIndex to a value other than -1. You specify the ordinal value corresponding to the item you want to edit, and the control takes care of the rest. To indicate that you want to display the Item/AlternatingItemTemplate, set the EditItemIndex property to -1 again.

In order to complete your page, follow these steps, adding the appropriate event handlers:

1. Use the View, Code menu item to display the page's code-behind file.

2. From the Class Name drop-down list (the list on the left) at the top of the code editor, select datEmps. From the Method Name list (the list on the right), select EditCommand. This inserts the stub for the datEmps_EditCommand event handler into the module.

3. Modify the new procedure so that it looks like this:

```
Private Sub datEmps_EditCommand( _
ByVal source As System.Object, _
ByVal e As System.Web.UI.WebControls. _
DataListCommandEventArgs) _
Handles datEmps.EditCommand

  datEmps.EditItemIndex = e.Item.ItemIndex
  DataListBind()
End Sub
```

4. Repeat the previous two steps, this time modifying the datEmps_CancelCommand procedure:

```
Private Sub datEmps_CancelCommand( _
 ByVal source As System.Object, _
 ByVal e As System.Web.UI.WebControls. _
 DataListCommandEventArgs) _
 Handles datEmps.CancelCommand

  datEmps.EditItemIndex = -1
  DataListBind()
End Sub
```

5. Repeat the previous two steps, modifying the datEmps_UpdateCommand procedure as shown in Listing 19.2.

TIP

Rather than typing this entire procedure, you can copy and paste it in from the Jumpstart\DataList\UpdateCommand.txt file.

LISTING 19.2   Update Data Using the UpdateCommand Event Handler

```
Private Sub datEmps_UpdateCommand( _
 ByVal source As System.Object, _
 ByVal e As System.Web.UI.WebControls. _
 DataListCommandEventArgs) _
 Handles datEmps.UpdateCommand

  Dim strSQL As String
  Dim strConn As String
  Dim strFirstName As String
  Dim strLastName As String
  Dim strPhone As String

  ' Retrieve values from e.Item
  strLastName = GetControlText(e.Item, "txtLastName")
  strFirstName = GetControlText(e.Item, "txtFirstName")
  strPhone = GetControlText(e.Item, "txtPhone")

  ' Build up the SQL string. Be careful about
  ' embedded apostrophes! That's what the QuoteString
```

LISTING 19.2   Continued

```
' method is for.
 strSQL = String.Format( _
  "UPDATE Employees " & _
  "SET FirstName = {0}, LastName = {1}, " & _
  "HomePhone = {2} " & _
  "WHERE EmployeeID = {3}", _
  DataHandler.QuoteString(strFirstName), _
  DataHandler.QuoteString(strLastName), _
  DataHandler.QuoteString(strPhone), _
  e.CommandArgument.ToString)


 ' Build Connection String
 strConn = Session("ConnectString").ToString

 Try
    ' Submit the SQL
    DataHandler.ExecuteSQL(strSQL, strConn)

 Catch exp As Exception
    lblError.Text = exp.Message

 End Try

 ' Cancel the edit mode.
 datEmps.EditItemIndex = -1

 ' Reload employee info. You can't simply
 ' rebind to the stored Session variable--
 ' its data is now incorrect.
 DataListLoad()
 DataListBind()
End Sub
```

6. This procedure is somewhat complex and requires some investigation. The
   datEmps_UpdateCommand procedure takes these actions when you click the
   Update link on the DataList control:

   - It retrieves the text from the three TextBox controls on the
     EditItemTemplate. This in itself requires a little explanation: Your event-
     handling procedure receives, as its parameter, the value e, which contains

information about the DataList control that triggered the event. The Item property of the object provides a reference to the active template, and you must somehow find the controls you need within this template. You can either refer to the controls by their ordinal position within the template (by number) or use the FindControl method to find the control you need, by name. We've used this technique here, and the GetControlText function (see the next step) calls the FindControl method for you and returns the value in the text box you request:

```
' Retrieve values from e.Item
strLastName = GetControlText(e.Item, "txtLastName")
strFirstName = GetControlText(e.Item, "txtFirstName")
strPhone = GetControlText(e.Item, "txtPhone")
```

NOTE

If you're paying attention, you may remember that we wrote very similar code in Chapter 16, "Using the DataGrid Control." In that case, however, we used the other technique—we simply used the ordinal value of the control we needed to find within the EditItemTemplate for the DataGrid control. Why handle this differently here? In the case of the DataGrid control, there were only two controls in the EditItemTemplate, and it was easy to determine the ordinal position of each within the template. In this case, there are a number of controls in the template, and it's risky to count on the particular position of any one control within the template. Although it's more effort, the FindControl method is safer—it doesn't depend on any hard-coded ordinal values.

- It builds the required SQL UPDATE statement, filling in values retrieved from the EditItemTemplate:

```
strSQL = String.Format( _
  "UPDATE Employees " & _
  "SET FirstName = {0}, LastName = {1}, " & _
  "HomePhone = {2} " & _
  "WHERE EmployeeID = {3}", _
  DataHandler.QuoteString(strFirstName), _
  DataHandler.QuoteString(strLastName), _
  DataHandler.QuoteString(strPhone), _
  e.CommandArgument.ToString)
```

- It retrieves the connection string from the Session variable:

```
' Build Connection String
  strConn = Session("ConnectString").ToString
```

- It calls the `ExecuteSQL` method you've seen throughout this book:

```
' Submit the SQL
DataHandler.ExecuteSQL(strSQL, strConn)
```

- It cancels "edit" mode and then rebinds and reloads the DataList control's data source:

```
' Cancel the edit mode.
datEmps.EditItemIndex = -1

' Reload employee info. You can't simply
' rebind to the stored Session variable--
' its data is now incorrect.
DataListLoad()
DataListBind()
```

7. To finish, add the following procedure to the class:

```
Private Function GetControlText( _
 ByVal Item As WebControl, _
 ByVal ControlName As String) As String
  ' This method will fail if you pass it a control
  ' that doesn't exist. But that shouldn't happen, since
  ' you created the controls.
  Return CType(Item.FindControl(ControlName), _
    TextBox).Text
End Function
```

The `GetControlText` procedure uses the `FindControl` method (given a control name), casts the resulting control as a text box, and calls its `Text` property to retrieve the results.

At this point, you've added all the functionality your page requires. Take a few moments and verify that you can view employees, edit the data, and either save or cancel the changes.

TIP

There's no reason you couldn't add functionality that would allow you to add or delete employees, using this same page. Deleting an employee would simply require adding a Delete link to the EditItemTemplate and then adding code to handle the `DeleteCommand` event of the control. You could model this code on the `UpdateCommand` code, although it would be much simpler. To add a new employee, you could place an Add link on the page (not on the DataList control) that could navigate to a page on which you could enter information about a new employee. The code to do all this would be quite similar to the corresponding code on the `ProductsEdit.aspx` page, as discussed in Chapter 17, "Editing Data Using the DataGrid Control."

Summary

The DataList control has a great deal of flexibility, but this flexibility means that you must do a little extra work to get the control laid out the way you want it. In this chapter, you learned the following:

- How to use the DataList control to display and edit data within a table-like display

- How to supply HTML templates for each of the "modes" you want to support (item display, alternating item display, edited item display, and so on)

- How to provide code that can handle editing and updating data within the DataList control

PART III

Web Development
Techniques

IN THIS PART

20

Using Crystal Reports

OBJECTIVES

- Learn to create simple reports using Crystal Reports for .NET

- Learn to display reports in the context of ASP.NET

- Filter rows within reports

At some point, you'll need to display data, gathered from some data source, in the context of an ASP.NET page. You might consider writing code to create the report yourself, but you'd soon realize that it's quite tricky to create your own report writer.

Luckily, you don't have to do all the work yourself. Visual Studio .NET provides Crystal Reports for .NET, and this tool can make it easy for you to design and display professional-looking reports from within your ASP.NET applications. In addition to the standard report-designing tools, Crystal Reports also provides some nice tools that allow you to group data in a hierarchical manner and to drill down to a specific grouping at runtime. In this chapter, you'll create a simple report and see how to display the output on an ASP.NET page.

The Crystal Reports designer is a *banded* report designer, meaning that there are nested bands where you create the various elements of your report. Much like the DataList and Repeater controls, where you supply content using various templates whose contents are rendered by the page framework as it displays the page, a banded report designer allows you to lay out report header and footer content, page header and footer content, and detail row content, all in separate areas of the designer.

Once you create your report, you can save it as a report template. Then, when you need the report, the Crystal Reports runtime engine can use the template you've created, fill it with the data that's currently available, and display the report. That is, you're not creating a finished report—just a template that can be "filled" with data as necessary.

The intent of this chapter is not to teach you everything about Crystal Reports—that could be the subject for a whole book. This chapter shows you how to create a very simple report and then how to display that report on a Web page. Because you'll almost always need to filter data, the chapter also shows how to restrict the amount of rows returned from a report by setting a property on the CrystalReportViewer control.

Creating a Report

To get the feel for how Crystal Reports works, you'll create a simple Products Listing report, as shown in Figure 20.1. This report will contain only a few fields, but it should give you a good idea about how to build a report for your project using Crystal Reports.

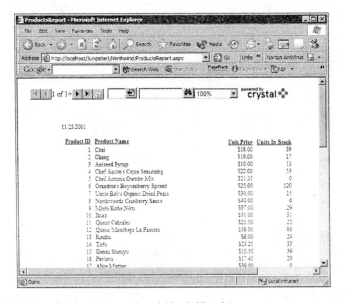

FIGURE 20.1   Your finished report should look like this.

To get started, follow these steps:

1. Select the Project, Add New Item menu item.

2. From the Add New Item dialog box, select Crystal Report. Set the name of the report to `ProductsReport.rpt`, as shown in Figure 20.2. Click Open to move on to the next step.

WARNING

The first time you use the Crystal Reports designer, you will need to register your product, and this requires a few minutes of your time and a live Internet connection.

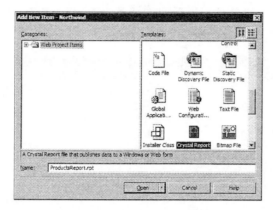

FIGURE 20.2   Use the Add New Item dialog box to add a new report to your project.

3. From the Crystal Report Gallery (see Figure 20.3), you can select how to create the new document and which Expert to use. For now, accept the defaults and click OK.

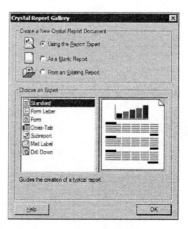

FIGURE 20.3   Select the style of report you'd like from the gallery.

4. From the Data page of the Standard Report Expert dialog box, you must select a data source. You have a lot of choices here, including OLE DB (ADO) sources,

ADO.NET DataSets, XML files, local database files, and more. For now, select OLE DB (ADO) and follow the prompts to add a connection to SQL Server and the Northwind sample database. (You'll need to supply the server name, login ID, and password in order to proceed.) Figure 20.4 shows the Standard Report Expert dialog box after you've selected the data source and drilled down into the list of tables.

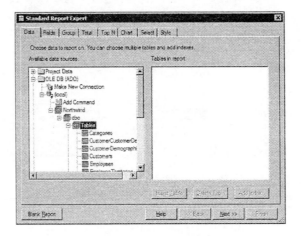

FIGURE 20.4   Start out by selecting your data source.

5. In order to tell the Expert which tables you need, select the Products table from the Available Data Sources list and then click Insert Table to add the table to the Tables in Report list. Click Next to move to the next page of the Expert.

6. On the Fields page, you must select the fields your report will require. In this case, select ProductID, ProductName, UnitPrice, and UnitsInStock, as shown in Figure 20.5. When you're done, click Finish to conclude making selections—you're now done making choices for this simple report.

TIP

If you investigate further, you'll find many more options buried in this Expert. You can set up groupings, totals, charts, subsets, and more—and this is just one of several Experts! As you can see, there are a lot of options when creating reports using Crystal Reports.

Now that you've finished specifying options, Crystal Reports displays its designer, allowing you to modify the layout of the report. Figure 20.6 shows the sample report in the designer.

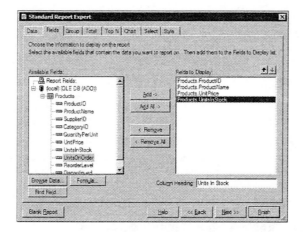

FIGURE 20.5   Select fields to add to your report.

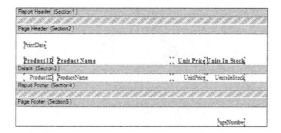

FIGURE 20.6   Use the Crystal Reports designer to lay out the report.

Viewing the Report

Before you can display the report from within an ASP.NET application, you'll need to embed the CrystalReportViewer control on a page. In this section, you'll learn to use the control and then to view the page you've created.

Creating a Report Viewer Page

Follow these steps to set up the CrystalReportViewer control on a page to display your report:

1. Use the Project, Add Web Form menu item to add a new page. Name the page ProductsReport.aspx.

2. Set the PageLayout property for this new page to flowLayout.

3. In the Toolbox window, double-click the CrystalReportViewer control to add an instance to your new page.

4. Set the new control's ID property to cvwProducts and its DisplayGroupTree property to False.

TIP

The viewer control's DisplayGroupTree property enables the display of a navigation tool on the report for working with groupings. If your report doesn't contain groupings (as is the case with this sample report), you'll save space on the screen by setting this property to False.

Displaying the Report

To actually display the report, you'll need to write a little bit of code. You must first set the ReportSource property to be the full path and filename of the saved report template. Next, you must call the DataBind method so that the control will render the report on the page. Follow these steps to display the report:

1. Double-click the page to load the page's code-behind file. Modify the Page_Load procedure so that it calls the ReportBind procedure (which you'll add in the next step):

```
Private Sub Page_Load( _
 ByVal sender As System.Object, _
 ByVal e As System.EventArgs) _
 Handles MyBase.Load

  If Not Page.IsPostback Then
    ReportBind()
  End If
End Sub
```

2. Add the ReportBind procedure, which sets the path and binds the data for your report:

```
Private Sub ReportBind()
  With cvwProducts
    .ReportSource = Server.MapPath("ProductsReport.rpt")
    .DataBind()
  End With
End Sub
```

To test out your new report, follow these steps:

1. Add a hyperlink to Main.aspx, which navigates to your new ProductsReport.aspx page.

2. Run the project and select the new link, which loads the report-viewing page.

3. If you've done everything right, your page should appear, displaying the finished report, as shown earlier in Figure 20.1.

TIP

Try out some of the features the control provides—you can browse through the pages of data on the report, and you can search for data. You can also control the "zoom" of the report, zooming in and out visually. All these features are controllable programmatically, and you can turn any of them off using properties at design time.

Selecting Specific Rows

Although you can apply a filter to your data at design time, you may not know which rows a user will want to view and must therefore allow for some filtering at runtime. You might want to supply a drop-down list of available suppliers, for example, and allow users to view a report based on a particular supplier.

Although there's not much new technology involved in filling a DropDownList control with a list of suppliers—you've seen how to do that in a number of other chapters—there is one issue that we've not mentioned previously. You may want to display an "empty" item in the list, allowing you to prompt the user to select an item, hiding the report until the user actually selects an item. Figure 20.7 shows how the DropDownList control will look with the "empty" item selected.

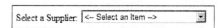

FIGURE 20.7 Create a drop-down list with an "empty" item requesting user input.

Once the user selects an item, you can set the CrystalReportViewer control's SelectionFormula property so that the control only displays rows that match the criteria you supply. If you only want rows where the SupplierID field contains the value 18, you can use code like this:

```
cvwProducts.SelectionFormula = _
  "{Products.SupplierID} = 18"
```

> **TIP**
>
> You must surround *Table.Field* names in your selection formula expression with braces. It's important that you include both the table and the field names. Also, in this example, you won't hard-code the supplier ID (18). Instead, you'll retrieve its value from the DropDownList control on the page.

To modify ProductsReport.aspx so that you can select a supplier and filter the report as well as to see how to add a "Select an item" entry in a drop-down list, follow these steps:

1. Open ProductsReport.aspx in the Visual Studio .NET page designer.

2. Click to the left of cvwProducts, moving the insertion point to the left of the control.

3. Press Enter to insert a "new line," making room for the DropDownList control.

4. Drag a Label control and then a DropDownList control onto the page. Set the properties for these controls as shown in Table 20.1. When you're done, the page should look like Figure 20.8.

TABLE 20.1   Set the Properties of the New Controls Using These Guides.

Control	Property	Value
Label	Text	Select a Supplier:
DropDownList	ID	ddlSuppliers
	AutoPostBack	True

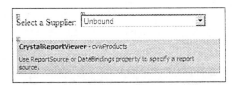

FIGURE 20.8   Add a label and a drop-down list to select a supplier.

5. Add the following procedure to your page's class. This procedure allows you to pass in a ListControl object (either a DropDownList or a ListBox control), and it adds a new item in the first position. In addition, the code sets the Value property of the new ListItem object to "-1":

```
Private Sub BlankRowAdd(ByVal lc As ListControl)
  Dim oItem As New ListItem()

  oItem.Text = "<-- Select an Item -->"
  oItem.Value = "-1"
```

```
   lc.Items.Insert(0, oItem)
End Sub
```

6. Add the `SupplierLoad` procedure to your page's class. This procedure loads the ddlSuppliers DropDownList control with a list of all the available suppliers:

```
Private Sub SupplierLoad()
  Dim strSQL As String
  Dim strConn As String
  Dim ds As DataSet

  strConn = Session("ConnectString").ToString()
  strSQL = "SELECT SupplierID, CompanyName " & _
   "FROM Suppliers ORDER BY CompanyName"

  ds = DataHandler.GetDataSet(strSQL, strConn)

  With ddlSuppliers
    .DataTextField = "CompanyName"
    .DataValueField = "SupplierID"
    .DataSource = ds
    .DataBind()
  End With

  BlankRowAdd(ddlSuppliers)
End Sub
```

7. Modify the `Page_Load` procedure to hide the report when the page first loads (forcing the user to select a supplier before the report displays at all) and to fill the list of available suppliers:

```
Private Sub Page_Load( _
 ByVal sender As System.Object, _
 ByVal e As System.EventArgs) _
 Handles MyBase.Load

  If Not Page.IsPostBack Then
    cvwProducts.Visible = False
    SupplierLoad()
    ReportBind()
  End If
End Sub
```

8. Add code to handle the `SelectedIndexChanged` event of the DropDownList control:

```
Private Sub ddlSuppliers_SelectedIndexChanged( _
 ByVal sender As System.Object, _
 ByVal e As System.EventArgs) _
 Handles ddlSuppliers.SelectedIndexChanged

  Dim id As String
  Dim strFormula As String

  id = ddlSuppliers.SelectedItem.Value

  ' See the comments below.
  If id = "-1" Then
    cvwProducts.Visible = False
  Else
    strFormula = "{Products.SupplierID} = " & id
    cvwProducts.SelectionFormula = strFormula
    ReportBind()
  End If
End Sub
```

This procedure first retrieves the `Value` property of the selected item in the DropDownList control:

```
id = ddlSuppliers.SelectedItem.Value
```

Then, the code hides the report viewer:

```
If id = "-1" Then
  cvwProducts.Visible = False
```

Alternatively, it creates a filtering formula, applies it to the control, and rebinds the report to its data source:

```
Else
  strFormula = "{Products.SupplierID} = " & id
  cvwProducts.SelectionFormula = strFormula
  ReportBind()
End If
```

Try out the page, and you should now be able to filter the report based on a supplier. If you select the "empty" item from the list, the report should disappear until you make a new selection. Figure 20.9 shows the page in use.

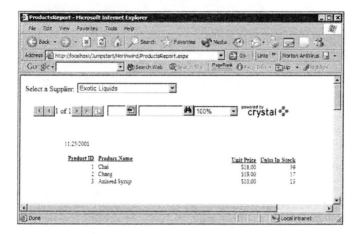

FIGURE 20.9   Use the DropDownList control to select a supplier.

Summary

In this chapter, you learned the following:

- How to create a report, using the Crystal Reports designer, from within the Visual Studio .NET design environment

- How to use the CrystalReportViewer control to display this report within an ASP.NET application

- How to restrict the number of rows displayed in the report using the SelectionFormula property of the CrystalReportViewer control

Clearly, there are many properties, methods, and events of the CrystalReportViewer control you'll want to investigate, and loads of options are available using the report designer. You've learned enough to get started—now you'll need to dig in and create your own reports.

21
Creating User Controls

- Learn to create user controls

- Learn to add user control properties and events

Microsoft provided a large set of server controls as part of ASP.NET, but it couldn't possibly imagine all the different scenarios that might require reusable "chunks" of user interface or code in your applications. ASP developers used "include files" as a way of encapsulating reusable functionality, but that technique had serious limitations. (If you've never dealt with the headache of scoping issues, public variable resolution, and the other problems involved with using include files, you won't see the joy in not having to do so. But believe us, include files were a mixed blessing.)

In order to allow you to create reusable ASP.NET components, Microsoft has provided two completely separate techniques:

- **User controls.** You can simply create a specially formatted page (with the .ascx extension) and embed it in other pages. These new controls are most like ASP's include files, but Visual Studio .NET provides a user interface for creating these components. Once you've created a user control and have added it to your project, you can simply drag and drop it onto as many pages as you want.

TIP

During the ASP.NET development process, user controls were originally called *pagelets*. During the process, the name was changed to *user controls*, but it may be beneficial to think of them as "pagelets"—little pages embedded within other pages—because that's really what they are.

- **Custom controls.** You can create a class that inherits from an existing control. Custom controls are, in essence, the same thing as server controls. You would use the same techniques to create your custom controls that Microsoft used to create all the controls in the Toolbox window. This technique is beyond the scope of this book, but you'll find many resources available to help you get started creating custom controls.

COMPARING USER CONTROLS AND CUSTOM CONTROLS

Several other differences exist between user controls and custom controls. For example, custom controls can appear in the Toolbox window; user controls cannot. Custom controls provide a user interface at design time; user controls display a gray box. Custom controls' properties appear in the Properties window; user controls require you to set properties at their design time or in code once they're hosted. Custom controls are globally available and can be used in any project; user controls must be copied into the project (which means you'll end up with multiple copies of the ASCX file on your server, if you use the same user control in multiple Web projects). User controls have one capability; however, that makes them special: They can provide page caching separate from the parent page. This allows you to play some neat tricks with output caching for your pages, if you want to dig into special caching techniques for user controls.

In this chapter, you'll create some simple user controls. You'll also learn how you can reuse one or more controls, with code you've written, on as many pages as you require.

Creating a Header Control

In this chapter, you'll be modifying the Main.aspx page. So that you can refer back to this page later, if necessary, follow these steps to preserve your original page:

1. In the Solution Explorer window, select Main.aspx.

2. Right-click the page and select Copy from the context menu.

3. Select the project, Northwind, in the Solution Explorer window.

4. Right-click and select Paste from the context menu.

5. In the Solution Explorer window, select Copy of Main.aspx, right-click, and select Rename from the context menu. Rename the page as MainOriginal.aspx.

6. Right-click again and select View Code from the context menu. Modify the class name declaration, near the top of the file (Public Class Main), so that it contains the new class name (Public Class MainOriginal).

7. In the Solution Explorer window, double-click `MainOriginal.aspx` to load it in the page designer. Click the HTML link at the bottom of the window to display the page in HTML view.

8. Verify that the `Page` directive at or near the top of the file looks like this (if not, change it manually):

```
<%@ Page Language="vb" AutoEventWireup="false"
Codebehind="MainOriginal.aspx.vb"
Inherits="Northwind.MainOriginal"%>
```

9. Close all the designer windows.

To get started creating user controls, in this section you'll create a simple control that contains an image and a label—just the sort of thing you might want to place at the top of each page on your site. Figure 21.1 shows the completed control.

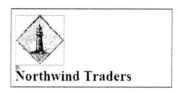

FIGURE 21.1   A user control can contain multiple server or user controls.

Follow these steps to create the simple user control:

1. Select the Project, Add Web User Control menu item.

2. Name the file `NWHeader.ascx` and then click Open to open the new file.

3. Using Windows Explorer, locate the `Jumpstart\CreatingControls\Northwind.gif` file. Press Ctrl+C to copy this file to the Windows Clipboard.

4. In Visual Studio .NET, in the Solution Explorer window, select the `Images` folder inside your project. Press Ctrl+V to paste the `Northwind.gif` image file into the folder.

5. From the `Images` folder, drag `Northwind.gif` onto the new user control.

6. On the page, click to the right of the image to set the insertion point. Then double-click the Label control in the Toolbox and set its properties as shown in Table 21.1.

TABLE 21.1   Use These Properties for the Label Control

Property	Value
Text	Northwind Traders
Font.Bold	True
Font.Size	X-Large

7. Save the project.

 Now that you've created the user control, follow these steps to try it out:

1. Open `Main.aspx` in the page designer.

2. Delete the Label control at the top of this page.

3. In the Solution Explorer window, select `NWHeader.ascx`. Drag and drop the user control onto the upper-left corner of `Main.aspx`. Your page should now look something like Figure 21.2.

FIGURE 21.2   The user control provides little design-time information.

4. Run your application. The main page should now look like Figure 21.3.

That's all there is to creating a simple user control!

TIP

One of the great features of adding user controls to your projects is that if you modify the design of the user control, all the pages that incorporate that control will automatically "see" those changes the next time anyone browses to the page. These controls provide a simple way to incorporate site-wide user interface changes.

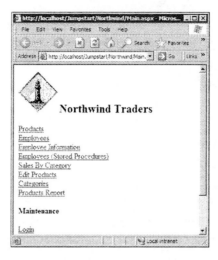

FIGURE 21.3   The finished page displays the user control at runtime.

Creating a Navigation Control

You may want to have the navigation list, shown on the left in Figure 21.3, on more than just the main page in your application. You might want to display the list of links on the left, with content filling the rest of the page.

To accomplish this goal, you might create a table on each page, with the navigation information in the first column and the rest of the content filling the second column of the table. In addition, it seems like a user control would be the simplest way to use the same set of links on all the pages of your application.

In this section, you'll create a new user control containing all the links from Main.aspx and then modify Main.aspx to take advantage of the new user control. Along the way, you'll see how to create a simple table on a page.

Follow these steps to create your user control:

1. Open Main.aspx in the page designer.

2. Select all the links on the page, including the Label control separating the two groups of links.

3. Press Ctrl+X to cut the controls to the Windows Clipboard.

4. Select the Project, Add Web User Control menu item. Name the new user control NWLeftNav.ascx. Click Open.

5. With the new user control open in the page designer, press Ctrl+V to paste the controls onto the new control.

6. In the Solution Explorer window, right-click Main.aspx and select View Code from the context menu.

7. Select the Page_Load and lnkLogout_Click procedures and press Ctrl+X to cut the procedures to the Clipboard.

8. In the Solution Explorer window, right-click NWLeftNav.ascx and select View Code from the context menu.

9. In the code window, select and delete the existing Page_Load procedure and then click Ctrl+V to paste the code you cut from Main.aspx.

10. Save the project and close all the designer windows.

Now that you've created the navigation control, add it to Main.aspx:

1. Load Main.aspx in the page designer.

2. Click the page, immediately below the existing NWHeader user control.

3. Select the Table, Insert, Table menu item.

4. On the Insert Table dialog box, set the BorderSize property to 0, the Rows property to 1, and the Columns property to 2. Click OK to insert the new table.

5. From the Solution Explorer window, click and drag NWLeftNav.ascx into the left column of the table.

6. Run the project and verify that Main.aspx looks and works just as it did before you added the user controls.

content on the page will "wrap" into the area where the navigation list displays, and the columns of the table can stretch as far, vertically, as necessary.

Creating More Complex User Controls

In the previous two examples, you created simple user controls that merely expose user interface elements. Neither user control required you to write any code, nor did either provide any interactive functionality.

What if you want to encapsulate often-needed functionality as well? For example, in previous chapters on more than one occasion, you filled a DropDownList control with data. You used a SQL string with two columns, filled a DataReader or DataSet, and then either looped through the data or bound the control to the data. If you need to do this same thing often, it's a candidate for creating a user control.

Your new control, the DataDropDownList control, will contain a standard DropDownList control and will provide the members shown in Table 21.2. You'll set the `DataTable`, `DataTextField`, and `DataValueField` properties; then you'll call the `DataBind` method to fill the control with its data. If you set the `AutoPostBack` property to True, you'll get an immediate postback when you select an item from the list. You can react to the control's `SelectedIndexChanged` event, and in your event procedure, you can retrieve the `SelectedItem` property from the control.

TABLE 21.2   The New User Control Supplies These Members

Member	Type	Description
AutoPostBack	Property (Boolean)	Exposes the DropDownList control's AutoPostBack property
DataBind	Method	Overrides the DropDownList control's `DataBind` method, effectively retrieving the data and calling the control's `DataBind` method
DataTable	Property (String)	Determines the table from Northwind supplying the data
DataTextField	Property (String)	Exposes the DropDownList control's `DataTextField` property
DataValueField	Property (String)	Exposes the DropDownList control's `DataValueField` property
SelectedIndexChanged	Event	Raised when the DropDownList control's `SelectedIndexChange` event occurs
SelectedItem	Property (ListItem)	Exposes the DropDownList control's SelectedItem property

The following sections walk you through creating your own DataDropDownList control.

First, follow these steps to get started:

1. Select the Project, Add Web User Control menu item. Name the new control `DataDropDownList.ascx`.

2. On the control's designer, add a DropDownList control. Set the new control's ID property to ddlList.

3. Use the View, Code menu item to view the code for the control and add a declaration for mstrDataTable immediately above the `Page_Load` procedure:

```
Private mstrDataTable As String
```

You'll use this member variable to maintain the name of the table that provides the data for the DropDownList control.

Creating Properties

Next, add the `DataTable`, `DataTextField`, and `DataValueField` property procedures for your control, as shown in Listing 21.1.

LISTING 21.1   Add Property Procedures to Your Control

```
Public Property DataTable() As String
  Get
    Return mstrDataTable
  End Get
  Set(ByVal Value As String)
    mstrDataTable = Value
  End Set
End Property

Public Property DataTextField() As String
  Get
    Return ddlList.DataTextField
  End Get
  Set(ByVal Value As String)
    ddlList.DataTextField = Value
  End Set
End Property

Public Property DataValueField() As String
  Get
```

LISTING 21.1   Continued

```
    Return ddlList.DataValueField
  End Get
  Set(ByVal Value As String)
    ddlList.DataValueField = Value
  End Set
End Property
```

> **TIP**
>
> If you look carefully, you'll see that the DataTextField and DataValueField properties simply
> get and set the corresponding properties of the DropDownList control contained within
> this user control. The DataTable property doesn't correspond to any property of the
> DropDownList control, so it requires a private variable in which to maintain its value.

Overriding the DataBind Method

Because you want your DataDropDownList control to behave as much like a standard DropDownList control as possible, you'll want to expose the same types of methods and properties as the standard control. With that in mind, your control should provide a DataBind method (a procedure that retrieves the data and hooks it up to the control). Because your control is inheriting from the base UserControl type, which provides its own DataBind method (this method doesn't actually do anything—you have to override it to provide the functionality), your DataBind procedure must use the Overrides keyword, indicating that it is overriding the base classes' implementation of the method.

Add this procedure to your class:

```
Public Overrides Sub DataBind()
  Dim strSQL As String
  Dim strConn As String

  strSQL = String.Format("SELECT {0}, {1} FROM {2}", _
  DataTextField, DataValueField, DataTable)
  strConn = Session("ConnectString").ToString

  With ddlList
    .DataSource = DataHandler.GetDataSet(strSQL, strConn)
    .DataBind()
  End With
End Sub
```

> **TIP**
>
> The DataBind method needs to retrieve values that are properties of the DataDropDownList control. When the code refers to the DataTextField property, for example, it's using the value of the property defined for the current instance of the class—the control whose code is currently running.

Rather than writing this same code for each DropDownList control you use, you can now simply add a DataDropDownList control to a page, set some properties, and get the functionality you need—all without having to worry about data retrieval each time you want to fill a DropDownList control.

Using the Control

In this section, you'll create a simple page to test out your DataDropDownList control. Follow these steps:

1. Select the Project, Add Web Form menu item to add a new page. Name the new page DataDropDownListTest.aspx.

2. From the Solution Explorer window, drag an instance of the DataDropDownList.ascx user control onto your new page. Set the name of the new control to dddlCategories.

3. Add a Label control immediately below the user control. Set the Label control's ID property to lblCategory and delete its Text property.

4. Double-click the page to display the code-behind file.

5. Although Visual Studio normally adds a member variable corresponding to each control you place on the page so that you can program against the control, it doesn't do this for user controls. You'll need to modify the class file so that it looks like this, so you can program against the new user control:

```
Public Class DataDropDownListTest
  Inherits System.Web.UI.Page

  Protected WithEvents dddlCategories As DataDropDownList
```

6. Modify the Page_Load procedure so that it looks like this, setting up the DataDropDownList control to display its data:

```
Private Sub Page_Load( _
  ByVal sender As System.Object, _
  ByVal e As System.EventArgs) _
```

```
    Handles MyBase.Load

    If Not Page.IsPostBack Then
      With dddlCategories
        .DataTable = "Categories"
        .DataTextField = "CategoryName"
        .DataValueField = "CategoryID"
        .DataBind()
      End With
    End If
End Sub
```

That's all it takes to load up the DataDropDownList control with data from the Categories table, and it's a lot less code than you'd otherwise have to write.

TRY IT OUT To test out your new page, right-click DataDropDownListTest.aspx in the Solution Explorer window and then select Build and Browse from the context menu. Your new user control should contain a list of categories from the Categories table.

Under the Hood

What actually happens when you drag a user control onto a page? Visual Studio .NET adds a Register directive to the HTML content of your page, looking something like this:

```
<%@ Register TagPrefix="uc1" TagName="DataDropDownList"
Src="DataDropDownList.ascx" %>
```

This directive includes three attributes:

- **TagPrefix (uc1 by default).** Provides a unique tag name for your control. In the HTML for the page, you'll find uc1:DataDropDownList as the full control tag name. You can change this item, if you like, when you drop the first instance of the control on the page. You'll need to fix up any existing control instances to match once you modify this value.

- **TagName (DataDropDownList).** Provides the control tag name. By default, this matches the name portion of the file containing the control. You can change this value, but you must change any existing elements within the page's HTML to match.

- **Src (DataDropDownList.ascx).** Provides the file containing your user control. Don't change this or else the page won't be able to find the content for your control.

Dragging the control onto the page added the following HTML representing the control to the page's content:

```
<uc1:datadropdownlist
 id="dddlCategories" runat="server">
</uc1:datadropdownlist>
```

If you know the properties you want to set, at design time, you can also set those properties here in the control's element. For example, instead of writing the code you had added previously, you could modify this tag to contain the information, like this:

```
<uc1:DataDropDownList id="dddlCategories"
 DataTextField="CategoryName" DataValueField="CategoryID"
 DataTable="Categories" runat="server">
</uc1:DataDropDownList>
```

Defining and Raising Events

By default, your user control doesn't raise any of its own specific events—it only raises events defined by its base class (UserControl), such as the Load and Unload events. If you want to add your own events, such as the SelectedIndexChanged event, you'll need to add a little more code to the user control's code-behind file.

You'll first need to define the event, adding a declaration for the event including its parameters and return value. Then, you'll need to manually raise the event so that the consumers of your control can react to the event.

> **TIP**
>
> The code you're about to add hasn't really changed from VB6, if you've ever raised an event from a class in VB6. You may have noticed the use of the WithEvents keyword when you declared the instance of the user control on the test page—it allows the page to react to events raised by the user control.

Follow these steps to add the SelectedIndexChanged event to the control:

1. In the Solution Explorer window, right-click DataDropDownList.ascx and select View Code from the context menu.

2. Immediately below the declaration for mstrTableName, add the following declaration:

```
Public Event SelectedIndexChanged( _
 ByVal sender As System.Object, _
 ByVal e As System.EventArgs)
```

Once you've declared the event, you must raise it. In this control, you'll need to raise the SelectedIndexChanged event when the user selects a value in the DropDownList control embedded within the user control. That is, in reaction to the SelectedIndexChanged event of the internal control, you need to raise the event to consumers of the user control.

Follow these steps to add code to raise the SelectedIndexChanged event:

1. From the Class Name drop-down list, at the top-left corner of the module editor window, select ddlList.

2. From the Method Name drop-down list, at the top right, choose the SelectedIndexChanged event.

3. Modify the procedure stub Visual Studio .NET creates for you so that it looks like this:

```
Private Sub ddlList_SelectedIndexChanged( _
 ByVal sender As System.Object, _
 ByVal e As System.EventArgs) _
 Handles ddlList.SelectedIndexChanged

  RaiseEvent SelectedIndexChanged(sender, e)
End Sub
```

NOTE

The RaiseEvent statement raises a declared event so that consumers of your class can "see" it and react to it. You must pass the parameters defined in the declaration; in this case, you're simply passing the parameters sent to the DropDownList control's event out to the consumer of the DataDropDownList control.

Allowing for Automatic Postback

Because your DataDropDownList control looks and feels like a standard DropDownList control, users will expect it to provide the same postback capabilities. In order to test the control, you'll want to be able to post back immediately after an item is chosen. To make this possible, you need to add an AutoPostBack property to your control, exposing the DropDownList control's AutoPostBack property to consumers.

Add the following property procedure near the other property procedures in the DataDropDownList control's code-behind file:

```
Public Property AutoPostBack() As Boolean
  Get
    Return ddlList.AutoPostBack
  End Get
  Set(ByVal Value As Boolean)
    ddlList.AutoPostBack = Value
  End Set
End Property
```

Retrieving the Selected Item

Your user control also needs to allow users to determine which item was selected, from the SelectedIndexChanged event. To do that, you must add a read-only property to your DataDropDownList class:

```
Public ReadOnly Property SelectedItem() As ListItem
  Get
    Return ddlList.SelectedItem
  End Get
End Property
```

Reacting to the Event

Now that you've completed all the properties, methods, and events necessary for your user control, you can try out the control on the test page. Follow these steps:

1. In the Solution Explorer window, right-click DataDropDownListTest.aspx and select View Code from the context menu.

2. Modify the Page_Load procedure by setting the AutoPostBack property to True:

   ```
   Private Sub Page_Load( _
   ByVal sender As System.Object, _
   ByVal e As System.EventArgs) _
   Handles MyBase.Load

     If Not Page.IsPostBack Then
       With dddlCategories
   ```

```
      .AutoPostBack = True
      .DataTable = "Categories"
      .DataTextField = "CategoryName"
      .DataValueField = "CategoryID"
      .DataBind()
    End With
  End If
End Sub
```

3. From the Class Name drop-down list, at the top left of the module editor window, select dddlCategories.

4. From the Method Name drop-down list, at the top right, choose the SelectedIndexChanged event.

5. Modify the procedure stub Visual Studio .NET creates for you so that it looks like this:

```
Private Sub ddlCategories_SelectedIndexChanged( _
 ByVal sender As System.Object, _
 ByVal e As System.EventArgs) _
 Handles dddlCategories.SelectedIndexChanged

   lblCategory.Text = dddlCategories.SelectedItem.Value
End Sub
```

6. In the Solution Explorer window, right-click DataDropDownListTest.aspx, select Build and Browse from the context menu, and try out the page. Select an item from the DataDropDownList control, and you should see the corresponding value displayed in the Label control on the page.

NOTE

It's important to understand that you wouldn't have been able to program against dddlCategories if you hadn't added the declaration in the code module manually. Visual Studio .NET doesn't do this for you when you add a user control. In addition, you can react to events of this control only because you included the WithEvents keyword in the declaration—this VB .NET keyword makes it possible for you to react to events of an object.

Summary

In this chapter, you investigated three user controls: The first merely displayed content, the second provided functionality, and the third encapsulated an existing control, adding new functionality. You might want to consider the techniques shown here any time you need to group controls together and use them more than once, or when you need to add your own functionality to an existing control or group of controls. For example, you might want to create the following items:

- A DataGrid control with sorting capabilities built in

- A LogIn control that handles authentication for you

- A data-driven menu system that reads menu items, and perhaps subitems, from a table (or tables)

The possibilities are endless. It is important to remember, however, that user controls don't provide much in the way of design-time experience. If you want to create controls that look and feel like the built-in server controls, you'll need to investigate creating custom controls—a much more difficult process.

22

Rich ASP.NET Controls

Throughout this book, you've worked with many different ASP.NET server controls, including the Label, TextBox, DropDownList, ListBox, and Button controls. Beyond the controls that map directly to HTML controls, ASP.NET offers a series of rich controls that provide functionality HTML controls simply can't provide.

In this chapter, you'll investigate several additional ASP.NET server controls, including the following:

- The CheckBoxList and RadioButtonList controls

- The Calendar control

- The AdRotator control

- The Literal control

- The PlaceHolder control

You can find a separate, prebuilt project that demonstrates these controls with the examples for this book in the `MiscWebControls` folder. Load the `MiscWebControls.sln` solution file, and you'll be able to follow along with the discussion in this chapter.

NOTE

We can't even begin to attempt to cover every detail of each of these controls in this chapter. We'll merely demonstrate the behavior of each control and how you might use it, and we'll leave the "heavy lifting" to you.

OBJECTIVES

- Choose from multiple items with the RadioButtonList and CheckBoxList controls

- Select dates using the Calendar control

- Display randomly selected images using the AdRotator control

- Insert HTML into a page using the Literal control

- Add controls at runtime using the PlaceHolder control

The CheckBoxList and RadioButtonList Controls

ASP.NET's RadioButton and CheckBox controls work fine, but they really provide no support for handling groups of related data. If you want to fill a list of either type of controls with data from a DataSet, for example, you'll need to fill each control's text individually. In addition, keeping track of which items in the list of individual controls have been selected is a chore.

To make working with groups of these controls easier, ASP.NET provides the CheckBoxList and RadioButtonList controls. Both controls allow you to bind their lists to data sources and fill these lists at runtime. The major difference between the two is that you can select as many items as you require using the CheckBoxList control, but you can only select a single item using the RadioButtonList control. (This behavior is most likely what you'd expect, given the usage of these two types of input controls.)

Imagine that you'd like to allow users to select a single region from a list of regions. You might like to allow a single selection (using a list of radio buttons) or multiple selections (using check boxes). The sample page, `ListControls.aspx`, provides this capability using both types of list controls (see Figure 22.1).

FIGURE 22.1   Use the CheckBoxList and RadioButtonList controls to allow selections from a list of options.

Each of the two buttons on `ListControls.aspx` calls a common procedure: `RegionLoad`. This procedure fills the list with data retrieved from the Regions table in the Northwind sample database.

```
Private Sub btnRegionCheckList_Click( _
  ByVal sender As System.Object, _
```

```
ByVal e As System.EventArgs) _
Handles btnRegionCheckList.Click

  RegionLoad(clstRegions)
End Sub

Private Sub btnRegionRadioList_Click( _
ByVal sender As System.Object, _
ByVal e As System.EventArgs) _
Handles btnRegionRadioList.Click

  RegionLoad(rlstRegions)
End Sub
```

The RegionLoad procedure accepts, as its parameter, a variable of the ListControl
type. Because both the CheckBoxList and RadioButtonList controls inherit from the
ListControl base class, either is a valid parameter for this procedure. (You could also
pass in a ListBox control or DropDownList control, because those controls also
inherit from the ListControl base class.)

The RegionLoad procedure shown in Listing 22.1 uses code exactly like you've seen
before for working with ListBox or DropDownList controls.

LISTING 22.1   Fill Lists with Region Information Using This Procedure

```
Private Sub RegionLoad( _
ByVal ctlRegions As ListControl)

  Dim strSQL As String
  Dim strConn As String
  Dim ds As DataSet

  ' Build Connect and SQL strings
  strConn = "Provider=sqloledb;" & _
    "Data Source=(local);" & _
    "Initial Catalog=Northwind;User ID=sa"
  strSQL = _
    "SELECT RegionID, RegionDescription " & _
    "FROM Region"

  ds = GetDataSet(strSQL, strConn)

  With ctlRegions
```

LISTING 22.1 Continued

```
    .DataTextField = "RegionDescription"
    .DataValueField = "RegionID"
    .DataSource = ds
    .DataBind()
  End With
End Sub
```

This procedure builds SQL and connection strings and then calls the `GetDataSet` procedure to retrieve a `DataSet` object. The code sets the `DataTextField` and `DataValueField` properties of the list control, sets the data source to the DataSet, and then calls the `DataBind` method to hook up the data and display the control.

The `GetDataSet` procedure should look completely familiar to you by this point. This procedure accepts SQL and connection strings and returns a `DataSet` object:

```
Private Function GetDataSet( _
 ByVal SQL As String, _
 ByVal ConnectionString As String) _
As DataSet

 Dim da As OleDbDataAdapter
 Dim ds As New DataSet()

 Try
    da = New OleDbDataAdapter(SQL, ConnectionString)
    da.Fill(ds)

 Catch
    Throw

 End Try
 Return ds
End Function
```

The Calendar Control

If you want to allow a user to select a date, displaying a calendar is the right way to do it. You could fashion your own calendar using an HTML table and a lot of scripting code (many developers have done this, in many different ways), but it's a lot of effort. Fortunately, ASP.NET handles this effort for you. The Calendar control, shown in Figure 22.2 (see the sample page `CalendarControl.aspx`) displays a neatly format-ted, bindable table-like view that provides for almost any "look" you need. (Actually, if you view the source for the page containing the Calendar control in the browser, you'll see that it actually is an HTML table, albeit a somewhat complex one.)

FIGURE 22.2   Use the Calendar control to select a date.

The Calendar control uses client-side script to trigger a postback to the server each time you click any of the dates, or other links, on the calendar. As you can see, in the status bar in Figure 22.2, each date calls a JavaScript procedure that raises an event on the server, thus allowing you to run code each time the user clicks a date.

When the user clicks a date, the `SelectionChanged` event is triggered. In this event procedure, you might retrieve the `SelectedDate` property of the Calendar control and use that date:

```
Private Sub cal_SelectionChanged( _
 ByVal sender As System.Object, _
 ByVal e As System.EventArgs) _
 Handles cal.SelectionChanged

  lblDate.Text = _
  String.Format("Selected date: {0:d}", _
   cal.SelectedDate)
End Sub
```

TIP

This example uses a format specifier in the `String.Format` placeholder: `{0:d}`. The formatting string, d, indicates that the date should be formatted using the short date format of the current locale. For more information on formatting strings, see the online help for the `String.Format` method.

If you click one of the links at the top of the control that moves you to a new month, you trigger the Calendar control's `VisibleMonthChanged` event. This event procedure receives, in its second parameter, a variable of the `MonthChangedEventArgs` type. This variable provides two unique properties, `NewDate` and `PreviousDate`, that allow you to determine the first day of the month that's currently showing and the first day of the month that was previously showing. The sample page uses the `NewDate` property to display the current month:

```
Private Sub cal_VisibleMonthChanged( _
 ByVal sender As System.Object, _
 ByVal e As System.Web.UI.WebControls. _
 MonthChangedEventArgs) _
 Handles cal.VisibleMonthChanged

  lblMonth.Text = _
   String.Format("Visible Month: {0:MMMM yyyy}", _
   e.NewDate)
End Sub
```

TIP

This example uses a user-defined formatting specification, MMMM yyyy, to display only the month name and the year. Again, see the online help for `String.Format` for complete information on its formatting capabilities.

Initializing the Calendar

The Calendar control provides two properties, `SelectedDate` and `TodaysDate`, that are closely related. The `SelectedDate` property (and its cousin, `SelectedDates`) allows you to specify or retrieve the selected date—that is, the date the user has selected. (The `SelectedDates` property allows you to set or retrieve a group of selected dates.) The `TodaysDate` property allows you to set or retrieve the date the calendar considers to be the current date, and this property will contain the server's date if you don't specify a date.

It's quite possible, and highly probable, that these two properties will contain different values. When you first load a page containing the Calendar control, however, you might like them to both contain the same value. (If you don't specify a value for the `SelectedDate` property, it contains the date 1/1/0001. If you don't specify a value for the `TodaysDate` property, it contains the current date on the server.)

To avoid any confusion that might occur if you want to allow a user to select the current date without actually clicking anything, you might want to initialize both these properties to the same date as your page loads:

```
Private Sub Page_Load( _
 ByVal sender As System.Object, _
 ByVal e As System.EventArgs) _
 Handles MyBase.Load

  cal.SelectedDate = cal.TodaysDate
End Sub
```

The AdRotator Control

The AdRotator control allows you to display a randomly selected image, selected from a list contained within an XML file, each time your page is rendered. You supply the images and the XML file containing information about the images, and the ASP.NET page framework handles the rest. You can apply filters dynamically so that you can limit the images to subsets of your choosing, as well. In the sample page, `AdRotatorControl.aspx`, you can select to show images of either male or female employees (or both) randomly selected from a list of images in an XML file (see Figure 22.3).

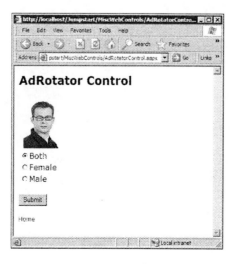

FIGURE 22.3   The AdRotator control allows you to cycle through a series of images.

To use the AdRotator control, you place the control on a page and set the control's
AdvertisementFile property to the location of the XML file containing the image
information. In addition, you can set the KeywordFilter property of the AdRotator
control at any time to filter the images based on the keyword you specify.

The sample advertisement file, Ads.xml, contains information about each of the
images to be displayed, like this:

```
<Advertisements>
<Ad>
  <ImageUrl>images/buchanan.jpg</ImageUrl>
  <NavigateUrl>
    ClickThrough.aspx?Name=Buchanan
  </NavigateUrl>
  <AlternateText>Buchanan</AlternateText>
  <Impressions>80</Impressions>
  <Keyword>Male</Keyword>
</Ad>
<Ad>
  <ImageUrl>images/callahan.jpg</ImageUrl>
  <NavigateUrl>
    ClickThrough.aspx?Name=Callahan
  </NavigateUrl>
  <AlternateText>Callahan</AlternateText>
  <Impressions>80</Impressions>
  <Keyword>Female</Keyword>
</Ad>
</Advertisements>
```

The Advertisements and Ad tags are required, and Table 22.1 describes each of the
elements within each ad.

TABLE 22.1   Use These Elements Within Your Advertisements File

Attribute	Description
ImageUrl	The URL of the image to display.
NavigateUrl	The URL of the page to navigate to when the AdRotator control is clicked.
AlternateText	The text to display if the image is unavailable. On some browsers, this text is displayed as a tooltip.
Impressions	A value that indicates how often an advertisement is displayed in relation to other advertisements in the XML file.

TABLE 22.1   Continued

Attribute	Description
Keyword	The category for the advertisement. This is used by the AdRotator control to filter the list of advertisements for a specific category.

TIP

The Impressions element is somewhat confusing. The values you enter here are relative. That is, you determine the scale for the meaning of these values. If all images have equal values for this element, they're all equally likely to appear. If you have five images, and the Impressions values are 5, 4, 3, 2, and 1, then the first image is five times more likely to appear than the last. In other words, out of 15 hits, the first image is likely to appear five times, the second four times, and so on. You would get the same behavior using values such as 100, 80, 60, 40, and 20. The magnitude of these values doesn't matter, only the relative weights.

In this example, clicking the AdRotator control takes you to ClickThrough.aspx, which displays the information passed to the page, using the Request.QueryString method (see the NavigateURL elements in the sample XML):

```
Private Sub Page_Load( _
 ByVal sender As System.Object, _
 ByVal e As System.EventArgs) Handles MyBase.Load

  If Not Page.IsPostBack Then
    If Not IsNothing(Request.QueryString("Name")) Then
      lblInfo.Text = "You clicked on " & _
        Request.QueryString("Name")
    End If
  End If
End Sub
```

Filtering the AdRotator Control

If you supply Keyword elements in the XML advertisements file, you can filter the images displayed in the AdRotator control. Set the KeywordFilter property of the control and only see images whose keyword matches the keyword you've specified.

In the sample advertisements file, all the images contain either "Male" or "Female" as their keyword values. The sample page allows you to specify whether you want male or female images, or both. (Specifying "Both" on the sample page sets the KeywordFilter property to an empty string, effectively allowing all images.)

```
Private Sub rblFilter_SelectedIndexChanged( _
 ByVal sender As System.Object, _
 ByVal e As System.EventArgs) _
 Handles rblFilter.SelectedIndexChanged

  Dim strFilter As String
  strFilter = rblFilter.SelectedItem.Text
  If strFilter = "Both" Then
    strFilter = String.Empty
  End If
  adEmp.KeywordFilter = strFilter
End Sub
```

The Literal Control

When you start creating data-driven ASP.NET sites, you'll often need to dynamically generate HTML content for your pages. Perhaps you need to store item description information, as HTML, in a database table. At runtime, you need to be able to display that content, rendered correctly as HTML. The Literal control can render HTML at runtime, allowing you to inject HTML into a page.

The sample page, LiteralControl.aspx, allows you to enter HTML into a TextBox control. When you click Display in Literal Control, you execute this event procedure, copying the text into a Literal control:

```
Private Sub btnAssign_Click( _
 ByVal sender As System.Object, _
 ByVal e As System.EventArgs) _
 Handles btnAssign.Click

  litHTML.Text = txtHTML.Text
End Sub
```

That's all it takes to insert HTML into a page at runtime. (Imagine that the HTML was coming from a table, rather than from a TextBox control. Things get awfully powerful, awfully quickly. You can render an entire page from a database, modifying the layout by changing the data in a table. The possibilities are huge.) Figure 22.4 demonstrates the technique, rendering a bulleted list from HTML entered into the text box on the page.

FIGURE 22.4   Use the Literal control to inject HTML into a page. The bulleted list on this page gets its HTML from the TextBox control at the top.

The PlaceHolder Control

Just as the Literal control allows you to inject HTML into a page at runtime, the PlaceHolder control allows you to inject new controls into a page, at a specific location, at runtime. Imagine that you have a table full of links, and you want to insert the series of links into a page between to static paragraphs of text. You don't want to render the entire page at runtime, only the list of links.

No problem—the PlaceHolder control comes to the rescue (working with its pal, the Literal control). We've used this technique to generate the content for Main.aspx in the sample project shown in Figure 22.5. At design time, there's really nothing on this page except a Label control and a single PlaceHolder control (see Figure 22.6).

The PlaceHolder control provides a collection property, the Controls property, that allows you to work with and add to the collection of controls contained within the PlaceHolder control. (The PlaceHolder control isn't the only control that provides a Controls collection—the GroupBox, RadioButtonList, and CheckBoxList controls, for example, also allow you to work with the subcontrols contained within the control. The PlaceHolder control, however, is the best control to use if you want to generate new content on a page at runtime.)

FIGURE 22.5   You can generate any control at runtime and use the PlaceHolder control to place the new control at a known location on the page.

FIGURE 22.6   The sample page doesn't contain much until runtime.

To add a new control at runtime, you can simply instantiate the type of control you want, set the properties you need, and then add the new control to the Controls collection of the PlaceHolder control. For example, the Main.aspx page needs four HyperLink controls, with <p> elements (paragraph breaks) between them. The page contains the AddLink procedure, shown in Listing 22.2, which adds a single link and a <p> element afterwards:

LISTING 22.2   Add HyperLink Controls to the Page Dynamically

```
Private Sub AddLink( _
 ByVal NavigateURL As String, _
 ByVal Text As String, _
 ByVal ID As String)

  Dim hyp As New HyperLink()
  Dim lit As New Literal()

  With hyp
    .NavigateUrl = NavigateURL
```

LISTING 22.2   Continued

```
      .Text = Text
      .ID = ID
   End With
   plcHyper.Controls.Add(hyp)

   lit.Text = "<p>"
   plcHyper.Controls.Add(lit)
End Sub
```

The AddLink procedure starts out by instantiating a new HyperLink control and a new Literal control:

```
Dim hyp As New HyperLink()
Dim lit As New Literal()
```

The procedure sets properties of the HyperLink control using parameters passed into the procedure:

```
With hyp
   .NavigateUrl = NavigateURL
   .Text = Text
   .ID = ID
End With
```

Once the hyperlink is all set up, the code adds the control to the Controls collection of the PlaceHolder control on the page:

```
plcHyper.Controls.Add(hyp)
```

The code then sets the Text property of the Literal control and adds it to the PlaceHolder, as well:

```
lit.Text = "<p>"
plcHyper.Controls.Add(lit)
```

The Page_Load procedure calls the AddLink procedure four times, once for each link it must add:

```
Private Sub Page_Load( _
 ByVal sender As System.Object, _
 ByVal e As System.EventArgs) _
 Handles MyBase.Load
```

```
If Not Page.IsPostBack Then
  AddLink("ListControls.aspx", _
    "List Controls", "hypListControls")
  AddLink("CalendarControl.aspx", _
    "Calendar Control", "hypCalendarControl")
  AddLink("AdRotatorControl.aspx", _
    "Ad Rotator Control", "hypAdRotator")
  AddLink("LiteralControl.aspx", _
    "Literal Control", "hypLiteralControl")
  End If
End Sub
```

Although the sample page uses hard-coded links, your page might use link information pulled from a database, thus allowing you to create totally dynamic pages at runtime.

Summary

Although many of the ASP.NET controls map directly to existing HTML controls, the controls shown in this chapter don't. Each of the controls shown here adds its own utility:

- The Calendar control aggregates existing HTML controls.

- The Literal and Placeholder controls allow you to create dynamic content.

You may not use these controls in every page you build, but it's useful to know that these extended controls are available, should you ever need them.

23

State Management in ASP.NET

OBJECTIVES

- Learn what state is and how you use it

- Learn different methods of state management

- Learn the advantages and disadvantages of each method

Web pages are, by definition, stateless. This means that as you move from page to page, the data from each page is automatically discarded. Because you might need data from one of these previous pages, you need to store that data (or state) as you move from one page to another. There are many techniques you can use to maintain state. Programmers today use Session variables, XML files, databases, and many other proprietary solutions.

State management capabilities are very primitive in ASP when compared to ASP.NET. In ASP, the Session object can only run in-process with the IIS server and does not have any Web farm capabilities. If you want to use a Web farm with ASP, you are forced to create some sort of COM component to store the state into a SQL Server database. You are able to use hidden input fields, but you don't get the automatic state management provided by the ViewState object, and you have to manage it all manually. Also, there are no built-in StateBag objects, so any state you need to keep while on a page has to be managed in hidden input fields, and you have to handle the encryption yourself.

In this chapter, you will learn how to use the various state-management techniques in your .NET Web applications. You will see how to use the Session object, StateBag objects, and the .NET Framework to manage state across a Web farm. You will also learn the advantages and disadvantages of each of these techniques.

State Management Techniques in Brief

You can manage state in your .NET Web applications using tools available in Internet Information Server (IIS) and within the .NET Framework itself. Many of the IIS tools have not changed for use with ASP.NET but have been updated to be more scalable. The .NET Framework has also added some additional tools you will learn about in this chapter. You'll find several options for managing state, for example:

- Using `Session` and `Application` objects to cache information

- Using memory and disk cookies to preserve information

- Using hidden input fields or the URL-embedded data to pass information from one page to another

- Using the `ViewState` property of the page to set and retrieve information stored in a `StateBag` object

- Using SQL Server to store state information

In each case, your goal is to take data from the current page and have that data available, on demand, either when you redisplay the current page or as a reference when you display a different page.

The `Session` and `Application` Objects

The `Session` and `Application` objects allow you to store name/value pairs. The `Session` object stores values between Web pages, maintained for each user. You use the `Application` object to store data that you want to make available across the whole site, for all users. You might use a `Session` variable to keep track of user identity, as the user navigates the pages of your application. You might use an `Application` variable to keep track of the number of times a page has been hit. Both of these objects, `Session` and `Application`, store the state information on the Web server.

The `Application` object is not well suited for state management because it's only a single object, for all users and sessions. Typically, applications manage state on a per-user basis; therefore, the `Application` object will not be discussed in this chapter.

Cookies

Some developers use memory cookies to reduce the amount of resources stored on the server. Memory cookies pass back and forth from the browser to the server, where they're maintained as the user moves from page to page on a site. When the user closes the browser, the cookie is released from memory.

Permanent (or *hard*) cookies allow you to save data on the users' local computers. If you know that a user will visit your site multiple times, it makes sense to save state information locally, if the user has allowed this option. The Web server sends permanent cookies to the user's browser, and the browser stores this data on the user's hard disk. The browser can retrieve this data from disk when the user revisits the Web site. The cookie is again passed from the browser to the server for each page.

Hidden Input Fields

Hidden input fields can be used to pass data from one page to another. When the user clicks a submit button, the form posts the data the user filled in, along with any hidden input fields. You create a hidden input field using a normal HTML tag, like this:

```
<input type="hidden" value="10" name="txtRate">
```

You can store data in a hidden input field to help maintain state from one page to another. In the preceding example, the value 10 is stored in the hidden field named txtRate.

Embedded URL Parameters

You may pass values on the URL by using value/data pairs. For example, you may call an ASP.NET page like this:

```
Main.aspx?CMD=1&ID=29398
```

When you navigate to Main.aspx, you pass two variables in the URL: CMD and ID. You can pass quite a bit of information on this URL, so this is a reasonably effective method of maintaining state.

WARNING

Passing parameter information in the URL displays the values for the user to see—that is, if the information is in the URL, it gets displayed in the browser. Therefore, don't plan on passing sensitive data in the URL.

The StateBag Class

The .NET Framework provides the StateBag class, which allows you to preserve view state while you are working within one page. If the user will be posting data back to the server while staying on the same page, you can use a `StateBag` object to hold multiple intermediate values for this page. You might use this technique when the user must choose a value from one combo box on a page, and then you want to fill the items in another combo box based on the selected item in the first combo box.

The sample project for this chapter is called `StateMgmt.sln`. You should create a virtual directory for this solution that points to the appropriate folder for its files. You can now load this project because many of the following sections will refer to these sample files.

Without some means of preserving the state between roundtrips to the Web server, the data that you've entered onto a Web page would disappear as you post back the page. If you click a button or take any other action that causes a postback to the server, without some help from ASP.NET, your data would be lost as the server re-sends the current page. ASP.NET takes care of managing this roundtrip postback state for you with no extra coding on your part.

ASP.NET keeps track of this data by adding a hidden input control on each page. This control (always named __VIEWSTATE) maintains all the information from all the controls on the page that have their `EnableViewState` property set to `True`. You can see this hidden input variable if you view the source for a Web page from your browser. ASP.NET compresses and encrypts the state information, so you won't be able to discern any of its contents.

SQL Server

In addition to all the other techniques available, you can store state information in a SQL Server database. If you need to maintain a lot of data between pages, this may be your best bet. If you're gathering a large amount of data about the user over several Web pages, you might consider storing this data in SQL Server. There are two techniques for using SQL Server: You can construct the session data and insert the data into the database yourself, or you can let the .NET Framework handle the job for you automatically.

Using the `Session` Object

The `ViewState` information is great for maintaining state across postbacks on a single page, but as you develop Web applications in .NET, you will find that there is a definite need to keep track of data from one page to another, not just on a single page. That's when you need a `Session` object.

Each time a new user comes into your site, IIS creates a new Session object. IIS automatically assigns a unique number to this session and places it into the `Session` object's `SessionID` property. You can use this SessionID to uniquely identify a particular user and create your own session variables to hold state as long as that user's session is active. IIS sends the value of the SessionID property to the browser as a dynamic cookie; each time the browser navigates to any page on the site, this cookie is sent to the server via the HTTP header.

NOTE

In order to make use of the Session object, your users must accept cookies. Although most users don't turn off this capability in their browsers, some do. You'll see, later in this chapter, how you can eliminate cookies when using Session variables.

Session Longevity

The Session object for a particular user does not live indefinitely. The ID only lives until one of the following conditions becomes true:

- Your code calls the Session.Abandon method.

- The Session object times out. The default timeout value is 20 minutes; therefore, if the user doesn't submit a request back to the site in that time, the Session object will be released. You can change this timeout value.

- The IIS Service shuts down.

NOTE

Users perceive that their sessions "die" when they close their browsers. This isn't actually the case. When a user closes his browser, all that's lost is the memory cookie that provided the link to the session on the server.

You can create your own session variables and assign values to these variables using code like this:

```
Session("Email") = "JohnDoe@yahoo.com"
```

This code creates a new session variable, named Email, which is unique for this user. Once you have created session variables, the values stay around until you explicitly set them equal to Nothing or until the session is destroyed, as explained in the previous section.

To retrieve the value of a session variable, use code like this:

```
txtPassword.Text = Session("Email").ToString()
```

Issues with Session Objects

You'll need to keep in mind several issues when you're using the Session object to maintain your application's state. Here are a few of these issues:

- **Memory on the server is limited.** Each session variable you create consumes memory on the server. Although the memory needed for one variable may not seem like much, when you multiply all the data in all your session variables by the number of users that might hit your site at one time, your session variables could be eating up quite a large amount of memory. This memory does not get released until the session is destroyed.

- **You'll need some security.** Once a session begins, the user works with the same SessionID value until the session times out. If a hacker is able to retrieve this value, he could potentially take over the user's session. If you were storing credit card information into a session variable, it's possible that the hacker could see this information, thus causing a security leak. Although this is unlikely, it isn't impossible. To get around this problem, you might wish to employ Secure Sockets Layer (SSL) when working with sensitive information.

- **Session variables don't scale.** A *Web farm* is a group of Web servers working together to service a particular Web site. Each time the user hits a page on your Web site, an IP router determines which machine is not being used too heavily and routes the request for the page to that machine. If the user is routed to a different machine than the one on which the Session object was created, the new server has no way to retrieve that state, and all that user's data is lost.

  To alleviate the problem of different machines serving different pages, you can set values in the application's Web.Config file that specify the name of the machine that stores all session variables. This way, you can dedicate one machine that will do nothing but manage session variables for your site.

  Although this helps with the problem of a Web farm, it introduces problems of its own. For example, this "session state" machine is one more machine that you need to keep up and running 24 hours a day. You might also need some redundancy for this machine to provide continuity while you perform maintenance tasks. In addition, the one main machine could cause performance problems, as one machine could be a bottleneck when many machines have to cross the network to get at the data. We'll discuss Web.Config settings in more detail later in the chapter.

- **Not all users accept memory cookies.** If you have users who will not accept memory cookies in their browsers, you need to set a specific configuration option in .NET to make the session variables work correctly. In the past, memory cookies were *required* on the client browser to make Active Server Pages hold state. The .NET Framework can preserve session state without memory cookies. See the section "Cookieless Sessions" later in this chapter, for information on setting this up.

Turning Off Cookies Page by Page

Whenever an ASPX page is hit, the .NET runtime will, by default, attempt to generate a cookie and send it to the browser. If you know that a page will not use any session state, you can set the EnableSessionState page directive to False to turn off this automatic generation on a page-by-page basis. At the top of every ASPX page, you will find a page directive that looks like the following:

```
<%@ Page Language="vb" AutoEventWireup="false"
 Codebehind="SessionTestError.vb"
 Inherits="StateMgmt.SessionTestError"
 EnableSessionState="False"
%>
```

If you add the EnableSessionState directive, no cookie will be generated for this page.

WARNING

If you attempt to use a Session object on a page that has the EnableSessionState page directive set to False, you will receive a runtime error.

Using Cookies

If you do not wish to store the state of your application on the Web server, you can send the state out to the client's browser. You do this by using *cookies*. You will most likely use a memory cookie because they are destroyed when users close their browsers. To create a memory cookie, you use the Cookies property of the Response object, as shown in the following code. In this example, the code creates a memory cookie named Email and assigns the e-mail address into the cookie:

```
Response.Cookies("Email").Value = "JohnDoe@yahoo.com"
```

Another method of creating a new cookie is to use the `Add` method of the `Cookies` collection, which is a property of the `Response` object. You can create a new `System.Web.HttpCookie` object and pass in the name and the value to the constructor for that object. Here's an example:

```
Response.Cookies.Add(New _
  System.Web.HttpCookie("Email", "JohnDoe@yahoo.com"))
```

Either method shown here will set a memory cookie in the user's browser for you. This assumes that the user allows memory cookies in his browser.

To retrieve a memory cookie on any subsequent page, or even on the same page, use the `Request` object. You should first check to see whether the memory cookie has been created yet. If you try to access the `Cookies` collection and pass in the name of a variable that has not yet been created, you will receive a runtime error:

```
If Not Request.Cookies("Email") Is Nothing Then
   txtEmail.Text = Request.Cookies("Email").Value
End If
```

The sample code checks to see whether the `Request.Cookies("Email")` object is `Nothing`. If it is, you won't be able to do anything with that cookie. If the object has something in it, you can retrieve the value and assign it to a text box on the form.

Permanent Cookies

If you wish to store a cookie to a user's hard disk, you need to set the `Expires` property on that cookie. The following code shows an example of how you create a cookie called EmailPerm and set the expiration date for 30 days in the future:

```
With Response.Cookies("EmailPerm")
  .Value = txtEmail.Text
  .Expires = Today.AddDays(30)
End With
```

By setting the `Expires` property to a date in the future, the browser stores this cookie in a folder on the user's hard disk. Users may set their browsers to only allow memory cookies and not allow permanent cookies. If the active browser won't allow permanent cookies, the data can't be stored. You will not receive an error that the cookie could not be stored, but you won't get the data back when you request the cookie. If you wish to remove a permanent cookie, set the `Expires` property to a date in the past.

Issues with Cookies

Using cookies gives you excellent state management capabilities because they are simple to implement and help you move resources off the server. Like almost any particular technique, cookies have some limitations:

- **Some users don't allow cookies.** Some users believe that viruses can be sent in a cookie and will not allow them on their computers. Although there have never been any documented cases of this happening (and no one could realistically send a virus through a cookie), a lot of users still turn off the ability to accept cookies. When this happens, the user will not be able to use your site if you use cookies for managing state.

- **Performance can deteriorate.** Imagine that a user walks through a wizard on your site, and you gather 100 pieces of data from that user over several pages. Each page needs to post gathered data to the server. If you wait until all 100 pieces of data are gathered, you need to store that data somewhere in the meantime. If you keep putting data into a cookie, a lot of data is being sent back and forth between the browser and the server. This will eat up a lot of bandwidth and could slow your whole site down. Remember, the data has to go both ways for each page the user hits on your site.

- **Cookies take up memory.** Some browsers impose a limit on the size of the cookie data they can accept or the number of cookies they can accept at one time. In addition, the amount of memory that you may chew up on the user's machine may cause his operating system to swap some memory to disk. Under this circumstance, the cookie has slowed down your user's machine as well as the server.

Using the `ViewState` Property

In some cases, you do not need to maintain state across pages but rather only between calls to the same page. If you need to do this, you can use a `StateBag` object provided by ASP.NET.

Using the `StateBag` Object

You can use the `ViewState` property of the page. The `ViewState` property is a `StateBag` object. That is, the property is defined `As StateBag`. In the Web page shown in Figure 23.1, you input three values. You can submit them to the server and display some data in the Result label. At the same time, you create three variables in a "state bag" using the `ViewState` object.

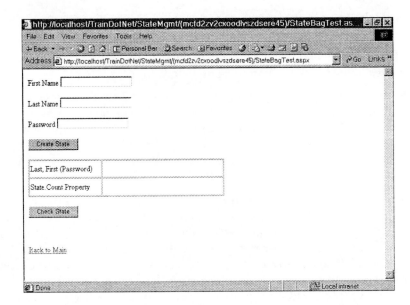

FIGURE 23.1   Use this screen to test the `StateBag` object.

In the `Click` event procedure of the Create State button, write the following code to display the data and create the `ViewState` object:

```
Public Sub btnSubmit_Click(ByVal sender As Object, _
ByVal e As System.EventArgs) Handles btnSubmit.Click
    ViewState("First") = txtFirst.Text
    ViewState("Last") = txtLast.Text
    ViewState("Password") = txtPassword.Text

    lblResult.Text = txtLast.Text & ", " & _
     txtFirst.Text & " (" & txtPassword.Text & ")"
    lblStateResult.Text = ViewState.Count.ToString()
End Sub
```

In this code sample, you use the `ViewState` object just like the `Session` object. Create a new variable just by supplying the name of the variable in parentheses and quotes and assigning a new value to it. Each of the values comes from the text boxes on the Web page.

While you are still on the same page, you can test to see whether the values in the state bag are really preserved during the roundtrip. You can click the Check State button to redisplay the values from the `StateBag` object (when you click the button, you're submitting the page to the server, forcing a roundtrip):

```
Public Sub btnStateCheck_Click(ByVal sender As Object, _
  ByVal e As System.EventArgs) Handles btnStateCheck.Click
    lblResult.Text = ViewState("Last").ToString() & _
    ", " & ViewState("First").ToString()
    lblStateResult.Text = ViewState.Count.ToString()
End Sub
```

StateBag objects are only valid while the page is active. As soon as you navigate to another page, the StateBag object is discarded. If you really wish to give the ViewState property a test, you could click the Create State button and then restart the IIS Service. After restarting the IIS Service, click the Check State button and see whether all your values have been preserved. The ViewState property, with all the data, has been preserved in a hidden field in your form. This is a nice feature—it means that restarting the Web server will not affect the data you are storing for that one page.

State Bag Issues

The StateBag object provides a nice mechanism for storing view state information: the ability to store state for an individual page across roundtrips to the server. However, like most techniques, it comes with its own set of issues:

- The ViewState property is only valid for a single page. For multiple pages, you need to use another structure.

- The more information you store in your StateBag object, the more data you have to exchange with your client's browser. This can cause performance problems across your whole site. Remember that the data must go back and forth with each post of the page back to the server.

- Memory could become an issue. Because pages could grow quite large, with many controls, the ViewState information can take up a large amount of memory on the user's machine. This may cause the user's operating system to swap some memory to disk and slow down the user's machine even more.

Cookieless Sessions

If you know you will be using a Web farm (described in the next section) or you do not want to take a chance on using cookies, you can configure ASP.NET to run without using cookies. You will still be able to use the Session object, but a memory cookie will not be generated. You can accomplish this by changing the Cookieless attribute in the SessionState setting in the Web.Config file associated with the project from `False` to `True`. Once you've set this option to `True`, the `SessionID` value is added to the URL as shown in the following example:

```
http://localhost/StateMgmt/(pe5t5r55ay2cqrfpu4tvgm45)/StateBagTest.aspx
```

The additional text (pe5t...) added to the URL contains the session ID value. IIS uses this number as the session ID when this page is resubmitted back to the server. If you are using any hyperlink elements or `<Form Action="">` tags in your HTML, .NET will add this session ID to each of these HTML tags as well. This works for all pages in your Web site, regardless of whether they are HTML or ASPX pages.

To enable cookieless sessions, you need to make one change in the `Web.Config` file in your ASP.NET application. Follow these steps to enable a cookieless session:

1. Open your application's `Web.Config` file in the Visual Studio .NET editor.

2. Locate the `<sessionState>` XML element.

3. Change the `Cookieless` attribute from `false` to `true`, as shown here:

```
<sessionState
    mode="InProc"
    stateConnectionString="tcpip=127.0.0.1:42424"
    sqlConnectionString="data source=127.0.0.1;user id=sa;password="
    cookieless="true"
    timeout="20"
/>
```

4. Once you have done this, run the application again and watch the URL. You will see a session ID appear with each page that is displayed. This ID is appended to each and every call to any page in this Web site. The ASP.NET engine handles all the details of sending this ID back to the `Session` object.

ASP.NET State Service

One of the problems you learned about earlier involved session state management across a Web farm. In particular, when users come to a Web site that uses several servers that can serve a particular user at any time, the session state does not automatically carry over from machine to machine. Another problem with session state is that it typically runs in the same process space as the IIS service. As a result, if your IIS service goes down, you also lose all session states.

Using a Separate State Server Machine

If you wish to solve both of these problems, you need to move the session state management to an out-of-process component that is separate from the IIS service.

When the .NET Framework is installed, a new service called ASP.NET State is installed on your server. This service manages the Session object in a separate process. This separate process can be located on the same machine as IIS or on a separate machine.

If you choose to use a separate server to be the state management machine, all the servers in your Web farm use this machine to store and retrieve the state information for a user. No matter which machine serves the user, the state is maintained on a separate machine, one from which all the Web servers can retrieve data.

You're probably thinking that this is all very difficult to set up and maintain. Nothing could be further from the truth! In fact, all you have to do is change one setting in each Web server's Web.Config file.

Follow these steps to enable an out-of-process session state manager:

1. Using the Services applet, start the ASP.NET State Service.

2. Open your application's Web.Config file in the Visual Studio .NET editor.

3. Locate the <sessionState> XML element.

4. Change the Mode attribute from InProc to StateServer.

5. Make sure the Cookieless attribute is set to True, as shown here:

```
<sessionState
    mode="StateServer"
    stateConnectionString="tcpip=127.0.0.1:42424"
    sqlConnectionString="data source=127.0.0.1;user id=sa;password="
    cookieless="true"
    timeout="20"
/>
```

6. After setting this attribute, you can test your changes.

7. Run some code that creates a session variable.

8. Stop and restart the IIS Admin and Web Publishing Services.

9. Go back to a page that retrieves the session variable that you previously set. You'll find that the saved variable still exists.

If you will be using a separate machine for state management, make sure that the ASP.NET State Service is running on this other machine. Next, set the stateConnectionString attribute in the <sessionstate> XML element to the name or IP address of the machine that will manage the state.

> **TIP**
>
> By default, the stateConnectionString attribute is set to 127.0.0.1, which corresponds to the current machine. If you want to manage state on a separate machine, you'll need to modify this value.

Issues with the ASP.NET State Service

Here are some issues with using this ASP.NET State Service:

- **Performance.** The performance of retrieving state information from an out-of-process service will be slower than from an in-process service. If you are retrieving data across the network to a state server, you also have the network traffic to contend with. This can slow your retrieval of state information significantly.

- **Redundancy.** If you use another machine to manage state, you will need to set up some redundancy for this machine in case it crashes. Of course, this redundancy will not help you if the original machine dies, because all the session data is stored in memory.

Automatic SQL Server State Management

If you have an installation of SQL Server available to you, you might want to consider moving your session state management to SQL Server, especially if session state is of critical importance to your application and you can't afford to lose the session state for a user. When you send persistent session data to a SQL Server database, the data not only will survive the restarting of Web services but also a restart of the whole machine.

Follow these steps to use SQL Server to manage your state:

1. Open the Web.Config file in the Visual Studio .NET editor.

2. Locate the <sessionState> XML element.

3. Change the Mode attribute to SQLServer.

4. Make sure the Cookieless attribute is set to True.

5. Change the `sqlConnectionString` attribute so the data source expression refers to your server. Add valid user ID and password values as well. You do not need to specify the name of a database because the tables that manage state are located in Tempdb. Here's an example:

```
<sessionState
    mode="SQLServer"
    stateConnectionString="tcpip=127.0.0.1:42424"
    sqlConnectionString="data source=(local);user id=sa;password="
    cookieless="True"
    timeout="20"
/>
```

After setting these attributes, you need to create the ASPState database with some stored procedures that the .NET Framework will use to manage state. Follow these steps to complete the installation:

1. Find the file named `InstallSqlState.sql` located in your `<systemdrive>\Windows\Microsoft.NET\Framework\<Version>` folder.

2. Load the `InstallSqlState.sql` file into SQL Query Analyzer and execute the statements. This creates the ASPState database and all the appropriate stored procedures.

After you have done these tasks, try running your code that creates a session variable. You can stop and start the IIS and Web Publishing Services, and once again, your state will remain. If you open SQL Server Enterprise Manager and navigate to the Tempdb database, you will find a table named ASPStateTempSessions. Open this table, and you will find a record with your session ID, the time this session was created, and when this session will expire. You will also see several binary fields. These fields contain the data for the session. You won't be able to look at this data, but then you don't really need to because the .NET Framework takes care of all this for you automatically.

Issues with Automatic SQL Server State Management

Although using SQL Server to store your session state relieves you of many difficult development issues, you'll still need to consider some important limitations:

- **You're limited to SQL Server.** This technique can only use SQL Server; no other server database will work. If you do not have a SQL Server installation available, you will be unable to use this solution.

- **Performance may suffer.** Like any of the state management techniques, using SQL Server to manage your application's state can cause your performance to degrade a little. Because it takes a little bit of time to make a connection and read and write state information in the database, there's no avoiding a small bit of overhead.

Summary

In this chapter you learned about the many ways you can maintain state on a Web site. In even the smallest of Web applications, you will most likely need to use one or more of these techniques. Storing state information in SQL Server offers flexibility and performance, although sometimes you might need to use a combination of the techniques presented. Being aware of all the possibilities is important, and you might consider each of these options as you plan for state management in your own applications. Here is some key information you should take away from this chapter:

- State is maintained using `Session` variables, SQL Server, and the ASP.NET State Server service.

- The .NET Framework allows you to code your application using `Session` variables yet change their method of storage using simple configuration file changes.

- Using SQL Server is probably the best way to manage state in terms of flexibility and performance.

24

Introduction to Web Security

OBJECTIVES

- Learn the basics of Web-related security

- Use forms-based authentication

- Authorize authenticated users

W hen you refer to security in a Web application, you're generally considering two basic issues: authenticating users (verifying that a user is someone you want to allow into your site) and authorizing users (granting rights based on the current logged-in user's identity). This chapter introduces both of these topics, providing an example based on the project you've been creating throughout the book.

> **NOTE**
>
> Security is a huge topic in ASP.NET, and in .NET in general. Because Microsoft has built security into every area of .NET, from code access to application deployment, full coverage of all the .NET security issues and their implications is far beyond the scope of this chapter and this book.

Forms-Based Authentication

Authentication refers to the process of identifying who a user is and whether he has rights to enter your system. How you authenticate a user is completely up to you: You can ask a user for his e-mail address and a password that you have assigned to him. You can ask him for a user ID and password, or you might ask him for his first name, last name, and Social Security number. It all depends on what type of site you are asking the user to log in to and what information is most relevant to you and to the user.

Authenticating users can be done in one of several ways, including the following:

- **Windows authentication.** Windows authentication allows you to use Basic or Digest security, or any of the built-in techniques Windows provides to authenticate users, such as NTLM or Kerberos. You'll most likely use Windows authentication in an intranet scenario, because every user you authenticate must be able to supply credentials within a Windows domain. It's unlikely that you'd use this technique for a public Web site.

- **Forms-based authentication.** When you use forms-based authentication, you can have ASP.NET automatically redirect a user to a specific page on which he must supply login credentials. Once you've validated the user (perhaps by looking up his information in a database), it's up to your code to indicate to the ASP.NET page framework that the current user is valid. Doing so assigns a cookie to the user. The ASP.NET page framework verifies whether the cookie exists, and if it does, displays the page the user originally attempted to view. If the cookie doesn't exist, ASP.NET redirects the user back to the login page. When you use forms-based authentication, it's up to your application to verify the validity of users. This behavior is different from what you'll see with Windows- or Passport-based authorization. In both those other scenarios, authentication is out of your hands—it's handled by Windows or by Microsoft's secure servers. You would most likely use forms-based authentication on an Internet site.

- **Microsoft Passport.** Microsoft Passport is a centralized authority that handles authentication for you. Passport requests credentials from users, and if they're part of the Passport system and are successfully validated, the Passport service sends your application a certificate so you can verify the users. Using Passport authentication requires a live Internet connection, of course, and it's unlikely you'll use this technique for intranet applications, where it would be simpler to use Windows authentication to validate your users.

Rather than attempting to cover all the issues involved with ASP.NET security (a topic that would require far more space and depth than this book can provide), this chapter focuses on adding a simple forms-based authentication scheme to your application. You'll allow certain users and disallow others, based on data in the Northwind sample database and in the Web.config file.

Denying Anonymous Users

Your first step in securing your site is to deny access to anonymous users. To do that, you'll need to modify the Web.config file as well as add a little code to the Login.aspx page you created earlier in this book.

To add support for denying anonymous users, follow these steps:

1. Open your project in Visual Studio .NET. In the Solution Explorer window, double-click the Web.config file to load it into the code editor window.

2. Find and modify the `<authentication>` element so that it looks like this:

```
<authentication mode="Forms">
  <forms name="NorthwindApp" loginUrl="Login.aspx" />
</authentication>
```

WARNING

XML is case sensitive! Make sure you type in the code exactly as you see it here.

3. If you set the `<authentication>` element's `mode` attribute to `Forms` (as you've done here), you must supply the `forms` element containing information about how you want to authenticate users. This element can contain several different attributes. In this example, the following attributes are used:

- `name`. Specifies the cookie to be sent in the HTTP header that will be used for authentication. By default, the cookie name is `.ASPXAUTH`. In this example, you'll use `NorthwindApp` as the cookie name.

- `loginUrl`. Specifies the page to redirect to if no valid login cookie is found. By default, ASP.NET will redirect to a page named `default.aspx`.

4. You also need to explicitly deny access to anonymous users to enable the redirection to the login page. To do that, modify the `<authorization>` element in `Web.config` so that it looks like this:

```
<authorization>
  <deny users="?" />
</authorization>
```

Inside the `<authorization>` element, you can allow or deny users by using the `<allow>` or `<deny>` element, respectively. In this case, you've selected to deny anonymous users. You have several options for building lists of users. Specifically, you can use the following to allow or deny access, depending on the element you include:

- **?.** Represents anonymous users.

- ***.** Represents all users.

- **A specific name.** Represents a specific user (`"George"`, for example).

- **DomainName\UserName.** Represents a Windows domain user.

- **DomainName\RoleName.** Represents a member of a particular Windows role.

When users attempt to browse to your site, they'll immediately be redirected to `Login.aspx` in order to log in. You must modify that page so that it informs the ASP.NET page framework that you've successfully validated the user.

> **NOTE**
>
> For now, `Login.aspx` won't attempt to perform any verification—it'll simply inform ASP.NET that any user who visits the page is indeed a valid user.

To add support for verification to your page, follow these steps:

1. In the Solution Explorer window, double-click `Login.aspx` to load it into the page designer.

2. On `Login.aspx`, double-click the Login command button, loading the code editor with the `btnLogin_Click` procedure displayed.

3. Scroll to the top of the file and add the following `Imports` statement:

```
Imports System.Web.Security
```

4. Modify the `btnLogin_Click` procedure so that it looks like this (removing the call to `Server.Transfer`):

```
Private Sub btnLogin_Click( _
 ByVal sender As System.Object, _
 ByVal e As System.EventArgs) _
 Handles btnLogin.Click

Session("LoginID") = txtLogin.Text
Session("Password") = txtPassword.Text

FormsAuthentication. _
 RedirectFromLoginPage(txtLogin.Text, False)
End Sub
```

The `FormsAuthentication` class provides an object with shared methods that makes it easier for you to manage authentication tickets. In this case, you're using `RedirectFromLoginPage`, a method that redirects a user back to the originally requested page (which was most likely, in this case, `Main.aspx`). When you call `RedirectFromLoginPage` here, you're passing two parameters:

- A string containing the name of the user (for cookie-authentication purposes).

- A Boolean value indicating whether ASP.NET should issue a durable cookie (a cookie that's saved across browser sessions). In this case, the code requests a memory cookie.

TRY IT OUT At this point, if you've followed the steps carefully, you should be able to run the application, see the Login.aspx page, and enter any value for the login ID. Once you click Login, you should be redirected to the main page.

Authenticating Employees

It's likely that you'll want to authenticate users within your environment based on some table containing information about valid users and their passwords. In this section, you'll add support for validating employees, using the phone extension as the password for each employee.

Adding an ExecuteScalar Method to DataHandler.vb

Given an employee name, you'll want to be able to retrieve the correct password for that employee from the Northwind Employees table. This requirement adds a need for a standard method you can call that will accept a SQL string and return a single value from a table. ADO.NET provides this capability in the ExecuteScalar method of its Command objects (OleDbCommand and SqlCommand). This method returns the value of the first column within the first row of its resulting set of rows, and that's exactly what you need in this case.

To add this functionality to your project, modify the DataHandler.vb class, adding the procedure shown in Listing 24.1.

LISTING 24.1   Retrieve a Single Value from an OleDbCommand Object

```
Public Shared Function ExecuteScalar( _
ByVal SQL As String, _
ByVal ConnectionString As String) As Object

  Dim dr As OleDbDataReader
  Dim cmd As New OleDbCommand()
  Dim Value As Object

  Try
    With cmd
      .Connection = _
        New OleDbConnection(ConnectionString)
      .Connection.Open()

      .CommandText = SQL
      Value = .ExecuteScalar()
      .Connection.Close()
    End With
```

LISTING 24.1 Continued

```
   Catch
      Throw

   End Try

   Return Value
End Function
```

Adding the LoginValid Method

Given a login ID and a password, you'll need to be able to validate a user. In this section, you'll add the LoginValid procedure, shown in Listing 24.2, to do the work for you.

1. In the Solution Explorer window, right-click Login.aspx and select View Code from the context menu.

2. Add the procedure shown in Listing 24.2, directly below the btnLogin_Click procedure.

LISTING 24.2 Use ExecuteScalar to Determine Whether a Login Is Valid

```
Private Function LoginValid( _
 ByVal LoginID As String, _
 ByVal Password As String) As Boolean

   Dim strSQL As String
   Dim strConn As String
   Dim boolFound As Boolean

   ' Retrieve connection string.
   strConn = Session("ConnectString").ToString

   ' Build SQL to count number of valid employees
   ' found with credentials.
   strSQL = "SELECT Count(*) FROM Employees " & _
      "WHERE LastName = " & _
      DataHandler.QuoteString(LoginID) & _
      " AND Extension = " & _
      DataHandler.QuoteString(Password)

   Try
```

LISTING 24.2   Continued

```
    'Execute query and return count of valid records
    boolFound = (CInt(DataHandler. _
    ExecuteScalar(strSQL, strConn)) > 0)

    If Not boolFound Then
      lblError.Text = _
        "Invalid Login ID/Password combination."
    End If

  Catch exp As Exception
    lblError.Text = exp.Message

  End Try

  Return boolFound
End Function
```

The LoginValid procedure does its work taking these actions:

- It retrieves the standard connection string:

```
' Retrieve connection string.
strConn = Session("ConnectString").ToString
```

- It builds the SQL string requesting the count of rows that match the ID and password supplied by the user:

```
' Build SQL to count number of valid employees
' found with credentials.
strSQL = "SELECT Count(*) FROM Employees " & _
  "WHERE LastName = " & _
  DataHandler.QuoteString(LoginID) & _
  " AND Extension = " & _
  DataHandler.QuoteString(Password)
```

- It executes the SQL, returns the count, and compares that count to 0. If the count is greater than 0, you've successfully found a match against the login ID/password pair:

```
boolFound = (CInt(DataHandler. _
  ExecuteScalar(strSQL, strConn)) > 0)
```

- If a match wasn't found, error text is displayed:

```
If Not boolFound Then
  lblError.Text = _
    "Invalid Login ID/Password combination."
End If
```

- In any case, the procedure returns the value of boolFound:

```
Return boolFound
```

Validating the User

Finally, you must modify the btnLogIn_Click procedure in the Login.aspx page so that it validates the user. Modify the procedure so that it looks like Listing 24.3.

LISTING 24.3 Use LoginValid to Validate a User

```
Private Sub btnLogin_Click( _
 ByVal sender As System.Object, _
 ByVal e As System.EventArgs) Handles btnLogin.Click

  Dim strID As String
  Dim strPwd As String

  strID = txtLogin.Text
  strPwd = txtPassword.Text

  If LoginValid(strID, strPwd) Then
    If Session("LoginID").ToString = String.Empty Then
      Session("LoginID") = strID
      Session("Password") = strPwd

      FormsAuthentication.RedirectFromLoginPage( _
        strID, False)
    End If
  Else
lblError.Text = "Invalid Login ID/Password."
  End If
End Sub
```

This code attempts to authenticate the user/password combination. If it succeeds, it checks the Session variable, LogID. If that variable is an empty string, the code fills in the Session variables LogID and Password with the newly entered values. The code then redirects to the main page, passing the user ID.

TRY IT OUT   Test out the sample application again. If you've entered all the code correctly, you should now only be able to authenticate employees and their passwords (using each employee's Extension field as the password). Table 24.1 lists the valid employee name/password combinations.

TABLE 24.1   Use One of These Employee/Password Pairs to Log in to the Sample Application

Last Name	Extension
Buchanan	3453
Callahan	2344
Davolio	5467
Dodsworth	452
Fuller	3457
King	465
Leverling	3355
Peacock	5176
Suyama	428

Logging Out

The main page of the sample application includes a Log Out link that allows users to log out from your application, redirecting them back to the main page (thereby allowing them to log in again) once they've logged out. Follow these steps to add support for logging out:

1. Display NWLeftNav.ascx in the page designer.

2. Double-click the Log Out LinkButton control, displaying the empty lnkLogOut_Click procedure.

3. Scroll to the top of the file and add the following Imports statement:

```
Imports System.Web.Security
```

4. Modify the lnkLogOut_Click procedure so that it looks like this:

```
Private Sub lnkLogout_Click( _
 ByVal sender As System.Object, _
 ByVal e As System.EventArgs) _
 Handles lnkLogOut.Click
```

```
FormsAuthentication.SignOut()
Session.Abandon()
Response.Redirect("Main.aspx")
End Sub
```

5. Save your project.

The lnkLogout_Click procedure executes three actions:

- It calls the shared SignOut method of the FormsAuthentication class. This releases the client authentication ticket on the server.

- It calls the Abandon method of the Session object. This cancels the current session, releasing any Session variables in use.

- It uses the Redirect method of the Response object to redirect back to the Main.aspx page (of course, the current user has now logged out, and the Session variable has been reset). Because the certificate for the client has been deleted, ASP.NET will redirect the user to the page defined in the loginUrl attribute within the authentication element in Web.config.

TRY IT OUT Once again, try out the sample application. This time, click the Log Out link on the main page and verify that you end up back on the login page, logged out and ready to log in again.

TIP

Why did we use Response.Redirect to take you back to Main.aspx? Imagine that once you log out, another user might like to step up to the terminal and interact with this application. Once the original user logs out, you've lost the authentication cookie for that user, and any attempts to browse to any page within the application would redirect the user back to the login page (because of the settings in Web.config). To avoid this, the sample application redirects the user to Main.aspx, which has two side effects: It displays Login.aspx immediately (because the authentication cookie has been lost) and also maintains the page to redirect to once another user logs in.

Supporting Authorization

Once you've authenticated a user (that is, determined that you know who the user is), you may want to restrict or deny access to various parts of your site, or to various activities on your site, based on the user's identity. This process is called *authorization*. As an example, you might want to allow supervisors and managers to access the Maintenance menu on your site but hide the menu from normal users. ASP.NET provides several techniques for managing authorization in your applications. This section investigates three different issues:

- Controlling authorization using Web.config

- Managing authorization dynamically

- Taking advantage of role-based authorization

Using Web.Config

You can use the authorization element in Web.config to determine exactly which users can enter your site. To try out this technique, follow these steps:

1. In the Solution Explorer window, double-click Web.config to load the file into the code editor window.

2. Modify the authorization element so that it looks like this:

```
<authorization>
  <deny users="?" />
  <deny users="Fuller" />
</authorization>
```

3. Run the application.

4. Attempt to log in as Fuller (password 3457) and verify that you cannot log in.

5. Attempt to log in using any other valid user ID/password combination from Table 24.1 and verify that you can log in successfully.

Because you added Fuller to the "deny" list, you won't be able to log in as that particular employee.

TIP

Although you can place names into the "deny" list in the Web.config file in the same folder as your application, it's not a likely scenario—you can just as easily control authorization directly in the login page you created earlier. If you create a separate virtual root for a specific "protected" section of your site (the maintenance section, for example), you could create a new Web.config file and place it into that root. Then, when ASP.NET attempts to load any page within that root, it will use the Web.config file it finds in that folder and then allow or deny users based on the Web.config file it finds there. Using separate Web.config files in individual folders allows you to maintain complete control over who you allow into various parts of your application.

Managing Authorization Dynamically

The Page object provided by the ASP.NET page framework provides the User property, which in turn provides the Identity property. This property allows you to find out the identity of the currently logged-in Windows user. The User property provides properties such as Name, IsAuthenticated (to determine whether the user is currently authenticated), IsInRole (to determine whether the current user is in a specified role), and more. If you wanted to take specific action based on the current logged-in user, you might modify the code in Main.aspx to look like this (not in the sample project):

```
Private Sub Page_Load( _
 ByVal sender As System.Object, _
 ByVal e As System.EventArgs) _
 Handles MyBase.Load

  Dim blnShow As Boolean
  blnShow = (Page.User.Identity.Name = "Davolio")

  lnkLogOut.Visible = blnShow
  hypEmpMaint.Visible = blnShow
  hypPwdChange.Visible = blnShow
End Sub
```

Role-Based Authorization

Just as you can work with users and roles in Windows, you can take advantage of the same technology to authorize users from within your ASP.NET applications. That is, you can authorize a user to take some action or view some information, based on the role the user has taken on—administrator or manager, for example.

To understand the use of roles in ASP.NET, you'll need to dig into a few concepts first.

Important Interfaces

In order for ASP.NET to be able to work with the various .NET classes that allow for authorization, the .NET Framework provides two important interfaces that other objects implement: IIdentity and IPrincipal.

> **TIP**
>
> When we say that one class "implements an interface," we're referring to the object-oriented technique called *interface inheritance*. One class (for example, IIdentity) defines the set of properties, methods, and events that are required by any class that claims to contain identity information. Given that class, any other class can implement the behavior defined by the interface in any way that's required. Although this sounds similar to inheriting from a base

class, the two techniques are different enough that there are good reasons to use one or the other. For more information, you'll need to find a good article or book on object-oriented programming techniques.

An object that implements IIdentity represents the current user on whose behalf the code is running. There are four .NET classes that implement this interface:

- GenericIdentity. A basic implementation of IIdentity that can represent any user.

- FormsIdentity. Represents a user who has been authenticated using forms-based authentication. This object provides a way for an application to interact with the cookie-authentication ticket.

- PassportIdentity. Represents a user who has been authenticated using Passport authentication. This class provides access to the Passport profile cookies.

- WindowsIdentity. Represents a user who has been authenticated using Windows authentication (in other words, a Windows user).

Each of these classes provides its own functionality, depending on its use. For example, the WindowsIdentity class provides information on whether a user is logged in to a System, Guest, or Anonymous account; the PassportIdentity class provides properties that allow you to interact with its Passport-authentication ticket.

An object that implements the IPrincipal interface represents the security context of the user on whose behalf the code is running. This context contains identity information (in the form of an object that implements IIdentity) and any roles to which the user belongs.

Two classes implement the IPrincipal interface:

- GenericPrincipal. This class simply allows code to check the role membership of a user represented by the GenericPrincipal object. If you use this class, you'll need to create the roles and add users to it yourself—it doesn't communicate with or have information about Windows roles.

- WindowsPrincipal. This class allows code to check the Windows role membership of the user represented by the WindowsPrincipal object.

Using Identities and Principals

Suppose you'd like to be able to assign users to particular roles (Users or Managers) and then be able to show or hide information and controls based on the role the current user is in. To do this, you'll need to work with some class that implements IIdentity (representing the user) and some class that implements IPrincipal (representing the user's security context).

In this example, you'll examine the identity of each user who logs in to your site, and based on the username (remember, you're only allowing in employees of the Northwind company) you'll add some employees to the Managers role and others to the Users role. Then, based on the role of the user, you'll show or hide controls on the main page.

> **TIP**
>
> Yes, you're unlikely to hard-code this information in a real application. You might, instead, use the Windows roles and the WindowsPrincipal class to work with the users. Alternatively, you might store information about the users' roles in your company's database. To keep things simple here, we're using the GenericIdentity and GenericPrincipal classes (although we could very easily have used the FormsIdentity object, because we know that in this application, we're using forms-based authentication to authenticate the user).

Normally, to work with identities and principals, you'll need to first create an object that implements IIdentity (one of GenericIdentity, FormsIdentity, and so on), supplying login information to identify the authentication ticket for the user. You'll then use the new IIdentity object, along with an array of strings containing the names of the roles assigned to the user, to create an object that implements IPrincipal (either GenericPrincipal or WindowsPrincipal).

You'll see code like this, later in this section:

```
Dim astrRoles(0) As String
Dim gid As GenericIdentity
Dim gp As GenericPrincipal

' Create Identity
gid = New GenericIdentity(LoginID)

' Create Principal
astrRoles(0) = "Managers"
gp = New GenericPrincipal(gid, astrRoles)
```

This example creates a new GenericIdentity object, given the login ID supplied by the user. The code sets the only role for this user (Managers) and then creates a new GenericPrincipal object, passing in the GenericIdentity object and the roles. This GenericPrincipal object identifies the security context for the logged-in user, including the login information and the roles.

Adding Support for Role-Based Authorization

TRY IT OUT To test out role-based authorization, this section walks you through inserting code to add role information to a `GenericPrincipal` object. You'll also see how to create the appropriate `GenericIdentity` object, corresponding to the logged-in user, and how to retrieve the security information when necessary.

In this example, the goal is to show the Employee Maintenance and Change Password links only if the logged-in user is a member of the Managers role. Otherwise, those links simply shouldn't appear on the page.

Follow these steps to add role-based authorization support to `Login.aspx` and `Main.aspx`:

1. In the Solution Explorer window, select `Login.aspx`. Right-click and select View Code from the context menu.

2. Scroll to the top of the file and add the following `Imports` statement:

```
Imports System.Security.Principal
```

3. Add the following procedure to the class:

```
Private Sub SetIDAndPrincipal( _
ByVal LoginID As String)

    ' This must be an array, but since you
    ' know you're only dealing with a single role,
    ' declare it to contain only the 0th element.
    Dim astrRoles(0) As String
    Dim gid As GenericIdentity
    Dim gp As GenericPrincipal

    ' Hard-code the roles, for this
    ' simple example.
    Select Case LoginID
      Case "King", "Buchanan"
        astrRoles(0) = "Managers"
      Case Else
        astrRoles(0) = "Users"
    End Select

    ' Create Identity
    gid = New GenericIdentity(LoginID)
```

```
' Create Principal
gp = New GenericPrincipal(gid, astrRoles)

' Store in a Session variable for later use.
Session("Principal") = gp
End Sub
```

The SetIDAndPrincipal procedure sets up the role information for authorization use, later in your application. For demonstration purposes, this procedure adds the Managers role to two employees (King and Buchanan) and the Users role to the rest. (Of course, your own applications could assign roles in other ways, including using Windows' own roles.) Along the way, this procedure takes these actions:

- It declares necessary variables. The code will need an array of strings containing role assignments. Because this example uses only a single role, the array can be preassigned to contain only a single element. In addition, the code needs GenericIdentity and GenericPrincipal objects, and it creates those variables here:

```
Dim astrRoles(0) As String
Dim gid As GenericIdentity
Dim gp As GenericPrincipal
```

- It hard-codes the roles for all the employees, making simple assumptions about the appropriate role for each, based on the login ID value:

```
Select Case LoginID
  Case "King", "Buchanan"
    astrRoles(0) = "Managers"
  Case Else
    astrRoles(0) = "Users"
End Select
```

- It creates the new GenericIdentity object, using the login ID. The code then creates the GenericPrincipal object using the new GenericIdentity object and the array of roles filled in previously:

```
' Create Identity
gid = New GenericIdentity(LoginID)

' Create Principal
gp = New GenericPrincipal(gid, astrRoles)
```

- Finally, because the rest of your application will need to be able to retrieve role information, the code stores the GenericPrincipal object into a Session variable:

```
' Store in a Session variable for later use.
Session("Principal") = gp
```

You'll need to add a call to the new SetIDAndPrincipal procedure. To do that, follow these steps:

1. Make sure the code-behind file for Login.aspx is still loaded in the code editor window. (It should still be loaded if you haven't closed it after executing the previous steps.)

2. Modify the btnLogin_Click procedure once again, adding the call to SetIDAndPrincipal, as shown in Listing 24.4.

LISTING 24.4 Add a Call to SetIDAndPrincipal

```
Private Sub btnLogin_Click( _
ByVal sender As System.Object, _
ByVal e As System.EventArgs) Handles btnLogin.Click

  Dim strID As String
  Dim strPwd As String

  strID = txtLogin.Text
  strPwd = txtPassword.Text

  If LoginValid(strID, strPwd) Then
    If Session("LoginID").ToString = String.Empty Then
      Session("LoginID") = strID
      Session("Password") = strPwd

      SetIDAndPrincipal(strID)

      FormsAuthentication.RedirectFromLoginPage( _
        strID, False)
    End If
  Else
    Server.Transfer("Main.aspx")
  End If
End Sub
```

Finally, you'll need to add support to the main page so that you can hide and show links on the page based on the current user's role. That code is in the `NWLeftNav.ascx` user control. Follow these steps to modify the navigation user control to hide links as necessary:

1. In the Solution Explorer window, right-click `NWLeftNav.ascx` and select View Code from the context menu.

2. Scroll to the top of the file and add the following `Imports` statement:

```
Imports System.Security.Principal
```

3. Modify the `Page_Load` procedure so that it looks like this:

```
Private Sub Page_Load( _
ByVal sender As System.Object, _
ByVal e As System.EventArgs) _
Handles MyBase.Load

    Dim blnShow As Boolean
    Dim blnIsManager As Boolean
    Dim gp As GenericPrincipal

    blnShow = _
      (Session("LoginID").ToString <> String.Empty)

    gp = CType(Session("Principal"), GenericPrincipal)
    blnIsManager = (gp.IsInRole("Managers"))

    lnkLogOut.Visible = blnShow
    hypEmpMaint.Visible = blnShow And blnIsManager
    hypPwdChange.Visible = blnShow And blnIsManager
End Sub
```

4. The new code you've added to this procedure retrieves the `Session` variable containing the `GenericPrincipal` object:

```
gp = CType(Session("Principal"), GenericPrincipal)
```

5. The code uses the `IsInRole` method of the `GenericPrincipal` object and determines whether the logged-in user is acting in the Managers role:

```
blnIsManager = (gp.IsInRole("Managers"))
```

6. Finally, the code determines whether to show the `hypEmpMaint` and `hypPwdChange` links, based on the role of the user:

```
hypEmpMaint.Visible = blnShow And blnIsManager
hypPwdChange.Visible = blnShow And blnIsManager
```

(In this code, the blnShow and blnManager values would have to be True in order to have the links appear on the page.)

To test out the role-based authentication, follow these steps:

1. Press F5 to run the project.

2. Log in as Buchanan, using 3453 as the password. You'll be redirected to the main page. Verify that you see the maintenance links, because you're currently logged in using the Managers role.

3. Click the Log Out link, and you'll be redirected back to the login page.

4. Log in again as Davolio, using 5467 as the password. On the main page, verify that you don't see the maintenance links, because you're now logged in using the Users role.

Summary

In this chapter, you learned to secure your Web application using forms-based authentication. You learned to authenticate users and how to authorize their access into certain areas of the system.

25

Creating Mobile Web Applications

OBJECTIVES

- Determine why you need the Microsoft Mobile Internet Toolkit (MMIT)

- Learn what's in the MMIT

- Create a sample page using several of the controls in the MMIT

Y ou can assume that anyone visiting your Web site has a full-featured browser, with a keyboard, a color screen of at least 640480 pixels, and reasonably wide bandwidth, right? Wrong! Not every visitor will be using a personal computer—the number of connected smaller devices increases each month, and you can no longer make these standard assumptions. Users who visit your sites might be using Pocket PCs, cell phones, or other limited-capability browsers, and they will need special consideration.

In addition, by creating only an HTML version of your site, you're missing out on the hordes of users attempting to visit your site using Web-enabled cell phones, pagers, and PDAs. These devices, in general, don't use HTML but rather some limited sort of markup language, such as Wireless Markup Language (WML), compact HTML (cHTML), or various subsets of HTML used by PDAs and pagers. How do you accommodate these visitors?

Before ASP.NET, the only reasonable solution was to create multiple versions of your site—one for full-featured browsers, one for down-level browsers, another for WML devices, another for cHTML devices, and so on. ASP.NET handles the rich versus down-level browser situation well, and it integrates with the Microsoft Mobile Internet Toolkit to support mobile devices.

Introducing the Microsoft Mobile Internet Toolkit

The Microsoft Mobile Internet Toolkit (MMIT) adds features to ASP.NET that support handheld and mobile devices. Using this toolkit, you can create a single application that targets multiple devices and standards. In general, the MMIT is an SDK that takes advantage of the features of ASP.NET as well as integrates tightly with the Visual Studio .NET development environment.

The MMIT provides useful features for Web developers. In specific, the MMIT does the following:

- **Creates write-once mobile Web pages.** Rather than requiring you to rewrite your pages for multiple devices, the MMIT allows you to create the pages once, and then the toolkit renders the pages according to the information passed to ASP.NET from the browser, in the HTTP request header information.

- **Supports multiple markup languages.** So that you don't have to create separate pages for HTML, WML, cHTML, and so on, the MMIT handles this detail as it renders the pages.

- **Supports a variety of devices.** Mobile browsers come in all sorts of devices, from Pocket PCs to pagers to e-mail devices. The MMIT handles them all, and it can be expanded by adding more device-configuration information.

- **Integrates with Visual Studio .NET.** The MMIT adds a new project type (Mobile Web Application) and page type (Mobile Web Page) to Visual Studio .NET. You use the tools you're accustomed to using to create Web pages that can be browsed from virtually any browser.

In this chapter, you'll use the Microsoft Mobile Internet Toolkit to create a simple page and then test it using one or more mobile device emulators. You'll learn about the controls provided by the MMIT and how to write code binding data to these controls.

Testing Mobile Pages

Unless you like collecting gadgets or have unlimited funds, you probably won't want to buy a device containing each different possible browser just to test your site. To make this task more reasonable, developers of each of the popular mobile browsers have released simulators that you can run on your development machine. You'll want to download or purchase simulators for all your target platforms. We tried four different simulators, as listed here:

- OpenWave's UP.SDK simulator for the Unwired Planet (UP) browser (http://developer.phone.com)

- Nokia's Mobile Internet Toolkit for its mobile phones (http://forum.nokia.com)

- Microsoft Mobile Explorer for phones using Microsoft's software (http://www.microsoft.com/mobile/phones/mme/mmemulator.asp)

- Microsoft's Pocket PC emulator for its Pocket IE (www.microsoft.com/mobile/developer)

Note that many of the simulators support "skins" (that is, graphics that make the simulator look more like a specific device) and may provide multiple skins.

TIP

If you're going to use the Pocket PC emulator, you'll need to also download a patch from Microsoft's Web site that allows JScript to work in the emulator. For more information, visit support.microsoft.com and look for Knowledge Base article Q296904.

Handling Mobile Requests

When a device makes a request against a Web site, that HTTP request makes its way through the Internet to your site. IIS renders a response, sent back to the browser, for display there. Cell phones, on the other hand, don't "understand" HTTP. Instead, must current cell phones use the Wireless Application Protocol (WAP) as their means of transmission. To hit current Web sites, cell phones pass their requests through a gateway (normally provided by the wireless ISP) that converts the WAP requests, using WML (Wireless Markup Language), to HTML and HTTP and then sends the requests on to the Web server. The Web server gets the requests, investigates the request header information to determine the source of the request (that is, the exact type of browser and its capabilities) and then generates a response. The response goes back to the browser; however, for cell phones, the response passes through the gateway again, which converts the HTML/HTTP information into WML/WAP.

The MMIT does the work of determining the capabilities of the requesting browser and renders the output of the controls you've placed on your pages so that it can be viewed on the host browser. If the browser doesn't support many lines, for example, the MMIT may render Command controls (seen as buttons on a standard browser) using the softkey on the device (the labeled button at the bottom of the screen with a software-supplied label).

Controls Supplied by MMIT

In its original release, the MMIT supplies controls that can be broken down into seven basic categories:

- **Container controls.** The Form and Panel controls contain other controls. The Form control is the basis for breaking up pages into smaller chunks. The

Panel control allows you to group controls so that you can treat them all as a programmable entity (to hide and show the entire group, for example).

- **Transfer controls.** The PhoneCall control allows you to initiate a voice call, if the device supports it. The Command control acts much like a Button control in ASP.NET pages, except that the Command control may be displayed as either a button on "large" browsers or as a softkey on compact browsers. The Link control acts as a hyperlink, allowing you to navigate from one form to another form or page, without having to write any code.

- **Text display controls.** The TextBox and Label controls work much like the ASP.NET equivalents. The TextView control works like a Label control, but it also allows you to display formatted and paginated text containing a limited subset of HTML attribute tags.

- **List and selection controls.** The List control allows you to display a list of items, and you can choose plain, bulleted, or numbered lists. You can react to the `ItemCommand` event when a user selects an item. The SelectionList control also displays a list of items, but this control also supports five different views (DropDown, ListBox, Radio, MultiSelectListBox, and CheckBox) and doesn't raise an event when you select an item. You'll need some other control (such as a Command control) to take an action after you've selected one or more items. The ObjectList control can be bound to a data source (that's the only way to supply it with data) and provides two views of the data—a table view and a details view. You'll investigate this complex control, in depth, later in the chapter.

- **Validation controls.** Provides much the same behavior as the parallel ASP.NET validation controls.

- **Image display controls.** The AdRotator and Image controls work much like their ASP.NET parallels.

- **Miscellaneous controls.** The DeviceSpecific control allows you to add property settings and behaviors that are specific to a single device, given characteristics that you specify. The MMIT supplies a number of predefined filters and specifications for devices. You can add your own, as well. The StyleSheet control allows you to bypass the otherwise missing support for Cascading Style Sheets in the MMIT. You can create named styles and associate them with controls' properties. The Calendar control allows you to request date information from users.

NOTE

The MMIT includes three predefined styles: error, subcommand, and title. You apply these styles to a control by setting the `StyleReference` property.

WARNING

Although the Calendar control's output looks great on "large" browsers, there's no room for a graphical calendar display on small browsers, and the whole interface works differently there. Make sure you investigate this before using the Calendar control on one of your pages.

Creating a Page for Mobile Devices

In this chapter, you'll walk through creating a reasonably complex page that's aimed specifically for mobile devices. Although the page works fine when browsed using Internet Explorer, its appearance is a little "tame" for standard browsing. Although we've attempted to have the page use as many different controls as is reasonable, there are several other controls we didn't cram into this example.

TIP

The first difference you'll notice between standard ASP.NET pages and mobile pages is that mobile pages are broken up into one or more forms. Each page must contain at least one form but can contain as many as you require. The Microsoft Mobile Internet Toolkit manages breaking the forms up, as required by the capabilities of the requesting browser.

To begin creating the example for this chapter, you will first need to have the Microsoft Mobile Internet Toolkit on your development machine. If you have not already done so, download the toolkit from the Microsoft Web site. Instead of publishing the URL on the Microsoft Web site (because Microsoft rearranges its site so often), we can only suggest that you browse to www.microsoft.com and perform a search for the Mobile Internet Toolkit. Follow the instructions to install this toolkit on your machine.

Creating the Page and First Two Forms

The page you'll build allows you to investigate customers in the Northwind sample database, filtering first by country and then by city. You'll view detailed information about the selected customer and will be able to view the total number of orders for the customer, as well. The page is broken up into five forms, and Figure 25.1 shows the first two, which allow you to enter a password and then select a country.

NOTE

These screenshots were taken using the Pocket PC browser—clearly, the display would be significantly different using any other browser.

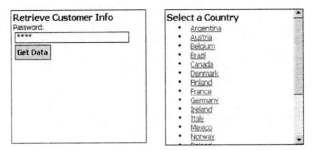

FIGURE 25.1   The first two forms allow you to enter a password and then view a list of countries.

Creating the Password Form

Follow these steps to create the page and the first form:

1. Open Visual Studio .NET and create a new Visual Basic .NET project, selecting Mobile Web Application from the Templates list. Name the new project **MMITSample**.

2. Find MobileWebForm1.aspx in the Solution Explorer window and change the name of the page to CustomerInfo.aspx.

3. Open CustomerInfo.aspx in Design view, and you should see a single form named Form1. Make sure the Properties window is visible and then select the form. Set the form's ID property to frmMain.

4. Add controls to frmMain using the controls and properties in Table 25.1 as your guide. When you are done, your form should look similar to Figure 25.2.

TABLE 25.1   Add These Controls, with the Listed Properties, to frmMain

Control	Property	Value
Label	StyleReference	Title
	Text	Retrieve Customer Info
Label	Text	Password:
TextBox	ID	txtPassword
	MaxLength	10
	Password	True
Command	ID	cmdGo
	SoftkeyLabel	Go
	Text	Get Data

As you add controls, note that you can only manage the order of the placement of the controls from top to bottom. If you follow the instructions, in order, you shouldn't have any troubles. Also, you won't add all the controls right now—you'll come back in later sections and add a few more, such as the RequiredFieldValidator control on frmMain.

FIGURE 25.2   The Password screen to enter the mobile application.

> **TIP**
>
> To place a control between two others, the simplest solution is to select the control preceding the location where you want the new control. Double-click the control you want to create in the Toolbox, and your new control will appear in the designer immediately following the selected control. If you accidentally place a control outside a form, simply drag it into the destination form. Don't spend any time attempting to resize or apply careful layout attributes to your controls. You simply don't get much control over the layout of the pages.

Creating the Country Form

On the second form, you'll use the List control to display a list of available countries. Follow these steps to set up the List control on the second form:

1. Click the page, outside frmMain, to place the insertion point.

2. Double-click the Form control in the Toolbox to add a new form to the page.

3. Set the new form's ID property to frmCountry.

4. Add controls to frmCountry using the controls and properties in Table 25.2 as your guide. When you are finished, your completed form should look similar to Figure 25.3.

TABLE 25.2   Add These Controls, with the Listed Properties, to frmCountry

Control	Property	Value
Label	StyleReference	Title
	Text	Select a Country
List	ID	lstCountry
	Decoration	Bulleted

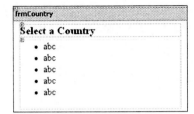

FIGURE 25.3   Display a list of countries using the List control.

Navigating from Form to Form

In order to navigate from one form to another, you must add one line of code to the Click event handler for the Command control on the first form. Follow these steps to hook up the navigation:

1. In the first form, double-click the Get Data button, loading the code editor with the cmdGo_Click procedure selected.

2. Modify the procedure so that it looks like this:

```
Private Sub cmdGo_Click( _
  ByVal sender As System.Object, _
  ByVal e As System.EventArgs) _
  Handles cmdGo.Click

    ActiveForm = frmCountry
End Sub
```

NOTE

We've modified the layout of the code so that it fits on the printed page. You needn't add the line-continuation characters in the procedure declaration—they don't affect the behavior of the code.

Setting the ActiveForm property of the page to a specific form causes the page to navigate to the selected form. In this case, clicking the Command control navigates to the frmCountry form.

Adding Data to the List Control

In order to display the list of countries in the List control, you'll need to add data-handling support. In this section, you'll get the data hooked up, and you'll fill the List control with its list of countries.

To add support for data handling, follow these steps:

1. Copy the `DataHandler.vb` file from your `Northwind.sln` solution into this project. (You can use Windows Explorer to help. Simply find the file, copy it to the Clipboard, and then paste it into your project.)

2. In the Solution Explorer window, right-click `CustomerInfo.aspx` and select View Code from the context menu. Add the following procedure, which fills lstCountry with a list of countries from the Customers table:

```
Private Sub FillCountry()
  Dim ds As DataSet
  Dim strConn As String
  Dim strSQL As String

  strConn = DataHandler.ConnectStringBuild("sa", "")
  strSQL = _
   "SELECT DISTINCT Country FROM Customers " & _
   "ORDER By Country"

  ds = DataHandler.GetDataSet(strSQL, strConn)
  With lstCountry
    .DataTextField = "Country"
    .DataValueField = "Country"
    .DataSource = ds
    .DataBind()
  End With
End Sub
```

TIP

By setting the List control's `DataTextField` and `DataValueField` properties, you're indicating to the control which fields from its data source it should use to represent the text displayed on the page (`DataTextField`) and the field it should use for the `Value` property of each list item. In this case, they're the same values—in many cases, you might display one string but use a different string to represent each item programmatically. (For example, you might want to display a customer name but use the CustomerID programmatically.) This code also sets the `DataSource` property of the control and calls its `DataBind` method.

3. You also need to call the `FillCountry` procedure as you navigate to the second form. Find the `cmdGo_Click` procedure and modify it so that it looks like this, calling the new procedure:

```
Private Sub cmdGo_Click( _
 ByVal sender As System.Object, _
```

```
ByVal e As System.EventArgs) _
Handles cmdGo.Click

    FillCountry()
    ActiveForm = frmCountry
End Sub
```

4. Use the Build, Rebuild All menu item to rebuild your project.

TRY IT OUT You are now poised and ready to try your first mobile Web application. If you've installed an emulator, you can use it to browse to your page at this location:

```
http://localhost/MMITSample/CustomerInfo.aspx
```

If you have not installed an emulator, just run the project within Internet Explorer or your local browser. The Microsoft Mobile Internet Toolkit renders output for full-featured browsers in addition to mobile browsers.

> **TIP**
>
> You may receive an error from Internet Explorer, complaining about a missing or expired cookie. You can either refresh the browser or reload the page to bypass the problem.

To try out the sample page, follow these steps:

1. Press F5 to run the application (or browse to the page from any device or emulator).

2. Fill in any password and click Get Data.

You should now see a list of countries displayed. You will notice that in the list of countries, the items aren't displayed as hyperlinks. The List control won't display hyperlinks for any of its data until you add code for the control telling it what to do when you select an item. You'll add this code in the next step.

Displaying Cities

Now that you have filled the List control with a list of countries from the Customers table, you can now drill down and view a list of cities from the selected country. Follow these steps to create the form containing the list of cities:

1. Click to the right of frmCountry and then double-click the Form control in the Toolbox window.

2. Set the ID property of this new form to frmCity.

3. Add controls to frmCity using the controls and properties in Table 25.3 as your guide. When you're finished, your form should look like Figure 25.4.

TABLE 25.3   Add These Controls, with the Listed Properties, to frmCity

Control	Property	Value
Label	ID	lblCity
	StyleReference	Title
	Text	Select a City
SelectionList	ID	slstCity
	SelectType	Radio
Command	ID	cmdCustomers
	SoftkeyLabel	GO
	Text	Customers
Label	ID	lblValidate
	ForeColor	Red
	Text	(empty)

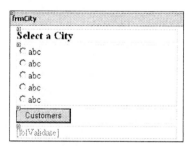

FIGURE 25.4   Use a SelectionList control to display a list of cities.

TIP

Investigate the other SelectType property values for the SelectionList control. Other values allow for multiple selections and other layouts. Note that the SelectionList control won't generate its own postback, so you'll need some mechanism for posting to the server—in this case, you're using a Command control.

NOTE

Why set the `SoftkeyLabel` property of the Command control? On some devices, the
Command control doesn't appear as a button but instead migrates to the softkey button—
this happens often on phones. There's not much space for text on the softkey label, so keep
this value very short.

Navigating to the City Form

Once you've selected a country, you can navigate to a form that displays cities
within that country. You'll need to supply a procedure to fill the SelectionList
control with a list of cities. In addition, you'll need to add code so that you navigate
to the page containing cities once you select a country.

Follow these steps to add these features:

1. Add the following procedure to your page's class:

```
Private Sub FillCity(ByVal Country As String)
    Dim ds As DataSet
    Dim strConn As String
    Dim strSQL As String

    strConn = DataHandler.ConnectStringBuild("sa", "")
    strSQL = String.Format( _
      "SELECT DISTINCT City FROM Customers " & _
      "WHERE Country = '{0}' ORDER By City", Country)

    ds = DataHandler.GetDataSet(strSQL, strConn)
    lblCity.Text = "Select a City in " & Country
    With slstCity
        .DataTextField = "City"
        .DataValueField = "City"
        .DataSource = ds
        .DataBind()
    End With
End Sub
```

TIP

The `FillCity` procedure sets the `DataTextField` and `DataValueField` properties of the
SelectionList control, just as the `FillCountry` procedure did for the List control. In this procedure, the `DataSource` property includes a `WHERE` clause that limits the cities to just the country
selected in the previous form.

---

2. From the Class Name drop-down list (the upper-left list at the top of the code editor window), select lstCountry. From the Method Name list (the upper-right list), select ItemCommand. The code editor creates the stub of the lstCountry_ItemCommand procedure for you.

3. Modify the lstCountry_ItemCommand procedure so that it looks like this:

```
Private Sub lstCountry_ItemCommand( _
  ByVal source As System.Object, ByVal e As _
  System.Web.UI.MobileControls.ListCommandEventArgs) _
  Handles lstCountry.ItemCommand

   FillCity(e.ListItem.Value)
   ActiveForm = frmCity
End Sub
```

TIP

When you select an item in a List control, the ItemCommand event procedure receives a parameter (e) of type ListCommandEventArgs. This object provides a ListItem property that represents the selected item. The Value property of this object provides the data in the selected row of the field you supplied in the DataValueField property. The corresponding Text property corresponds to the value in the field you specified in the DataTextField property.

 You can now try out all three pages to see how you navigate from one form to another in your mobile Web application. To do so, follow these steps:

1. Press F5 to run the application (or browse to the page from an emulator).

2. Enter any password and click Get Data.

3. Click a country to view all the cities for the selected country.

Different Views

Depending on the emulator or actual device you use, the forms on your page display differently. Figure 25.5 shows all the forms on the finished page using the UP.SDK emulator. Figure 25.6 shows the same forms using the Pocket PC browser. (You'll add the rest of the pages shown in these figures in the following sections.)

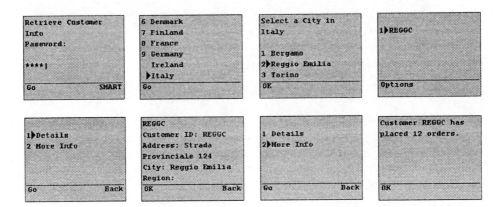

FIGURE 25.5   The sample ASP.NET page displayed on the UP.SDK browser.

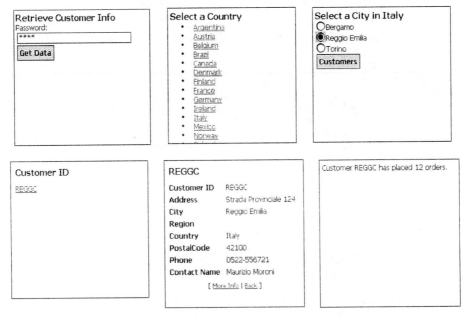

FIGURE 25.6   The same application looks much different when you use the Pocket PC browser.

In the next section, you'll learn to use the most powerful control in the Microsoft Mobile Internet Toolkit toolbox—the ObjectList control.

Working with the ObjectList Control

The ObjectList control allows you to bypass a lot of work you would otherwise have to do yourself. Once you've set the appropriate properties and have bound the control to some data source, the control can display both a table and a details view of your data. You supply the fields to be displayed in the table view as well as the exact information and formatting you want to use in details view, and the control does its work.

In this example, the goal is to display customer IDs and phone numbers in the table view and list complete information in the details view. This requires nothing more than setting a few properties.

Follow these steps to add the fourth form to your page:

1. Click to the right of frmCity and then double-click the Form control in the Toolbox window.

2. Set the ID property of this new form to frmCustomers.

3. Add an ObjectList control to frmCustomers and set its ID property to olstCustomers. You'll come back later and set the various properties of this somewhat-complex control.

Setting Up Fields in the ObjectList Control

Follow these steps to manage how the ObjectList control does its work:

1. Select the ObjectList control, olstCustomers, and set its AutoGenerateFields property to False. (If you allow the control to generate its own list of fields to display in its details view, you can't manage any properties of the data, such as its formatting, or the headings for the fields.)

2. Set the LabelField property to CustomerID. This property indicates which field you want to use as the title in the table view.

3. Set the TableFields property to CustomerID.

4. Now the tricky part: Select the Fields property and click the builder button (...). In the Field Name list, add one entry for each of the fields you want displayed in the details view and then fill in the rest of the properties as shown in Table 25.4. (Note that you're not setting the DataFormatString or Visible property of any of the fields, although you could.)

TABLE 25.4 Use These Settings for the `Fields` Property of the ObjectList Control

Field Name	Data Field	Title
CustomerID	CustomerID	Customer ID
Address	Address	Address
City	City	City
Region	Region	Region
Country	Country	Country
PostalCode	PostalCode	Postal Code
Phone	Phone	Phone
ContactName	ContactName	Contact Name

Filling the ObjectList Control with Data

Follow these steps to fill the ObjectList control with data (you should be intimately familiar with this code by now, because it's similar to much of the code you've seen throughout this book):

1. Add the following procedure to your page's class:

```
Private Sub FillCustomers(ByVal City As String)
  Dim ds As DataSet
  Dim strConn As String
  Dim strSQL As String

  strConn = DataHandler.ConnectStringBuild("sa", "")
  strSQL = String.Format( _
    "SELECT CustomerID, Address, ContactName, " & _
    "City, Region, PostalCode, Country, Phone " & _
    "FROM Customers " & _
    "WHERE City = '{0}'" & _
    "ORDER By CustomerID", City)

  ds = DataHandler.GetDataSet(strSQL, strConn)
  With olstCustomers
    .DataSource = ds
    .DataBind()
  End With
End Sub
```

2. Select cmdCustomers and its `Click` event from the drop-down lists at the top of the code module.

3. Modify the `cmdCustomers_Click` procedure so that it looks like this:

```
Private Sub cmdCustomers_Click( _
 ByVal sender As System.Object, _
 ByVal e As System.EventArgs) _
 Handles cmdCustomers.Click

  If slstCity.SelectedIndex >= 0 Then
      lblValidate.Text = String.Empty
      FillCustomers(slstCity.Selection.Text)
      ActiveForm = frmCustomers
  Else
      lblValidate.Text = "Please select a city first"
  End If
End Sub
```

Because it only makes sense to fill the ObjectList control if you've specified a city, the code that calls FillCustomers needs to verify that you've selected a city first. You can't use a RequiredFieldValidator control here, because that control won't validate a SelectionList control. Therefore, you need to take matters into your own hands.

The preceding code first checks to make sure one of the radio buttons has been selected in the SelectionList control. If it has, the code calls the `FillCustomers` procedure, passing in the city name selected from the SelectionList control.

TRY IT OUT Run the project once again, enter a password, and then select a country. Finally, select a city, and you should see a list of customers in that city. Select a customer, and you should see detailed information about the customer.

Adding a Custom Command

The ObjectList control also allows you to add custom commands (in addition to the default Back link) to its details view. In this case, you're going to add a link (More Info) that calculates the total number of orders for the selected customer and displays this information on a new form. You specify the `CommandName` and `Text` properties, and the control does the rest—you can check to see which command the user has clicked from the ItemCommand event handler.

Follow these steps to add the custom command:

1. Add a new Form control to your mobile Web page.

2. Set the `ID` property of this new form to frmOrders.

3. Add a Label control to this new form. Set the `ID` property to lblOrders and delete the default value for the control's `Text` property.

4. Back on the previous form, select the ObjectList control's `Commands` property. Click the builder button (...) to display the olstCustomers Properties dialog box.

5. Click Create New Command and set the `Command Name` text to **Orders** and the `Text` property to **More Info**.

6. Press F7 to load the code window and add this procedure to the page's class. The `CountOrders` procedure uses a Command object, calling its `ExecuteScalar` method, to retrieve the total number of orders for the specified customer:

```
Private Sub CountOrders(ByVal CustomerID As String)
  Dim strSQL As String
  Dim strConn As String
  Dim intCount As Integer

  strConn = DataHandler.ConnectStringBuild("sa", "")

  strSQL = String.Format( _
    "SELECT COUNT(*) FROM Orders " & _
    "WHERE CustomerID = '{0}'", CustomerID)

  intCount = CInt( _
    DataHandler.ExecuteScalar(strSQL, strConn))

  lblOrders.Text = String.Format( _
    "Customer {0} has placed {1} {2}.", _
    CustomerID, intCount, _
    IIf(intCount = 1, "order", "orders"))
End Sub
```

7. Press Shift+F7 to return to design view. Double-click the ObjectList control, loading the code module with the `ItemCommand` event procedure created for you. Modify the procedure so that it looks like this, calling the `CountOrders` procedure:

```
Private Sub olstCustomers_ItemCommand( _
ByVal source As System.Object, _
ByVal e As System.Web.UI. _
MobileControls.ObjectListCommandEventArgs) _
Handles olstCustomers.ItemCommand

  If e.CommandName = "Orders" Then
    CountOrders(e.ListItem.Item("CustomerID"))
```

```
    ActiveForm = frmOrders
   End If
End Sub
```

NOTE

In the `ItemCommand` event procedure, the code uses a `Select Case` construct to check the `CommandName` property of the parameter to the procedure. Because your control might include multiple custom commands, you should always check the command name before executing any code. In this case, the code counts the orders and navigates to the final form on the page.

8. Test your page. Verify that you can browse from one form to another and that selecting a customer in the table view of the ObjectList control displays details for that customer. Selecting the More Info link should display the total number of orders for the selected customer.

As you can see, with very little effort, you've created a full-featured mobile Web application, using the Microsoft Mobile Internet Toolkit!

Adding Validation Controls

When you're creating mobile Web pages, you're likely to want to validate user input before submitting it to the server. The Microsoft Mobile Internet Toolkit provides the same set of validation controls you'll find in standard ASP.NET pages.

NOTE

Unlike standard ASP.NET validation controls, the Microsoft Mobile Internet Toolkit's validation controls perform no client-side validation. All validation for these controls takes place on the server.

On the first form, you might want to require that the user supply a password before retrieving other information. You can use the RequiredFieldValidator control to accomplish this. Follow these steps to add this control to your page:

1. Select frmMain.

2. Click txtPassword so that it has the focus.

3. Double-click the RequiredFieldValidator control in the Toolbox to add a new control immediately beneath the text box.

4. Set the properties for the new RequiredFieldValidator control as shown in Table 25.5.

TABLE 25.5   Use These Properties for the RequiredFieldValidator Control

Property	Value
ID	rvalPassword
ControlToValidate	txtPassword
ErrorMessage	Enter a password

5. Unless you check for the validity of the data programmatically, nothing keeps the code in the page from navigating from one form to another. Therefore, modify the cmdGo_Click procedure so that it looks like this:

```
Private Sub cmdGo_Click( _
 ByVal sender As System.Object, _
 ByVal e As System.EventArgs) _
 Handles cmdGo.Click

    If rvalPassword.IsValid Then
        FillCountry()
        ActiveForm = frmCountry
    End If
End Sub
```

6. Test the project: Browse the page within Internet Explorer, a handheld device simulator, or a real device. In any case, you should be required to enter a password (any password), and you should see the data loaded into the controls.

Summary

The Microsoft Mobile Internet Toolkit (MMIT) makes it easier for you to create Web applications that support mobile devices. In this chapter, you learned:

- The Microsoft Mobile Internet Toolkit provides extensible support for multiple devices and protocols so that you don't have to write multiple sets of pages to accommodate all the devices.

- Under the covers, the MMIT supplies a group of controls that render themselves differently, depending on the browser posting the request.

- You can use a variety of browser simulators to avoid buying every single device. Don't take the simplicity of the toolkit for granted, however! Be warned that you should test on the real devices as much as possible.

26

Development and Deployment Techniques

OBJECTIVES

- Learn additional "best prac-tice" development techniques

- Deploy ASP.NET Web applica-tions

Building a Web application takes a bit more effort than simply creating the pages: You must consider the best way to package your code and how to actually deploy the pages. In this chapter, we'll tackle two important topics. We'll introduce some important development techniques that will streamline your development process, and we'll discuss how to deploy your Web applications, once you have them completed.

Development Techniques

What's one of the first rules you'll learn, as you build large maintainable applications? You'll learn to break your appli-cations into manageable chunks, or *components*. By break-ing your application into multiple components packaged as DLLs, you'll find that your application will be easier to develop. (Multiple developers working on different portions of an application, based on a specification that links the various components, makes for a productive working environment.) When you're maintaining your applications, being able to focus on specific components that provide various small well-understood blocks of func-tionality will make the job easier, as well.

In the sample application you have built so far throughout this book, you have kept all the functionality within a single project. It might be better to separate one or more of the components from the project into another project, compiled as a separate DLL. For example, the DataHandler and DataHandlerSqlClient classes can easily be split out into a separate DLL. These classes can be reused in many different projects, including both desktop and Web appli-cations.

As you become more experienced creating .NET applications, you'll want to take advantage of the power provided by the Common Language Runtime and the .NET Framework. In this section, you'll investigate several common techniques, including the following:

- Using components to make it easier to manage development and deployment

- Creating your own namespaces so you can unambiguously refer to components that share the same names

- Adding assembly information so you can embed information about you, your company, and your project within the assemblies you create

Along the way, you'll break the data-handling classes in your sample application into their own project and call the classes from the original Northwind sample project.

Creating a Class Library

In this portion of the chapter, you'll create a separate class library containing the data access code. Follow these steps:

1. Open the Northwind.sln project you've been building throughout the book.

2. Select the File, Add Project, New Project menu item, displaying the New Project dialog box.

3. Select Class Library from the Templates list.

4. Name the project **DataClasses**. Click OK to add the new project to your solution.

5. In the Solution Explorer window, select Class1.vb within the new project. Delete Class1.vb—you won't need it.

6. In the Solution Explorer window, select both DataHandler.vb and DataHandlerSqlClient.vb (click one and then Ctrl+click on the other).

7. In the Solution Explorer window, drag the selected files into the new project. (The files should appear within the new project and be removed from the original project.)

You've now created the new project, which will create DataClasses.dll—a separate component you can use from within multiple applications. You still have a few issues to tackle before using this component, however. You must set a reference to the component as well as fix up code errors, because the classes are no longer local to the Northwind project.

Adding a Reference

Just as VB6 developers used COM type libraries to add references to COM components to their applications, .NET developers can use the metadata included in .NET assemblies to reference the functionality in those external components. Follow these steps to add a reference to `DataClasses.vb`, to your Northwind project:

1. In the Solution Explorer window, right-click the DataClasses project and select Build from the context menu. (This step creates `DataClasses.dll`.)

2. In the Solution Explorer window, right-click the Northwind project and select Add Reference from the context menu, displaying the Add Reference dialog box.

3. On the Add Reference dialog box, select the .NET tab and then click Browse. Navigate to the `DataClasses\bin` folder, select `DataClasses.dll`, and click Open to select the file. Figure 26.1 shows the Add Reference dialog box after you've selected the new DLL.

4. Click OK to dismiss the dialog box.

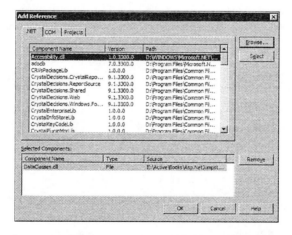

FIGURE 26.1   Select the new DLL to add its reference to the current project.

Once you've added the reference, your Solution Explorer window should look something like Figure 26.2. With this reference set, you can refer to the members of the `DataHandler` and `DataHandlerSqlClient` classes as if they were still part of the current project, without having to explicitly load the files into the project.

The one big problem that's still left is that your code can't determine how to find the various members, without taking one more step. If you attempt to compile your

application at this point, you'll receive all sorts of errors, indicating that either
DataHandler or DataHandlerSqlClient is not declared. You'll fix this problem in the
next section.

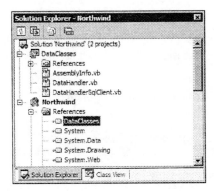

FIGURE 26.2   After adding the reference, DataClasses appears in the References list.

Accounting for Namespaces

When you're working within a single project, every public member of every class is
available to any other class or file within the project. Because, by default, every item
within a single project shares the same namespace—the same "naming context" (a
term we've made up)—any item can find any other. By default, this namespace has
the same name as the project. You were previously able to call the GetDataSet
method of the DataHandler class from anywhere within the Northwind project
because your code and the GetDataSet method existed within the same namespace.
When you entered code such as

```
ds = DataHandler.GetDataSet(<parameters here>)
```

you were actually using this code instead:

```
ds = Northwind.DataHandler.GetDataSet(<parameters here>)
```

Because your code and the GetDataSet method both existed within the same namespace, leaving out Northwind didn't matter—the .NET runtime was able to determine
which method you were calling and take care of the details for you.

Now that you've split the code out into separate projects, your code is still looking
for GetDataSet within the current namespace, but it exists within a separate namespace. To find the GetDataSet method now, you need to write code like this:

```
ds = DataClasses.DataHandler.GetDataSet(<parameters here>)
```

When you write code in Visual Studio .NET, you have three choices as to how you handle this namespace fixup:

- You can add the `DataClasses` prefix to each and every reference to the classes and their members. (This is a tedious prospect, at best.)

- You can add an `Imports` statement at the top of each file in your project that needs to refer to these classes, like this:

```
Imports DataClasses
```

- You can modify the Northwind project so that it automatically sets up the `Imports` statement "under the covers" for every file in the project.

Looking for the lowest-impact solution, we recommend the third solution. Follow these steps to finish creating and consuming the `DataClasses` component:

1. In the Solution Explorer window, right-click the Northwind project.

2. Select Properties from the context menu.

3. In the Northwind Property Pages dialog box, select the `Imports` node. Type the namespace (**DataClasses**), as shown in Figure 26.3.

4. Click Add Import to add the new namespace to the Project imports list.

5. Click OK to dismiss the dialog box.

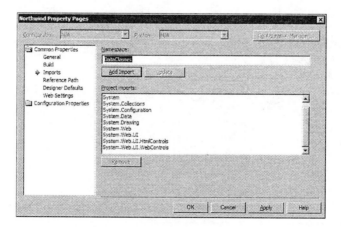

FIGURE 26.3   Add the project-wide `Imports` statement.

Once you've resolved all the namespace issues, you should now be able to run the project, just as you did before breaking the data classes out into their own assembly.

Were you to use the `DataClasses` assembly in a different project, you would just need to repeat the steps shown here, and the members of the assembly would be available to your new project.

More on Namespaces

When you separated the data-handling classes into their own class library, Visual Studio used the name of the project as the namespace for all classes contained within the new project—this is the default behavior. Why do namespaces exist? Imagine that your application already contains a class named `DataHandler`, and you add a reference to the `DataClasses` assembly. How would your code differentiate between the `DataHandler` classes in the two projects? Using separate namespaces for the two classes removes the ambiguity. If your project shares a namespace with the `DataClasses` assembly, your code wouldn't be able to compile. Unless the compiler can unambiguously determine which class you're referring to in your code, it can't compile the code.

When creating your own assemblies, you'll want to assign a unique root namespace for the classes you'll expose. (Many developers use their company's URL as part of the name—that URL is guaranteed to be unique.) To assign a root namespace for an entire project, you can use the project's property pages, as shown in Figure 26.4. The name you place here becomes the root namespace for the classes in the project. Rather than referring to `DataHandler.GetDataSet`, you could use `DataClasses.DataHandler.GetDataSet` (the full name, including the namespace).

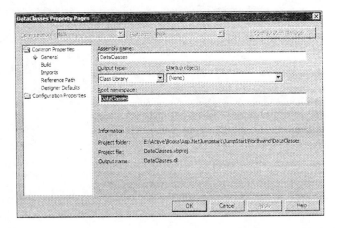

FIGURE 26.4   Use the project's property pages to modify the namespace for the project.

You can also assign namespaces to subsets of your project (one or more classes within a file, or even multiple files) by adding namespace declarations in your code.

For example, imagine that your application's root namespace is NorthwindSales. Your project includes Customer and Invoice classes, and you want to group them both within the Data namespace.

You could create the Data namespace like this (leaving out all the nonrelevant code here):

```
Namespace Data
   Public Class Customer
   End Class

   Public Class Invoice
   End Class
End Namespace
```

With this setup, you could refer to the LastName property of the Customer class like this:

```
strLastName = NorthwindSales.Data.Customer.LastName
```

INVESTIGATING ASSEMBLIES

What exactly is an assembly, anyway? Although you might think of an assembly like a DLL, it's more than this. Generally, Microsoft describes an assembly as "the .NET unit of reuse, versioning, security, and deployment." The simplest assembly actually will be a single DLL or EXE file, but assemblies can consist of multiple files.

In addition to the results of compiling your code, each assembly contains information that describes the assembly—that is, a manifest containing information about the locale, the procedures, and the dependencies of the assembly. You can think of an assembly's manifest information as being analogous to COM's typelibs, but there's much more information in a manifest than in a typelib.

By default, assemblies are private—that is, they're stored in the same file system "tree" as the code using the contents of the assembly. When you build your Web project, you'll find a DLL file in the \bin folder within the folder with your ASPX files. The .NET CLR doesn't require this behavior, however—you can create public assemblies, as well, by placing them in the Global Assembly Cache (GAC). Visual Studio .NET's Setup and Deployment projects can install assemblies there for you, or you can use the .NET Frameworks' GacUtil.exe program to do it. You can't simply copy files into the GAC, however. Because of the versioning information .NET maintains for you, you must use the utility.

Managing Assembly Information

Each assembly you create has space set aside within the compiled assembly for version information. You can store version numbers, copyright information, and more within the assembly. To make it easy for you to control this information, each project you create within Visual Studio .NET contains a file, `AssemblyInfo.vb`, that contains nothing but attributes that describe your assembly, as shown in Listing 26.1.

LISTING 26.1   The Default Contents of `AssemblyInfo.vb`

```
<Assembly: AssemblyTitle("")>
<Assembly: AssemblyDescription("")>
<Assembly: AssemblyCompany("")>
<Assembly: AssemblyProduct("")>
<Assembly: AssemblyCopyright("")>
<Assembly: AssemblyTrademark("")>
<Assembly: CLSCompliant(True)>

'The following GUID is for the ID of the typelib if this
'project is exposed to COM
<Assembly: Guid("1298341F-35DF-4D2E-ADB1-646CE8A0C3E5")>

' Version information for an assembly consists of the
' following four values:
'
'       Major Version
'       Minor Version
'       Build Number
'       Revision
'
' You can specify all the values or you can default the
' Build and Revision Numbers
' by using the '*' as shown below:

<Assembly: AssemblyVersion("1.0.*")>
```

You fill in the values within the attributes, and the compiler does the rest of the work. For example, you might modify the first block of attributes, setting information about your organization:

```
<Assembly: AssemblyTitle( _
 "Northwind Traders Web Application")>
<Assembly: AssemblyDescription("Sample Northwind Site")>
<Assembly: AssemblyCompany( _
 "PDSA, Inc. and KNG Consulting, Inc.")>
<Assembly: AssemblyProduct("Northwind")>
<Assembly: AssemblyCopyright("Copyright 2002")>
```

The `AssemblyVersion` attribute, at the bottom of the `AssemblyInfo.vb` file, allows you to set a version number for your assembly. By default, Visual Studio assigns the value `1.0.*` to your project. The asterisk indicates that you want the compiler to automatically increment the version number (for example, to increment from 1.0.7 to 1.0.8) each time you compile the DLL. You can elect to hard-code a complete version number by simply entering its value into this attribute.

After you compile the resulting DLL, you can retrieve this information in Windows Explorer by right-clicking the DLL and selecting the Version tab to view the assembly attributes. Figure 26.5 shows the Windows Explorer Properties dialog box, after setting the version number to `2.0.*`.

FIGURE 26.5   You can view assembly information from Windows Explorer.

Deploying ASP.NET Applications

Once you've created your ASP.NET application, you'll most likely need to deploy it onto a different server than your development server. Somehow, all the pages and DLLs used by your application need to be placed onto the public server where your application will be hosted.

The .NET Framework supplies two different ways to deploy your applications:

- **XCOPY deployment.** This Microsoft-generated term doesn't require the XCOPY DOS utility; Windows Explorer will do fine. You don't use XCOPY, really. The name simply implies that you can copy a folder and all its subfolders to a root on the new server, and your application should run. You'll need to create the virtual root(s) yourself.

- **Windows Installer technology.** The Microsoft Windows Installer technology allows you to create full executable installation packages. You can create an installation project in Visual Studio that will handle the installation details for you. Using this technique, you can perform a totally "hands-off" installation— any user can install your application onto a server, with no manual intervention required.

The following sections compare the two techniques and dig into using the Windows Installer to create an easy-to-install MSI file for your project.

XCOPY Deployment

Because of the self-describing nature of .NET assemblies (all the information about the contents of the assembly is included within the assembly itself), it's really possible to deploy an ASP.NET application to a new virtual root without requiring any tedious installation or registration. In this section, you'll create a new virtual root and test deploying your sample application by simply copying it into the new folder.

> **TIP**
>
> One really big issue we haven't discussed is that of replacing existing components while your Web site is running. In the bad old days, if you had created components called by ASP pages, you were required to shut down IIS in order to update the components. With ASP.NET, it's simpler—because ASP.NET doesn't lock the files it has in use, you can place the new components into the site right on top of the existing, running components. The next time a request comes in for the page requiring the component, ASP.NET will spin up the new component. When the last current user finishes using the existing component, it's removed from memory.

Although your development server contains all the source files for your site (`*.aspx`, `*.vb`, and so on), as well as the compiled version of your source code (the `Northwind.dll` file in the `bin` folder), you don't need to deploy (nor should you deploy) the source code (that is, the `*.vb` files). The files you will need to deploy include, at least, the following:

- `*.aspx`
- `global.asax`
- `web.config`
- `*.dll` from the `\bin` folder
- `images\*`

When you build your project, Visual Studio .NET compiles the code into
Northwind.dll for you—that's the file that contains the event handlers and other
procedures you've written.

Imagine that you'd like to copy the site from Jumpstart\Northwind to a new virtual
root, NorthwindSales, so that you can browse to the site directly by typing this URL:

```
http://localhost/NorthwindSales/main.aspx
```

> **TIP**
>
> Although it isn't required, we recommend that you create new virtual roots outside of the
> inetpub\wwwroot folder. By placing the site at a different location, you take complete control
> over the accessibility and availability of your site. In this example, we'll instruct you to create a
> new folder for the sample project outside this folder.

Follow these steps to test XCOPY deployment of your sample site:

1. Using Windows Explorer, create a new folder somewhere in your file system.
   For the sake of discussion here, we'll refer to the folder as C:\NorthwindSales.
   (You may use this path, if you like.)

2. Start the Internet Information Services console. (You may find this under the
   Windows Start, Administrative Tools menu, or you may find it within the
   Windows Control Panel.)

3. Drill down into the nodes in the left pane of the console, until you locate the
   Default Web Site node.

4. Right-click the Default Web Site node and select New, Virtual Directory from
   the context menu.

5. Create a new virtual directory named NorthwindSales, pointing to the folder
   you created earlier in these steps. Accept all the default options. Once you're
   done, the IIS console should look something like Figure 26.6.

6. Using Windows Explorer, browse to the folder where you intend to deploy
   your project (C:\NorthwindSales, if you've followed the suggestion).

7. Open a separate copy of Windows Explorer and browse to the folder containing your sample Northwind project.

8. Sort the Explorer window by file type and then select and copy the following
   groups of files to the new folder:

   - *.aspx

   - *.ascx

- `*.resx`

- `*.rpt`

- `styles.css`

- `global.asax`

- `web.config`

- `\images\*.*`

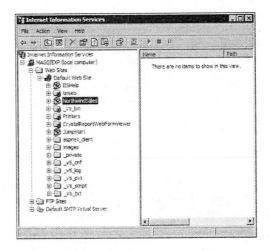

FIGURE 26.6   Create a new virtual root in IIS.

9. Copy the `\bin` folder to the new location. (You don't actually need the debugging files, `*.pdb`, within the `bin` folder. You can delete those, if you like.)

10. Open a browser window and browse to `http://localhost/NorthwindSales/main.aspx`. If you've copied all the files correctly, you should see the sample page, deployed without any special tools to a new location.

That's all there is to XCOPY deployment—just copy the necessary files (and perhaps subfolders) to the new location. In this example, you deployed to a new virtual root on your local machine, but you could just as easily have deployed your site to a remote server using the same technique.

TIP

If you want to set up the site so that users don't have to specify the start page, you can add `main.aspx` to the list of default documents within IIS. Right-click the NorthwindSales root, select Properties from the context menu, and select the Documents tab on the NorthwindSales Properties dialog box. Add `main.aspx` to the list, and you'll be able to browse directly to `http://localhost/NorthwindSales`.

Although XCOPY deployment is simple, it's not perfect for every scenario. If your folder structure is complex, or if you need several virtual roots as part of your project, it's more trouble than it's worth. In particular, here are several scenarios in which you'll want to consider not using this simple deployment technique:

- If your application uses COM components. In that case, you'll still need to register them in the Windows Registry.

- If you want to precompile an assembly to native code on the target machine. By default, the .NET CLR compiles your assembly into native code the first time it runs—the code is distributed in Microsoft Intermediate Language (MSIL) format. Precompiling it on the target machine requires extra work not possible in XCOPY deployment.

- If you want control over the placement of the assemblies. By default, ASP.NET's assemblies are private—in the same folder tree as the application. You can also make assemblies global by placing them into the Global Assembly Cache, but that requires running extra utilities. XCOPY deployment simply can't do this.

- If you want to update files that are locked by the operating system. For example, if your application includes databases or a Windows service, you can't simply copy the files to their new locations.

- If you need to automatically create IIS virtual roots or set properties of these roots as part of your installation.

If you need to handle any of these situations, you'll need to investigate using the Microsoft Installer technology, which is covered in the next section.

Windows Installer Deployment

If your Web application requires any extra handling or needs to be installed by a user (rather than by an administrator or developer), you'll want to investigate using the Windows Installer technology provided by Windows 2000 and later. You can create a Setup and Deployment project in Visual Studio .NET to walk you through creating the deployment package, in the form of an MSI file. You can give the MSI file to end users, who can simply click and install.

Introducing Microsoft Windows Installer

Microsoft Windows Installer is an installation and configuration service that originally shipped as part of Windows 2000 (later operating systems incorporate the technology, as well). The Microsoft Windows Installer Service keeps track of all the applications that it has installed on a computer, as well as all the components of the applications. When it comes time to uninstall an application, the installer can detect whether no other application is using a shared component, and only then will it delete the component.

In addition to standard installation duties, Microsoft Windows Installer has been extended to support these requirements of .NET assemblies:

- Installation, repair, and removal of assemblies in the Global Assembly Cache.

- Installation, repair, and removal of private assemblies.

- Transacted installs, repairs, and removals. If an entire set of steps fails, all intermediate steps can be rolled back to the original state.

- Install-on-demand for both public (in the GAC) and private assemblies.

In addition to the features supplied by Microsoft Windows Installer's technology, Visual Studio .NET's Setup and Deployment projects supply standard setup functionality, such described here:

- Reading and writing Registry keys

- Directory (and virtual root) creation

- Registration of components

- Managing conditional deployments based on operating system, rights of the users, and more

- Running a custom program after installation is complete

To demonstrate the use of Visual Studio .NET's Setup and Deployment projects, the next section will walk you through packaging the Northwind sample project into a Microsoft Installer (MSI) file.

Selecting Output Content for the MSI File

To illustrate creating an MSI file, this section walks you through adding a Setup and Deployment project to your Northwind solution as well as adding content to the file. Once you're done with the following sections, you can try deploying the sample ASP.NET Web application. Again, in this case, you'll create a virtual root named NorthwindSales.

> **TIP**
>
> If you want to really test out the installation capabilities, before you start this exercise, you'll need to delete the C:\NorthwindSales folder and remove the virtual root from within IIS.

Everything will continue to operate correctly if you skip this step, but you just won't prove much. You may need to pause Internet Information Server, using the IIS console, in order to delete the folder.

NOTE

There are seemingly millions of options when creating Setup projects. In this example, you'll take a linear path through one possible set of options, simply building an installation file for your sample project. Digging into the intricacies of creating Setup projects could fill an entire book (and probably does). If you're interested in all the details, start with the online documentation and then research from there.

Follow these steps to creating the MSI file:

1. Make sure the Northwind.sln sample solution you've been creating throughout this book is open within Visual Studio .NET.

2. Select the File, Add Project, New Project menu item.

3. From the Project Types list, select Setup and Deployment Projects.

4. From the Templates list, select Web Setup Project.

5. Set the name of the project to **NWSetup**. Figure 26.7 shows the Add New Project dialog box, with all options selected. Click OK when you're done.

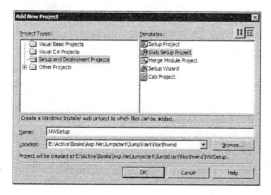

FIGURE 26.7   Select these options to add a new Setup project.

6. At this point, you should see the File System window (see Figure 26.8). You'll add the files you want to deploy to this window in the next few steps.

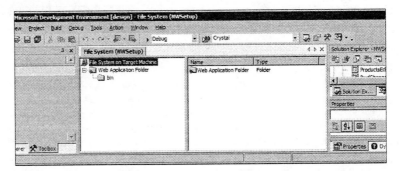

FIGURE 26.8   The File System window allows you to add content to your Setup project.

7. In the File System window, select the Web Application Folder node in the left pane—you'll be adding content to the Web application itself, represented by this node.

8. Select the Action, Add, Project Output menu item, which displays the Add Project Output Group dialog box, shown in Figure 26.9.

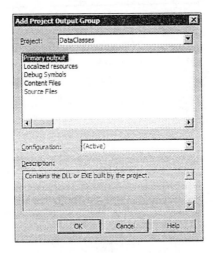

FIGURE 26.9   Use this dialog box to select output groups.

9. Select the project you want to deploy (Northwind, in this case) from the Project drop-down list.

10. Select both Primary Output (DLL/EXE files) and Content Files (*.aspx, *.ascx, *.xml, and so on) from the list of content groups. Click OK when you're done. Now the File System window should look like Figure 26.10.

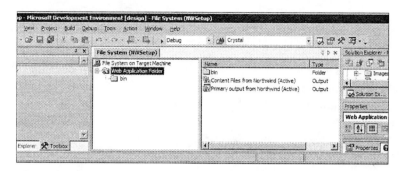

FIGURE 26.10   After adding the output, you should see the listed content files from your site.

11. To add `ProductsReport.rpt` (which isn't included in either content or primary output), select the Action, Add, File menu item and then select `ProductsReport.rpt` from the Add Files dialog box. Click Open when you're done.

12. Verify the list of files to be deployed by right-clicking the Content Files from Northwind (Active) item and selecting Outputs from the context menu. You should see a dialog box like the one shown in Figure 26.11. Repeat this for the primary output files, as well.

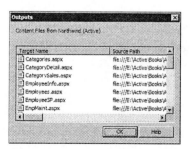

FIGURE 26.11   You can peruse the list of pending output files.

Configuring the Web Site Information

Once you've selected the content to be deployed by your Setup project, you can set up the name of the virtual root you'll want to use for your application. Follow these steps to input this important information:

1. Select the Web Application Folder node in the File System window.

2. Right-click and select Properties Window from the context menu.

3. In the Properties window, set the `DefaultDocument` property to `main.aspx`.

4. Set the `VirtualDirectory` property to `NorthwindSales`. When you're done, the Properties window should look like Figure 26.12.

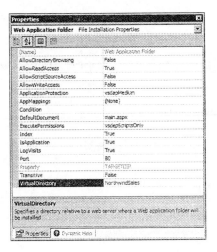

FIGURE 26.12   Set the VirtualDirectory property.

The Windows Installer uses the properties you set to create the virtual directory and set the start page on the target server.

> **TIP**
>
> You can use relative paths in the `VirtualDirectory` property to create a virtual directory under an existing virtual directory. For example, imagine that you've already created a virtual root named `CustomApps` on your server that points to the physical path `D:\CustomApps`. You could set the Web Application Folder's VirtualDirectory property to `CustomApps\NorthwindSales`. Now the NorthwindSales project files would be installed under `D:\CustomApps`, and the `NorthwindSales` virtual root would be a child of the existing virtual root `CustomApps`.

Building and Testing the MSI

Now that you've added all the output and properties settings, you can build and test the MSI file. Follow these steps to finish your Setup project:

1. Select the Build, Build NWSetup menu item. This may take a few minutes, as Visual Studio .NET rebuilds all the projects in your solution.

WARNING

By default, the output MSI file won't contain the .NET Framework. If you need to install your site on a server that doesn't yet include the .NET Framework, you'll need to include it with your installation. When you create your MSI file, the exact warning looks like this:

This setup does not contain the .NET Framework which must be installed on the target machine by running dotnetfx.exe before this setup will install. You can find dotnetfx.exe on the Visual Studio .NET 'Windows Components Update' media. Dotnetfx.exe can be redistributed with your setup.

2. Visual Studio .NET creates `NWSetup.msi` in the `JumpStart\Northwind\NWSetup\Debug` folder. (It also creates other subsidiary files, which you don't need to distribute.)

3. To test out the MSI file, double-click to run it from its current location. The installation program walks you through setting up the virtual root, and you should be able to run the application by simply browsing to the site, like this (if you've installed the MSI file on your local computer):

```
http://localhost/northwindsales
```

TIP

If you run `NWSetup.msi` again, it will offer to repair or remove the files and settings it installed originally. You can get the same effect using the Control Panel options to add or remove software.

Summary

In this chapter, you learned some useful development techniques, including the following:

- Creating and using class libraries so you can encapsulate commonly used functionality

- Creating and using namespaces

- Adding assembly information so you can identify your applications

You also learned two ways to deploy ASP.NET applications:

- XCOPY deployment (not really reliant on the old DOS XCOPY command but rather more focused on file and folder copying) is possible because of the metadata stored in all .NET assemblies. However, it provides no support for anything besides file placement.

- Microsoft Installer technology supports full setup programs with many additional features. You'll use this technique when you have anything but the simplest of applications to deploy.

PART IV

Web Services

IN THIS PART

27

Introduction to XML

U nless you've been living under a rock for the past five years, it would be hard to have missed the emergence of Extensible Markup Language (XML) as a standardized format for transporting data. Although there have been other data-transport mechanisms in the past, none has garnered as much support as XML.

Over the next few chapters, you'll be investigating both creating and consuming XML Web Services. In order to understand how and why XML works, you'll need some background on XML and why it's so popular. In this chapter, you'll review the basics of XML, learn how XML is constructed, and learn how to format XML data using an XML grammar, Extensible Stylesheet Language, XSL.

The Power of XML

You might wonder why XML is suddenly so popular. To understand the popularity, you must consider the alternatives. Humans and computers need some standardized way of moving data from one application to another or from one computer to another. The transport mechanism needs to have the following qualities:

- **Self-describing.** It must require no external support to "understand" the data.

- **Able to maintain full data integrity.** It must transport all the information about the data, including types, relations, and so on.

- **Able to move through firewalls and across the Internet.**

- **Extensible.** You must be able to extend the standard without breaking existing uses.

- **Universally understood and subscribes to an open standard.**

OBJECTIVES

- Learn why you should care about XML

- Learn how to create well-formed XML

- Validate XML using XML Schema

- Use Visual Studio .NET's XML tools to create and modify XML

- Bind a DataGrid to XML data

Think of some common mechanisms for transporting data:

- Comma-delimited text files

- ActiveX Data Objects (ADO) recordsets

- Hypertext Markup Language (HTML)

- Electronic Data Interchange (EDI)

Each of these is popular and in wide use. However, each fails the requirements in at least one way. Comma-delimited text files can't really include full information about data and relations—they simply maintain a set of rows and columns. Recordsets can provide full data integrity, but because they're binary objects (and limited to Windows and COM), they aren't universally understood—nor can they pass through firewalls easily. HTML is great for displaying content, but it can't be extended and is just a bit too flexible for data management. EDI is totally proprietary, and many different, incompatible "flavors" are currently in use.

XML solves all these problems by providing text-based data in a standard, yet totally extensible package. In this chapter, you'll begin to see how XML makes it possible to describe just about any type of data, and it can be used to transport that data over the Internet (and within applications, as well).

NOTE

Although you won't often need to investigate the inner workings of XML for most of your applications, most applications use XML "under the covers" in one way or another. The .NET Framework uses XML to transmit data between tiers of a multitiered application, and .NET handles this data transfer for you. If you want to step in and modify the XML being sent from one place to another, you can. When you return a DataSet from a component, or when you return data from a Web Service (coming up in the next chapters), you're sending XML from one component to another.

What About HTML?

You might be confused as to the differences and similarities between HTML and XML. Perhaps you thought that XML was a "superset" of HTML, but that's not true. HTML is a markup language devised for including layout and style information—it provides little or no information about its actual content. For example, the following HTML indicates how the text should be displayed but conveys no information about what the information actually is:

```
<b>May 16 1956</b>
```

The <b> and </b> tags indicate that the text within should be displayed in boldface, but nothing more than that.

XML, however, can convey information about the content; using XML "helpers" such as XSL (a set of elements created in XML specifically geared toward formatting XML data), you can include formatting information as well. For example, this XML indicates the usage of its content:

```
<birthdate>May 16, 1956</birthdate>
```

This fragment doesn't contain any formatting information (you'll learn a little about XSL later in the chapter), but it does at least indicate the significance of its contents.

XML's Helpers

XML itself is quite simple—it's just a combination of elements, attributes, and text, for the most part. On its own, it doesn't seem all that powerful. The most powerful part about XML, however, is that it's not just a language: It's a language for defining *other* languages. For example, developers have already created the following list of grammars of XML (languages created in XML), and this is a tiny subset of a growing list of specific tools created in XML:

- **XML Schema.** Defines a custom markup language created in XML. Just as a database schema defines the columns of a database table, XML Schema defines what content can appear within an XML file. Without a schema, XML data is really nothing more than structured text. With a schema, XML data is a representation of structured data.

- **XSLT (Extensible Stylesheet Language–Transformation).** Defines a language that allows you to format and transform XML data into any other format. Using XSLT, you can shape and format the data any way you require. You'll see an example later that uses XSLT to transform XML data into an HTML table.

- **XPath.** Defines a language that allows you to search within a set of XML data for elements meeting specified criteria. Much as you use SQL to query relational data, you use XPath to query XML data.

TIP

For more information on XML and the growing set of grammars created using XML, visit the World Wide Web Consortium site at http://www.w3.org. You'll find white papers, specifications, training, up-to-the-minute documentation, and more.

Getting Started with XML

In its simplest sense, XML is a markup language that uses tags to describe elements, much like HTML. Unlike HTML, however, XML doesn't contain any predefined tags—in XML, you make up your own tags to describe your data.

Take a look at some simple XML data, as shown in Listing 27.1. (You can find this content in Jumpstart\XMLIntro\EmployeeData.xml.)

LISTING 27.1   This Simple XML Document Shows off Many of the Important XML Syntax Features

```xml
<?xml version="1.0" encoding="utf-8" ?>
<!-- Employee Information -- >
<EmployeeData>
  <Employee ID="1">
    <FirstName>Davolio</FirstName>
    <LastName>Nancy</LastName>
  </Employee>
  <Employee ID="2">
    <FirstName>Fuller</FirstName>
    <LastName>Andrew</LastName>
  </Employee>
  <Employee ID="3">
    <FirstName>Levering</FirstName>
    <LastName>Janet</LastName>
  </Employee>
</EmployeeData>
```

This example shows off a number of XML features, including the following:

- **XML declaration.** The first line of text declares the version of XML you're using (generally 1.0, at this point) and other information about how the XML should be handled by the XML processor:

  ```xml
  <?xml version="1.0" encoding="utf-8" ?>
  ```

- **Comments.** You can include comments anywhere within the XML content, using the <!-- and -- > symbols:

  ```xml
  <!-- Employee Information -- >
  ```

- **Tag syntax.** Each element has a beginning and ending tag, which must match exactly, like this:

  ```xml
  <EmployeeData>. . . </EmployeeData>
  ```

- **Attributes.** Elements can contain one or more attributes, which are nothing more than name/value pairs in which the value must always be a string surrounded by quotes. The xml declaration element contains two attributes, and the Employee elements each contain one attribute:

```
<?xml version="1.0" encoding="utf-8" ?>
<Employee ID="1">. . . </Employee>
```

- **Elements that contain other elements.** The Employees element contains a group of Employee elements, each of which contains FirstName and LastName elements:

```
<EmployeeData>
  <Employee ID="1">
. . .
  </Employee>
  <Employee ID="2">
. . .
  </Employee>
  <Employee ID="3">
. . .
  </Employee>
</EmployeeData>
```

- **Elements that contain text.** The FirstName and LastName elements each contain information:

```
<FirstName>Davolio</FirstName>
<LastName>Nancy</LastName>
```

TIP

A few other lexical issues are involved in creating XML text, but not many. Any good text on XML will be able to help fill in the rest of the details.

XML Element Rules

XML is very strict about the names you choose for your elements. Here are some specifics:

- Tags can contain letters, numbers, and colons (:).

- Tags must contain at least one letter.

- Tags must begin with a letter or underscore.

- Tag names cannot contain spaces but can include hyphens and periods.

- Most important, tag names are case sensitive.

This last rule is hard to get used to, especially when you're used to working in a non–case-sensitive world.

Normally, elements contain data or other elements. If you have an element with neither, it can appear either like

```
<EmptyElement></EmptyElement>
```

or, equivalently, like this:

```
<EmptyElement/>
```

TIP

Beginning XML developers often ask, "How can I tell whether I should place information in elements or in attributes?" Although you're unlikely to be creating raw XML at this point, you still may be wondering how to best structure XML. Here's a simple answer: Think of XML elements as the data, and attributes as properties of the data. That's a nebulous distinction, but it helps to consider the issue this way. You might think of each element as an object, and the attributes of the element as its properties.

XML Document Structure

Every XML document should contain the same basic contents: the XML declaration, a single root element, and elements and attributes, as necessary. If you look carefully at the code shown in Listing 27.1, you'll find all three of these items:

- The XML declaration:

```
<?xml version="1.0" encoding="utf-8" ?>
```

- The root element:

```
<EmployeeData>
. . .
</EmployeeData>
```

- Elements and attributes:

```
<Employee ID="1">
  <FirstName>Davolio</FirstName>
```

```
    <LastName>Nancy</LastName>
  </Employee>
  <Employee ID="2">
    <FirstName>Fuller</FirstName>
    <LastName>Andrew</LastName>
  </Employee>
```

We used the term *well-formed* on purpose. When you describe XML data as being "well-formed," you're indicating that the content follows all the XML structure rules. This is the minimum requirement for any XML document—if the content isn't well-formed, there's no chance that any XML processor will be able to consume your XML. Although the XML version declaration isn't required, a well-formed document will have only a single root element, and all elements will follow the XML syntax rules.

TIP

XML elements must be nested completely. That is, you cannot begin element A, begin element B, end element A, and then end element B. For this content to be well-formed, you must end element B before you end element A. In other words, the following isn't well-formed:

```
<A><B></A></B>
```

However, this is:

```
<A><B></B></A>
```

TRY IT OUT Although there are many tools you can purchase to help you work with XML data, Visual Studio .NET provides very solid, basic XML-handling functionality built in. Follow these steps to use Visual Studio .NET to load and check the "well-formedness" of an XML document (*well-formedness* sounds awkward, but it's really the correct terminology for describing a well-formed XML document):

1. Load the `Northwind.sln` solution you've been working on throughout this book.

2. Select the Project, Add Existing Item menu item and browse to the `Jumpstart\XMLIntro` folder.

3. With the Files of Type drop-down list set to "All Files (*.*)," select `EmployeeData.xml`. Click Open to add the file to your project.

4. In the Solution Explorer window, double-click the `EmployeeData.xml` item to load it into the XML editor, as shown in Figure 27.1.

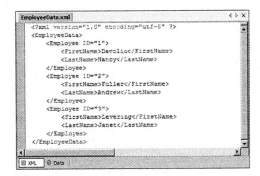

FIGURE 27.1   You can load XML data directly into a Visual Studio .NET project.

5. In addition to the standard XML view you see in Figure 27.1, you can also use Visual Studio .NET's data editor to view the XML. Click the Data tab at the bottom of the window to switch to Data view, as shown in Figure 27.2.

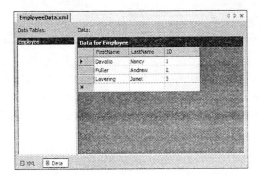

FIGURE 27.2   Use Data view to see a more traditional view of your XML data.

6. You can use the data editor to modify, add, and delete rows of data from your XML file. Try adding a new row for employee 4, Margaret Peacock. When you're done, switch back to XML view and verify that Visual Studio .NET added the new row to the XML source.

7. To test what happens if your XML isn't well-formed, once you're back in XML view, try changing the name of a tag so that it doesn't match its ending tag. For example, try changing the beginning <Employee> tag for Margaret Peacock to <Employees> instead.

8. Switch back to Data view, and you'll see an error message like the one shown in Figure 27.3.

9. Switch back to XML view and repair your change so that the data works correctly.

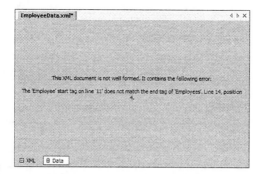

FIGURE 27.3   XML that isn't well-formed can't be displayed in Data view.

10. Try viewing the XML in Internet Explorer (which contains support for displaying XML natively). In the Solution Explorer window, right-click `EmployeeData.xml` and select View in Browser from the context menu. If you've correctly fixed the XML syntax so that the content is well-formed, you should see the browser window shown in Figure 27.4.

```xml
<?xml version="1.0" encoding="utf-8" ?>
- <EmployeeData>
  - <Employee ID="1">
      <FirstName>Davolio</FirstName>
      <LastName>Nancy</LastName>
    </Employee>
  - <Employee ID="2">
      <FirstName>Fuller</FirstName>
      <LastName>Andrew</LastName>
    </Employee>
  - <Employee ID="3">
      <FirstName>Levering</FirstName>
      <LastName>Janet</LastName>
    </Employee>
  - <Employee ID="4">
      <FirstName>Margaret</FirstName>
      <LastName>Peacock</LastName>
    </Employee>
  </EmployeeData>
```

FIGURE 27.4   Internet Explorer can display formatted XML.

XML Schema

If you're like most other beginning XML developers, you might have asked yourself "How can anyone communicate using XML? Since every set of XML data uses different tags, how can anyone know what's supposed to be in the data?" You won't have been alone in asking yourself these questions.

The answer is that without more information, XML is just data, and there's no way to determine whether it's the correct data. Sure, you can tell whether the XML is well-formed (you saw how you can verify that in the previous section). But you need more information to determine that the contents of the data are valid.

The XML Schema specification provides XML elements that describe the contents of other XML data. XML Schema is a rich specification, allowing for simple and complex data types, including all the standard types you're used to working with, and many more. An XML Schema corresponding to the XML data you've been working with so far might look like the XML shown in Listing 27.2.

As you can see, the XML Schema document shown in Listing 27.2 contains specifications for data types, the minimum number of occurrences, element and attributes names and types, and the XML root element.

> **TIP**
>
> Although it's not required, most XML Schema documents are saved in files with the `.xsd` extension. For a file named `EmployeeData.xml`, you will most likely see a corresponding schema named `EmployeeData.xsd`. This convention isn't required but is very common.

LISTING 27.2   XML Schema Completely Defines the Contents of XML Data, in XML Itself

```xml
<?xml version="1.0" ?>
<xs:schema id="Employees"
 targetNamespace="http://tempuri.org/EmployeeData.xsd"
 xmlns:xs="http://www.w3.org/2001/XMLSchema"
 attributeFormDefault="qualified"
 elementFormDefault="qualified">
  <xs:element name="Employees">
    <xs:complexType>
      <xs:choice maxOccurs="unbounded">
        <xs:element name="Employee">
          <xs:complexType>
            <xs:sequence>
              <xs:element name="FirstName"
                type="xs:string" minOccurs="0" />
              <xs:element name="LastName"
                type="xs:string" minOccurs="0" />
            </xs:sequence>
            <xs:attribute name="ID" form="unqualified"
              type="xs:string" />
          </xs:complexType>
        </xs:element>
```

LISTING 27.2   Continued

```
      </xs:choice>
    </xs:complexType>
  </xs:element>
</xs:schema>
```

Although you can create XML Schema content yourself, doing so is tedious and error prone. You're more likely to create the data (or simply receive the XML data from another source) and have some tool or another generate a starting point schema for you. Visual Studio .NET does a good job at inferring schema, and in the next section you'll work through the details of creating a schema based on the XML data you've been working with in this chapter and then modifying the schema to add more information.

TIP

For more information about XML Schema, and about XML in general, drop by Microsoft's XML site: `http://msdn.microsoft.com/xml`. As is the case with `http://www.w3.org`, you'll find the Microsoft site full of information about all aspects of XML, but from a slightly Microsoftian perspective.

 Follow these steps to create, modify, and test an XML Schema corresponding to the XML data you've been using so far in this chapter:

1. In the Solution Explorer window, double-click `EmployeeData.xml`, loading the data into the XML editor window.

2. Select the XML, Create Schema menu item. You should immediately see `EmployeeData.xsd` in the Solution Explorer window.

TIP

Your XML data should now include a reference to the newly generated schema, in the `Employees` root element. This reference links the two files together.

3. In the Solution Explorer window, double-click `EmployeeData.xsd`, displaying the designer shown in Figure 27.5.

TIP

If you click the XML tab at the bottom of the schema designer window, you'll see the same XML shown in Listing 27.2—the XML providing the schema for the `EmployeeData.xml` data.

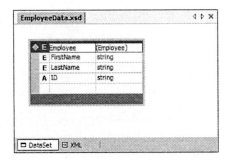

FIGURE 27.5   Visual Studio includes a full-featured schema editor.

Over the next few steps, your goal will be to make the ID attribute required (that is, any Employee element that doesn't contain an ID attribute will cause the document to be invalid) and to add an optional element named Phone. Follow these steps to modify the schema and then test it:

1. Click the DataSet tab at the bottom of the window to make sure you're viewing the XSD designer. In the final, empty row in the schema designer grid, click the first column.

2. Click the arrow next to the cell and select Element from the drop-down list. (Note that the designer moves your new row up, above the ID attribute.)

3. Enter **Phone** for the name of the element and select string for the data type.

4. Select the ID attribute in the grid and then press F4 to display the Properties window (you can also use the View, Properties menu item).

5. Set the use property to required.

6. Save the changes to your schema.

7. In the Solution Explorer window, double-click EmployeeData.xml to load the file back into the XML editor window.

8. Click the XML tab at the bottom of the window to ensure that you're working with the XML data directly.

9. Below the final </Employee> tag (the end of the last employee in the data), create a new employee named Stephen Buchanan. Enter only the first and last names. When you're done, the new element should look like this:

```
<Employee>
  <FirstName>Stephen</FirstName>
  <LastName>Buchanan</LastName>
</Employee>
```

TIP

Amazed to see IntelliSense support in the XML editor? Why is it available now when it wasn't available earlier? The answer is simple: an XML Schema. Because you've associated a schema with the XML document, the editor can now help you out as you type. This is exactly the same thing that happens when you enter HTML data directly into the HTML view of an ASP.NET Web form—the designer looks up the schema for the page, including all its controls, in an XML Schema document that ships with Visual Studio .NET.

10. Choose the XML, Validate XML Data menu item, which attempts to validate the data against the schema. It should fail, because you haven't supplied the required ID attribute for the new employee.

11. Add the ID attribute (Stephen Buchanan is employee 5) and then validate the data again. This time, it should succeed.

12. Although the schema supports an optional Phone element, it won't allow you to enter any other elements. Try adding an Address element within an Employee element, and the editor will immediately prompt you with a warning. Remove the offending element and then save the project.

Using XML Schema

Once your project contains both XML data and a schema, you have everything you need to take advantage of XML on an ASP.NET page. You could, for example, bind a DataGrid control to the contents of the XML file.

In order to use the XML data, you'll need to generate a typed DataSet class based on the XML data/schema. Follow these steps to create the DataSet and then bind a DataGrid to the data:

1. In the Solution Explorer window, double-click EmployeeData.xsd to load the schema into the Schema Designer window.

2. Select the Schema, Generate DataSet menu item, creating a code-behind file for the schema. (Use the Project, Show All Files menu item to see the new EmployeeData.vb file.)

3. Select the Project, Add Web Form menu item to add a new page to your project. Name the new page EmployeesXML.aspx.

4. In the Toolbox window, select the Data tab.

5. Drag a DataSet object onto your page. This displays the Add DataSet dialog box. In the dialog box, select the typed DataSet named Northwind.EmployeeData1 that you created in an earlier step. Click OK to

dismiss the dialog box, and your page should now include a `DataSet` object named EmployeesData1 in its tray area.

6. In the Toolbox window, select the Web Forms tab.

7. Place a DataGrid control on your new page. Set the DataGrid control's `DataSource` property to EmployeeData1 (the `DataSet` object you just created).

8. Double-click the page (not on the DataGrid control) and modify the `Page_Load` procedure so that it looks like the code in Listing 27.3.

LISTING 27.3   Bind a DataGrid to the Contents of an XML File

```
Private Sub Page_Load( _
 ByVal sender As System.Object, _
 ByVal e As System.EventArgs) _
 Handles MyBase.Load

  If Not Page.IsPostBack Then
    EmployeeData1.ReadXml( _
     Server.MapPath("EmployeeData.xml"))
    DataGrid1.DataBind()
  End If
End Sub
```

9. In the Solution Explorer window, right-click EmployeesXML.aspx and select Build and Browse from the context menu. The page should display the contents of the XML file in the DataGrid control, as shown in Figure 27.6.

FIGURE 27.6   It's easy to display the contents of an XML file within a DataGrid control.

What's going on in the code? The second line (calling the `DataBind` method of the DataGrid control) looks familiar, but what about the call to the `ReadXml` method of the DataSet?

When you created the `DataSet` object (`EmployeesData1`) on the page, Visual Studio .NET created a reference to the `EmployeeData.vb` class you created when you selected the Generate DataSet menu item. You can see this in the page's code-behind file, near the top of the code:

```
Protected WithEvents EmployeesData1 As Northwind.Employees
```

Normally, you fill a DataSet using the `Fill` method of a `DataAdapter` object. In this case, because you're reading data from an XML file rather than from a database, you simply call the `ReadXml` method of the DataSet, passing in the name of the XML file to read from.

You must also indicate the full path of the XML file. The `Server.MapPath` method takes as its parameter the name of a file in the application's folder and returns the full path for the file within the file system. Calling the `ReadXml` method, given the full path of the XML file, loads the DataSet so that the DataGrid can display the data.

> **TIP**
>
> It's interesting to note that you see the Phone column in the grid, even though none of the elements within the XML file contain this information. How did the DataGrid find this column? Obviously, when you created the typed `DataSet` object from the XML Schema in which you added the `Phone` element, that information was copied into the DataSet. Although you've read the actual data from the XML file, the schema was set at the time you created the typed DataSet.

Summary

In this chapter, you learned (or reviewed) the basics of XML, including the following:

- Why you might run across XML as a developer

- Why you might want to use XML rather than other data-transport mechanisms

- How XML data is constructed

- The rules of creating XML data

- How XML Schema defines the content of XML data

- How to use Visual Studio .NET's XML-related tools

- How to bind a DataGrid control to XML data

28

Introduction to XML Web Services

In the .NET development world, developers use software components as part of most (if not all) of their applications. Generally, those components exist on the same computer, or within the same network, as the application that consumes them.

What happens when you need to consume functionality provided by a software component that "lives" somewhere across the Web? Although classic COM provides for distributed components using Distributed COM (DCOM), DCOM doesn't work well across the Internet because of its reliance on connected behavior.

What you need is some way to communicate with components over HTTP, without a constant connection. In a perfect world, you'd be able to make a request, and you'd be notified when the response had come back from the remote object.

Imagine this scenario: Your company sells computers, and you'd like to be able to indicate the availability of the computers on your Web site. Of course, you don't actually stock the computers—you order them from the wholesaler, who drop-ships them for you to the client. What you really need is some way to perform real-time queries against the wholesaler's inventory so you can post the information on your site.

If the wholesaler provides some sort of component you can program against, perhaps calling the GetInventory method and passing in the ProductID value for the product you need, you could retrieve the available inventory for the product as users browse to the page for the product. Of course, you'd need this object to be available across the Web, because you don't have direct access to the supplier's database.

This chapter introduces XML Web Services—one possible solution to this development requirement. In this chapter, you'll see how and why XML Web Services provide a reasonable solution to the need for disconnected programmability.

> **NOTE**
>
> We use the specific term *XML Web Services* here because there are other types of Web services available. Specifically, XML Web Services (note the uppercasing) refers to Web Services that use the SOAP specification to communicate. To simplify matters, however, we'll often use *Web Service* as a synonym.

Web Service Requirements

In order for XML Web Services to exist, there needs to be some sort of universal programmatic access. That is, there needs to be some way for an application on one computer to "talk" with an application running on another computer, perhaps across the Internet. This access mechanism really needs to be independent of the operating system or development tools used on either end. Developers using Visual Studio .NET should be able to consume XML Web Services created by developers using a completely different set of tools, on a non-Windows operating system, if necessary.

In addition, to be able to create and consume Web Services, you must have available the following items:

- **A way to find service providers.** Without this, how would you know what XML Web Services are available?

- **A way to discover services a specific provider exposes.** Once you've found the provider, you'll need to know exactly what's available on the server.

- **A common, extensible service description format.** With this, the consumer can determine how to call the service, what parameters to send, and what data to expect in response. Even if you know that a server provides a particular method, what good is it if you don't know what parameters to send or what information it returns?

- **A common, extensible message format.** With this, the consumer can construct a request for data, and the service can respond with the results. You'll need to construct a packet of information containing your request, and the service will do the same with the response. If you both don't format your packets in a mutually agreed-upon format, how will you and the server be able to decipher the information?

- **A standard way to represent data.** With this, Web Service creators and consumers can understand the information going back and forth. Without some standard mechanism for representing text in the request and response packets, how can your code and the server communicate?

In order to see how XML Web Services satisfy these needs, let's start at the end of the list, working backwards from the smallest issue (data representation) to the biggest (determining available providers):

- **Representing data.** Clearly, XML is the solution (they'd hardly be called *XML* Web Services if they didn't use XML, right?). Because XML is extensible and supports namespaces that allow developers to specify the context for elements within the body of the text, XML makes a perfect solution to the problem of how to transport requests and responses over the Internet. In addition, because XML always consists of text (not binary information), you're guaranteed that XML can pass through firewalls—something you can't say for binary-encoded information.

- **Message format.** Because the sender and receiver must agree on a common request/response mechanism, you need some standard XML schema describing the method name, parameters, and so on, when making a method call. The Simple Object Access Protocol (SOAP) specification provides the standard messaging format (for more information, browse to http://www.w3.org/2000/xp/). The SOAP specification indicates exactly how to create the XML request and response packets and has no reliance on any particular transport (although you'll most likely be using HTTP), tools (you'll probably be using Visual Studio .NET), or operating system (we're guessing you'll be using Windows). The SOAP specification only requires XML containing particular elements—because it doesn't require HTTP transport, you could just as well create SOAP requests over e-mail or some queuing mechanism.

- **Service description format.** Web Service consumers require some way to determine what messages the Web Service understands. That is, Web Services need some way to document a "contract" that contains information about how consumers can call methods, what parameters the methods expect to receive, and what the methods return. The Web Services Description Language (WSDL) does this job for you. This XML grammar contains all the information your Web Service consumers need in order to communicate with the XML Web Service. Without this information, your consumers would have no idea how to construct method calls to the server.

- **Finding service providers.** How do you find plumbers in your local area? You look in the phone book, of course! It's not so obvious where to look, though, if you want information on XML Web Services. To make it possible for you to find out what's available, a group of companies (including Microsoft and IBM) have crafted Universal Description, Discovery, and Integration (UDDI). This specification provides a mechanism so that Web Service providers can "expose" their services. UDDI isn't part of Visual Studio .NET, but you can take advantage of this service. (See http://www.uddi.org or http://uddi.microsoft.com for more information.)

Table 28.1 summarizes this discussion, listing the requirements and solutions for you.

TABLE 28.1   In Order for Web Services to Exist and Function, Developers Must Take Advantage of All These Technologies

Requirement	Technology/Solution
Representing data	XML
Message format	SOAP
Service description format	WSDL
Discovering service providers	UDDI

XML Web Services Then and Now

There's not much new to creating and consuming XML Web Services, in theory. Developers have been using these exact techniques for years—but as you'll see, it used to be a lot more difficult than it is now.

Doing XML Web Services the Hard Way

In a normal SOAP-based Web Service application, the client application is responsible for creating the XML request and the SOAP envelope for transporting this XML across HTTP. On the receiving side, there must be a SOAP listener, waiting for SOAP requests. This listener will open the SOAP "envelope," process the contents, and invoke the appropriate object on the server. It must wait for the object to finish its job and then send the XML result back to the client machine. The client must then parse the XML, retrieving the results from the Web Service. Figure 28.1 diagrams this sort of application.

In the pre-.NET days, most developers who wanted to use Web Services in their applications wrote most of this code themselves. It's painstaking work, requiring a good understanding of creating and parsing XML and a careful reading of the SOAP specification.

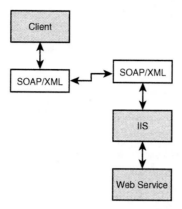

FIGURE 28.1   Using SOAP the hard way requires careful coding on both the client and the server.

Doing XML Web Services the Easy Way

Using Visual Studio .NET and the .NET Framework, creating and consuming XML Web Services couldn't be much simpler. The .NET Framework wraps classes around both the client and server sides of Web Services, so you don't need to know anything about either XML or SOAP in order to create and consume Web Services. As you'll see in the next chapter, exposing a method within a Web Service is simply a matter of adding a procedure attribute to the method, and consuming the Web Service is no more difficult than setting a reference.

Figure 28.2 shows how the .NET Framework makes it easier for you to interact with Web Services from within your client applications. Instead of requiring you to create SOAP messages using XML yourself, you simply call methods in the Web Service. The .NET Framework wraps up the SOAP information for you in both directions, so your applications aren't even aware that they're communicating with the server using XML.

TIP

If you find that you must consume XML Web Services from a non-.NET client (such as VB6 or Microsoft Office), you can take advantage of Microsoft's SOAP Toolkit 2.0, available at http://msdn.microsoft.com/xml. This toolkit provides a COM object that does much of the work provided by the .NET Framework.

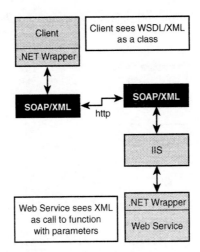

FIGURE 28.2   Calling Web Services in .NET still uses XML, but you can simply interact with objects provided by the .NET Framework that hide all the details from you.

Web Services in Action

Although Web Services and their use are relatively new, many businesses are beginning to understand the impact of being able to expose functionality for use in distributed applications across the Web. As you develop your own applications, you'll want to consider how you can take advantage of this technology. If you're thinking about ways you might use Web Services, here are some services you might want to create or consume:

- Address normalization functions

- Currency exchange rate converter

- Credit card authorization

- Shipment status

- Order confirmations

- Stock quote lookups

- Catalog/product information

- Weather information

Obviously, the list is endless. In any situation where you might want programmatic access to information on a remote computer, XML Web Services can provide the functionality you need.

TRY IT OUT Although you'll spend time creating and consuming your own XML Web Services in the next chapter, it's a good idea to "get your feet wet" and work through a simple example first, before digging into the more complex examples in the next chapter. In this section, you'll create a page that consumes an existing XML Web Service. We won't explain any of the details here—you'll learn what's going on in the next chapter.

Because this example uses an XML Web Service that we don't control, we can't guarantee that it will be available (or at the same location) or provide the same functionality by the time you try it. We've included this particular example here because we know the service's author and believe that he intends to maintain the service indefinitely. Obviously, we can't predict the future, but we hope you'll be able to try out this service before creating your own in the next chapter.

> **NOTE**
>
> This example requires a live Internet connection. Without the ability to retrieve the Web reference and then contact the XML Web Service, you'll be relegated to the sidelines, following the example and its figures without retrieving the actual data.

In this example, you'll create a page that allows you to enter a United States ZIP code and retrieve the current temperature (in Fahrenheit degrees) for the specified location. It's certainly not an Earth-shattering use of the technology, but it does show off the capabilities of consuming XML Web Services from within .NET applications.

Follow these steps to create a simple page that consumes an XML Web Service:

1. Create a new ASP.NET Web project or add a new page to an existing project.

2. Add Label, TextBox, and Button controls to the page. (For this simple demo, simply use the default names for the controls.) Delete the contents of the Text property for the Label control.

3. Select the Project, Add Web Reference menu item.

4. In the Add Web Reference dialog box, shown in Figure 28.3, click the Test Microsoft UDDI Directory link.

5. In the Business Name text box, enter **vbws** (the name of the company providing the sample service) and then click Search.

6. Once you see a list of available services in the left pane, select the Weather Service Registered Through VS .NET link.

7. Under the tModel label, select the Weather Service Registered Through VS .NET WSDL-Interface link (see Figure 28.4).

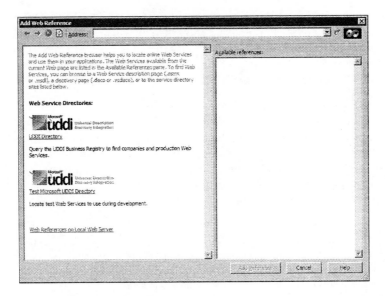

FIGURE 28.3   Use the Add Web Reference dialog box to add a reference to an XML Web Service.

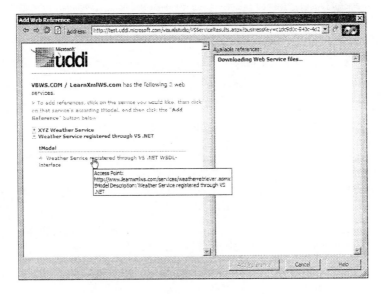

FIGURE 28.4   Select the specific service from the list of available services.

8. Once you see the WSDL information in the left pane, click the Add Reference button (see Figure 28.5).

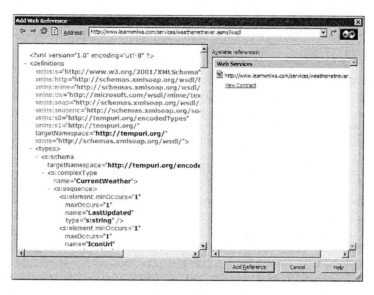

FIGURE 28.5 Once you've download the WSDL (the XML Web Service contract information), you can add the reference to your project.

9. Once you've added the Web reference, it shows up in the Solution Explorer window (in this case, as com.learnxmlws.www). Right-click the new reference, select Rename from the context menu, and rename the reference to **vbws**.

TIP

You don't really have to rename the Web reference. We've added this step here because you'll need to interact with this object programmatically, and the shorter name is easier to manage from within your code.

10. Double-click the button control on your page, bringing up the code editor. Modify the Button1_Click procedure so that it looks like this:

```
Private Sub Button1_Click( _
 ByVal sender As System.Object, _
 ByVal e As System.EventArgs) _
 Handles Button1.Click
```

```
Dim ws As New vbws.WeatherRetriever()
Label1.Text = ws.GetTemperature(TextBox1.Text)
End Sub
```

11. In the Solution Explorer window, right-click your page and select Build and Browse from the context menu.

12. Enter a U.S. ZIP code into the text box (enter **98052** to retrieve the temperature at the Microsoft home office) and then click the button.

13. After a few seconds, you should see the current temperature appear in the label control (see Figure 28.6).

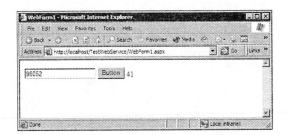

FIGURE 28.6   The WeatherRetriever service does its job.

What happened here? When you added a Web reference to your project, you added a few new files (and some code) to your project so that you could interact with the remote service programmatically. In your code, you called a method of the remote service, passing in a parameter. The .NET Framework stepped in and created XML to send to the service, which expects a request formatted using the SOAP specification. The .NET Framework sent the XML information remotely and waited for a response. The service did its job, retrieving the temperature for the requested area, and returned XML back to your project. The .NET Framework again stepped in, retrieving just the results you needed from the XML sent back from the service, and returned that string as the return value of the method you called.

All in all, this was hardly a difficult task for you, the developer! The .NET Framework did a lot of work on your behalf, but you managed to call a remote service as if it were a local object.

Summary

XML Web Services may revolutionize distributed application development because of their ease of use and .NET's support for creating and consuming these services. In this chapter, you learned the basics of working with XML Web Services:

- In order for XML Web Services to exist in the current environment, developers require a data format, a transfer mechanism, a document specifying the contents of the service, and a mechanism for discovering services. XML, SOAP, WSDL, and UDDI satisfy these requirements.

- Calling XML Web Services without .NET requires a great deal of effort, but it's possible. You just need to create and parse a lot of XML data yourself.

- Using .NET, it's simple to both create and consume Web Services.

- You can use the UDDI service to retrieve a Web reference to an existing service. Once you've set the reference, you can program against the remote object as if it were part of your project.

29

Creating and Consuming XML Web Services

In this chapter, you'll create two XML Web Services. The first, in this section, will be quite simple: Its goal will be to add two numbers together that you supply. The second, in the next section, will retrieve requested information back from SQL Server. In both cases, you're creating functionality that resides remotely—any application that has access to the Internet could consume the resulting Web Services and use the functionality remotely. Although you've already created a very simple Web Service in the previous chapter, the examples presented here begin to demonstrate the kinds of things (for example, calculations) you might actually want to do with XML Web Services.

Creating a Simple XML Web Service

Although the Web Service you create in this section is really simple, it shows off many of the issues you'll face when creating any Web Service, and its simplicity makes it a good example to get you started.

Follow these steps to create your first XML Web Service:

1. In Visual Studio .NET, create a new project. Select ASP.NET Web Service from the list of project templates.

2. Set the location of your service to `http://localhost/Jumpstart/MathService`. Click OK to create the project.

3. By default, the Web Service project template creates a component named `Service1.asmx`. Find this component in the Solution Explorer window and rename it to **Adding.asmx**.

OBJECTIVES

- Learn how to create Web Services

- Create a simple Windows application that consumes a Web Service

- Create Web Service methods that expose data

- Bind a DataGrid to the results of a Web Service method

NOTE

If you double-click `Adding.asmx` to display it in the designer, you'll note that it's empty but that there is a designer surface for the object. You might wonder why, given that you can't place Web Form controls on the designer. Microsoft supplies this designer so that you can use items on the Data and Components tabs of the Toolbox window. You can drag a `SqlDataAdapter` object onto the designer and have access to data from within your service. The same goes for all the objects provided on the Components tab. It's worth your time to investigate what tools Microsoft has provided on this tab—perhaps they can save you some time in a future application.

4. In the Solution Explorer window, right-click `Adding.asmx` and select View Code from the context menu. The code should look like Listing 29.1. (We've removed the hidden region and reformatted the code a bit to make it fit on the printed page.)

LISTING 29.1   When You First Create a Web Service Component, You'll Find This Code Inside

```
Imports System.Web.Services

<WebService(Namespace := "http://tempuri.org/")> _
Public Class Service1
    Inherits System.Web.Services.WebService

    ' WEB SERVICE EXAMPLE
    ' The HelloWorld() example service returns the string
    ' Hello World.
    ' To build, uncomment the following lines then save
    ' and build the project.
    ' To test this web service, ensure that the .asmx file
    ' is the start page
    ' and press F5.
    '
    '<WebMethod()> Public Function HelloWorld() As String
    '    HelloWorld = "Hello World"
    ' End Function

End Class
```

NOTE

Isn't it nice that Microsoft supplied a sample Web Service method for you? Too bad it doesn't do anything even vaguely useful. You'll always want to remove the sample template code.

5. Modify the class name from `Service1` to **Adding**.

6. Modify the default namespace (`http://tempuri.org/`) and replace it with **http://www.northwind.com/ws** instead. When you're done, the attribute should look like this:

```
<WebService(Namespace:="http://www.northwind.com/ws")> _
Public Class Adding
...
End Class
```

NOTE

The `WebService` attribute, associated with the class itself, allows you to specify information about the Web Service class. In this case, you're specifying the namespace associated with the class. Every Web Service must have some name tied to it (its *namespace*—the SOAP specification requires this), and by default, Visual Studio .NET uses a sample namespace, `http://tempuri.org/`. For any real Web Service, you should replace this with a unique name—normally a name that represents your organization. If your company's URL is `http://www.northwind.com`, for example, you could be guaranteed that no other company would use the same URL as its own namespace. Of course, there's no rule that forces developers to use a unique name here, and it's not crucial at this point that you do, but as Web Services proliferate, it will be useful if you identify your services with some unique "tag" in the service's `Namespace` property. If you don't modify the default namespace name, you'll see warnings later on, as you test your Web Service.

7. Delete the commented-out sample procedure, if you like.

8. Add the following code to the `Adding` class:

```
' Code Fragment 1.
<WebMethod()> _
Public Function AddTwoNumbers( _
 ByVal Number1 As Integer, _
 ByVal Number2 As Integer) As Long

   Return Number1 + Number2
End Function
```

If you take a moment to investigate the AddTwoNumbers method, you'll see that it's just standard VB .NET code. Nothing special is going on here, yet you're creating an XML Web Service that can work across the Web, using HTTP to transport values in and out of the method. How does this work? The answer is in the one extra attribute you've added to the procedure: The WebMethod attribute indicates to the compiler that your procedure is to be treated specially. It will send and receive its input and output using XML (encased in SOAP packets), and Visual Studio .NET will take extra steps to expose the functionality of the method inside an XML Web Service for you.

What can you do in a Web Service method? You can do just about anything you might do in any other code, except that you can't display a user interface. Obviously, because the Web Service method will be running on a remote computer, you don't want it to have any user interaction. Other than that, however, you can use any of the .NET Framework and its objects within your Web Service method.

Testing the Web Service

Although you'll generally consume the Web Service methods you create from within real applications, it's easy to test your method without needing to create a new application. When you simply browse directly to the Adding.asmx page you've created, ASP.NET renders a test page for you. Try it out by following these steps:

1. Press F5 to run the project.

2. Visual Studio .NET displays the test page with a link for each method you've created, as shown in Figure 29.1.

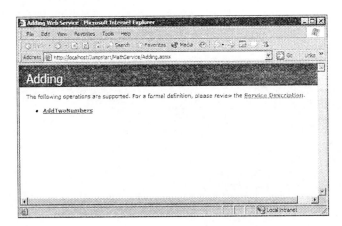

FIGURE 29.1   The test page for your Web Service allows you to try out the methods provided by the service.

3. Click the AddTwoNumbers link, bringing up the test page shown in Figure 29.2.

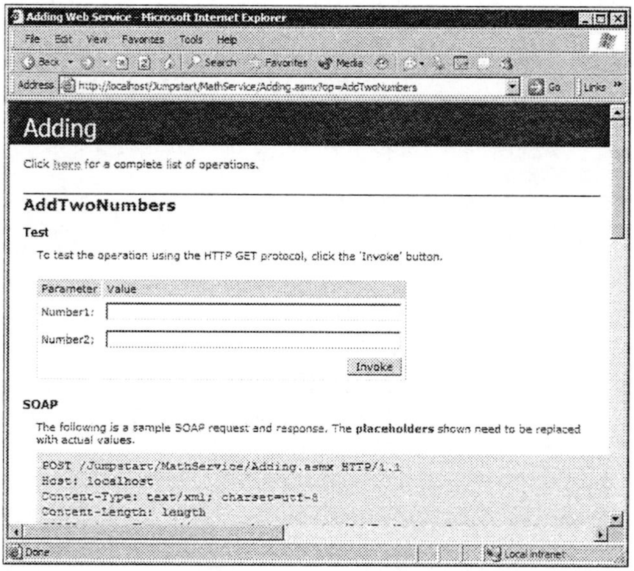

FIGURE 29.2   ASP.NET provides a test page for each Web Service method.

TIP

You might find it interesting to scroll your test page down and view the information about the SOAP packets created for you by the .NET Framework. Isn't it nice to know about all the work you *don't* have to do?

4. Provide the two requested numeric values and then click Invoke to test your method.

5. Once you're done, you'll see a page like the one shown in Figure 29.3, containing the results of your Web Service method call. (For this example, we entered 12 and 13 into the two text boxes on the previous page.)

Before you close the browser window, investigate the URL in the Address text box. You should see text like this:

```
http://localhost/Jumpstart/MathService/Adding.asmx/
➥AddTwoNumbers?Number1=12&Number2=13
```

You can test a Web Service method directly, if you know the name of the method and its parameter names, simply by entering a URL like this one. If you need to consume a Web Service from a non-.NET client, for example, you could create an

HTTP request within your code, using a URL like this one as your target. The response would contain the results shown in Figure 29.3.

FIGURE 29.3   The Web Service method returns its value in XML.

Consuming a Web Service

Although Web Services are formally a part of ASP.NET, you can write client applications that take advantage of the Web Services that run either on the client or on a Web server. In this section, you'll create a client-side application, using Windows Forms, to demonstrate the techniques involved in consuming an XML Web Service.

When you decide to consume a Web Service as part of your application, the Web Service might be located on your local intranet, it might be located at a corporate office that's only accessible through the Internet, or it might be a public service. Whatever the scenario, the steps to consume the service are the same. In general, you'll always need to perform these steps:

1. Add a Web Reference, retrieving information about the Web Service.

2. Create an object in your code that corresponds to the service.

3. Call a method of the object that's created in the previous step.

Creating a Client Application

In this section, you'll create a simple Windows Forms application that calls the Web Service you created earlier in the chapter. Follow these steps to create the new project and test the service:

1. Open a second instance of Visual Studio .NET. (You're leaving the first instance open only for convenience. If you don't want to run two copies of Visual Studio .NET concurrently, you can close the previous instance.)

2. Create a new project, selecting Windows Application from the list of project templates.

3. Set the name of the project to **WebServiceClient** and the location to any convenient location (perhaps within the Jumpstart folder, to keep all your examples in one place).

4. Click OK to create the project.

5. Use the View, Properties Window menu item to display the Properties window.

6. Set the Text property for the form to Add Two Numbers.

7. Add three Label controls, three TextBox controls, and button so that the form looks like Figure 29.4.

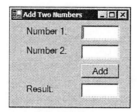

FIGURE 29.4   The finished form should look like this.

8. Set the Name properties for the TextBox controls to **txtNum1**, **txtNum2**, and **txtResults**, respectively.

9. Set the Name property for the Button control to **btnAdd**.

Adding the Web Reference

Now that you've created the basic form, you can hook up the Web Service. Follow these steps to add the Web reference:

1. In the Solution Explorer window, right-click the project. Select Add Web Reference from the context menu. (You could also select the Project, Add Web Reference menu item.)

2. Visual Studio .NET displays the Add Reference dialog box, shown in Figure 29.5. You could search for a service using UDDI (as you did in the previous chapter), but this time, you'll enter the exact address of the service you created in the previous section. Enter a full address, like this, into the Address text box and then press Enter:

```
http://localhost/jumpstart/mathservice/adding.asmx
```

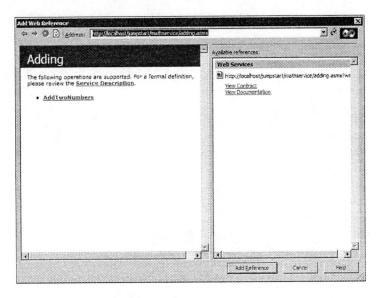

FIGURE 29.5   Enter the address of the Web Service you'd like to use.

3. Click Add Reference to add the reference to your project.

4. Take a look at the Solution Explorer window—it should look something like Figure 29.6 (we've expanded the node corresponding to the new Web reference). Note that adding the reference also added a few new files to your project—most notably, the adding.wsdl file, which contains information about the methods, parameters, and return values in the Web Service.

FIGURE 29.6   Adding a Web reference adds other files, as well.

TIP

Although you could rename the Web reference (you did this in the previous chapter), it's not required. If you'd like to rename localhost to some other name, feel free, although you'll need to modify any code in the rest of this example that refers to localhost explicitly.

Calling the Web Service Method

Once you've added the Web reference to your project, you can call the methods provided by the Web Service from within your project's code. Follow these steps to test calling the AddTwoNumbers method from your form:

1. On your form, double-click the Add button.

2. Modify the btnAdd_Click procedure so that it looks like this:

```
' Code Fragment 2.
Private Sub btnAdd_Click( _
 ByVal sender As System.Object, _
 ByVal e As System.EventArgs) _
 Handles btnAdd.Click

  Dim ws As New localhost.Adding()
  txtResults.Text = ws.AddTwoNumbers( _
   CInt(txtNum1.Text), CInt(txtNum2.Text)).ToString
End Sub
```

3. Press F5 to run the application.

4. Enter two values into the text boxes on the form, press Add, and, after a few seconds, you'll see the results appear on the form. When you're done, the form should look like Figure 29.7.

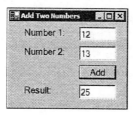

FIGURE 29.7   The sample form displays the results of calling the Web Service method.

5. Close the form when you're done.

What's going on in the code? The code starts by instantiating a `localhost.Adding` object:

```
Dim ws As New localhost.Adding()
```

The procedure finished by calling the `AddTwoNumbers` method of the object you created, passing in the `Text` properties of the two TextBox controls on the form. It converted the result into a `String` value for display in the Result text box, like this:

```
txtResults.Text = ws.AddTwoNumbers( _
 CInt(txtNum1.Text), CInt(txtNum2.Text)).ToString
```

The remaining question is, Where did the `localhost.Adding` object come from? How did your project know how to find this remote object? The simple answer is, of course, that when you added the Web reference to your project, you added code that takes care of these details for you.

If you use the Project, Show All Files menu item, you'll see that the `Reference.map` item in the Solution Explorer window includes a code-behind file named `Reference.vb`, as shown in Figure 29.8. This file contains a namespace that matches the name of your reference (`localhost`, in this case) and a class with the same name as your Web Service class (`Adding`, in this case).

FIGURE 29.8   Adding a Web reference adds a new code file, as well.

Therefore, when your code refers to `localhost.Adding`, you're actually working with the `Adding` class within the `localhost` namespace in the `Reference.vb` file in your project, not within a remote Web Service class. (This class is often called a *proxy class*, because it acts as a proxy for the real class in the remote Web Service.) If you examine the code within the `Adding` class in `Reference.vb`, you'll find an `AddTwoNumbers` procedure (which explains how your code can call the method named `AddTwoNumbers`). This local `AddTwoNumbers` procedure includes code that manages the call to the real Web Service procedure, so you don't need to worry about how it all happens. If you're interested, dig into the code in `Reference.vb`, although it's not important to understand all the details at this point.

> **NOTE**
>
> Perhaps you're wondering how you managed to get IntelliSense tips as you were typing the code that called the Web Service method. Because adding the Web reference adds the local proxy class containing the same information as in the Web Service, Visual Studio .NET can provide design-time help just as it does with local objects.

As you've seen, the most exciting feature of Web Services is that you don't have to know who created the service, or even in what language, development environment, or operating system. To your client applications, all that matters is the WSDL—the information about what methods are available, what parameters to send, and what data to expect back. If you've selected a Web Service from a reputable source, you can consume it just like any local object.

> **TIP**
>
> You've seen how to create a simple Windows application that consumes an XML Web Service. Creating a Web application that consumes a Web Service is no more difficult—as a matter of fact, it takes exactly the same steps to create a Web application that consumes a Web Service. You might want to try re-creating the consumer application you just created as a Web page. You'll see that you can follow the same exact steps and achieve the same results.

Creating a Useful Web Service

Although a service that adds two numbers together has its uses (although it might be difficult to determine those uses, except for demonstration purposes), you might be more likely to create a Web Service that interacts with a data source and provides information based on that data. In this section, you'll create a Web Service that retrieves information from the Northwind sample database in SQL Server. You'll provide two methods:

- `GetInventory`. This method returns the current, available inventory for a specific product.

- `GetAllInventory`. This method returns a DataSet containing the inventory level for all products.

There really isn't much new in these procedures, because the techniques you've already learned for manipulating data all apply here. To get started creating your service, follow these steps:

1. Create a new project in Visual Studio .NET, selecting the ASP.NET Web Service project template.

2. Set the location for your service to **http://localhost/JumpStart/InventoryService**.

3. Rename the Service1.asmx file to **Inventory.asmx**.

4. Select the View, Code menu item and modify the class name from Service1 to **Inventory**.

5. Modify the default namespace (http://tempuri.org/) and replace it with **http://www.northwind.com/ws** instead.

6. Delete the commented-out sample code within the class. When you're done, the class should look like Listing 29.2.

LISTING 29.2   The Starting Point for Your Web Service Looks Like This

```
Imports System.Web.Services

<WebService(Namespace:="http://www.northwind.com/ws")> _
Public Class Inventory
  Inherits System.Web.Services.WebService

End Class
```

7. Scroll to the top of the file and add the following Imports statement:

    ```
    Imports System.Data.OleDb
    ```

8. Add the following code to the Inventory class:

    ```
    Private Const CONNECTION_STRING As String = _
      "Provider=sqloledb;" & _
      "Data Source=(local);" & _
      "Initial Catalog=Northwind;" & _
      "User ID=sa;Password="

    <WebMethod()> Public Function UnitsInStock( _
      ByVal ProductID As Integer) As Integer
    ```

```
Dim strSQL As String = _
  "SELECT UnitsInStock FROM Products " & _
  "WHERE ProductID = " & ProductID

Dim cnn As OleDbConnection
Dim cmd As OleDbCommand
Dim intUnits As Integer

Try
  cnn = New OleDbConnection(CONNECTION_STRING)
  cnn.Open()
  cmd = New OleDbCommand(strSQL, cnn)
  UnitsInStock = cmd.ExecuteScalar()

Finally
  If cnn.State = ConnectionState.Open Then
    cnn.Close()
  End If
End Try
End Function
```

The UnitsInStock method opens a connection to the data source and executes a Command object that returns the single required value—the available units in stock for the requested product. To test your Web Service method, follow these steps:

1. Press F5 to run the project.

2. On the test page, click the UnitsInStock link.

3. Enter a value (say, **12**) into the ProductID text box. Click Invoke to test the method.

4. You should see the results, formatted as XML, within the browser window.

Returning a DataSet from a Web Service

Every sample method exposed in a Web Service that you've seen so far returns a single value. There's no reason, however, that a Web Service method can't return a complex result, such as a DataSet. To finish this chapter, you'll create a Web Service method that returns a complete DataSet, and then you'll create a simple page that displays the results of calling the Web Service method in a DataGrid control.

Follow these steps to create and consume the Web Service method:

1. Add the following method to the Inventory class in Inventory.asmx:

```
<WebMethod()> Public Function GetAllInventory() As DataSet
  Dim strSQL As String = _
    "SELECT ProductID, ProductName, " & _
    "UnitPrice, UnitsInStock " & _
    "FROM Products ORDER BY ProductName"

  Dim da As OleDbDataAdapter
  Dim ds As New DataSet()

  Try
    da = New OleDbDataAdapter(strSQL, CONNECTION_STRING)
    da.Fill(ds)
  Catch
    Throw
  End Try
  Return ds
End Function
```

2. Test your method, just as you did in the previous section. The return value should contain a large amount of XML data, as shown in Figure 29.9. This XML contains the DataSet returned by your Web Service method.

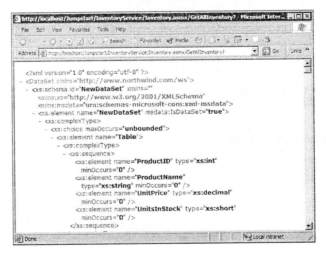

FIGURE 29.9   A Web Service method that returns a DataSet creates output like this.

3. Save your project.

4. Create a new ASP.NET Web Application project, selecting the location `http://localhost/JumpStart/WebServiceConsumer` for your project.

5. Add a Web reference to your project using this URL:

```
http://localhost/jumpstart/inventoryservice/inventory.asmx
```

TIP

Refer back to the previous example for complete steps and hints on adding a Web reference to your project.

6. Add a DataGrid control to your page. Set the control's `ID` property to `grdInventory`.

7. Double-click the page (not the control) and modify the `Page_Load` procedure so that it looks like this:

```
Private Sub Page_Load( _
ByVal sender As System.Object, _
ByVal e As System.EventArgs) _
Handles MyBase.Load

  If Not Page.IsPostBack Then
    Dim ws As New localhost.Inventory()
    grdInventory.DataSource = ws.GetAllInventory()
    grdInventory.DataBind()
  End If
End Sub
```

8. Press F5 to run the project. You should see the inventory data displayed in the grid.

What happened here? When your page loaded, it called the Web Service method, which returned a DataSet. Your code set the DataGrid control's `DataSource` property to the DataSet returned from the method and displayed the data. Couldn't be much easier than that, could it?

Of course, between the Web Service and the consumer application, the .NET Framework serializes the DataSet as XML—you saw that in Figure 29.9. Once the consumer application receives the XML, however, the proxy class indicates that the application should retrieve a `DataSet` object, and the .NET Framework converts the data back into its original data type, ready to be bound to the DataGrid control's `DataSource` property.

Summary

In this chapter, you saw how easy it is to create and consume XML Web Services. You created a few simple services and consumed services from both Windows applications and Web applications. In addition, you learned the following:

- How to create a simple XML Web Service.

- That you should add your own namespace instead of accepting the common namespace provided for you.

- That you can test your Web Service using the page the .NET Framework creates for you.

- How to add a Web Reference to a project.

- How to create a Windows application that consumes an XML Web Service.

- How to create a Web application that consumes an XML Web Service.

- That you can return either a simple or complex value as the return value of a Web Service method. You can return something as simple as an integer or as complex as a DataSet. The .NET Framework handles the conversions to and from XML as necessary.

30

Investigating Web Service Consumers

OBJECTIVES

- Compare synchronous and asynchronous calls to Web Service methods

- Learn to create the required procedure for callbacks in order to call a Web Service asynchronously

When you create a client application that consumes a method from a Web Service, most likely your application simply calls a method in the object provided by the Web Service—or so it would seem. Your code doesn't actually call a method in some remote object—that wouldn't make any sense. Under the covers, your code is calling a method in a local object that knows how to contact the remote Web Service and execute the method using SOAP. This local object then retrieves a return value from the remote Web Service method and returns that value back to you.

In this chapter, you'll first create an XML Web Service consumer that calls the method of the Web Service synchronously, much as you might have done previously. Then, you'll learn how to call a Web Service method asynchronously. This allows your application to return immediately after calling the method and await the results while accomplishing other tasks.

Consuming a Web Service Synchronously

In this section, you'll create a standard synchronous Web Service consumer. You'll also investigate how the proxy class makes it look like you're working with a local object and its methods when you make method calls in the Web Service.

The Sample Web Service

For this example, you'll modify the InventoryService Web Service you created in the previous chapter. This service provides a simple UnitsInStock method, which returns the available inventory for a product matching the ProductID value your method call supplies. In the following steps, you'll add code that causes the method to delay 10 seconds before returning its value to simulate the behavior of a Web Service that takes measurable time to do its work.

Follow these steps to slow down your Web Service method:

1. In Visual Studio .NET, load the InventoryService project you created in the previous chapter. You should be able to locate the project in the `Jumpstart\InventoryService` folder.

2. View the code for the `Inventory.asmx` file.

3. Modify the code in the `UnitsInStock` procedure so that it looks like this (we only show a few lines of code here to indicate the context for the new line of code):

```
cmd = New OleDbCommand(strSQL, cnn)
UnitsInStock = cmd.ExecuteScalar()
' Wait for a few seconds...
System.Threading.Thread.Sleep(10000)
```

To call this Web Service method, you pass in a product ID, and the method returns the number of items currently in inventory.

The code that you've added pauses the thread for 10 seconds. This code uses the shared `Sleep` method of the `Thread` object provided by the .NET Framework, emulating a long-running Web Service method.

WHAT'S A THREAD?

A *thread* is a single path of execution within an application. Each application must contain at least one thread, and many applications use more than one thread to do their work. Your Web Service only uses one thread, unless you write code that creates more, and the call to `Thread.Sleep` causes the single thread in use to block for the specified number of milliseconds. The outcome of this is that the caller, waiting for a response from this method, waits for 10 seconds for the function's return value. You won't normally add code to your applications to slow them down, but in this case, it helps test the concept of asynchronous Web Service consumer applications.

To verify that the sample Web Service works, follow these steps:

1. Press F5 to run the project.

2. Click the UnitsInStock link on the page that's displayed.

3. On the test page, enter a number between 1 and 15 or so in the text box, click the Invoke button, and verify that 10 seconds or so later, you get the available inventory for the item you requested.

4. Save your project.

Calling the Web Service

To create the sample page, for both this section and the next, follow these steps:

1. Create a new ASP.NET Web Application project. Set the location to
   `Jumpstart\AsyncConsumer`.

2. Add the controls shown in Figure 30.1 to the `Webform1.aspx` page. Set properties
   for these controls as shown in Table 30.1.

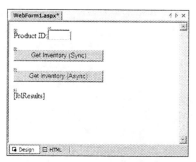

FIGURE 30.1   Your sample page should look like this.

TABLE 30.1   Set These Control Properties on the Sample Page

Control	Property	Value
Label	Text	Product ID:
TextBox	ID	txtProductID
	Text	1
Button	ID	btnSync
	Text	Get Inventory (Sync)
Button	ID	btnAsync
	Text	Get Inventory (Async)
Label	ID	lblResults

3. Add a Web reference to your project, referring to the InventoryService Web
   Service you modified in the previous section.

4. Select the Project, Add Web Reference menu item and enter the address for the
   InventoryService Web Service, using this address:

   `http://localhost/jumpstart/inventoryservice/inventory.asmx`

5. Select the Add Reference button once you've found the Web Service.

6. Right-click the name of the newly added Web Service, select Rename from the
   context menu, and rename the service to **InventoryService**.

7. Select the Project, Show All Files menu item so that you can view all the files added to your project.

8. Next, you'll add code to your page, calling the newly added Web Service. To begin, double-click btnSync and modify the btnSync_Click procedure, adding the following procedure call:

```
TestSync()
```

9. Add the TestSync procedure, shown in Listing 30.1, to your class.

LISTING 30.1   Add Code to Handle the Synchronous Call to the Web Service

```
Private Sub TestSync()

  Dim ws As New InventoryService.Inventory()
  Dim intResults as Integer
  Dim intProductID as Integer

  intProductID = CInt(txtProductID.Text)
  intResults = ws.UnitsInStock(intProductID)
  lblResults.Text = FormatResults( _
    intProductID, intResults)
End Sub
```

10. Add the FormatResults procedure shown in Listing 30.2, which formats the item number and inventory for display on the page (and for the Event Log item, later).

LISTING 30.2   Format the Results Using This Procedure

```
Private Function FormatResults(ByVal Item As Integer, _
ByVal ItemCount As Integer) As String
  Dim blnSingular As Boolean

  ' Format the results.
  blnSingular = (ItemCount = 1)
  Dim strResults As String = _
    String.Format( _
    "There {0} currently {1} {2} of item {3} in stock.", _
    IIf(blnSingular, "is", "are"), _
    ItemCount, _
    IIf(blnSingular, "unit", "units"), Item)
  Return strResults
End Function
```

NOTE

The FormatResults function you just added doesn't do much besides "prettify" the output. It accepts the item number and the item count as parameters and then creates a string such as "There are currently 4 units of item 12 in stock." The code takes into account the embarrassing singular versus plural issue.

11. Finally, you can test the page. Press F5 to run the project.

12. Enter a value into the Product ID text box, click Get Inventory (Sync), and wait for the response. After 10 seconds or so, you should see the results displayed in the Label control on the page.

13. Close the Browser window and save your project.

What's Going On?

If you look carefully at the code in the btnSync_Click procedure, you'll see that you're creating an instance of the InventoryService.Inventory class:

```
Dim ws As New InventoryService.Inventory()
```

Where did that namespace and class come from? They're both provided by the proxy class created for you when you added the Web reference. To check it out, open the Reference.vb file, hidden as a code-behind file for Reference.map in the Solution Explorer.

TIP

You won't see Reference.vb in the Solution Explorer if you didn't select the Project, Show All Files menu item. If you can't find Reference.vb, make sure you show all the files first.

If you investigate the Reference.vb file, you'll find code like this:

```
Namespace InventoryService
  Public Class Inventory
    Inherits System.Web.Services.Protocols. _
    SoapHttpClientProtocol
```

(Note that we've removed the distracting procedure attributes, which don't add much to our explanation here.) As you can see, the file provides a namespace (InventoryService) and a class (Inventory). The class inherits from SoapHttpClientProtocol, so it can call any of the methods provided by that base class. This will be important, in just a few paragraphs.

Because your project includes a file that creates the namespace and class, your code can refer to InventoryService.Inventory as if that were a local object, *because it is*. Even though it looks like you're referring to the Web Service class, you're actually working with the local class (often called a *proxy class*, because it stands in place of, as a proxy, for the real Web Service).

Now let's get back to the procedure you added. Next, the procedure calls the UnitsInStock method of the proxy class, like this:

```
lblResults.Text = ws.UnitsInStock( _
  CInt(txtProductID.Text)).ToString
```

Looking in the proxy class, you'll find a UnitsInStock procedure, like this (again, we've removed procedure attributes that affect how SOAP handles the procedure, but that doesn't affect anything at the moment):

```
Public Function UnitsInStock( _
ByVal ProductID As Integer) As Integer
  Dim results() As Object = _
    Me.Invoke("UnitsInStock", New Object() {ProductID})
  Return CType(results(0), Integer)
End Function
```

This method, which is actually what your code is calling, calls the Invoke method provided by the base class (SoapHttpClientProtocol), which uses the URL provided in the class's constructor to call the actual Web Service method:

```
Public Sub New()
  MyBase.New()
  Me.Url = _
    http://localhost/jumpstart/inventoryservice/" & _
    "inventory.asmx"
End Sub
```

The Invoke method expects that you'll pass it two parameters:

- The name of the method to call (UnitsInStock, in this case).

- An array of Objects, containing the parameters to be passed to the method. In this case, it's just an array with a single element—the ProductID value passed as a parameter to the procedure.

Consuming a Web Service Asynchronously   571

The `Invoke` method returns an array of Objects, and the `UnitsInStock` method retrieves the first item in the array (index 0), converts it to a `Short`, and returns the value as its return value.

As you can see, when you instantiate and make a call to a Web Service method, you're actually instantiating a local object and calling a method of that object that knows how to call the Web Service for you. This proxy class makes your interaction with the Web Service much simpler.

Consuming a Web Service Asynchronously

In the previous section, because you're calling the Web Service method directly, your page must wait for the return value before it can display the results. Most commercial Web sites don't require you to sit and wait until the page has completed its processing before displaying confirmation information.

For example, imagine a site where you register for a conference and request a hotel room for the conference at the same time. The conference site might be calling an XML Web Service provided by the hotel, and calling that Web Service might take measurable time. The conference site can't confirm your hotel room—they must have the hotel chain do this for you. Rather than forcing you to wait while the conference site works with the hotel chain to get you a confirmation number, they might simply indicate success on the Web page and then send you an e-mail confirmation once they have the hotel information.

In the previous example, you saw that you were required to wait 10 seconds when you requested the inventory level for a specific product. In a real Web site, you might be more likely to return immediately, with a response on the page, and send some notification later once you had gathered the information you needed. In this example, you'll do just that—rather than waiting the 10 seconds, you'll return immediately and write to a text file the results of the method call once you receive the information.

TIP

You might want to modify this example to send e-mail rather than writing to a text file. You can use the `System.Web.Mail` namespace, and its objects, to send a mail message. Because we can't guarantee that you have an available SMTP mail server, we opted to use a text file instead.

Adding the Method Call

Follow these steps to complete the asynchronous example:

1. Make sure WebForm1.aspx is open in the page designer.

2. Double-click btnAsync and add the following procedure call to the
   btnAsync_Click procedure:

   ```
   TestAsync()
   ```

3. Add the TestAsync procedure, shown in Listing 30.3, to your class.

LISTING 30.3   Add Code to Call the Web Service Method Asynchronously

```
Private Sub TestAsync()

  Dim ws As New InventoryService.Inventory()
  Dim acb As New AsyncCallback(AddressOf HandleCallback)

  ws.BeginUnitsInStock( _
   CInt(txtProductID.Text), acb, ws)

  lblResults.Text = "Thanks for your request. " & _
   "Check the text file "WebLog.txt" for the results."
End Sub
```

4. Add the procedure shown in Listing 30.4, which the .NET Framework calls
   once the Web Service method call has completed.

LISTING 30.4   Add This Callback Procedure, to Be Called by the .NET Framework

```
Private Sub HandleCallback(ByVal ar As IAsyncResult)
  Dim ws As InventoryService.Inventory
  Dim intProductID As Integer = CInt(txtProductID.Text)
  Dim intResults As Integer

  ' Get the Web Service object.
  ws = CType(ar.AsyncState, _
   InventoryService.Inventory)

  ' Call the End... procedure.
  intResults = ws.EndUnitsInStock(ar)
```

LISTING 30.4 Continued

```
WriteTextFile(FormatResults(intProductId, intResults))
End Sub
Private Sub WriteTextFile(ByVal Value As String)
   Dim sw As StreamWriter

   If Not File.Exists(Server.MapPath("WebLog.txt")) Then
     sw = File.CreateText(Server.MapPath("WebLog.txt"))
   End If
   sw.Write(Value)
   sw.Close()
 End Sub
```

5. Press F5 to run the project.

6. Enter a value into the Product ID text box, click Get Inventory (Async), and wait for the response. The page should post back almost immediately, asking you to check the text file for the results.

7. Close the Browser window and save your project.

8. Load the Jumpstart\AsyncConsumer\WebLog.txt file in Notepad and you should see the ProductID and the results written in this file.

What's Going On?

Calling a Web Service asynchronously, not waiting for the results, requires a few more steps and a little more care than calling the method synchronously. In the previous example, you did all the work to call a method asynchronously. What did you actually do?

First of all, it's important to investigate the code in the Web Service proxy class, just as you did when creating the synchronous method call. In the `Reference.vb` file, you'll find the two methods shown in Listing 30.5 (note that the procedure attributes have been removed and the methods have been reformatted for easier reading).

LISTING 30.5   The Proxy Class Contains These Two Methods

```
Public Function BeginUnitsInStock( _
 ByVal ProductID As Integer, _
 ByVal callback As System.AsyncCallback, _
 ByVal asyncState As Object) As System.IAsyncResult
  Return Me.BeginInvoke("UnitsInStock", _
   New Object() {ProductID}, callback, asyncState)
End Function

Public Function EndUnitsInStock( _
 ByVal asyncResult As System.IAsyncResult) As Integer
  Dim results() As Object = Me.EndInvoke(asyncResult)
  Return CType(results(0), Integer)
End Function
```

These two procedures (`BeginUnitsInStock` and `EndUnitsInStock`) call back to the Web Service method (again, using the URL property of the base class). The `BeginUnitsInStock` procedure sets up the callback, and you call the `EndUnitsInStock` procedure when the Web Service method call has completed its work. These two procedures are created for you in the proxy class—your job is to call them correctly.

When you create an asynchronous callback, you'll always work through these issues:

- **Creating two procedures.** You provide two procedures—a "start" procedure (`TestAsync`, in this example) and an "end" procedure (`HandleCallback`, in this example). You call your start procedure to call the proxy class's `Begin...` method (`BeginUnitsInStock`, in this example). Your start procedure can display a status message on the page and allow the output page to display in the user's browser.

- **Setting up the callback.** The start procedure registers a callback to your end procedure. Basically, you pass the address of your end procedure to the .NET Framework, which calls your end procedure when the Web Service has finished its work.

- **Handling the callback.** When the Web Service method is complete, the .NET Framework calls your end procedure, which calls the `End...` method in the proxy class (`EndUnitsInStock`, in this example). In this case, the end procedure writes information to the WebLog.txt text file, although it could e-mail it as well.

The .NET Framework makes it easy for you to create this callback mechanism. The framework supplies two classes specifically for this purpose:

- AsyncCallback. Describes the exact procedure signature required by the callback procedure. If you want your end procedure to be called by the .NET Framework when the asynchronous method is complete, it must be of this type.

- IAsyncResult. Contains information about the state of the asynchronous callback. You'll use this type as the parameter to your callback procedure—the procedure that the .NET Framework calls when the asynchronous method call has completed.

INTRODUCING DELEGATES

The AsyncCallback type defines a *delegate*. You may have heard this term before and wondered what it means. When you create a variable of this type, you can only assign the address of a procedure that meets the delegate's exact signature into the variable. In this case, the AsyncCallback delegate type requires any variable of this type to refer to a procedure that

- Is a Sub
- Accepts one parameter of type IAsyncResult

Think of it this way: You register your callback procedure with the .NET Framework. It needs to call your procedure when the Web Service method has completed. If your procedure didn't accept the correct parameters, the call from the .NET Framework would fail. Therefore, the framework needs some way to verify, at compile time, that your callback procedure can "answer the call." That's the point of the Delegate data type: You guarantee, at the time you compile the code, that your procedure meets the needs of any other procedure that calls it.

The "Start" Procedure

The code in TestAsync (your "start" procedure) that sets up the callback looks like this:

```
Dim ws As New InventoryService.Inventory()
Dim acb As New AsyncCallback(AddressOf HandleCallback)

ws.BeginUnitsInStock( _
 CInt(txtProductID.Text), acb, ws)
```

This code takes these actions:

- It creates a new instance of the InventoryService.Inventory class, just as your code might if calling the method synchronously.

- It creates a new instance of the AsyncCallback class, passing the address of your "end" procedure (HandleCallback) to the constructor.

- It calls the BeginUnitsInStock method, provided by the Web Service proxy class.

The `BeginUnitsInStock` procedure accepts three parameters: the ID of the product you're investigating, the address of the procedure to be called once the asynchronous method is complete, and an object of your choosing (it can be `Nothing`, if you like). The .NET Framework passes this object on to you at the other end—when you're handling the results of the method call. In this case, the code passes the ws object so that your `HandleCallback` procedure can work with the same `Inventory` object, retrieving the inventory for the item you requested.

The "End" Procedure

The `HandleCallback` procedure (your "end" procedure) includes this code:

```
Dim ws As InventoryService.Inventory
Dim intProductID As Integer = CInt(txtProductID.Text)
Dim intResults As Integer

' Get the Web Service object.
ws = CType(ar.AsyncState, _
 InventoryService.Inventory)

' Call the End... procedure.
intResults = ws.EndUnitsInStock(ar)

WriteTextFile(FormatResults(intProductId, intResults))
```

This code takes these actions:

- It declares a variable as `InventoryService.Inventory`. This variable will refer to the Web Service object created in your "start" procedure and will allow you to call the `EndUnitsInStock` method.

- It declares variables to hold the item and item count:

  ```
  Dim ws As InventoryService.Inventory
  Dim intProductID As Integer = CInt(txtProductID.Text)
  Dim intResults As Integer
  ```

- It retrieves a reference to the original Web Service object, created in the "start" procedure. Because you passed the `BeginUnitsInStock` method a reference to this object as a parameter, the .NET Framework passes this along to your callback procedure in the `AsyncState` property of the `IAsyncResult` object. You must cast this property to the correct type (using the `CType` function):

  ```
  ws = CType(ar.AsyncState, _
   InventoryService.Inventory)
  ```

- It calls the EndUnitsInStock method of the Web Service object, which retrieves the return value from the Web Service, cached by the .NET Framework (note that you must pass the IAsyncResult object you received as a parameter to the EndUnitsInStock method):

```
intResults = ws.EndUnitsInStock(ar)
```

- It writes the results to the Event Log, using the WebLog.txt file located in your Jumpstart\AsyncConsumer folder.

```
WriteTextFile(FormatResults(intProductId, intResults))
```

Summary

It's easy to call a Web Service method synchronously: Simply create a new instance of the proxy class created for you when you add a Web reference and then call the appropriate method. You will, however, have to wait until the results come back from the Web Service before posting your page, and this may be unacceptable to your users.

If you don't want to wait, you can call a Web Service method asynchronously, as well. It seems like a lot of effort to call a Web Service asynchronously, but it's really just a few more steps. In summary, here's what you must do:

- Create a "start" procedure that calls the proxy class's BeginXXX procedure, where XXX is the name of the method you want to call in the Web Service. Pass BeginXXX a reference to your "end" procedure so that the .NET Framework can call your procedure when the Web Service has returned a value.

- Create an "end" procedure to handle the callback from the .NET Framework. In this procedure, call the EndXXX procedure provided by the Web Service proxy class in order to retrieve the return value from the Web Service.

31

Securing Web Services

OBJECTIVES

- Learn to secure a Web Service
- Learn about Windows Authentication
- Learn to use SOAP headers

Securing a Web Service is very similar to securing an ASP.NET application. The programming will be slightly different because there is no user interface to prompt the user for a login ID and password. You will need to call a method that allows you to pass the login ID and password to the Web Service in order to authenticate the user. How you do this depends on the technique you opt to use for authenticating and authorizing the user of the Web Service.

This chapter describes different ways in which you might administer authentication and authorization. (For more information on authentication and authorization, refer back to Chapter 24, "Introduction to Web Security.") You will first learn to use Windows Authentication to secure your Web Service; then you will learn how to use SOAP authentication.

Security Mechanisms

Many methods of securing Web applications and Web services are available. You can use the built-in features of IIS, you can use options available through the ASP.NET Framework, and with either one you can use secure sockets to ensure transmissions that are not easily readable. The following subsections will give you an overview of each of these mechanisms before you learn how to set up the different options using ASP.NET and IIS.

Using Secure Sockets Layer (SSL)

If you wish to ensure that all transmissions between the client and the server are encrypted, you can choose to use Secure Sockets Layer (SSL). Be aware that although this technique ensures that no one can view the data going across the connection, it will slow the performance of your Web site.

To set up SSL on a Web site, you will need to obtain a secure server certification through VeriSign or other certification authority. See the IIS online help for more information on how to secure a Web site using SSL.

Using IIS

One way you might secure the Web Service is through IIS properties. Simply select a Web site in IIS and open the Properties dialog box. Then select the Directory Security tab and click the Edit button in the Anonymous Access and Authentication control section (see Figure 31.1).

FIGURE 31.1   Click the Edit button to change the security for this Web site.

Clicking the Edit button displays the dialog box shown in Figure 31.2 (this dialog may look slightly different, depending on your version of IIS).

FIGURE 31.2   Choose an authentication method for your Web site from this dialog box in IIS Administrator.

Using ASP.NET

You can change settings in Web.config files to secure individual Web sites. The <authentication> and <authorization> XML tags in this file manage the corresponding features. When using a Web Service, you can set the authentication element to either Windows or None. (You can't use Forms, because Web Services provide no user interface, so you can't redirect to a specific page and force a user to log in.)

Windows Integrated Authentication

If you wish to use Windows Integrated Authentication, you are assuming that the user who will be connecting to the Web server has a domain account with that Web server and will supply the correct credentials to that server. If the correct credentials are not supplied, the user will be denied access to the Web Service. Credentials can only be supplied through creating an instance of the NetworkCredential class in the .NET Framework and supplying a user ID, password, and domain name.

You will now create a very simple Web Service that will be used to test our integrated security. This Web Service will simply return a string and the name of the process under which this service is running. Follow these steps:

1. Create a new Web Service named WSSecure.

2. Create a method as shown in Listing 31.1.

LISTING 31.1   Create a Simple Web Service That Returns the Identity of the Process Under Which the Web Service Is Running

```
<WebMethod()> Public Function WindowsSecure() As String
  Dim id As WindowsIdentity = WindowsIdentity.GetCurrent

  Return "Hello from Windows Secured Service: " & _
    id.Name()
End Function
```

3. Make sure you build this Web Service project before proceeding with the next steps. You will now create a client-side application to connect to this service.

4. Start a new instance of VS .NET and create an ASP.NET Web application. Name this application Jumpstart/TestSecurity.

5. Add a button to the default Web page. Set the name to **btnTest**.

6. Add a label below this button and set the name to **lblResponse**.

7. Add a Web reference in this project to the WSSecure Web Service.

8. Double-click the Button control and write the code shown in Listing 31.2.

LISTING 31.2   Call a Secure Windows Service by Creating Credentials and Passing Them to the Service

```
Private Sub btnTest_Click( _
 ByVal sender As System.Object, _
 ByVal e As System.EventArgs) Handles btnTest.Click
 Dim ws As New WebSecure.Service1()
 Dim cc As CredentialCache = New CredentialCache()
 Dim nc As NetworkCredential

 lblResponse.Text = ""
 ' Create a new instance of NetworkCredential
 ' using the client credentials.
 nc = New _
  NetworkCredential("AUser", "password", _
  "CORP-WEBSERVER")

 ' Add the NetworkCredential to the CredentialCache.
 cc.Add(New Uri(ws.Url), "Basic", nc)
 cc.Add(New Uri(ws.Url), "NTLM", nc)

 ' Add the CredentialCache to the
 ' web service class credentials.
 ws.Credentials = cc

 Try
     ' Call the Web Service
     lblResponse.Text = ws.WindowsSecure()

 Catch exp As Exception
     lblResponse.Text = exp.Message

 End Try
End Sub
```

NOTE

You will need to replace `"AUser"`, `"Password"`, and `"CORP-WEBSERVER"` with a valid user ID, password, and domain, respectively, that will authenticate on your machine.

9. You now need to turn off the anonymous access to your Web Service site in the IIS Properties dialog box.

10. Bring up IIS, right-click your Web Service Web site, and select Properties.

11. Click the Directory Security tab.

12. Click the Edit button under the Anonymous Access and Authentication Control frame.

13. Uncheck the Anonymous Access check box.

You are now ready to test the Web Service and see whether you can connect to it. Run your test project and click the button. If you have entered a valid user ID, password, and domain, you should see a response come back, such as CORP-WEBSERVER\ASPNET. If you change the user ID to an invalid user on your system, you should see an error message such as "Access Denied."

This tells us that even though you are passing valid credentials to IIS, the site will not run under those credentials; it will normally run under the "ASPNET" user credentials. This is a user created when the .NET Framework is installed.

> **TIP**
>
> You'll want to include some sort of exception handling, either displaying an error message (as in this example) or redirecting the user to another page, in case an error occurs. You really don't want general users to see the error message they'd otherwise receive.

Authentication Modes

No changes need to be made to the Web.config file because the default authentication mode when you create a Web Service project is Windows. If you open the Web.config file in your Web Service project and locate the <authentication> tag in this file, you should see something like the following:

```
<authentication mode="Windows" />
```

The only authentication modes you can use with a Web Service are Windows and None. You cannot use the Forms-based authentication because there is no user interface and no forms to redirect a user to. Passport-based authentication is not an option because it is also not set up to authenticate users without a user interface.

Authorization of Users

By default, all users are authorized by ASP.NET to access a Web Service if they are authenticated. If you locate the <authorization> tag in the Web.config file, you will find that it looks like the following code fragment:

```
<authorization>
<allow users="*" /> <!-- Allow all users -->

<!--   <allow users="[comma separated list of users]"
            roles="[comma separated list of roles]"/>
       <deny users="[comma separated list of users]"
            roles="[comma separated list of roles]"/>
  -->
</authorization>
```

By leaving "*" in the <allow users> tag, you are letting anyone with valid credentials run any Web Service in this site. If you are using Windows integrated security, you may specify only certain users and/or roles within the domain to run the Web Services within this site. For example, if you wanted to restrict a user named Charlie within the domain CORP-WEBSERVER, you would change the <authorization> tag as shown in the following code fragment:

```
<authorization>
  <deny users="CORP-WEBSERVER\Charlie" />
  <allow users="*" /> <!-- Allow all users -->
</authorization>
```

You must explicitly deny access to a user by placing the deny tag before the <allow users="*"> tag. If you do not, the allow all users tag will take precedence.

There are many scenarios in which you might allow or restrict access to users and/or roles in your Web Service. You will have to decide what will be the best for your particular situation.

Custom SOAP Authentication

You may not wish to use any of the Windows authentication modes because you do not want to create each user who logs into your site as a user on your domain. If this is the case, you will need to build your own custom security mechanism. The SOAP protocol has already defined a SOAP header that can pass credential information. You can implement that in an XML Web Service by creating a custom class with login ID and password properties.

Creating a SOAP Header Class

You will now learn to create a SOAP header class in your Web Service project. To do this, you will need to create a new class that inherits from the .NET Framework

SoapHeader class. The SoapHeader class is located in the
System.Web.Services.Protocols namespace, so it is a good idea to import this
namespace. Follow these steps:

1. Open your WSSecure Web Service project.

2. Open the Service1.asmx code-behind file and add the following line of code to
the top of the file:

```
Imports System.Web.Services.Protocols
```

3. Now you will create the new class just below the Service1 class in this file.

4. Move your cursor to the line after End Class in the Service1 file.

5. Create the class shown in Listing 31.3.

LISTING 31.3   The Simplest SoapHeader Class

```
Public Class LoginInfo
  Inherits SoapHeader

  Public UserName As String
  Public Password As String
End Class
```

You can add any custom properties you need to this class in order to authenticate
your user. For example, a simple class like the one shown in Listing 31.3 uses public
variables to maintain UserName and Password properties. You can add as many additional properties as you want to this SoapHeader class, and they will be passed to
your Web Service for you to extract them.

You will now create a new method in your Service1.asmx file to test out this
SoapHeader class. To use this class, you will need to add some additional attributes to
the WebMethod attribute of your Web Service function. In addition, you need to create
a public member variable of the type LoginInfo. Here are the steps to follow:

1. Just above the WindowsSecure method, add the following public variable:

```
Public LoginCredentials As LoginInfo
```

2. Now you will create your new method, as shown in Listing 31.4.

LISTING 31.4   This Simple Example Shows How You Can Use the *SoapHeader* Attribute

```
<WebMethod(), _
SoapHeader("LoginCredentials", _
Direction:=SoapHeaderDirection.InOut, _
Required:=True)> _
Public Function SOAPSecure() As String
  If LoginCredentials Is Nothing Then
    Return "Invalid User"
  Else
    Return "Hello " & LoginCredentials.UserName
  End If
End Function
```

The SoapHeader attribute specifies the name of the class to use (LoginCredentials),
the direction (InOut, indicating that the header will be sent to both the Web Service
and to the client), and that the header is required. The name in the SoapHeader
attribute "LoginCredentials" must match the name of the object you create in the
Public variable. This method returns either "Invalid user" or text that includes the
username, if the client passed in a LoginInfo object.

Calling the SOAP Method

When you call the SOAPSecure method of this Web Service, you will need to create a
LoginCredentials object and fill in its UserName and Password properties. You
then set the LoginInfoValue property of your Web Service to this new object. The
LoginInfoValue property is automatically created whenever you have a class within
a Web Service that uses a SOAP header. It will create a "Value" property, so you may
create an instance of that class and pass the class to the Web Service.

After you fill in the LoginInfo object, .NET will serialize the information in this
object and pass the header information with your request to the SOAPSecure Web
Service method. Here's an example of how you might make this call to the secure
Web Service:

```
Private Sub btnTestSoap_Click( _
 ByVal sender As System.Object, _
 ByVal e As System.EventArgs) Handles btnTestSoap.Click
  Dim ws As WebSecure.Service1
  Dim lc As WebSecure.LoginInfo
```

```
Try
    ' Create the Service
    ws = New WebSecure.Service1()
    ' Create the Login Credentials
    lc = New WebSecure.LoginInfo()

    ' Fill in the credentials
    lc.UserName = "Bill"
    lc.Password = "Gates"

    ' Place credentials object into web service
    ws.LoginInfoValue = lc

    ' Call the Web Service
    lblResponse.Text = ws.SOAPSecure()

Catch exp As Exception
    lblResponse.Text = exp.Message

End Try
End Sub
```

After running this code, you would see the words "Hello Bill" appear in the Label control. This shows that the information got passed from the client to the Web Service via the LoginInfo object.

NOTE

The information in the SOAP header is passed as an XML string in clear text across the Internet. As such, you should make sure you are using SSL if this information needs to be secure.

Client Certificates

You can also use client certificates to authenticate users. A *client certificate* is a digital ID that is passed from the client machine to the server. This ID is "signed" with a digital signature that is verified by a third-party certification authority. This third party is someone you trust to check out users prior to issuing a client certificate.

A digital signature is basically a hash of a message (in this case, the certificate) that is encrypted with the sender's private key. IIS can be configured to ignore, accept, or require client certificates. It's important to understand how each setting changes how IIS responds to client certificates:

- **Ignore certificates.** IIS doesn't care if a user sends his certificate with a request; IIS will simply authenticate the user using another method, such as Challenge/Response.

- **Accept certificates.** If a client certificate is sent, IIS will use this certificate information to authenticate the user. If no certificate is sent, IIS will use another method.

- **Require certificates.** IIS will only fulfill requests from users with valid certificates.

IIS client certificate mapping associates (or maps) client certificate information with Windows NT user accounts. This form of authentication can be very secure and flexible, and most newer browsers support the use of client certificates.

The certificate itself is a special text file that contains two sections: a clear text section (readable by humans) containing the information about the owner, issuer, and so on, and an encrypted section (not readable by humans) that contains the digital signature and public key of the certification authority.

The text file is given the .cer extension so that when you open it, the operating system uses whatever certificate utility it has to view the file. If you open one of these files in Notepad, it will look something like this:

```
-----BEGIN CERTIFICATE-----
CBHcm91cCBDQS5jcmwwRqBEoEKGQGZpbGU6Ly9cXEN
FU1RTU1ZcQ2VydFNyd1xDZXJ0RW5yb2xsXE1TIEN1
cnRTcnYgVGVzdCBHcm91cCBDQS5jcmwwCQYDVR0TB
AIwADBiBggrBgEFBQcBAQRWMFQwUgYIKwYBBQUHMAK
GRmh0dHA6Ly9DRVJUU1JWL0N1cnRTcnYvQ2VydEVuc
m9sbC9DRVJUU1JWX01TIEN1cnRTcnYgVGVzdCBHcm
91cCBDQS5jcnQwDQYJKoZIhvcNAQEEBQADQQAhq70
nR1se0u1PstU+IWdjeNj5p
-----END CERTIFICATE-----
```

IP Address Restriction

In a typical server-to-server exchange of information, you will most likely know the IP address of the machine that will be requesting information from your machine. If this is the case, you can restrict your Web site to only accept requests from this IP address. Simply select a Web site in IIS and then open the Properties dialog box. Then, select the Directory Security tab and click the Edit button in the IP Address and Domain Name Restrictions section (see Figure 31.3).

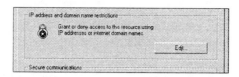

FIGURE 31.3   Click the Edit button to edit IP addresses you want to restrict.

When you click the Edit button, you will see a dialog box similar to the one shown in Figure 31.4. This dialog box allows you to choose to grant access to the list of specified IP addresses. You may also choose to deny access to a specified list of IP addresses. This is a somewhat confusing dialog box because you will have a list of both granted and denied IP addresses listed in the list box.

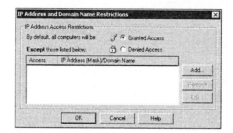

FIGURE 31.4   This dialog box allows you to grant or deny access to certain IP addresses.

If you have the Granted Access option button selected and then click the Add button, you will be presented with a dialog box in which you enter a single IP address. This IP address will be the only one granted access to this particular Web site. You may add one or many IP addresses to this list, as you want.

If you click the Denied Access option button and then click the Add button, you will be presented with a dialog box like the one in Figure 31.5.

When you choose the Group of Computers option button, you can specify a specific network ID and even a subnet mask, as shown in Figure 31.6. This is a little more flexible and would be ideal for an intranet scenario.

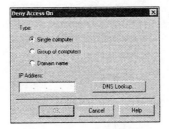

FIGURE 31.5   You can deny access to one computer, a group of computers, or a specific domain name.

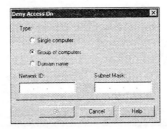

FIGURE 31.6   Specifying a group of computers is easy with this dialog box.

> **WARNING**
>
> Although you can also choose a domain name, this requires a reverse DNS lookup operation and can significantly slow down the performance of your Web site.

Summary

You can configure the security of your Web sites that host Web Services using many different methods. For example, you can use IP address restrictions, client certificates, Windows integrated security, or a custom approach to security. You also have the option of setting up security either within IIS itself or by changing the Web.config file in your Web site.

In this chapter, you were introduced to many security concepts, including the following:

- Using Windows Authentication

- How to use IP restrictions in IIS

- How to pass SOAP headers

A

Programming Standards

OBJECTIVES

- Learn why programming standards are important

- Learn how to set up your computer and Visual Studio .NET

- Learn suggested naming and programming conventions

Programming standards are created for many reasons. Most mainframe shops have had programming standards for years. Unfortunately, most PC programmers have forgotten standards they might have used, or have never worked in a formal programming shop and will often overlook this important step in application development.

Creating a programming standard does not limit your creativity, as most programmers seem to think. Instead, programming standards help you focus your creativity where it is really needed. You can concentrate on the program itself, instead of having to always think about what name to give a procedure or variable. Think about the Windows environment (or even the Macintosh): Every program written for Windows has a consistent look and feel. This is why users like using Windows programs, because they do not have to learn everything about how a new program works. They already know how to use most of the features of it. By using standards in your programming, you can also keep your code's "look and feel" consistent. This means you spend less time figuring out what the variables are or how many indents some other developer might have used, and you can focus more on the logic of the program.

The use of standards can lead to reduced maintenance costs as well, due to a consistent look and feel. This means you can move from one project to another very easily, even one someone else wrote, and immediately read and understand the code. Programming standards are used to help programmers create a consistent structure, coding style, and naming convention for variables within an application. Standards help a programmer create code that is unambiguous, easy to read, and easy to maintain by other developers.

We use the standards described in this appendix when developing applications for our clients. These rules aren't "set in stone," however. They're just the ones used in our organizations. Feel free to modify them to suit your own organization's needs.

> **TIP**
>
> The developers at PDSA, Inc., have created a full document describing the programming practices in use at their company. You might want to stop by www.pdsa.com and download this useful document.

Setting Up Your Environment

Before you can begin coding, you'll need to set up your computer, and Visual Studio .NET, to make the best use of your time and the tools. The next few sections discuss the details of architecting a maintainable desktop computer environment and choosing the important Visual Studio .NET options.

Computer Setup

It's important that you configure your development system appropriately. If you're working with multiple developers, this is especially important, because you want all computers to be configured similarly.

We've found that it's crucial for developers to be able to rebuild machines, from scratch, with a minimum of effort. This means that it's imperative that data be stored separately from the operating system. This way, you can "blow away" the operating system at any time without losing data.

We suggest the following strategy, which has worked well for us:

- Create a partition just for the operating system. This partition should be at least 4 to 6GB. This partition will be your C: drive. Make sure you use an efficient file system, such as NTFS. FAT and FAT32 are both inefficient and unsecurable.

- Install an appropriate operating system (Windows 2000, Windows XP, or Windows .NET) onto your C: drive.

- Once Windows is installed and running, rename your CD-ROM (or DVD, or other optical drive used for installations) to a "high" drive letter (we use X:) so that other installed drives won't move the drive letter for the optical drive later on.

- Create two more partitions. The first, D:, will be used for your data, projects, and applications. You should use NTFS for this partition, as well. The other partition, E:, should be the same size as your C: drive and must be formatted using FAT or FAT32. You'll use this drive to create an image of your C: drive.

- Install all your standard applications. Make sure any personal data files (such as an Outlook PST file) are stored on the D: drive. (We suggest you also set your My Documents folder to point to a folder on the D: drive.)

- Once you have all your standard applications installed, you can create an image copy of your C: drive. Using a tool that creates exact images of drives (such as Norton Ghost(C) or PowerQuest's DriveImage(C)), create an image of your C: drive and store it on the E: drive.

Your machine is now ready to be used. If you ever need to restore your C: drive to a working configuration, you can simply restore the saved image, which takes minutes rather than the original hours you invested in creating and installing your C: drive.

Visual Studio .NET Options

Visual Studio .NET includes many options that define the behavior of the environment and the features in new projects. You'll want to make sure developers within your organization have set up their environments in the same way. We've outlined, in the following list, some important settings you'll want to consider. Each heading lists settings within the Options dialog box (use the Tools, Options menu item to display this dialog box):

- **Environment, Projects and Solutions.** Set the Visual Studio Projects Location property to the location where you will be creating all your Visual Studio projects. This will ensure that the SLN file is located in the same location as your project files.

- **Text Editor, Basic, General.** Unselect the Hide Advanced Members option. Some members will not show up in the IntelliSense lists if you do not do this. (We have no idea why Microsoft included this option. How can you program with some of the options missing from the IntelliSense? We just don't understand this one.)

- **Debugging, Edit and Continue.** Select the Allow Me to Edit VB Files While Debugging option. This is a big change for VB6 developers—in that environment, you could change code while in Break mode and have your code changes compiled and added to the project debugging session immediately. In Visual Studio .NET, you can't even make changes to the files while debugging unless you select this option. Even after selecting this option, you'll need to rebuild your project after making changes during a debugging session.

  You may also want to select the Always Ignore Changes and Continue Debugging option. Without this change, you'll either need to respond to an alert each time you make changes during debugging, or even worse, restart debugging immediately after making a change.

Option Strict

In VB .NET, Option Strict is off by default—this is a poor decision, in our eyes, because it allows the same sort of code you might have written in VB6, including embarrassing type conversions. As it is, you must open the project properties for each new project you create in order to turn on Option Strict (or, you can manually add it to the top of each file, which is certainly an onerous task).

You can set Option Strict on in VB .NET for all new projects you create, but it's a nontrivial task. Although there may be a simpler way, we've found that you can modify the project templates themselves, adding the instruction to include this directive for each new project you create.

To do this, find the folder containing all the project templates. If you followed the preceding convention for setting up your machine, this folder is located under `C:\Program Files\Microsoft Visual Studio.NET\Vb7\VBWizards`. You'll find a number of subfolders within this folder, but you're looking for files named `*.vbproj` within this location. (You need to modify each of these, indicating that you want to turn on Option Strict for each project template.) Table A.1 contains a list of the folders and their corresponding project templates.

TABLE A.1   List of Folders Where Project Templates Are Located

Folder Name	Project Template
`ClassLibrary`	Class Library
`ConsoleApplication`	Console Application
`MobileWebApplication`	Mobile Web Application
`WebApplication`	ASP.NET Web Application
`WindowsApplication`	Windows Application
`WindowsService`	Windows Service
`WindowsControl`	Windows Control Library
`WebService`	ASP.NET Web Service
`WebControlLibrary`	Web Control Library

The simplest way to find each project file is to use Windows Explorer's Search tool. Once you've browsed to the correct folder (`C:\Program Files\Microsoft Visual Studio .NET\Vb7\VBWizards`), click the Search button in Windows Explorer, and enter **`*.vbproj`** as the search criterion. Once Windows Explorer has found the list of VB projects, load each file into a text editor and modify the XML at the top of the file so that it looks something like this:

```
<VisualStudioProject>
    <VisualBasic>
        <Build>
```

```
<Settings
  OptionExplicit = "On"
  OptionStrict = "On"
```

You'll find a lot more XML in the templates—we've removed all the nonessential information here. Leave the rest of the XML elements alone. We've also added the OptionExplicit setting here, because you're likely to want that on, as well.

Save each file, and the next time you create a project based on one of these templates, Option Strict will be on, by default. You will definitely want to have Option Strict on for your development in VB .NET, and you'll forget to turn it on manually if you do not perform these steps to add it to each project template.

Naming Conventions

While you're developing new code, you'll spend a large portion of your time naming things. You'll need to propose names for variables, procedures, and more. The following sections propose standards for providing names, thus allowing for consistency in your code.

Naming Variables

Although it's subject of much debate, we believe you should adopt a strict and consistent naming convention for variables in your applications. Because variables describe the behavior of your code, it's useful to be able to glance at a variable and determine its type (and perhaps its use) just given its name. We've adopted a commonly used convention, starting variables with a two- or three-letter prefix that indicates the data type of the variable.

TIP

We've found one programming convention that consistently leads to confusion—the habit of using single-letter variable names. We can't suggest strongly enough that you avoid the temptation. The only place we'll allow this (and it's still a matter of contention) is in simple integer values used for looping counters.

Taking into account our own coding styles, we suggest you consider adopting these same rules when naming variables:

- Avoid one-letter variables.

- Make all variable names mixed case. That is, each word or abbreviation within the variable name should be capitalized. This technique is often referred to as *camel case*, because you end up with "humps" in your names, like this: intTotalValue.

- Do not use the underscore character in a variable name. (There's no point if you use mixed-case names.)

- Preface each variable name with a two- or three-letter prefix indicating the type of data it contains.

- Abbreviate names in variables only when absolutely necessary.

Hungarian Notation

Hungarian notation is a variable-naming scheme created by a Microsoft developer of Hungarian nationality (hence, the name). Originally developed for C language programmers, it has now been successfully applied to many other development languages. The use of Hungarian notation in a program will give developers useful information about a variable simply by inspecting the name of the variable. A variable that has been named using the Hungarian notation scheme indicates the variable's scope (Global, Member or Local), what data type it contains (Integer, Long, and so on), and, of course, the purpose of the variable.

Although originally created for C developers, Hungarian notation is just as useful in Visual Basic applications, and we endorse its use. Although we don't adhere to it "religiously," you will find that all the variables used throughout this book do include data type information, and we suggest that you follow at least this part of the naming convention.

Hungarian notation can be useful within your code, but there are places where it can be confusing or misleading. You should not use Hungarian notation when naming any of the following variables:

- Public property names

- Public method names

- Public event names

- Parameters to procedures

- Properties in a structure

- Enumerations

Basically, we suggest that you don't use Hungarian naming on any name that's publicly viewable in any IntelliSense list.

Data Type Prefixes

Table A.2 lists the standard variable data types in Visual Basic, along with suggested prefixes for these data types.

TABLE A.2   Data Type Prefixes

Data Type	Prefix	Example
Boolean	bool or bln	boolIsValid or blnIsValid
Byte	byt	bytValue
Char	chr	chrLetter
Date	dt	dtStart
Decimal	dec	decValue
Double	dbl	dblValue
Integer	int	intLoop
Long	lng	lngValue
Object	o	oValue
Short	srt	srtValue
Single	sng	sngValue
String	str	strName

Scope Prefixes

A variable's *scope* defines the locations within your application where a particular variable may be inspected or modified. For example, a local variable is one declared within a procedure. This variable may only be read or modified while code is executing within the particular procedure. A member variable, on the other hand, may be used from within any method within the same class. Global or public variables (whose use you should consider restricting, for maintainability reasons) may be referenced from any procedure or function within the same project. We suggest using the single-letter prefixes shown in Table A.3.

TABLE A.3   Variable Scope Prefixes

Prefix	Description
g	Global or Public scope throughout the entire project.
m	Member variable within a class definition. This variable has scope throughout the whole class.

Local variables should not have a prefix. This will distinguish them as being local and not having a scope outside of the current procedure:

```
Public gintLoop As Integer  ' Public variable
Private mstrName As String   ' Member variable
Dim boolOpen As Boolean ' Local variable
```

> **TIP**
>
> You can declare member variables (variables that exist within a class, outside a procedure) using the `Dim` keyword or the more explicit `Public`, `Private`, `Friend`, or `Protected` keyword. We strongly suggest you never use `Dim` to declare a member variable—always use the explicit modifiers so that it's never a guess as to how a variable is exposed to other classes.

Naming Controls and Menus

Just as you use prefixes indicating the type of variables, we suggest using a prefix to indicate the type of controls you use on your user interface. That way, it's easy to tell from within your code exactly what type of control you're working with. Table A.4 lists the Web Form controls and the suggested prefixes for those controls. Table A.5 suggests prefixes for use with Windows Form controls.

TABLE A.4   Web Form Control Prefixes

Control	Prefix
Label	lbl
TextBox	txt
Button	btn
LinkButton	lnk
ImageButton	img
HyperLink	hyp
DropDownList	ddl
ListBox	lst
DataGrid	grd
DataList	dlst
Repeater	rep
CheckBox	chk
CheckBoxList	cbl
RadioButtonList	rbl
RadioButton	rdo
Image	img
Panel	pnl
PlaceHolder	plc
Calendar	cal
AdRotator	ad
Table	tbl
RequiredFieldValidator	reqv
CompareValidator	cmpv
RangeValidator	rngv
RegularExpressionValidator	rexpv

TABLE A.4   Continued

Control	Prefix
CustomValidator	custv
ValidationSummary	vsum
Xml	xml
Literal	lit
CrystalReportViewer	crv

TABLE A.5   Prefixes to Use with WinForm Controls

Control	Prefix
Label	lbl
LinkLabel	lnk
Button	btn
TextBox	txt
MainMenu	mnu
Checkbox	chk
RadioButton	rdo
GroupBox	grp
PictureBox	pic
Panel	pnl
DataGrid	grd
ListBox	lst
CheckedListBox	clst
ComboBox	cbo
ListView	lvw
TreeView	tvw
TabControl	tab
DataTimePicker	dtp
MonthCalendar	cal
HScrollBar	hscr
VScrollBar	vscr
Timer	tim
Splitter	spl
DomainUpDown	dup
NumericUpDown	nup
TrackBar	trk
ProgressBar	prg
RichTextBox	rtxt
ImageList	ilst
HelpProvider	hlp

TABLE A.5   Continued

Control	Prefix
ToolTip	tip
ContextMenu	cmnu
ToolBar	tbar
StatusBar	sbar
NotifyIcon	nic
OpenFileDialog	ofd
SaveFileDialog	sfd
FontDialog	fd
ColorDialog	cd
PrintDialog	pd
PrintPreviewDialog	ppd
PrintPreviewControl	ppc
ErrorProvider	errp
PrintDocument	pdoc
PageSetupDialog	psd
CrystalReportViewer	crv

If you take care to name your controls with these common prefixes, you'll be able to identify the type of a control reference in your code without having to refer back to the page or form.

Windows Forms Menu Naming Conventions

When creating Windows applications, you'll often use menus on your forms. Just like custom controls, all the various menus you create should also be prefixed appropriately. The prefix mnu should be used on all menus. This prefix should be followed by the caption of the menu. For each pull-down menu under the main menu item, use the first letter of the top-level menu. Table A.6 lists some standard menu items and how you might name them.

TABLE A.6   Menu File Naming Conventions

Menus	Name
File	mnuFile
File, New	mnuFNew
File, Open	mnuFOpen
Edit	mnuEdit
Edit, Copy	mnuECopy
Edit, Paste	mnuEPaste

When you use this convention, all members of a particular menu group are listed next to each other in the object drop-down list boxes (in the Code window and Property window). In addition, the menu control names clearly document the menu items to which they are attached.

Naming Conventions for Other Controls

For new controls not listed in the tables, try to come up with a unique three-character prefix. Note, however, that it is more important to be clear than to stick to three characters.

For derivative controls, such as an enhanced list box, extend the prefixes listed earlier so that there is no confusion over which control is really being used. A lowercase abbreviation for the manufacturer could be added to the prefix, for example.

Naming ADO.NET Objects

Although thousands of objects are available as part of the .NET Framework (and we wouldn't even consider providing naming standards for more than a few of the framework classes), you're likely to use ADO.NET as part of your applications, and we'd like to suggest some naming standards for the common ADO.NET objects. Table A.7 lists the prefixes we use throughout this book.

TABLE A.7   Prefixes for ADO.NET Classes

Class	Prefix for Object
DataSet	ds
DataTable	dt
DataView	dv
DataRow	drw
Connection*	cnn
Command*	cmd
DataAdapter*	da
CommandBuilder*	bld
DataReader*	dr

* Each of these objects would be prefixed with OleDb, SQLClient, or some other namespace, depending on the driver used to access your data source.

We use an additional convention when working with ADO.NET objects: If a scope contains only a single instance of a particular type of object, we'll use just the prefix as the variable name. Here's an example:

```
Dim dr As New SqlDataReader()
Dim ds As DataSet
```

Of course, if you need two or more of the same data type in the same scope, you can use the prefixes listed in Table A.7 as part of variable names.

Coding Conventions

In addition to other naming conventions, we suggest carefully naming data structures and procedures. We also suggest specific conventions for indentation and commenting.

Naming Data Structures

The following subsections describe how we name other types of objects within projects, such as classes, interfaces, enumerations, and so on.

Classes and Structures

Although it is, again, a matter of contention, we suggest using nonprefixed names for classes (some developers insist in prefixing classes with C). We also suggest that you create property procedures for all properties within your classes (as opposed to using public variables), because this grants you greater flexibility as you continue to evolve your class implementation. Feel free to use Hungarian notation for any and all private data, but we suggest that you don't expose any public members with prefixed names. Here's an example:

```
Public Class Customer
    Public Property Name() As String
    End Property
...
End Class
```

Interfaces

Begin interface names with I. Here's an example:

```
Interface ICustomers
...
End Interface
```

In this case, ICustomers defines an interface that would be implemented by other classes.

Enumerations

An enumeration should have a descriptive name, followed by the suffix Enum. Here's an example:

```
Public Enum GridTypesEnum
    All = 0
```

```
    ListOnly = 1
End Enum
```

To use this enumeration, you could write code like this:

```
Dim gt As GridTypesEnum = GridTypesEnum.All
```

Constants

Constant names should be uppercase with underscores (_) between words. This will help distinguish your constants from any other type that you might use in your application. Be sure to supply a data type for your constants—of course, with Option Strict on, you won't be able to leave out the data type. If you do not type your constants, they will be of the type Object. Your constant declarations might look like this:

```
Public Const TAB_ADDRESS As Integer = 0
Public Const TAB_PHONES As Integer = 1
```

Conditional Compile Constants

For conditional compilation constants, use the prefix cc followed by all uppercase letters. Separate words with an underscore character, just like regular constants:

```
#If ccDEMO Then
    ' Perform some code here
#End If
```

Exceptions in Try/Catch Blocks

Although many error-handling examples you'll see use e as the name of the Exception object handled within a Catch block, you'll find that this name conflicts with the parameter passed into many event-handling procedures. We suggest using the exp prefix (or simply the name exp, on its own) to avoid the conflict.

Here's an example:

```
Try
    ...
Catch exp As Exception
    ...
End Try
```

If you create your own classes, inheriting from the Exception object, make sure you follow the same convention used by Microsoft: Give the class a meaningful name, followed by Exception. For example, your exception class that handles the "file too large" exception might be named FileTooLargeException.

Naming Procedures

Naming procedures comprise another area in which careful planning will help make your applications more understandable and more maintainable. Selecting a standard within your development organization will make it easier for all your developers to work together.

We've gathered a list of suggestions, and we've found that these suggestions make our development tasks go more smoothly. When naming procedures, we follow these rules in general:

- Use mixed case, where each word in the procedure is capitalized.

- Begin functions and procedures with a noun.

- Follow the noun with the action that will be performed on the object represented by the noun.

- Avoid using underscores in your function names, because it becomes hard to determine which procedures are yours and which are event-handling procedures.

Here are some examples of procedure names that follow these conventions:

- `FormShow`

- `FormInit`

- `StateLoad`

- `EmployeeLoad`

As you can see, these examples place the noun, or object, first. This convention mirrors the way that in object-oriented languages the object name is placed first, followed by the method or action you wish to perform on that object. Objects are always nouns, and actions are verbs. Therefore, we suggest you follow this coding style when creating names for your procedures.

> **TIP**
>
> This coding style has an added benefit. When you use a cross-referencing tool or are looking in the Procedure drop-down box in Visual Studio .NET, you will see all functions that operate on a particular object grouped in one place. Because you've named your procedures so that all the actions associated with a given object begin with the name of that object, they'll all be sorted together within the list.

Commenting Your Code

All procedures and functions should begin with a brief comment describing the functional characteristics of the routine (that is, what it does). This description should not describe the implementation details (that is, how the procedure does its work) because the implementation often changes over time, resulting in unnecessary comment-maintenance work—or worse yet—erroneous comments. The worst possible case is one in which the procedure comments describe how the procedure works, but the comments and the actual procedure don't match. The code itself and any necessary inline or local comments should describe the implementation.

Here are some additional suggestions involving comments:

- Parameters passed to a routine should be described if their use isn't obvious and when the routine expects the parameters to be in a specific range. (We also suggest the use of the Debug.Assert method, if it's important that parameters meet specific criteria.)

- Function return values and global variables that are changed by the routine (especially through reference parameters) must be described at the beginning of each procedure.

- Every nontrivial variable declaration should include an inline comment describing the use of the variable being declared.

- Variables, controls, and routines should be named clearly enough that inline commenting is only needed for complex or nonintuitive implementation details.

Indentation

Consistent code indentation can mean the difference between easily readable code and a hopeless nightmare. Happily, indentation has become a nonissue in Visual Studio .NET. If you allow Visual Studio .NET to perform its smart indenting, it will take care of the indentation for you. We strongly suggest that you allow Visual Studio .NET to handle the indentation chores. The standard indentation depth is four characters, and we don't see any reason to change it to a larger value. For the purposes of fitting more code into the limited space in this book, we've set this value to 2 in many cases. The good news is that it doesn't matter: If you simply select an entire procedure and then press Shift+Tab, Visual Studio .NET will reformat the code for your particular tab setting, making it easy to adapt code formatted for a different tab size to your own preferences.

Summary

Programming standards are imperative for multideveloper organizations and will make the job of even a single developer much easier. Because much of your development time is spent in maintenance mode, you'll want to adopt standards that make it easier for you to maintain and manage your projects. In this chapter, we've suggested some easily adopted standards that can by adapted for your own needs, including the following:

- Computer setup
- Visual Studio .NET options
- Option Strict support
- Naming conventions
- Coding style conventions

Index